The Hudson

YALE UNIVERSITY PRESS / NEW HAVEN & LONDON

Tom Lewis

The

A History

Hudson

Quotations on the dedication page are from "The Municipal Gallery Revisited" by W. B. Yeats, and "The Sleepers" by Walt Whitman.

Excerpts on pp. 195, 197, and 202 from poems by Thomas Cole. Copyright 1972 by George Shumway. Reprinted by permission of George Shumway.

Excerpt on p. 223 from "Flow Gently, Sweet Etymology, Ornithology, and Penology" by Ogden Nash. Copyright 1950 by Ogden Nash. Reprinted by permission of Curtis Brown, Ltd.

Excerpt on p. 282 from "The Lordly Hudson" by Paul Goodman. Copyright 1972, 1973 by the Estate of Paul Goodman. Reprinted by permission of Sally Goodman.

Published with assistance from the foundation established in memory of Amasa Stone Mather of the class of 1907, Yale College.

Frontispiece: "The *Half Moon* at the Highlands," engraving by Robert Hinshelwood after a painting by Thomas Moran, ca. 1870s.

Designed by Nancy Ovedovitz and set in Mrs Eaves type by Duke & Company, Devon, Pennsylvania. Printed in the United States of America by R. R. Donnelley, Harrisonburg, Virginia.

The Library of Congress has cataloged the hardcover edition as follows:

Lewis, Tom, 1942–
The Hudson : a history / Tom Lewis.
    p.   cm.
ISBN 0-300-10424-3 (cloth : alk. paper)
1. Hudson River (N.Y. and N.J.)—History.
2. Hudson River Valley (N.Y. and N.J.)—History.
I. Title.
F127.H8L49 2005
974.7'3—dc22   2005015120

A catalogue record for this book is available from the British Library.

The paper in this book meets the guidelines for permanence and durability of the Committee on Production Guidelines for Book Longevity of the Council on Library Resources.

ISBN 978-0-300-11990-9 (pbk. : alk. paper)

10 9 8 7 6 5 4

For

Robert and Peggy Boyers

And say my glory was I had such friends

and to the memory of

William Draper Lewis, Jr.

The father holds his grown or ungrown son in his arms with measureless love,

and the son holds the father in his arms with measureless love

Contents

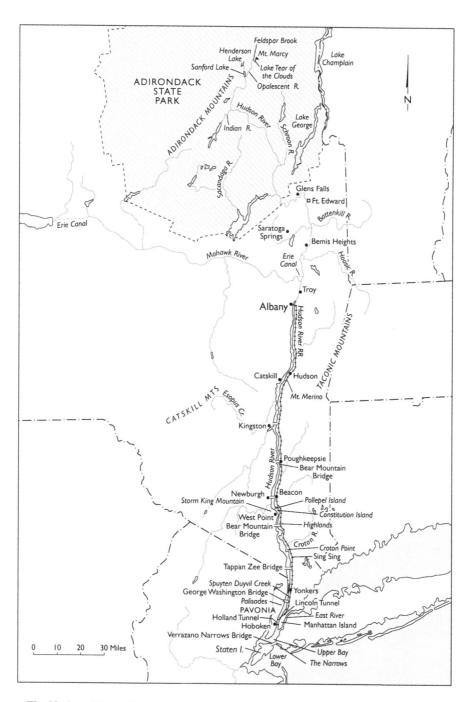

The Hudson River valley

Introduction

In 1900 Francis Bannerman faced a dangerous problem. The dealer in military surplus, who had begun trading in armaments after the Civil War, had just purchased 90 percent of the munitions and matériel left over from the Spanish-American War, a rich horde of small arms, cannon, ammunition, and gunpowder. The supplies were far too hazardous to stockpile in his store at 501 Broadway in New York City. His son, who had recently returned from a canoe outing on the Hudson, told him of seeing Pollepel Island in the river's highlands about fifty miles above Manhattan and just south of the city of Beacon. The island, Bannerman learned, belonged to a local family and was for sale.

Native Americans, according to the local lore, believed that Pollepel was possessed by evil spirits and refused to spend the night there. Legend also had it that Dutch captains thought the island to be inhabited by goblins and sometimes put off unruly or stubborn sailors there to discipline them. During the Revolution the American forces built a chevaux-de-frise from Pollepel Island to the western shore. In the mid nineteenth century a fisherman lived there with his insane wife, who imagined herself to be the Queen of England. Matthew Vassar considered building a great memorial commemorating Henry Hudson on Pollepel, but the Poughkeepsie brewer decided instead to endow a college for women in his name. Bannerman thought the nearly seven acres of land a thousand feet from the east bank of the Hudson would be just the place to store his newly acquired weapons as well as the black powder, shot, and shells from the Civil War. He bought the island for one thousand dollars.

For eighteen years Francis Bannerman erected buildings on his island. A Scottish immigrant, he decided to honor his heritage by creating a fortress compound that included three warehouses, houses for guards and workers, and a large residence for his family. He surrounded his compound with brick and concrete walls and adorned many of them with a concrete garland of thistle leaves and flowers. On the north wall he proclaimed in bold concrete letters: BANNERMAN'S ISLAND ARSENAL. The compound's portcullis, crenelated towers, and turrets, all of his own design, reminded him of castles he had seen in his native land. Although Pollepel is an island in the Hudson River, he even planned to surround it with a moat. And as no self-respecting Scotsman in America would be content without a heraldic device, he designed his own coat of arms.

As military adventures escalated in the early years of the twentieth century, the arsenal became the center of a worldwide arms trade, and Francis Bannerman thrived. He sold the recycled surplus munitions, cannon,

Overleaf: Bannerman's Island Arsenal on Pollepel Island. Between 1900 and 1918 Francis Bannerman designed and built this arsenal for war-surplus matériel he had purchased from the federal government after the Spanish-American War. For its design Bannerman drew from his Scottish heritage, creating his vision of a baronial castle complete with turrets, a portcullis, and a moat. (Courtesy of Neil Caplan, Bannerman Castle Trust for the New York State Office of Parks, Recreation, and Historic Preservation)

saddles, rifles, bayonets, knapsacks, and uniforms to emerging armies. Foreign ships arrived regularly at Bannerman's castle to pick up arms for Russia, Mexico, or countries in Europe. During World War I, Bannerman sent ships laden with rifles and military supplies for Scottish and British troops in Dundee and London.

After Bannerman's death in late 1918, the armaments business passed to his family, who continued to operate the arsenal on Pollepel Island and live there during the summer. In 1920 an explosion in one of the munitions buildings hurled a large section of a castle wall onto the nearby railroad tracks. After that the family moved most of its operation to Long Island, but they were still storing munitions on the island until 1950. Family members continued to summer at their castle until 1967, when they sold it to New York State. Two years later a fire, started perhaps by an arsonist, left Bannerman's castle a forsaken shell. In the years that followed, vandals regularly looted the castle of souvenirs and scarred its walls with graffiti. Today Amtrak train passengers on their way to and from New York look upon a scene that is more reminiscent of Scotland than the Hudson River valley.

The story of Francis Bannerman's fantasy in the Hudson River suggests four themes that thread their way through this history of the river and the valley: utility, individuality, community, and symbol. As is the case with all rivers, the Hudson's foremost purpose is utilitarian. Beyond the obvious example of those who paddled, sailed, and steamed north, south, and across the river with passengers and cargo are those who have brilliantly exploited its topography for defense, or fished it each spring for shad, or blasted its rock outcroppings for brownstone houses and a prison, or harvested its ice each winter for refrigeration, or, alas, considered its rolling waters to be little more than a vast dumping ground for countless toxic substances. Bannerman, too, recognized that the Hudson is a river of utility. He selected Pollepel Island for his arsenal because it was accessible to deepwater shipping.

Bannerman was just one of numerous individuals who saw the river and the valley as a place where they might thrive for good or ill, people like DeWitt Clinton, the governor of New York who long championed and later built the narrow ribbon of water connecting the Hudson River with Lake Erie, or Adriaen van der Donck, who came to the valley as the representative of the van Rensselaer interests in New Netherland and later wrote an elaborate description of the flora, fauna, and native people that he saw. But it has been home to others who exploited the river and the land for their own gain, people like William Edwards and Zadock Pratt, whose leather tanning operations in the Catskill Mountains accounted for the denuding of whole hillsides of hemlocks, or New York's corrupt mayor Robert A. Van Wyck, who made a fortune by fixing the price of Hudson River ice.

As is the case with so many other individual acts on the Hudson, Francis Bannerman's romantic creation had an impact on the valley's community and culture. No mean storage shed, Bannerman's Island Arsenal was a delight for the eye; today its ruin inspires the imagination. Nor is it alone. One need only consider the stark fortress at West Point, or Frederic Edwin Church's orientalist house, Olana, at the city of Hudson, Henry Burden's iron works at Troy, or the suspension bridge at Bear Mountain to understand the intimate connection between individuals, their creations, and the larger valley.

Bannerman planned his arsenal to stand proudly as a symbol of the strength and power that he associated with his ancestors, but in its own way, and even in its derelict state, it suggests the mystery of the great river, a mystery found in the paintings of Thomas Cole or the writings of Washington Irving, and the sublime character of the landscape. Always those who came to the river and its valley were moved by what they saw. Natty Bumppo, the hero of James Fenimore Cooper's Leatherstocking novels, put it best. Looking down from high in the Catskills, he saw the river "for seventy miles, looking like a curled shaving under my feet." To Bumppo the Hudson and the view of the valley were nothing less than "Creation . . . all creation."

Why the Hudson?

This continent's great rivers have in large measure defined and shaped American history and culture. The West belongs to the roiling red waters of the Colorado. It is the river of John Wesley Powell, who first explored its gorges and canyons in the 1870s. It is the site of prodigious engineering feats like the Hoover and Glen Canyon dams; for better and worse its waters helped to turn the deserts of the Southwest into farmland. The middle of the country belongs to the swift, forever shifting currents of the Mississippi. It is the river of Mark Twain, who believed it had a new story to tell every day. It serves the great ports of the Midwest, St. Louis, Memphis, and New Orleans, and its waters supply the rich lands of its bird's-foot delta.

The East belongs to the Hudson. Far more than a short river flowing through New York state, the Hudson is a thread that runs through the fabric of four centuries of American history, through the development of American civilization—its culture, its community, and its consciousness.

For those living in the United States the Hudson is the river of firsts: the first great river that explorers came upon when they arrived in the New World; the first river that led explorers into the continent's uncharted interior; the river that was the first line of defense in the American Revolution; the river of America's first writers, the river that inspired America's first great painters; the river millions of immigrants first encountered when they stepped off their boats onto their new land; the river whose deep-water port helped New York City become the nation's foremost financial center; the river that inspired America's first conservationists. And in the late twentieth century, after suffering extraordinary degradation, the river became the first battleground of environmentalists. All these firsts in a landscape that authors as disparate as James Fenimore Cooper, Edith Wharton, Walt Whitman, Henry James, and T. Coraghessan Boyle have noted for its mystery, romance, and ineffable beauty. Surely the writer Paul Goodman was correct when he called it "our Lordly Hudson."

The river is crucial to the history of Portuguese, French, Dutch, and English exploration. It served as the road to some of the first American fortunes made through the trade in furs and lumber. Its valley saw the first Dutch settlements in the New World at Beverwyck, now Albany, and New Amsterdam, now New York; and later, the vast feudal manors of Dutch and English families like the Van Rensselaers and Livingstons. Those settlements in turn had a profound impact on the Native Americans who had inhabited the land for centuries, but who yielded it to the Europeans for wampum, blankets, guns, powder, pipes, and rum.

Nearly one-third of the battles in the American War for Independence took place on or near the banks of the Hudson, because control of the river and its valley held the key to winning the war. The British general Sir

William Howe realized this when he captured Long Island and Manhattan at the mouth of the Hudson. George Washington knew it when he secured the fort at West Point, the narrowest place in the river, and strung a chain from shore to shore to prevent British ships from sailing north. The revolutionary patriot and traitor Benedict Arnold also understood the Hudson's importance when he hatched a plot to capture West Point. Had he succeeded, Arnold might well have changed the outcome of the war. And at Bemis Heights, a high bluff overlooking the Hudson at Saratoga, American forces did change its outcome when they won the most important battle of the Revolution, a victory that secured not only the river north of New York City for the colonies but also French support to fund their cause.

In the history of technology, engineering, and business enterprise, the Hudson has played a singular role matched by few places in the nation. The depth of New York's port attracted commerce and millions of immigrants in the nineteenth and twentieth centuries. The river has been the setting for revolutionary developments in transportation—the steamboat, the Erie Canal, and the railroad—as well as for the great engineering accomplishments of its bridges and tunnels.

Millions of men and women have taken advantage of the natural corridor through the valley in order to make their way into the West, and later, to ship the crops and goods they produced there back to the East. Each advance has changed the river and its economic significance as well as the fortunes of the communities on its shores.

The Hudson holds a unique place in the history of American art, architecture, and literature. It inspired the imagination of Thomas Cole, Asher B. Durand, Jasper Cropsey, and Frederic Edwin Church, among many others, who produced paintings that began a native tradition in American art popularly known as the Hudson River school. The river, the mansions that line its shores, and the stones and plants of its dramatic hills infused Andrew Jackson Downing's landscape architecture and his writings on the theory and practice of house design and gardening in North America. It is the river and the valley that provided Irving, Cooper, and Melville with a physical and spiritual setting for many scenes in their stories and novels.

The lower Hudson—the name often given to the last 150 miles of the river from Troy to Manhattan—commands the most attention and has become an American icon. From the time that Henry Hudson proclaimed its valley "as pleasant a land as one can tread upon," the lower Hudson has captured the imaginations of travelers. This is the river valley where statesmen and public figures—Robert Morris, Alexander Hamilton, DeWitt Clinton, and Franklin and Eleanor Roosevelt, among others—have lived and earned their reputations. This is the river valley where some of the nation's most important merchant princes—Astors, Morgans, Belmonts, and Vanderbilts among them—have earned great fortunes and built majestic houses. This is the river valley of legends and mansions and sublime scenery.

Lured by the Hudson's unusual botanical, geological, and environmental features, scientists have long been drawn to the river. In the eighteenth century the Swedish naturalist Peter Kalm and the American naturalists John and William Bartram came to the valley to discover new specimens of flora and fauna for their collections. Kalm named the American mountain laurel that he discovered there after himself: *Kalmia latifolia.* In the nineteenth century the eminent British geologist Sir Charles Lyell and a fledgling American scientist, Amos Eaton, traveled the Hudson. Eaton's discoveries served as the basis for American geology. Both men marveled at the river's great fjord that accounts for the tides that extend upstream to Troy.

Early in the twentieth century the Hudson served as the cradle for early environmental advocates, including John Burroughs and Edward Henry Harriman. They awakened citizens to the ravages of lumbermen who were systematically clear-cutting their way through the Adirondacks and the Catskills, and quarriers who sought to carve up the Palisades and the Highlands. More recently the river has become a battleground for environmental activists who have stopped one hydroelectric and seven nuclear power plants from being built on its banks. In the course of these battles they have helped to establish legislation and prompted landmark legal decisions that have affected environmental policy for the entire country. Today activists are dedicating themselves to restoring the river and its tributaries—along with their wildlife habitats—after hundreds of years of bacterial and chemical pollution, including the dumping of countless tons of raw sewage, garbage, and PCBs.

This is not a conventional full-scale history. Such a work would encompass numerous volumes and many of the disciplines in the humanities, sciences, and social sciences. It would consider literature and botany, geology and architecture, environment and myth, military strategy and technology—along with countless other subjects. Readers will not find a complete history of Henry Hudson's explorations, or the Livingston family, or the Battle of Saratoga, to name just three examples. Although I write about each of these topics and many more, there is still much more that might be said.

But it is a personal history that has been growing, albeit unconsciously, in my mind for four decades. It began in 1964, in my almost daily walks in Manhattan's Riverside Park. They afforded me a view of the great sweep of the river: Riverside Church, Grant's Tomb, the Palisades, and the George Washington Bridge to the north; the boat basin, the docks, and Weehawken and Hoboken to the south. Later, in connection with another book I wrote on the inventors of radio, I was able to climb the three-armed FM tower atop the Palisades at Alpine, New Jersey. From that vantage point nearly a thousand feet above sea level, I could follow the Hudson north to Newburgh and south to the Verrazano Narrows Bridge and New York Bay. I could take in the sweep of the valley, the Tappan Zee, the Bear Mountain Bridge, West Point, and the reaches of the river beyond. Moving to Saratoga Springs thirty years ago afforded me an entirely new perspective of the Hudson. Over the years I have taken countless train and automobile trips following the eastern and western shores of the river between Albany and New York City. As Saratoga Springs is situated ten miles from the Hudson, close to the foothills of the Adirondacks, I learned about the upper river. I've followed the Hudson's course north from Bemis Heights, the site of the Battle of Saratoga, to Fort Edward, Glens Falls, Hudson Falls, Warrensburg, North Creek, and on into the high peaks of the Adirondacks, until high on Mount Marcy, New York's highest peak, I arrived at the Hudson's source, Lake Tear of the Clouds.

"But that same image, we ourselves see in all rivers and oceans," Herman Melville reflected after telling the story of Narcissus in the opening chapter of *Moby Dick*. "It is the image of the ungraspable phantom of life; and this is the key to it all." In many ways the Hudson, which Melville knew intimately from Albany to Manhattan, reflects ourselves, our grace and our greed;

our virtue and our vices. Its waters are the key to much of America's past and present. The cities and towns that appear briefly in this history—New York, Yonkers, West Point, Poughkeepsie, Hudson, and Albany, among others, are places where men and women gathered to take advantage of nature's abundant spoils. Through fishing and commerce, community and civilization, they used the river to sustain their lives.

The one constant in this story is the Hudson itself, the valley where nature's creation and human creation meet, the river that connects so much of America's past with its present and future; unchangeable in its presence, yet always changing. This is a chronicle of those changes.

CHAPTER 1

The River and the Land

The landscape of the Hudson is a giant palimpsest, a great parchment on which the hand of nature has written and rewritten her bold signature for more than a billion years. As we look upon the nearly vertical cliffs of New Jersey's Palisades from Manhattan's Riverside Park, or take in the view of Rip Van Winkle's Catskill Mountains from the shore of Robert Livingston's Clermont estate in Columbia County, or step across the swift waters of the Opalescent River on the slope of Mount Marcy, we see just the top layer of writing on the land of the Hudson.

A closer inspection reveals traces of earlier scripts. When the last glacier scraped across the land less than twenty thousand years ago, it garbled the order of the writing one last time, leaving fragmentary codes of the past that scientists have been struggling to understand.

A shell heap left on the shore of the Hudson by Native Americans perhaps ten thousand years ago tells us that humans have contributed their own writing to the landscape. In the last four hundred years our writing has become more violent. We have blasted marble from Mount Pleasant in Westchester County for buildings and monuments in New York, Albany, and the great Sing Sing State Prison at the water's edge; we have dug enormous deposits of clay from the riverbanks for brick making; we have added hundreds of acres of land to the shores of the lower Hudson at Manhattan Island and New Jersey; we have dredged a wide channel for deep-ocean vessels to penetrate northward as far as Albany; we have erected forts along the riverbanks, including the great citadel at West Point; and we have deposited huge amounts of contaminants, including polychlorinated biphenyls (PCBs), mercury, garbage, and human waste, into the water. Each of our actions has changed the surface of the landscape.

For many the Hudson we see today appears to be two distinct rivers. The first belongs to the mountains. It begins in small Adirondack streams that appear as little more than faint squiggles on maps. The true rising takes place about ten miles southeast of the village of Lake Placid at Lake Tear of the Clouds on the southwestern slope of Mount Marcy, 4,322 feet above sea level. The lake might better be called a pond that depends primarily on runoff from the steep mountain slope above. Its meager outflow at the western end feeds Feldspar Brook. Children who climb to this spot will often use their feet to dam the trickling water, declaring to all the world that they alone have stopped the mighty Hudson.

Lake Tear of the Clouds is the place where the river's life begins.

Opposite: Lake Tear of the Clouds on the southwestern slope of Mount Marcy, the highest peak in the Adirondacks. One of hundreds of images of the Adirondacks captured by Seneca Ray Stoddard in the late nineteenth century, this photograph echoes the earlier landscape paintings of Thomas Cole or Asher B. Durand, as can be seen by comparing this view of Lake Tear of the Clouds with Cole's *Lake with Dead Trees* in Chapter 7. (Library of Congress)

Surrounded by evergreens and decaying trees, the lake appears a desolate, forbidding, even a prehistoric place. Its water supports no fish and, other than an occasional duck, little wildlife. But as the flow into the Feldspar attests, Lake Tear of the Clouds marks the first generation of the great river.

Life quickens in the brook. In the space of a mile the waters drop about a thousand feet down a deep declivity to join the Opalescent River. The Opalescent then charts a twisted path between Mount Colden and Cliff Mountain, plunging five hundred feet before broadening at the base of the mountains into a marsh known as the Flowed Land. Along the way, numerous springs make their own small, but pure, contributions to the current. The outflow from the Flowed Land drops about a thousand feet more before joining the outflow of another narrow sliver of water, Sanford Lake.

Sanford Lake also collects the waters from the slopes of other Adirondack peaks—Mount Adams, Mount Andrew, and Popple Hill among them—as well as from Lake Sally to the east and Henderson Lake to the north. It is the mile-long outflow connecting Henderson and Sanford lakes that cartographers have designated as "the Hudson River."

In its first fifty miles, the Hudson drops an average of sixty-four feet each mile. From Sanford Lake the river flows south and east while taking in a number of creeks, as well as the Indian, Schroon, and Sacandaga rivers; and it drops over a number of falls, including a fifty-foot plunge at Glens Falls. The waters head eastward to Hudson Falls and then turn due south through Fort Edward, Schuylerville, Stillwater, and Mechanicville. Still more tributaries, including the Battenkill, Fish Creek, and the Hoosic River, join the Hudson on its way to Troy. There the river meets its greatest tributary, the Mohawk, which more than doubles its volume. South of Troy the waters broaden dramatically for their final 150-mile journey to the sea.

This second river, often called the lower Hudson, is actually a fjord, a deep-valley channel where the fresh waters from the north and west mix with the tidal waters of the Atlantic Ocean. Indeed, this part of the Hudson is actually a long and broad tidal estuary. The scenery ranks with the most dramatic in North America. This is the river that lured countless artists to settle on its shores, attracted always by its extraordinary beauty.

Other tributaries, including the Esopus, the Catskill, the Wallkill, and the Croton, feed the second Hudson. The Catskill Mountains dominate the western shore, while to the east and well back from the water's edge lie the gentler hills of the Taconic range. At West Point the valley narrows to fifteen hundred feet. On the western shore opposite Yonkers and the northern part of Manhattan Island the land rises to form a sheer cliff known as the Palisades. At the southern tip of Manhattan, the Hudson merges with the East River at the Upper Bay before slipping through the Narrows between Brooklyn and Staten Island into the Lower Bay, and, ultimately, the Atlantic Ocean.

In the lower Hudson salt and fresh waters in the fjord battle for dominance. In seasons of drought the salt tides force their way as far north as Poughkeepsie, while spring freshets push the salt line below West Point. Even the winds of the valley are in contention. Atlantic breezes blowing north up the valley from New York harbor subside when they meet the cooler climate of the Highlands at Iona Island. There salt water and warm breezes from the Atlantic contend with fresh waters and cool winds from the north to determine from season to season the species of plants and fish that will live there. Arrowroot and pinweed thrive to the south, while black spruce and bog moss flourish to the north.

The relatively straight path of this lower Hudson never failed to impress Europeans in the seventeenth and eighteenth centuries. It seemed so different from the rivers they knew: the Danube that rises in Germany and winds its way across Austria, Hungary, and Romania before emptying into the Black Sea; or the Rhine that has so many twists, turns, and deflections in its course from Switzerland through Germany and Holland that at one point it flows east rather than west before it finally discharges its waters from the Alps into the North Sea; or the Dälaven that begins in the mountains on the Norwegian border with Sweden and cascades over falls and rapids flowing southeast in a circuitous fashion to the Baltic Sea.

"Why does this river go on in a direct line for so considerable a distance?" the Swedish naturalist Peter Kalm wondered when he sailed up the Hudson in June of 1749. Kalm was taken with the length of the Hudson's reaches, those straight stretches of water between two bends or points.

The Dutch called them "racks," and in many cases they still bear names given them in the seventeenth century. Captains sailing north from

Manhattan Island encounter the Great Chip Reach, bordered on the west by the cliffs of the Palisades; it extends from Weehawken to about Yonkers. From there they pass into the Tappan reach, the Tappan Zee of today. At Croton Point they meet the Haverstraw Reach, which extends to Stony Point. From the vantage at Stony Point sailors can see three and a half miles across the bay, making the Hudson seem more like a lake. The next four reaches—Seylmakers, Crescent, Hoge's, and Martyr's—challenge sailors. They lie in the Highlands where the currents, the winds, and the river's depth can be treacherous. So deep and narrow is the passage here that Herman Melville chose it as a metaphor of Captain Ahab's "deepeningly contracted" lunacy: "like the unabated Hudson, when that noble North-man flows narrowly, but unfathomably through the Highland gorge."

The next reaches—Fisher's, Lange Rack, Vasterack, and Claverack—fall between Storm King Mountain and the city of Hudson and are relatively long. But from Hudson north to Albany, the reaches, including Backerack, Jan Playsier's, and Hart's, become shorter as the navigable river narrows to restrict the vision of sailors. The Hudson of these last reaches is dominated by marshlands, or "flats," and islands, including Coxsackie, Rattlesnake, Houghtaling, and Lower and Upper Schodack.

The geological forces that made the first marks upon the great landscape of the Hudson began over a billion years ago in the Grenville orogeny, the oldest mountain-building period. We see evidence of those forces in the ancient metamorphic and igneous Precambrian rocks of the high-peak region of the eastern Adirondacks. Even to geologists, who talk of years in terms of tens and hundreds of millions, these rocks are very old. They should have worn away hundreds of millions of years ago, yet they are still rising at the rate of about three centimeters a year, as though a great cyclopean fist continues to push from beneath the surface to raise still higher the great peaks we call the Adirondacks.

It wasn't until the middle of the twentieth century that plate tectonic theory enabled geologists to explain the twists and contortions of the landscape. About 1.3 billion years ago, a slow tectonic collision of the continents of North America, Africa, and Europe folded, compressed, heated, and broke the rocks into high ancestral Adirondack peaks, towering mountains that rose perhaps fifteen miles from their base, three times the height of

Mount Everest. Erosion over the next 650 million years wore those peaks down to a relatively flat layer of Precambrian root rocks.

And all the time the continents were in a great slow-motion dance of separation and collision. Separation allowed the sea to flood in and deposit sediments, which became the sedimentary rocks, limestone, shale, and sandstone that we see today around the edges of the Adirondack dome. But then the continental plates collided once again to create more mountains and a supercontinent. About 220 million years ago they split apart once more to create North America, the Atlantic Ocean, Europe, and Africa much as we know them today. About 65 or 75 million years ago, the giant fist began to push upward, eventually forcing those ancient, billion-year-old root rocks of the Adirondacks into the mountains of today. On the slopes of those high peaks cascading streams have eroded channels in the softer sedimentary rocks. Among those streams are the ones that feed the Hudson.

In the tidal estuary of the lower Hudson, especially in the Highlands, nature's hand twisted the land in similar ways. The same separation of the continents that created the Atlantic Ocean helped to set the Hudson's course. But the landscape has been so changed that even today geologists can't agree completely on the events that shaped the valley. Most believe that beginning about 475 million years ago, as the entire coast lay under a sea that steadily deposited the detritus of algae and other ancient forms of life, the crusts of the continents collided again to deform and metamorphose the Precambrian rocks of the Grenville orogeny, and fold and uplift them with immense pressure and temperature into the schist, gneiss, slate, and marble that we can find in the Catskills, the Highlands, and the Palisades on the west side of the river and the Taconic range on the east side.

These mountain-building periods are difficult to interpret. We see signs of great metamorphic events in the durable granite-rich hills and mountains lining the river like North Beacon, Breakneck, Storm King, Bear, and Dunderberg, as well as in the weaker marble belts of Mount Pleasant behind Sing Sing. In Central Park, Manhattan's eight-hundred-acre bay window onto millions of years of the past, the boulders of Manhattan Schist are also evidence of mountain building.

Still, the geologic evidence is difficult to interpret. At the cliffs near Peekskill, in the midst of the metamorphic rock, an igneous intrusion of nearly black norite granite and nearly white Peekskill Granite appears.

Its writing upon the landscape is more recent, perhaps about 435 million years ago. These granites are 40 million years younger than the rocks around them. The evidence of Manhattan and the Palisades opposite the island is similarly confusing. It suggests a splitting of the continents 220 million years ago. The Hudson River cleaves the landscape at the point of the split.

The most recent rending of the land occurred about an hour ago in geologic time. Roughly 22 million years ago the earth's climate began to cool; by about 2 million years ago the path of the Hudson Valley lay under a thick sheet of ice that covered even the high peaks of the Adirondacks. At times the glacier advanced; at others it receded; and each time it left its mark upon the landscape. The last ice sheet, the Wisconsin, culminated about 20,000 years ago. It had the greatest impact on our present land, eliminating and reworking earlier glacial deposits. It was possibly 350 feet thick, exerting extraordinary pressure that actually flattened the land. The Atlantic Ocean was perhaps 400 feet lower than today, exposing about 100 miles of the continental shelf. The receding sheet eased the pressure on the land, allowing it to rise, with the result that the valley of the Hudson that had been created over a hundred million years earlier became both wider and deeper.

As the southern edge of the Wisconsin ice sheet receded, glacial ice also flowed south to create an immense terminal moraine of sand and gravel that we know as Long Island. Today the Hudson passes from the Upper to the Lower Bay through the Narrows, but this wasn't always the case. The moraine of Long Island once extended west, damming the waters from the glacier to create Glacial Lake Hudson. The lake very possibly extended northward to the Tappan Zee and spilled through the Sparkill Gap into New Jersey. Into this glacial lake streams and rivers often deposited layers of sand, gravel, and clay left by the glacier. Glacial Lake Hudson lasted for thousands of years before the force of the water finally cut a path through the Narrows to the ocean. Today we see unmistakable signs of this geologic event in the clays, sands, and sediments like those found at Croton Point, where the present-day Croton River meets the Hudson.

The narrow passage of the Hudson through the Highlands that we see today did not exist under the Wisconsin ice sheet. At that point a barrier of rock arose as the ice retreated to create another huge lake—Glacial Lake

Albany—that extended from the Highlands northward to Glens Falls and westward into the region of the lower Mohawk valley. Again, streams and rivers that emptied into the lake marked their union with deposits of sediments. Like Glacial Lake Hudson to the south, Lake Albany scoured its way through the metamorphic rock barrier at the Highlands to complete the river's present course to the sea.

Scientists have found another, unseen, Hudson that takes an important place in the geological story. After the waters flow through the Narrows between Brooklyn and Staten Island, and southeast toward the Ambrose Light, the river seems to end. Twenty thousand years earlier, when the Wisconsin ice sheet was receding and the continent extended about 130 miles farther, to the rim of the continental shelf, the river could be seen flowing through a channel before dropping into a deep gorge. Since the waters from the receding ice sheet made the Atlantic Ocean about 400 feet deeper, the floor of this great submerged gorge—geologists call it "Hudson Canyon"—lies between 9,000 and 15,000 feet beneath the ocean's surface. Other East Coast rivers, the Delaware and the Potomac, have similar canyons, but the Hudson Canyon is the greatest of them all.

In this underwater Grand Canyon, so deep that plant life cannot survive there, fish swim that are rarely seen elsewhere. Many are large and predatory. A species of tilefish weighing as much as thirty pounds burrows into the sloping sides of the Hudson Canyon before the water plunges into the cold darkness. There, leatherback turtles may be found, as well as whales, five-hundred-pound tuna, and the nasty, six-foot-long lancet fish, which features a tall dorsal fin, wide mouth, and fanglike teeth.

About halfway to Bermuda, at the bottom of the continental shelf and deep in the ocean, at a place fittingly called the Abyssal Plain, the water of the Hudson that began its journey on the slope of Mount Marcy in the Adirondacks and gathered the waters of countless rivers, streams, brooks, and springs along its journey, deposits the last traces of debris from the Hudson Canyon. It is there on the Abyssal Plain, about 895 miles southeast of Lake Tear of the Clouds, that the Hudson River ends its journey at last.

The Hudson River and its valley are part of a vast web of natural life. In the river, simpler life forms—plankton, diatoms, and algae—abound. Enriched by the sun and floating on the tide, they nurture larvae, worms, and amphipoda that join plankton on the banquet table for sunfish, shiners, and bass, among others. Fish take their place as the food of choice for gulls, herons, eagles, and ospreys—and of course, humans. The land contributes to the infinite cycle, too. Nitrogen from soil bacteria and plants leaches into streams that feed the Hudson to nurture aquatic life. Phosphorous, an essential mineral required by every cell membrane, leaches from weathering rocks into plants and watershed runoff. The cycle of birth, growth, death, and rebirth is infinite.

Late in the twentieth century scientists counted 206 species in the Hudson estuary. Five different classes of fish are present: freshwater, including small and largemouth bass and silver, white, and yellow perch; catadromus, fish that migrate from fresh water to the sea to spawn, including the American eel; anadromus, saltwater fish that ascend the Hudson to spawn in fresh water, including shad, striped bass, Atlantic sturgeon, and tomcod; saltwater fish, which spend their first year feeding in fresh water, including bluefish; and estuarine, which live mainly in the brackish waters of the lower Hudson, including hogchokers. Most have originated in the river's mouth, but some, including the spotfin shiner (*Notropis spilopterus*) and the central mudminnow (*Umbra limi*), swam east from Lake Erie through the Erie Canal.

The sheer number of fish is astonishing. In the 1980s scientists found that 3 to 4 million shad came to spawn in the Hudson each year, and, depending on the time, the number of striped bass jumped from a million in the late summer and fall to tens of millions in the late spring when their eggs hatched.

The Hudson estuary allows "almost any species that occurs in the nearby Atlantic" into the river, as one ichthyologist wrote, and marine strays are more the rule than the exception; one count in 1995 found seventy-seven such stray species from the ocean. Sharks swim upstream from time to time, as do the occasional skate, conger eel, striped anchovy, Atlantic cod, Atlantic mackerel, lined seahorse, Atlantic herring, and scores of others. Occasionally an eddy from the Gulf Stream that passes by the Lower Bay proves particularly warm in August, which lures striped mullets, ladyfish, and lookdowns into the river. Should they find a discharge pipe from a power plant, they have been known to survive the winter.

Fish aren't the only creatures to swim into the Hudson. In the mid seventeenth century, Adriaen van der Donck, one of the first to describe the Hudson Valley in detail, reported that in March 1647 several whales swam upriver as far north as Troy. One met its end when it became stranded at the Cohoes falls, making the river "oily for three weeks, and covered with grease," and filling the air with its stench "for two miles to leeward." In 1693 a royal charter gave Trinity Church the right to any whale that washed onto Manhattan's shore. Trinity did not exercise its right in 1983, when a dead forty-foot finback whale was found off Sixty-fourth Street. Occasionally an alert stroller in Riverside Park or a police diver will spot a whale, a harbor seal, or a sea turtle. Peter Kalm reported that "porpoises played and tumbled in the river." Late in the last century a school of dolphins swam almost to Albany before heading back downriver.

The rich diversity of the Hudson's aquatic and plant life brings birds and beasts to feast on the fruits of the waters. Amphibians—especially frogs and toads—live along the entire river, particularly in the shallow waters of the Adirondacks. The Flowed Land of the Opalescent teems with toads; the brackish waters of the lower Hudson, however, are not hospitable to amphibians. As we see from the snapping turtles around Constitution and Iona islands, they prefer the tidal marshes of the estuary.

Other animals, including many black bears, numerous deer, moose, raccoons, foxes, and beavers, are prevalent in the Hudson Valley as well. It was the abundance of this last animal that lured many of the colonists from Europe to New Netherland. Scientists estimate that there were about 60 million beavers in New England and New York at the beginning of the seventeenth century, and perhaps 20 million of them lived in the Hudson Valley. That was before the killing began. "We estimate that eighty thousand beavers are annually killed in this quarter of the country," wrote van der Donck. Then he added, "There are some persons who imagine that the animals of the country will be destroyed in time, but this is unnecessary anxiety."

Along with humans, these large rodents are nature's great colonizers and builders. They look to the marshes and tributaries of the Hudson as places to build their domed lodges. With their huge incisors, whose orange color reveals a heavy concentration of iron, they can fell aspen and birch trees with extraordinary swiftness.

The beaver is one of nature's more efficient creatures. Its short legs and front feet with claws are ideal for grooming, manipulating food, and gripping branches. Its webbed rear feet make it a powerful swimmer. Its fur has two layers: The grayish brown under fur, short, fine, and dense, keeps water from reaching the skin. The reddish brown outer fur, long, coarse, and glossy, protects the animal from the underbrush. With its front paws and incisors, the beaver spreads oil secreted through its skin pores on the coarse hairs to keep the outer coat shiny and waterproof. It is the beaver's fur that brought the Hudson's other great colonizers, the Europeans, to its valley.

"The whole country is covered with wood," van der Donck reported. For him the Edenic land of the Hudson only wanted to be tamed. Huge oaks ("sixty to seventy feet high") with great boles ("two to three fathoms thick") equaled any that might be found on the Rhine. Nut-wood, "tough and hard," served for "cogs and rounds in our mills and for threshing-flails, swivel-trees, and other farming purposes." So great was the abundance of wood that, "unless there are natural changes or great improvidence, there can be no scarcity of wood in this country."

In a crude but ecologically sound form of forest management, which also made the hunting easier, the Native Americans burned the woods and meadows in the fall or spring. In Rensselaerwyck, abundant with pine, the scene from the deck of a boat in the Hudson was sublime: "When the woods are burning on both sides of the [river] . . . we can see a great distance by the light of the blazing trees, the flames being driven by the wind, and fed by the tops of the trees." But there were times, van der Donck reported, when the fires got out of hand and consumed houses, barns, and fences.

Peter Kalm expressed similar awe when he visited the Hudson nearly a century later. On his leisurely three-day journey up the river to gather seeds and specimens of plants and trees for the Swedish Academy he made a record of what he saw—the flora, fauna, and fish—along with the general features of the landscape. As he traveled by boat rather than on foot or horse, he had the perspective of both shores as well as the water itself.

To Kalm everything seemed to be in abundance. He visited islands cultivated with grain. He saw several kinds of apple trees ("they bear as fine fruit as in any other part of North America"), farms that grew hemp, flax, and corn. Dutch and German farmers, he reported, produced great quantities of peas and potatoes. He was told that the wheat near Albany made the best flour "in all North America, except that from Sopus [Esopus] or King's Town [Kingston]." Grapevines grew "on the steep banks of the river in surprising quantities," sometimes climbing and pulling down nearby trees. Sword grass covered the meadows near the water and in several places formed small islands. As Kalm looked into the dense woods that in many places came to the shoreline, he noted sassafras and chestnut trees, red flowering and sugar maples, red cedars and white oaks, water beech and elms, sumac and water poplar, as well as examples of the mountain laurel that he discovered.

Natives and Europeans, residents and visitors, have always appreciated the remarkable natural abundance and beauty of the Hudson Valley. Starting in the eighteenth century, people like Jane Colden, Amos Eaton, and Verplanck Colvin began to appreciate the landscape scientifically. Colden studied the valley's flora for Carolus Linnæus. Eaton was the first to make a systematic study of the geology of the Hudson River valley. Colvin tramped through the Adirondacks, found the source of the Hudson, and understood better than anyone of his time the ecology of the river and the land. Each of these pioneers stood at the dawn of our understanding of the Hudson's natural history, and their personal histories tell us much about the culture of the valley and the nature of the early republic.

On his trip up the Hudson, Kalm had stopped at Coldengham, the three-thousand-acre manor northwest of Newburgh that belonged to Jane Colden's father, Cadwallader Colden, the philosopher, scientist, and sometime lieutenant governor of New York. A product of the Enlightenment, Colden embraced the scientific and intellectual developments of the seventeenth century, especially the discoveries of Isaac Newton and Edmund Halley, and the empiricism of Francis Bacon. Mixing intellectual inquiry and political ambition, he wrote numerous reports as well as a history of the Iroquois and served various royal governors. In 1728, he moved his wife and children to Coldengham, "a small spot of the world which when I first entered upon it was the habitation of wolves and bears," Colden reflected some years later. He tamed the wilderness of his small spot with a fine stone house and devoted his life to farming and the pursuit of useful knowledge. From Coldengham, where he was free to indulge his "humor in philosophical amusements more than I could while in town," he carried on a steady correspondence with men like Benjamin Franklin, Linnæus, and the first president of New York's King's College, Samuel Johnson, the Philadelphia naturalist John Bartram, and the Charleston doctor Alexander Garden.

It was Colden's study of botany that brought Kalm to Coldengham. He arrived with two books, gifts from Linnæus, including one describing a new plant genus, Coldenia. Colden had been quick to recognize the importance of Linnæus's simple yet elegant binomial structure for botanical classifications, and he "resolved" to apply it to the plants growing near his own house. Colden's flora, the first such classification of New York flora, so impressed Linnæus that he published it through the Swedish Royal Society as "Plantæ Coldenghamiæ," and named a new genus that Colden had discovered in his honor.

But Cadwallader Colden had entered his seventh decade by the time of Kalm's visit, and he found himself unable to "bear the fatigue which accompanies botanical Researches." Yet the letters from London, Leiden, Uppsala, Philadelphia, and Charleston, each with a request for a description or a specimen, kept arriving. In desperation he turned to his daughter Jane for help. Jane was then twenty-eight, the fifth of Cadwallader's ten children. Though she lacked formal schooling she possessed a natural "inclination to reading" and a "curiosity for natural philosophy," as Colden reported to a botanist in Europe. Endowed with "a sufficient capacity for attaining a competent knowledge," she could become his plant gatherer and cataloger. With some initial tutoring from her father, Jane learned the principles of Linnæan classification—albeit in English, because she knew no Latin. Colden procured the best botanical books from Europe for his daughter, "as she cannot have the opportunity of seeing plants in a botanical garden." After some initial explorations around the property yielded descriptions of common plants—dandelion and hollyhock—she was ready to venture farther into the countryside. By 1753, Jane had cataloged and described in detail 142 specimens; by her death the number had grown to 352. With each description she included a simple ink drawing of a leaf from the plant.

The quality of Jane Colden's descriptions is remarkable, not so much for the number of plants she presented but for the astuteness and detail as well as the sensuousness and charm of her observations. Thus the cup or calyx of red mint (*Monarda didyma*), commonly known as "bee balm," is "a Long Tube, with many Streaks, mouth cut into 5 sharp pointed teeth"; its flower "one long Ripe shaped leaf, widen'd towards the top, its brim cut deep into two, the upper Lip upright, sharp pointed." The brim of the flower of Virginia snakeroot (*Aristolachia serpentaria*) "forms two blown up roundish hollow Lips, which nearly close the upper one resembling the Lip of a Hare." Jane was careful to note the medicinal qualities of her specimens. "NB. The Root of this Asclepias taken in powder, is an excellent cure for the Colick," she writes of silk grass (*Asclepias tuberosa*), commonly known as butterfly weed. "About halff a Spoonfull at a time," she suggests, reporting that the cure came from a "Canada Indian" and had been confirmed "by Dr. Porter of New England, and Dr. Brooks of Maryland."

Nor was she reluctant to challenge the one who had created the system: "Linnæus describes this as being a Papilionatious Flower, and calls the two largest leaves of the Cup *Alae*," she wrote in her entry on snakeroot (*Polygala*), "but as they continue, till the Seed is ripe and the two flower Leaves, and its appendage fol[d] together. I must beg leave to differ from him." And then, adding an additional, sweet, persistent barb to her disagreement: "the Seed Vessell, differs from all that I have observed of the Papilionatious Kind."

Cadwallader Colden soon found that his daughter's acquiescence in his desires reinforced and even expanded his place in the intellectual fraternity of naturalists. He became her champion, writing of her accomplishments to his correspondents in America and Europe. "She has already a pretty large volume in writing," he wrote to a scientist in Leiden. "She has the impression of three hundred plants in the manner you'll see by the samples." Addressing her as "Respected Friend Jane Colden," John Bartram wrote in his best Quaker prose of "ye viney plant thee so well discribes. . . . I never searched ye characters of ye flower so curiously as I find thee hath done." William Bartram sent her some of his own drawings. Along with the Bartrams, Alexander Garden visited Cadwallader and Jane at Coldengham; Garden wrote glowingly of her accomplishments to Charles Alston, director of the Botanical Gardens in Edinburgh. He sent Jane seeds of a shrub he had found in New York, which he named Cape Jasmine (*Hypericum virginicum*), only to learn that she had discovered it before him, and "using the privilege of first discoverer" she named the plant gardenia. Small matter that still another naturalist, John Ellis, had actually discovered the bush before her. He too prevailed upon Linnæus to name it gardenia. Later, Jane wrote an article about gardenias that was published in Edinburgh. From London Peter Collinson wrote Cadwallader Colden in admiration of his "ingenious daughter"; Collinson and Ellis each praised her work to Linnæus.

In the woods of the Hudson Valley, Jane Colden had established a botanical idyll known to important naturalists throughout the colonies and Europe. But when Britain declared war on France in 1756, the idyll came to an abrupt end. The French and Indian War, as it came to be known, curtailed Jane's excursions into the countryside to hunt for specimens; visits to Coldengham by fellow naturalists ceased. The following year Cadwallader Colden moved his family to the safe haven of Manhattan and turned his attentions once again to politics and serving the British crown.

Unable to gather plants in the field, Jane devoted her time to rewriting, indexing, and providing Latin names for the 340 descriptions of Hudson Valley plants in her manuscript. (Her attempts at illustrations of her flora however, show that her talents lay in verbal rather than visual description; her drawings appear as basic renderings.) She also found time to be courted by William Farquhar, a widowed doctor and Scotsman. When they married in 1759, she was in her thirty-fifth year, her husband in his fifty-fifth. With her marriage, Jane Colden's botanical studies ceased. Perhaps Cadwallader Colden's political activities precluded his need for the intellectual companionship that his daughter's work had provided; perhaps she felt her duties to her husband and to their only child barred such study. On March 10, 1766, Jane Colden, the first female botanist in America, died in New York City.

Amos Eaton was born with the promise of the republic: at sunrise on May 17, 1776, into a third-generation family of farmers in the Hudson Valley hamlet of Chatham in Columbia County. His early schooling showed his potential: he excelled in Latin and Greek, mathematics, and natural philosophy; he designed and built his own compass and surveying instruments; and he graduated "with reputation" from Williams College in 1799. That year Eaton married a childhood friend, fathered a son, and moved to New York to study law with New York's attorney general, Josiah Ogden Hoffman, and later, it is said, with Alexander Hamilton. A close friend and fellow student in Hoffman's office was Washington Irving.

The natural sciences, however, not the law, inspired Eaton's imagination and captured his intellect. He spent much of his time outside Hoffman's offices studying informally with two of the nation's foremost physicians and scientists, David Hosack and Samuel Latham Mitchill. Hosack and Mitchill were what we might call scientific generalists today. At Columbia College they were professors of "materia medica"—the botanic substances used in medicine and chemistry. Hosack had an extensive mineral collection and established a large botanical garden three miles north of the city on the site of present-day Rockefeller Center. Mitchill established and edited the first professional journal of medicine, was the first professor of chemistry in the country, and wrote a basic survey of the geology of the Hudson. Hosack and Mitchill welcomed the serious young man, and encouraged his study of botany and mineralogy. It was a time, Eaton remembered, when "Fortune seemed to smile on every side." Only at the end of his studies in New York did his fortunes change, for shortly before he was admitted to the bar in October 1802 his wife died of consumption.

Undaunted by his loss, the young widower moved to Catskill, a village a hundred miles north of Manhattan on the west bank of the Hudson, to take a position as attorney and land agent for John Livingston. It was in Catskill that Amos Eaton's misfortunes increased. Livingston proved to be a difficult employer, rich in land and arrogance, but poor in cash and spirit. "Collect money as fast as possible," he wrote to his agent, goading Eaton to make economies on the property and raise the rents. Eaton decided to become a landowner himself and joined with his father to purchase five thousand acres in the town of Catskill.

It was the natural history of the land rather than land speculation that quickly began to consume most of Eaton's time. The botany and geology of the Hudson landscape soon obsessed him. By 1806 he was devoting every spare moment to walking through the valley, collecting and classifying plant and rock specimens, recording observations in voluminous notebooks, and corresponding with the leading scientists in Europe and America. When he delivered a series of lectures on the botany of the Hudson to small groups of interested villagers, he also discovered he was a natural teacher. With the encouragement of his mentors Hosack and Mitchill, Eaton began a botanical school at Catskill "to make practical Botanists of young persons of all conditions and pursuits."

Perhaps it was his increasing interest in natural history that made Eaton so blind to the machinations of Nathaniel Pendleton, who sold him land in Catskill in 1805. Later it seems Pendleton wanted the land back and brought a charge of forgery against Eaton. As the penalty for forgery was life in prison, it was not unusual for a person accused of the crime to flee the state, thereby leaving his property in the hands of his accuser, and there is some evidence that Pendleton expected to "frighten [Eaton] to New Orleans, or to some other great distance."

By today's standards the outcome of the case was a flagrant miscarriage of justice. The documents Pendleton brought forward as "evidence" of forgery had themselves been forged. Moreover, Pendleton alleged that Eaton committed his crime 145 days *after* the indictment, a remarkable inconsistency that neither the judge nor the jury seems to have taken into account.

There can be no question that Eaton was a victim of connivance. But he was guilty of his own failure to take the charges against him seriously until it was too late. By then he was bankrupt and disgraced. Hosack and Mitchill had abandoned him, as had judges and fellow lawyers. Only his second wife, whom he had married shortly after arriving in Catskill, stood by his side. She was pregnant with his third child when the sentence was delivered: "hard labor for and during his natural Life."

At Newgate Prison in Manhattan, however, Amos Eaton was not a typical prisoner. Recognizing his abilities, Newgate's agent, William Torrey, granted him unusual liberties. Torrey appointed him clerk of the shops to keep account of "all the articles manufactured" and saw to it that Eaton took his meals with the guards. Whenever he wanted to break from his work, Eaton was free to walk about the prison yard and stroll with a guard on the banks of the Hudson. Of all the liberties William Torrey afforded his unique prisoner, the most important was the freedom to teach. The prison agent established classes in botany and geology for his son John as well as the children of Newgate's committee of overseers. When he wasn't teaching, Eaton devoted himself to study. John Torrey, the prison agent's son, provided him with books; Eaton invented new botanic classifications based on notes about plant specimens he had gathered before his imprisonment; and he wrote a three-hundred-page treatise titled "A System of Mineralogy."

It wasn't until November 1815 that Governor Daniel Tompkins chose to release Eaton, but the governor extracted a condition: "that . . . he depart from the state of New York and never thereafter return to the same." Banished from New York and the Hudson Valley where he had spent most of his life, Eaton turned to New England, first to New Haven and Yale University, where he attended lectures on chemistry, mineralogy, and botany; then to Williamstown and Williams College, where he lectured on zoology, botany, and geology. With his Williams students he published a comprehensive botanical dictionary.

Eaton remained an exile until 1817, when DeWitt Clinton became governor of New York. As mayor of New York City at the time of Eaton's incarceration, Clinton likely came to know about the quiet man at Newgate Prison, the one who many said was falsely accused, who had earned the trust of the warden and guards and who even taught natural science to the overseers' children. Through Torrey, Clinton himself gave the prisoner access to his own library of scientific books. Just six months after he was sworn in as governor, Clinton granted the forty-one-year-old Eaton unconditional pardon.

There appears to have been, however, one unwritten condition: Eaton would deliver a series of lectures to the state legislature on the geology of New York. Work had just begun on "Clinton's ditch," the Erie Canal between the Hudson and the Great Lakes, which would change the fortunes of the Hudson Valley, the state, and the nation. The governor himself sponsored Eaton's lectures on natural history to the "state sachems," as Eaton described them. More lectures followed, so many that by 1819 Eaton described himself as a "scientific peddler." "I have learned to act in such a polymorphous character," he wrote, "that I am, to men of science a curiosity, to ladies a clever schoolmaster, to old women a wizard, to blackguards and boys a shewman and to sage legislators *a very knowing man.*"

But Amos Eaton also knew of his abilities in geology. "I tell you I am the best *practical* geologist in the U.S.!!!!!!!!!!!!" exulted a confident and headstrong Eaton to a friend in 1818. He was right. Though primitive and mistaken by today's standards, his understanding of geology was far advanced for the time. From observations he made on walking trips through the Hudson Valley and the Taconic Mountains, he theorized that the land had undergone cycles of change, that periods when marine sediments were being deposited by ocean floods had been supplanted by plant deposits as the floods receded. The cycle continued as the land was flooded again. The theory seems quaint, but for the time it was ambitious. While most scientists were content simply to note the appearance of various rocks, Eaton did not rest until he had studied the place of rocks in strata, which meant observing and comparing them in "fifty or a hundred localities" and recording his findings in detailed geological maps as well as *An Index to the Geology of the Northern States.*

Among the legislators who heard Amos Eaton's lectures was Stephen Van Rensselaer, eighth Patroon of Rensselaerwyck, owner of much of Rensselaer County on the eastern shore of the Hudson, including the city of Troy, and much of Albany County on the western shore. Understanding the importance of the Erie Canal, Van Rensselaer saw the economic benefits that would accrue to him and the region from a scientific understanding of the land. He hired Eaton to produce *A Geological Survey of the County of Albany* in 1820, which collected and arranged "geological facts with a direct view to the improvement of agriculture." Companion surveys of Rensselaer County and the lands along the route of the canal followed. With Van Rensselaer's money and support, Eaton completed a transverse section of landscape from Boston to Buffalo, some 550 miles long and 50 miles wide.

In 1824, Eaton turned to the patroon, or "The Patron" as he aptly called Van Rensselaer, to help create what became his most enduring legacy: a school in Troy "for the . . . application of science to the common purposes of life." The Rensselaer School, later named Rensselaer Polytechnic Institute, embodied Eaton's pedagogical belief that students learn best by performing scientific experiments and lecturing on their experience. The patron supported Eaton's school with ten thousand dollars in its first three years, which effectively gave him control of the enterprise. In one of his first acts, Van Rensselaer appointed Eaton "professor of chemistry and experimental philosophy, and lecturer on geology, land surveying, and laws regulating town officers and jurors." The graduates of Eaton's course of study soon established themselves in their profession, and for more than a generation the school produced most of the nation's geologists. Rensselaer alumni headed county and state geological surveys across the land and published geology textbooks that influenced the thinking of even more students in America. One outstanding graduate, Washington Roebling, served as chief engineer on the Brooklyn Bridge. Although Rensselaer did have other professors, Eaton himself supervised every department of the school and presented full courses on geology, botany, and civil engineering, as well as condensed courses on subjects as disparate as astronomy and rhetoric. And, though he was far in advance of public opinion and doomed to failure, Amos Eaton made a bold proposal to open Rensselaer's education to women students.

"If I am to be remembered for anything," Eaton wrote to a friend at the height of his success, "it will be geology and *geology* only." He was right. So important were his contributions to the study of geology and his training of geologists that historians of science celebrate him as the "Father of American Geology" and fondly give a geological appellation to the period of his investigations: the Eatonian Era.

Amos Eaton confined his geological and botanical investigations to the lower Hudson; Verplanck Colvin, another nineteenth-century lawyer turned scientist, investigated the river's upper reaches. As had been the case with Eaton, his research soon became an obsession; but in Colvin's case the obsession took several strange turns.

Like so many whose families had lived in the Hudson Valley for centuries, Colvin carried himself with proud self-assurance, and he was quick to embellish his numerous achievements. The motto on his family's crest, *In hoc signo vinces,* or "Under this sign you will conquer," set the tone of his every act. In an 1882 sketch he wrote about himself (in the third person) for a biography of New York state's public servants, he reveals that assurance. Not content just to record his birth in Albany in 1847, he traced his forebears to the *Mayflower* on his father's side and to Dutch emigrants from Holland on his mother's. Vanity also compelled him to note that the maternal side of his family had settled on the east shore of the Hudson about thirty-five miles north of Manhattan, at a place they named Verplanck Point. Colvin's father, a state senator and Albany city attorney, groomed his son for a career in the law, but the youth had other ideas. Chemistry was an early interest until an explosion leveled the laboratory he had built behind his parents' house. Prudently, the young scientist turned to the calmer pursuits of geology, surveying, cartography, and preservation in the Adirondack wilderness. Colvin concluded his autobiographical sketch with a sentence that betrayed all of his virtues and vanities: "He is a young man of thirty-five years of age, and un married; is nearly six feet in height, muscular, and erect; in manner quiet, but in spirit and determination indomitable."

At the time he wrote his own profile, Colvin had been demonstrating his spirit and determination for more than a decade in New York's largely uncharted Adirondacks, which at the time were being ravaged by lumbermen. Erosion from the denuded mountains was silting the region's streams and rivers, and ultimately threatening the flow of the Hudson. The state had taken possession of most of the Adirondacks after the Revolution, but no one had any idea of the region's size and importance, the number of its lakes and ponds, or the number and height of its mountains. Surely, Colvin argued, the state should make a survey to learn exactly what it did own. He hounded and cajoled, using his family's position and his good Dutch name to gain entry to the offices of the state's assemblymen. In 1872 his efforts paid off. That year the assembly voted "Verplanck Colvin . . . ten hundred dollars, to aid in completing a survey of the Adirondack wilderness."

Colvin was appointed at a time when Americans wanted to learn more about their land. Colonel Frederick W. Lander had brought the artist Albert Bierstadt with him to record the splendors he encountered on a railway survey in the Far West. In 1863 Bierstadt awed crowds in a New York City gallery with his majestic painting *Rocky Mountains, Lander's Peak*. In 1869, Major John Wesley Powell and a small party successfully navigated the rapids of the Colorado River through the Grand Canyon. As Colvin was beginning his survey of the Adirondacks the artist Thomas Moran was exhibiting his huge (seven feet tall and twelve feet long) *Grand Canyon of the Yellowstone* in New York City. (The critic for the *Times* proclaimed it "splendid.") Though the emphasis on exploration was to the west, in New York about a third of the state also lay uncharted. Like Powell in the West, Colvin set out to record the largely unknown territory. In the next three decades of tramping through the 8 million acres of wilderness, Colvin would discover new lakes, new mountains, and the source of the Hudson River.

With just a thousand dollars to "aid" his work, Colvin began the project that would occupy him for the next twenty-eight years. The funding was never steady or certain. Sometimes he could hire but a few guides and surveyors and had to forgo any pay for himself; at other times, he could hire large parties with a dozen men or more. Colvin proved a stern and eccentric taskmaster. In the late spring, he marched his men and hundreds of pounds of equipment through the Adirondack wilderness. He demanded the men be "strong in constitution and spirit and morals," and he forbade them from using "spirituous liquor." Each Sunday morning he led them in a lengthy service of prayers and Bible readings, usually on the shore of a newly charted lake or pond. No weather, not freezing temperatures, snow, or ice, would deter Colvin from his mission.

Surveying 8 million acres of wilderness tested Colvin's ingenuity. The equipment had to be portable and relatively easy to carry over rough terrain. To make his measurements he relied on triangulation, the elementary geometry rule that knowledge of the length and angles of one side of a triangle will enable one to determine the length of the other two sides. Starting at the summit of a mountain within sight of two lighthouses on the shore of Lake Champlain, Colvin created a network of triangles that located the place of every feature of the landscape. On each of the two mountaintops that formed the distant points of his triangle through space, he erected a "Stan Helio," a tower of his own devising with tin reflectors that could be seen by the naked eye twenty miles away.

The tin reflectors for the Stan Helio were light in comparison with the hundreds of pounds of equipment—theodolite or transit to measure the summits of mountains through trigonometry, a sextant, glass mountain barometers that also measured altitudes, and red, white, and black signal flags—as well as food. In order to cross remote lakes and ponds Colvin invented a canvas boat weighing but a few pounds that could be carried easily into the wilderness. For this he received a patent in 1874.

He climbed and mapped all the high peaks: Big Slide and Kempshall, Gore and Seward, Colden and Wright, and the highest of all, Mount Marcy. He followed the waters: Mill and Stony creeks; the Schroon and Sacandaga rivers; Trout and Feldspar brooks. And he surveyed all the lakes:

Verplanck Colvin (left) with an assistant surveying the
Adirondacks from a summit station in the mountains.
From 1872 to 1900 Colvin charted 8 million acres of
the wilderness. He frequently submitted reports to the
state legislature condemning the reckless and shortsighted destruction being carried out by tannery owners
and lumbermen. It was Colvin who discovered the rising
of the Hudson on the slope of Mount Marcy. He called
it "the *summit water* of the State," a "minute unpretending
tear of the clouds." (Adirondack Museum)

Tupper and Saranac; Raquette and Long. In just one year, Colvin and his surveyors paddled on and mapped 250 hitherto unexplored lakes. Many of the ponds, lakes, streams, brooks, and rivers, Colvin carefully noted, made up the vast watershed that emptied into the Hudson.

It was in 1872, the first year of his survey, that Verplanck Colvin made his most important contribution to knowledge of the Hudson when he discovered its source. Before Colvin's accurate measurement of the elevations in the Adirondacks, opinion was divided on the origin of the Hudson. Some spoke of Hendrick Spring that feeds Round Pond as the remote source. The waters from Round Pond flow into Catlin Lake and from thence into the Hudson. Others considered Lakes Avalanche and Colden fed by the Opalescent. But Colvin's surveying found these assumptions to be wrong. On September 16, descending from the summit of Mount Marcy he came upon "a little lake," as Colvin described it in his report to the state legislature. It was "the *summit water* of the State." But then he became more poetic. The *"Summit Water,"* Colvin said, was a "minute unpretending tear of the clouds . . . a lonely pool, shivering in the breezes of the mountains, and sending its limpid surplus through Feldspar Brook, to the Opalescent River, the well-spring of the Hudson." Even the state legislators were moved by the surveyor's description of the brilliant teardrop from the heavens. They named Colvin's "Summit Water" Lake Tear of the Clouds.

We may trace New York State's creation of the Adirondack Park to the efforts of Verplanck Colvin. For a quarter of a century, the surveyor used his annual reports to the assemblymen to tell them of the magnificent wilderness at their back door, and to condemn the reckless and shortsighted destruction being carried out by tannery owners and lumbermen. Tanneries were abundant in the southern part of the Adirondacks, especially in Warrensburg, a small town on the Hudson in the midst of a hemlock forest. Tanners simply felled the trees and stripped the bark—the source of tannic acid used in leather making—and left the trunks to rot. Worse for the Hudson, the tanners dumped the poisonous wastewater from their tanning vats into the river.

Lumbering proved even more destructive. Early in the century, speculators like Amos Eaton's nemesis Nathaniel Pendleton, who built a dam and a mill in the town of Newcomb, had trees cut and lumber sawn on the spot. The product then was almost entirely board lumber for construction. But by the time Colvin's surveying party arrived in the Adirondacks, the destruction brought by the ax had become more wanton. Sawmills were located downriver at places like Albany, closer to the markets for lumber. The development of pulp papermaking after the Civil War brought huge mills and wealth to Hudson River towns like Corinth and Glens Falls, and by the end of the century, Mechanicville. To feed the insatiable saws and pulp vats, lumbermen now routinely moved deeper into the wilderness, cutting every spruce, balsam, pine, and hemlock in sight. (They left hardwood trees—walnut, ash, cherry, maple—because the logs are difficult to float.) The state seemed all too ready to oblige the lumber companies. It declared Adirondack rivers, including the Hudson, to be private highways for logs and allowed a log boom to be set up in the oxbow of the river just above Glens Falls. The state also sold lumber companies tract after tract of Adirondack forest land, sometimes for as little as five cents an acre. Lumbermen quickly denuded each acre of forest and, once the land was cleared, moved on.

The lumbermen always felled trees in winter and skidded them over the snow and ice to the banks of the rivers and lakes that feed the Hudson. With the breakup of the ice in the spring, drivers pitched the logs into the waters for their journey to the Hudson mills. Even comparatively narrow rock-filled rivers like the Schroon became lucrative highways for logs. Loggers for lumbermills took trees with boles of at least nineteen inches and cut them into thirteen-foot lengths; loggers for pulp mills took every evergreen in sight, no matter the length or girth. By 1890, a particularly destructive year, there were few conifers with a girth greater than six inches in diameter on the southern and western slopes of Mount Marcy.

Lumbering did more than destroy the forests; it upset the entire ecology of the Hudson from its headwaters to the Atlantic. After the cutting spree of 1890, so many logs choked Lake Harris near the town of Newcomb that it became impossible for fish to swim or spawn. Birds left the area because they couldn't use the lake as a source of food. Lumbermen sometimes built dams on rivers like the Opalescent in order to float the logs over the rocks, and they thought nothing of blasting away any natural obstructions in the rivers that might hinder the progress of the logs on their journey to the Hudson.

Colvin's message in each of his reports on the Adirondacks was always the same: the practices of tanners and lumbermen were nothing less than "forest slaughter," compromising what is "perhaps the most remarkable watershed of the eastern half of North America," a watershed that feeds the St. Lawrence River to the north as well as the Hudson and the Erie Canal. Denuding the forests exposed vast tracts of the land to evaporation of rainwater, which consequently caused streams and creeks throughout the region to run dry. "Upon the Hudson River," Colvin wrote, "the destruction of the Adirondack forest would have a calamitous effect." The federal government was expending "vast sums in the improvement of the navigation of the Hudson," he wrote in his 1875 report, "yet the secret origin of the difficulty seems not to have been reached."

In 1883 state legislators finally acted on Colvin's repeated appeals to preserve the Adirondacks. That year they barred lumber companies from buying any more state lands, and two years later they created a Forest Preserve and Forest Commission. Whenever a lumber company defaulted on its land taxes, which usually happened after it had toppled every tree, the state quietly acquired the land. In 1892 the assembly created the stunning 2.8-million-acre Adirondack Park, and two years later New York ratified an article of the state constitution that declared the land would remain "forever wild." Over time, trees would return to the ravaged landscape and with them the streams that feed the lordly Hudson. Colvin had prevailed.

After the state created the Adirondack Park, Colvin's life took some improbable turns. The state legislators had not always been pleased with the odd man who by this time dressed in a wing collar, Prince Albert coat, and beaver top hat. Over the years he had acquired a suite of offices in the state capitol that he decorated to resemble a private Adirondack hunting lodge. Stuffed animals, rustic chairs and tables, pack baskets, and snowshoes competed for space with maps, surveying equipment, drawings, and reports. Occasionally, a few legislators would protest that the politically appointed state engineer should take over the Adirondack Survey. In 1898 the legislature abolished the survey completely, only to find two years later that Colvin was still firmly entrenched in his offices and drawing his five-thousand-dollar annual salary, which they had neglected to stop. That year he even tried to recruit a regiment of Adirondack mountain men to fight in the Spanish-American War. Finally, on April 25, 1900, Governor Theodore Roosevelt, the hero of that war, had Colvin removed from his office and demanded that he return all files, maps, and equipment to the state. Colvin was fifty-three.

Curiously, Colvin took up another project in the Adirondacks that alarmed his friends and former associates. A syndicate of investors planned a rail link between New York City and Ottawa, Canada, that would cross through the Adirondack wilderness. Verplanck Colvin not only invested in a venture that would destroy the land he had fought so hard to keep forever wild, but in 1902 he became the company's president. Fortunately for the wilderness Colvin had saved, the New York and Canadian Pacific Railway, as he called the venture, never laid a foot of track.

Verplanck Colvin's bizarre actions suggest he was trapped in an early stage of dementia. The signs became ever more ominous as the years wore on. The once neatly dressed man who would stride confidently into the state capitol after a brisk walk down Washington Street now shuffled aimlessly about the town dressed in shabby clothes, muttering to himself about betrayal. Paranoia set in. Neighbors sometimes heard him firing shots inside his house as he fought off illusory attackers. In February 1919, Colvin's friends had him committed to an asylum in Troy. When he died thirteen months later, few seemed to notice. The *New York Times,* which had often championed Colvin's survey, neglected to write an obituary; newspapers in Albany failed to mention the role Verplanck Colvin had played in the creation of the Adirondack Park and the preservation of the Hudson River watershed.

"It is by far the most interesting river in America," wrote the illustrator and essayist Benson Lossing of the Hudson over a century ago. From the beginning the water and the land, the flora and the fauna, the geography and the geology, the light and even the smells, have combined to make the Hudson River valley a unique place in America. The natural river and the valley through which it flows have served as a vast stage on which we have acted out our ambitions and desires, however noble or ignoble they might be. And always the Hudson's rich landscape has helped to shape our actions.

CHAPTER 2

Explorers and Traders

He was fired by a single passion, to find a way to reach Cathay, a passion
fed by the widespread fiction that somewhere over the top of the earth,
or even *through* the land we know as North America, the passage to the East
awaited discovery. His passion made him willful and headstrong; it brought
him into conflict with his sailors as well as the companies that supplied him
with ships and provisions. Such affairs mattered little to his determined
nature; he would explore the globe on his own terms and gain the fame that
awaited the one who found the route he knew was there. Only the reality
of an impassable continent and impenetrable ice would thwart him. But
he earned his fame nonetheless: on the second day of September 1609,

passion and fiction conspired to bring Henry Hudson to the river that now bears his name.

Most of Henry Hudson's life before his last five years remains shadowy and uncertain. He was born in London, about 1570, perhaps, to a family possibly connected with the Muscovy Company, England's great syndicate that held a monopoly on trade with Russia. In the late sixteenth century Queen Elizabeth ordered the company to raise an expedition in search of a northern passage to Asia. Hudson himself may have sailed on an early voyage for the company. He might have visited Richard Hakluyt, whose *Divers Voyages Touching the Discovery of America* had been published in 1582. He definitely made two voyages for the company in the first decade of the seventeenth century.

The fiction that inspired Hudson first came to life in 1527 in the mind of a merchant and amateur geographer named Robert Thorne. While Thorne was tending to his family's business in Seville, he saw firsthand the power that accrued to the Spanish and Portuguese from their monopoly over the trade routes through the Strait of Magellan and around the Cape of Good Hope. Thorne also understood the power of cartography. Maps held the knowledge of the world's surface; by guarding them as state secrets the Iberians and Portuguese had effectively cornered the world's economic resources. They had earned their charts, too, for they were the products of their great explorers, men like Bartholomeu Dias, Cristoforo Colombo, and Vasco Núñez de Balboa. So valuable were these maps that in 1592 a group of Amsterdam merchants sent two Dutch navigators to Lisbon to steal a set; they were caught.

Spanish domination of the trade route around the Cape of Good Hope effectively penned England and the Netherlands in the North Atlantic and forced both nations to seek an alternate route to the Orient. Preferably it would be one that would take them there quickly, for a faster route meant lower costs for the journey, and less exposure for a ship, its crew, and its cargo to the perils of the sea or pirates. It is probably for these reasons

Overleaf: A nineteenth-century engraving after Robert W. Weir's depiction of Henry Hudson's arrival in the river, showing a highly fictionalized scene of welcoming for the strangers to the New World.

that the English, and very likely Henry Hudson, gave so much credence to Robert Thorne.

Possessed of a rich imagination and unimpeded by any knowledge whatsoever, Thorne proposed to King Henry VIII a passage to the east by way of the North Pole, and he drew his own crude map purporting to show the way. Cold would not be an impediment, he assured the king, for "there is no land unhabitable, no sea innavigable." When it was found, he promised, the passage would cut "almost two thousand leagues" from the trip. Although Thorne died soon after making his declaration, his words and his map lived on. Henry VIII dispatched several parties of explorers to find the route, and Richard Hakluyt included Thorne's letters and map in his *Principal Navigations, 1598–1600*.

Inspired by Thorne and Hakluyt and lured by the prospect of expanding its trade, the Muscovy Company hired Hudson in 1607 and 1608 to lead expeditions to find the passage. First he explored the east side of Greenland, but met the great ice barrier stretching to Spitzbergen; then he tried a route between Spitzbergen and Novaya Zemlya. This time two seamen reported sighting a mermaid ("From the Navill upward, her backe and breasts were like a womans . . . her skin was very white; and long haire hanging down behinde, of colour blacke; in her going downe they saw her tayle, which was like the tayle of a Porposse, and speckled like a Macrell"). Hudson saw only a field of ice. The company declined to bankroll a third voyage.

Not to be thwarted, Hudson turned to the Netherlands and the Dutch East India Company for a ship and crew that would seek the passage. His choice of a sponsor was pragmatic and shrewd. The Dutch had successfully challenged the Portuguese domination of the sea lanes, but the route around the cape or through the Strait of Magellan was still fraught with peril. If a northern route to the East did indeed exist, so the directors of the Dutch East India Company reasoned, they should be the ones to control it. To this end the States General in the Netherlands had offered a prize of twenty-five thousand guilders to the explorer who discovered the way.

Money more than pride had driven the Dutch to seek the passage. For fifty years a nasty and bloody war against the dominion of the Spanish and the Catholic Church had burned up the resources of the seven northern provinces (Holland, Zeeland, Utrecht, Gelderland, Groningen, Friesland,

and Overijssel), but now both sides were deep in deliberations that resulted in the Twelve Years' Truce. The coming peace would give the merchants of the Dutch East India Company the opportunity to make money; Henry Hudson's plan to find a northern passage would give them a chance to make it faster.

So desperate were the Dutch to find the passage that they paid Hudson in advance of his trip, gave him a boat and crew, and contracted to pay his wife a bonus should her husband not return. For his part, Hudson seemed to have no reservations about signing a contract that directed him to steer his boat over the northeastern route "by way of Nova Zembla" and that "under no circumstances" should he attempt to find a passage by sailing west. Hudson probably knew from the start that he would keep his own counsel about the best route to the East. Should he succeed, all concerns about the contract would disappear.

It had been a rough and often terrifying journey. Hudson's mixed crew of about eighteen Dutch and English seamen sailed from the Netherlands on the *Half Moon* in early April 1609. The ship was cramped—just eighty-five feet long on the upper deck with a beam of seventeen feet—and the men, perhaps because they did not share a common language, disliked one another and detested their captain. By mid-May, surrounded by ice floes in the Barents Sea, they threatened mutiny if he did not abandon the quest and head to more temperate lands. And so, after stopping a day at the Faroe Islands to take on fresh water, the *Half Moon* sailed directly for North America. Along the way a violent storm toppled the main mast, forcing the men to anchor in Penobscot Bay off Maine so that carpenters might fashion a new one. When they landed, some of the sailors "behave[d] badly" with the Native Americans they encountered, killing twelve and taking their property. Once repaired, the *Half Moon* sailed slowly south-ward along the coast until she reached the mouth of a large river—the Hudson—surrounded by "a very good Land to fall with, and a pleasant Land to see."

In the nineteenth century, as Native Americans were fast vanishing from much of the landscape, Hudson's arrival served as a fitting and sentimental subject for artists. A painting by Robert W. Weir depicted the explorer standing in the stern of a small boat being pulled into a quiet bay by welcoming natives. Hudson, arms outstretched, holds his plumed hat, another in the party carries a flag, and a third announces the Europeans' arrival with a trumpet. In the foreground a native stands, arms outstretched, holding corn and tobacco leaves. Still other natives approach the *Half Moon* anchored in the river. From the viewer's perspective on the shore, no doubt surrounded by fellow natives gazing at the strange vessel, the gestures are all of wonder and peace. The engraving is, of course, a fantasy, a nineteenth-century vision based on facts and fictions distilled through the refulgence of time and various histories, of the way Hudson's coming to the New World may have appeared.

The natives, too, had a myth, and like the myths of Hudson and other explorers, theirs combined fact with fiction, reality with the fantastic. Over the years natives passed its words orally from generation to generation, from village to village, and from tribe to tribe: Some natives, fishing "where the sea widens," saw "something remarkably large swimming or floating on the water." Returning to the shore of "York Island," where they joined their chiefs and warriors, they beheld:

> a large house of various colors, full of people, yet of quite a different color than they [the natives] are of; that they were also dressed in a different manner from them, and that one in particular appeared altogether in red, which must be the *Mannitto* himself. . . . The house . . . stops, and a smaller canoe comes ashore with the red man and some others in it, some stay by this canoe to guard it. The chiefs and wise men . . . had composed a large circle, unto which the red clothes man with two others approach. . . . He must be the great *Mannitto* (supreme being) [the natives] think, but why should he have a *white skin*?

Over the years the story had obviously shifted as events changed the river's history. It might be the story of a single sighting of the white man, or an amalgam of several. The island of Manhattoes had become York Island. The color of the man's coat might well be a later addition, but he was also a Manitou, a powerful deity either of good or evil who traverses the earth governing all things. Whatever the circumstance, the central truth remained the same: Europeans had arrived at the river.

It is clear, too, that by 1609 Native Americans had been seeing white sailors in the Hudson River for at least eighty-five years. The Italian Giovanni da Verrazano had arrived in 1524. Sailing for the French on the ship

Dauphine, Verrazano found "a very agreeable place between two small but prominent hills; between them a very wide river, deep at its mouth, flows out into the sea; and with the help of the tide, which rises eight feet, any laden ship could have passed from the sea into the river estuary." Verrazano and his men went ashore where the natives, "dressed in birds' feathers of various color," greeted them joyfully. Across the river came "about 30 small boats" to see them. Though the explorers were tantalized by the hills, which "showed signs of minerals," a sudden squall forced them to leave. The captain and his crew sailed no farther than the river's mouth.

The Portuguese sailor Estevan Gomez, sailing for the Spanish, followed Verrazano in 1525, though no record of his journey survives. French traders possibly penetrated the interior, but they, too, failed to document their experience. The first true European discoverer of the river, if only because he and a crew member recorded their journey to its headwaters in the early autumn of 1609, was Henry Hudson.

Not all of the natives' contacts with Europeans were as pleasant as Weir's engraving suggests. While the sailors who shipped with the famous navigators were brave men who embraced the perils of crudely charted seas and unknown lands with extraordinary daring, they were an unpleasant, undisciplined, and often violent lot. The taking, or even killing, of natives was simply part of their work, like shooting a deer or even a beaver. The scant journals they left—for few could read or write—suggest that they did not think twice about it. The sailors were of a single mind: to gain the spoils of conquest and the cornucopia of wealth to be had from a direct passage to the East. For this they were willing to endure all hardships. If butchery and slaughter were necessary for them to reach their goal, so be it.

Hudson's sailors regarded the inhabitants of the river valley with suspicion and mistrust. To his Dutch deckhands the Native Americans were "Wilden," that is, wild men, neither tame nor domesticated, living in a state of nature; to his English hands they were "savages," also wild and undomesticated, but with a hint of the fang and claw. Bearing such an attitude as the Europeans did it is little wonder that the slightest misunderstanding or provocation could easily lead to violence.

Such was certainly the case with Henry Hudson's crew members. One of Hudson's English sailors, Robert Juet, kept a journal that gives a chilling account of the carnage they wrought. Near the Narrows, Juet reported, the natives came on board, "some in Mantles of Feathers, and some in Skinnes of divers sorts of good Furres," but, he added, the sailors "durst not trust them." Distrust very possibly caused the bloodletting that occurred the following evening. A scouting party of five was taking soundings near Newark Bay, when "night came on, and it began to rayne, so that their Match went out." Two boats of natives approached; a fight ensued in the murky shadows; two of the party were wounded and another lay dead with an arrow through his throat.

Just off Yonkers two days later, Hudson and his men abducted two men whom they dressed in "red Coates," and tried to abduct two others. Other parties of natives approached the ship as it proceeded north; some attempted to come aboard, "but," writes Juet in what is almost a mantra for his journal, "we durst not trust them." Several days later "our two savages" escaped out a porthole and "called to us in Scorne" from the shore.

Once in the mountains of the Highlands, the Europeans found "a very loving people" who traded beaver and otter pelts for "Beades, Knives, and Hatchets." Juet reports getting the "chiefe men of the Countrey" drunk; one had to stay the night. At one point the men from the *Half Moon* anchored on the east bank at a spot just north of the present-day city of Hudson. "I sailed ashore in one of their canoes," Hudson wrote, "with an old man, who was the chief of a tribe, consisting of forty men and seventeen women; these I saw there in a house well constructed of old bark, and circular in shape, with the appearance of having a vaulted ceiling. It contained a great quantity of maize and beans of the last year's growth." That evening Hudson and his hosts dined on "a pair of pigeons" and "a fat dog," but the explorer declined an invitation to stay the night and insisted on returning to his boat.

The hostility of some of the natives wasn't the only challenge that Hudson and his crew faced. As they moved farther north, the river was getting narrower and shallower with each league. Shoals were becoming more frequent; at one point the *Half Moon* ran so "neere the shore, that we grounded."

We can only imagine what went on in the minds of Hudson and his crew, navigating from one reach to another, anticipating around each bend the promised vista of the Pacific Ocean, yet seeing only another bend, more mountains and wooded hills, and another reach of the river. Yet as long as the waters remained navigable through each of the reaches, their vision of the ocean remained fixed in their mind's eye. But on September 22 the explorers' imaginations met reality: While the *Half Moon* lay off Albany, a scouting party went upriver in a small boat to reconnoiter. At Cohoes they "found it to bee at an end for shipping to goe in" and turned back. There was nothing for Hudson and the sailors to do but return.

On their way downstream the crew experienced the bloodiest encounter of the trip. South of the Highlands one of the crew spotted a native making off with Juet's "pillow, two shirts, and two bandeleeres," and shot him through the breast. Another native tried to overturn the boat sent out to retrieve the stolen property, but "our Cooke took a swaord and cut off one of his hands, and he was drowned." The following day saw more ferocious fighting. Hudson's men killed "two or three" men who attacked the ship with bows and arrows, and Juet fired a small cannon from the deck, killing others who had gathered on the shore and approached in canoes. Still more died when his companions fired their muskets at an approaching canoe. When it was all over Juet counted at least eight dead, possibly more.

Although Hudson and Juet, along with the other Europeans who followed them to the river, did not realize it, the natives they encountered in the southern part of the valley were of the Algonquin linguistic stock and had lived there since the Wisconsin ice sheet receded at the end of the Ice Age. Europeans later called them the Delaware, a name they gave to all the tribes, but in fact the natives called themselves the Lenni Lenape, and within the Lenni Lenape there were a number of smaller autonomous communities or bands bound together by common cultural ties.

Arrowheads in Orange County and oyster shells at Croton Point suggest they arrived as early as 10,600 BCE. For centuries they had depended on the river for much of their food and as an avenue for their communication, trade, and culture. During the Woodland period (1500 BCE to the seventeenth century) possibly as many as twelve thousand people of the Lenni Lenape developed a substantial culture in the Hudson Valley. They often gathered in small, and sometimes fortified, villages. They caught game (bear, turkey, deer), fish (shad, sturgeon, eels), and ate vegetables (corn, beans, and squash) that they had cultivated.

Those whom Hudson and later Dutch colonizers called "Savages" or

"Wilden" were actually various bands of the Delaware. They lived in a number of separate locations on both shores of the river. Indeed, through much of the valley, the river also served to separate them. Sailing north in 1609 Hudson saw not just "Indians" but numerous independent bands of natives. Among the most important on the west shore were the Navasink at Sandy Hook, the Raritan at the southern end of Staten Island, the Hackensack at Jersey City, the Tappan at the Palisades, the Haverstraw at the bay that bears their name; and, farther north still, the Esopus, the Catskill, and the Mahicans. The Mahicans also had a number of separate bands on both sides of the river. On the eastern shore Hudson encountered the Canarsee at Brooklyn and southern Manhattan, the Wecquaesgeek on northern Manhattan and Westchester, and farther north the Nochpeem, Wappinger, and Mahicans.

The fact that by the seventeenth century the Mahicans were not the only ones in the valley, as well as the Europeans' suspicion of the "savages," might have contributed to the battles that Juet recorded in his journal. Beginning about 1300, drought and poor hunting in the Mississippi Valley drove the nations of the Iroquois eastward along the Ohio and Allegheny rivers and eventually into what is now New York. By the mid sixteenth century the Iroquois had formed the League of Five Nations—made up of the Seneca, Cayuga, Onondaga, Oneida, and Mohawk peoples. The League—especially the Mohawks—pressed farther east, to the banks of the Hudson, where the Algonquins had lived a peaceful existence of hunting and fishing for thousands of years. The Mohawks would not be denied the valley's fertile land and the woods abundant with game, and they would live up to their name, which means, roughly, "eaters of people." Hudson and his crew had sailed into a war zone.

Despite Juet's repeated pronouncement, "we durst not trust them," and Hudson's declaration, "[they are] much inclined to steal and adroit in carrying away whatever they take a fancy to," the natives were objects of great fascination for the Europeans. Exotic and unusual, they were the extraterrestrials of the seventeenth century. Stories of their habits, dress, eating, mating, and dying captured the popular imagination. When he landed at Kitty Hawk, North Carolina, Verrazano kidnapped "a child from an old woman" to bring home as a souvenir of his trip. Sixty years later, in 1584, a captain sailing for Sir Walter Raleigh returned from a trip to

Roanoke Island with two Algonquins. Raleigh brought them to court and Parliament to promote his venture in America.

No Dutch sailor ever succeeded (either through kidnapping or persuasion) in bringing a Native American back to the Netherlands, although Hudson's crew certainly tried. Still, Netherlanders did read reports of the strange race across the sea. Johannes de Laet included Hudson's descriptions of the "Folk of the Great River of Mountains" in his *New World, or Description of Dutch West-India,* as well as an account of their language and customs. But de Laet had never been in North America. For an account from one who actually lived among them, we must turn to Adriaen van der Donck.

The Wilden are Wilden because they are "*wild men,*" asserts the Dutchman with a clarity that only circular logic can attain. As the word "Wilden" was the first thought of those who encountered them in 1609, it must be so. They have very little religion, "and that is very strange"; their marriages "differ from civilized societies"; and their laws are "wild regulations." As the appellation helps to distinguish them from other heathens and Negroes, van der Donck concludes, it is still appropriate. With dark prescience, he declares his account is to be a "memorial" to them "after the Christians have multiplied and the natives have disappeared."

Primitive anthropologist that he was, van der Donck proceeded to describe the natives' habits: They neither eat nor drink to excess, "even in their feast days"; their various languages have no words for "drunkenness"; they grow maize in their rich fields near the river and grind it into a mush that they often mix with meat or fish, though on "extraordinary occasions" they eat "beavers' tails, bass heads, with parched corn meal"; they have "pensive dispositions" and speak slowly and with well-considered words; their clothing is usually of one fashion, for "they are not proud"; their women "appear . . . as if they possessed no amorous feelings; They however only thus disguise nature"; they have "no miserly desire" for precious metals. They do not earn their money, but "make" it from black and white shells, which they call "wampum"; they live in long houses with as many as eighteen families in a house and a "fire kept in the middle"; they "generally marry but one wife," and "to be unchaste during wedlock is held to be very disgraceful"; they look with "contempt" upon "romping, caressing, and wanton behaviour . . . [and] if they observe such behaviour among the Netherlanders, they reprove the parties."

For all his talk of the wild man, van der Donck presents the Native American as a noble savage. Although he reports that they are "thievish," "slovenly," "dirty," "revengeful and obstinate even unto death," he also describes their simpleness and purity, which sets them apart from the Europeans. Van der Donck's natives are Montaigne's cannibals; their nation has been "fashioned very little by the human mind" but they are "still very close to their original naturalness. The laws of nature still rule them."

It is likely that Hudson first believed—and certainly he hoped—on his arrival at the river's mouth that he had discovered the elusive passage to India, for he spent three weeks exploring its waters until he reached the shoals just north of Albany. The record of this 150-mile journey sets Hudson apart from others who preceded him. His trip gained fame from three chroniclers: Emanuel van Meteren of Amsterdam, who had been in England when Hudson arrived from America, published a brief account in 1610, in the last edition of his *History of Netherlanders.* Robert Juet's day-by-day account of the exploration of the river appeared probably no later than the spring of 1610. Finally, Johannes de Laet included portions of Hudson's own journal in his *New World, or Description of Dutch West-India,* published in 1625.

The accounts suggest that the Europeans had discovered a wondrous sweet-smelling land covered with vegetation. The wilderness, which often came to the very edge of the river, held an abundance of "great and tall Oakes . . . Grasse and Flowers, and goodly Trees" as Juet reported, "Wal-nut trees, and Chestnut trees, Ewe trees, and trees of sweet." Grapes and pumpkins (Juet called them "pompions") were abundant, too. Hudson reported that the land was "the finest for cultivation that I ever in my life set foot upon." The colors of the mountains suggested that "some Metall or Minerall were in them." The smell from the land was strong and sweet.

Of course in many respects the landscape of the river and valley that Hudson and Juet saw differed greatly from today's. Manhattan Island was narrower and its southern tip more pointed; Water Street on the eastern shore was *under* water, and the place where the first World Trade Center stood was part of the Hudson River. Manhattan Island had many more hills, most of which have since been leveled. With the exception of an occasional hut usually built of bark and brush, there were no buildings, and as the Native Americans regarded the island as their summer game preserve, there was far more vegetation. North of Manhattan the land was dense with trees, which made it an ideal hunting ground for the natives.

But in other ways the features of the river landscape—the hills and mountains, the sheer cliffs of the Palisades, the "high Mountains" of the Catskills, and "the channell very narrow" at the headwaters—were much the same. The tides, the winds, and the reaches that the *Half Moon* made use of were much the same, too. Juet often writes of taking advantage of the "flood" to advance upriver, or the "twelve, thirteene and fourteene fathoms" off West Point, or the shallow tidal waters farther north where they were grounded and forced to wait for the tide before "heav[ing] of againe."

The *Half Moon*'s return to Europe did not proceed as the directors of the Dutch East India Company or Henry Hudson would have wished. Hudson had clearly violated the provisions of his contract directing him to sail north and forbidding him from sailing west. The directors had another reason to be unhappy with the explorer. On returning, he sailed the *Half Moon*, which was *their* boat, to England rather than the Netherlands, and the English barred the ship and its captain from leaving.

If we are to believe van Meteren, Henry Hudson and his crew did not want to be in England either. He had set his compass for Ireland, but on November 7, "by the Grace of God," as Juet put it, he landed at the port of Dartmouth in Devonshire. The English Crown promptly seized the *Half Moon* and its charts, and forbade Hudson's return to Holland. To the Crown's thinking, an Englishman was sailing for a group of foreign merchants to discover a passage and riches that would increase Dutch commerce. Furthermore, the English claimed that the land and the river that Hudson had explored belonged to them. In 1606 the Crown had granted sovereignty to the London and Plymouth companies for the North American coastline between Chesapeake Bay and the St. Lawrence River. No matter that the English had explored but few miles of this land; they presumed it to be theirs. Though the Dutch East India Company was able to recover its ship the following year, and though the errant captain appears to have sent the directors an account of his voyage, Henry Hudson never returned to Holland.

Hudson's voyage of 1609 was the last that either the explorer or Robert Juet lived to tell about. In April 1610, Hudson, with Juet as his mate and a crew of twenty-two, sailed from London for a group of English adventurers on the ship *Discovery*. Again, the explorer was indulging his passion to find a Northwest Passage to the riches of the Orient. At the end of summer he piloted the *Discovery* between Baffin Island and Labrador, arriving ultimately at what he called "a sea to the Westward," now Hudson's Bay. But the weather closed in; by November the *Discovery* was caught in ice for the winter.

The following June, Juet led a mutiny of the starving crew. Near New-foundland, the brigands set Hudson, his son, John, and seven others adrift in a small open boat "without food, drink, fire, clothing or other neces-saries" and sailed for home. Hudson and his party were never heard from again. When the mutineers, a remnant of the former crew, sailed into the Thames River, their leader was not among them. Robert Juet had died from wounds suffered in a fight with a band of Eskimos, so the survivors said. They had cast his body into the sea.

The directors of the Dutch East India Company were unhappy that Hudson had ignored the terms of his contract and failed to find a way to the East through the barrier of North America. Though they refused to engage in any further ventures with him, the Amsterdam merchants be-lieved that the navigator in his failure might well have discovered a source of great wealth, for reports from the sailors told of a giant rodent, the beaver, much prized in Europe, that was abundant in the new land.

In addition to showing land forms, seventeenth-century maps of the New World often present a virtual bestiary, a cartographic graffiti of ga-zelles, deer, bears, herons, cormorants, and turkeys, trekking across the landscape or standing in the waters. Illustrations were often similar. One even depicts a unicorn strutting across a terrain filled with both moun-tains and palm trees. Such pictures helped the Dutch to conjure up exotic images of the strange land that awaited them across the sea. The beaver stirred the imaginations of Amsterdam merchants, for it promised them great wealth.

"Wild Animals of New Netherland," engraving by J. E. Gavit, ca. 1850s. Palm trees, a ferocious beaver, a stag gnawing on a horse, and an eagle attacking a unicorn are all part of the scene in the New World, but there is also at the left rear of the engraving a sophisticated structure, a barn perhaps, to suggest human control of the wilderness.

Seventeenth-century Europe regarded beavers as a most important commodity. Used for centuries in coats, beaver fur, especially the densely matted, soft underbelly, had also proven to make excellent felt. The market for wide-brimmed felt hats and winter coats was building while European sources of beaver pelts were diminishing. The French had cornered the beaver trade in Canada and refused to let others into the territory; the Russians had a source on their own lands, and they were willing to sell to the Dutch, but the price was dear. Perhaps, so the merchants reasoned, the lands just below those claimed by the French, where van Meteren reported "good skin and furs . . . were to be got at a very low price," would bring them riches. The risks were enormous, but the even greater rewards made the venture worthwhile.

The Amsterdam merchants sent Hendrick Christiaensen to the river in 1610 or 1611 to confirm Hudson's discovery, replicate his charts (which the English had confiscated), and see for himself the land, the natives, and the abundance of the wilderness. In 1611, at about the same time that Robert Juet and his fellow mutineers were abandoning Henry Hudson and his son somewhere off Newfoundland, a syndicate of three merchants chartered a vessel to sail to "Terra Nova." Since they financed more voyages in the following years, we may presume that the ships returned with their hulls filled with furs. Soon the syndicate acquired another partner, sent even more ships to the river, and filled its warehouses in Amsterdam with beaver pelts. The van Tweenhuysen syndicate, as it came to be known after the name of its leading partner, tried in vain to conceal its new source of wealth. Dissembling proved futile. A challenge from another merchant syndicate was inevitable.

The challenge came on the shores of the Hudson in the late summer of 1612. Adriaen Block, captain of the van Tweenhuysen syndicate's boat, appropriately named the *Fortuyn,* was completing his third voyage and for two months he had enjoyed great success trading with the natives. Experience had taught Block that these exchanges went far more smoothly if instead of trinkets he offered more practical items like cloth and cooking utensils, or more deadly ones like liquor and guns. As the skipper was preparing his ship for the return voyage, the *Jonge Tobias,* a vessel belonging to a new rival, the Hans Claesz syndicate, sailed into the river.

It was bad enough to have competition, of course, but even worse, Thijs Volckertsz Mossel, the skipper of the *Jonge Tobias,* was "spoiling" the trade that Block's syndicate had established by offering more goods for the furs. To add to the confusion, as soon as the *Jonge Tobias* landed, a West Indian mulatto member of the crew named Juan Rodrigues slipped into the forest with his own store of weapons, planning to become a freelancer in the fur trade.

In Amsterdam that winter the rival syndicates rejected all attempts at compromise and instead prepared for the next spring's skirmish on the Hudson. This time the van Tweenhuysen syndicate outfitted not a single boat but a squadron to trade on the Hudson and explore elsewhere on the coast. Adriaen Block, who was to be the captain of a new ship, the *Tijger,* armed it with several heavy swivel deck cannon he had borrowed from the Dutch Admiralty. The captain made sure that Mossel and the Hans Claesz syndicate learned of his new firepower.

In the summer, fall, and winter of 1613 the dispute among the competing syndicates threatened to become violent, but it ended in comedy. The first to arrive was Hendrick Christiaensen sailing the *Fortuyn* for the van Tweenhuysen syndicate. Christiaensen quickly connected with Rodrigues, the West Indian deserter, who had spent his winter in the valley concocting deals and scheming with the natives. Mossel arrived on the Claesz syndicate's *Nachtegael* a few weeks later. He became furious to learn that Rodrigues had turned traitor and immediately began to offer still more goods for the pelts. When Block sailed into the river a few weeks later, he found Mossel and Christiaensen locked in a full-scale bidding war that could only bankrupt both companies. Filled with rage, he threatened to attack them. And Block had the swivel deck cannon.

But Adriaen Block never got to use his cannon. Late that fall, as ice began to appear in the river and the three captains, their crews, and the deserter Rodrigues continued their squabble over pelts, the *Tijger* accidentally caught fire and burned to the waterline as it lay at anchor in the Hudson off lower Manhattan.

Block was in serious trouble. He and his men were stranded on the forbidding shore without a ship. Christiaensen's ship had neither the stores nor the space to take on all of his men for the return passage. Mossel offered to split the crews between his and Christiaensen's ships, provided that Block and Christiaensen's syndicate give him half the pelts when they reached Amsterdam. As intransigent as ever, Block refused. No matter that he'd lost his ship, his cargo, and his cannon. He laid the keel for a new vessel, one he aptly named the *Onrust,* or "restless."

The members of Block's crew proved less stubborn than their captain. But many were restless. Seeing no reason to mutiny against Block, who after all didn't have a ship, they joined with crew members from the other two ships to commandeer Mossel's *Nachtegael,* and sailed to the West Indies for the rest of the winter. Block, Christiaensen, Mossel, and a number of crew members were left to winter in the New World.

With help from the Lenapes, who provided him "with food and all kinds of necessaries . . . through a dreary winter," Block completed the

The charred keel and ribs of what is likely Adriaen Block's boat the *Tijger*, found in 1916 by a crew of workmen who were digging a new subway tunnel under what eventually became the location of the first World Trade Center. The lines in the image are cracks in the glass plate negative. (Museum of the City of New York; gift of the New York City Department of Parks)

Onrust that winter and launched it in the spring. On its maiden voyage, the captain piloted his small vessel through the Hell Gate and into Long Island Sound and then Narragansett Bay, where he discovered the island that bears his name. But the *Onrust* had a keel of just forty-four feet, which made it too small for a transatlantic passage. Block returned to the mouth of the Hudson to meet Christiænsen.

Christiænsen himself had been on a voyage. Sailing up the river to Castle Island, at the present-day Port of Albany, the captain and his men had built a small stone house inside a fifty-foot-square wooden blockade. Equipping it with two cannon and eleven guns, Christiænsen gave it the grand name of Fort Nassau. It was the first permanent Dutch settlement in the New World and a trading post to which the Mohawks and Mahicans would bring their furs. But early in 1614 the few men Christiænsen had left on the island learned of the destruction that spring freshets could bring to the Hudson. Their fort was under several feet of water and had to be abandoned for higher ground.

Fortunately for Block and Mossel and their surviving crew, two ships arrived the following spring to carry the stranded traders back to the Netherlands. But the Dutch Admiralty sued Adriaen Block for losing its cannon.

The final scene for the *Nachtegael* and its crew was comic. While the mutineers' abilities as pirates were superior, their skills as navigators were decidedly inferior. After wintering in the West Indies, they returned to the Hudson only to find that Mossel, Block, and Christiaensen had left for the Netherlands. They decided to pilot the *Nachtegael* to Newfoundland but quickly lost their way. Then they set their compass for Spain, probably thinking that their best chance of survival would be to sail into the port of a country hostile to the Netherlands. Some months later they landed in Ireland.

Even the most stubborn among Amsterdam's merchants found the trials of 1613–14 on the shores of the Hudson too great to endure. They joined as "diverse merchants" to petition the States General for the exclusive right to trade with the natives. Four syndicates, including those of van Tweenhuysen and Claesz, formed the new partnership, which the States General formally called the New Netherland Company. Over the next three years, before its charter expired in 1618, the New Netherland Company made four voyages to the New World. When the grant to the New Netherland Company expired in 1618, Dutch merchants continued to trade informally with the natives.

In 1916, while excavating for a new subway tunnel twenty feet beneath Greenwich and Dey streets in lower Manhattan, workers discovered the charred keel and ribs of a ship, along with a double-bladed Dutch ax, beads, pot shards, a length of chain, and a cannonball. In the seventeenth century Greenwich Street had marked the edge of Manhattan Island; there could not be much doubt that these were the remains of Adriaen Block's *Tijger*. There was little interest in and no money to preserve such artifacts, but a foreman who happened to be an amateur historian retrieved an eight-and-a-half-foot section of the relic and eventually gave it to the Museum of the City of New York. In 1968, workers excavating for an office building near the same spot uncovered one of the cannon Block had installed on the *Tijger*. It, too, went to the museum. The gun and charred timbers are the earliest artifacts of European culture to be found in the Hudson Valley. But the rest of the *Tijger* was never found. Several hundred years after the ship burned, the place became the site of the North Tower of the World Trade Center.

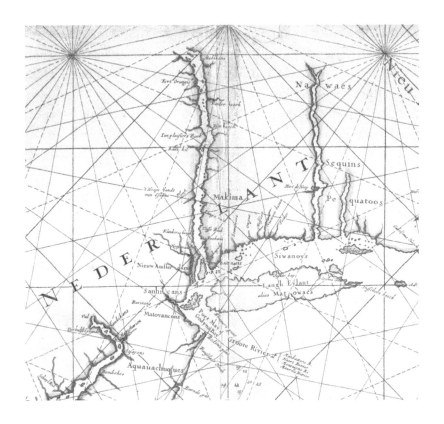

CHAPTER 3

The Colonizers Arrive

In many ways the Dutch had the good fortune to establish the center of their North American colony in the Hudson River valley, for the rhythms of the Hudson's tidal estuary proved to be similar to the waters that had surrounded them in Europe. From their experience with their great rivers, the Rhine, the Maas, and the Scheldt, they understood drainage and agriculture. The protection that the Narrows and the Upper Bay of the Hudson gives to Manhattan Island is similar to the effects of the Zuider Zee in Amsterdam. The abundance of fish in the river's estuary, especially at Haverstraw and the Tappan Zee, no doubt reminded the Netherlanders of the marshes they knew in Holland. By adapting the sloops they had created for Holland's waters, they used the Hudson to best advantage for their commerce and communication.

In spite of these obvious analogies with their experience in Europe, the Dutch never fully appreciated the importance of their investment of money and human lives in the Hudson River valley. Their merchants sought to exploit the land commercially, and to enhance their profit as much as possible the States General in Holland created the Dutch West India Company, a trading firm that brought business and privateering together in the service of the state. The time was propitious. The Twelve Years' Truce with Spain was due to end in 1621; renewal of war looked increasingly certain. The Dutch peace party was in eclipse; its aging leader, who had championed the Twelve Years' Truce, had been sent to the scaffold in 1619 on a charge of treason.

The Dutch West India Company would trade in places like Guiana (called the Wild Coast), Brazil, and the New Netherlands, and its backers believed it would garner great profits. Like its model, the Dutch East India Company, it could sail the high seas in search of Spanish merchant vessels and harry Spanish strongholds in the Americas. And some directors of the new company, though not all, believed that it would enable the Dutch to share in the colonization of the New World.

The Dutch East India Company served as a shining example of all that merchants could accomplish for the state and for themselves. To preserve the flow of trade, the company had subsidized occasional military exploits of privateering. Its profits, as much as 162 percent return on investment,

Opposite: Detail from Arnold Colom's map of "Nieu Nederlandt," from 1658, showing the Hudson (left) and Connecticut rivers. The famed cartographer labeled the Hudson as the "Groote Rivier," along with several other names, and also showed the locations of "Nieuw Amsterdam" and "Fort Orangie." The map was included in his *Zee Atlas,* one of the most important compilations of Dutch sea charts of the time. (I. N. Phelps Stokes Collection, Miriam and Ira D. Wallach Division of Art, Prints, and Photographs, The New York Public Library, Astor, Lenox, and Tilden Foundations)

warmed the hearts of every trader on the Bourse. Recently it had established a major trade center at Batavia (now Jakarta), and in 1659 it would take control of the Cape of Good Hope.

Chartered in June 1621, the Dutch West India Company was to be managed from Amsterdam by nineteen directors, known as the "Assembly of XIX" or simply as "the Nineteen." In North America the company was to control the province of New Netherland between the Delaware and Connecticut rivers (then called the South and Fresh rivers), and New France to the north. The Hudson, then called the Mauritius or the Nordt river, at the center of the province became the great highway of the company's operations and the center of most trade. As naturally as water flowed from the interior down the Hudson, so did furs—pelts of beaver, otter, and mink—gathered in the interior flow down the great river on Dutch ships. On Manhattan Island, the natural place for it, the Dutch established Fort Amsterdam, for the residence of the Dutch West India Company's director-general.

The first true settlers in New Netherland—thirty families, mostly French-speaking Belgians known as Walloons who had been driven by the Spanish into the Netherlands—give a clue to the peculiar character of the nascent colony. They weren't Dutch, and they possibly were not the first choice of the Nineteen to populate their new land. But realizing that Hollanders, enjoying the emoluments of their own wealthy land, were not interested in emigrating to an unknown and possibly hostile New World "uncertainty," the directors settled on transporting the Walloons. Eight of the Walloons stayed on Manhattan Island, eighteen families sailed up the Hudson to the head of navigation at Fort Orange, the successor to Fort Nassau at Albany, but built on higher ground, while the rest decided to resolve their destinies on the shores of the Delaware and Connecticut rivers.

For their first shelters the new emigrants created "dug outs"—pits "six or seven feet deep, as long and broad as they think proper," cased and floored with wood, and covered "with bark or green sods." After several years, they would often erect houses over their holes. By 1626, settlers in New Amsterdam had upgraded to crude bark-covered houses; a recent arrival reported that some were even replacing those hovels with more

The Seal of New Netherland, one of several
used by the Dutch West India Company. This
one features a rampant beaver at its center
(signifying the colony's principal activity of
fur trading) encircled by a string of wampum
(signifying its wealth). Above these the crown
suggests the company's royal charter, while
the words SIGILLUM NOVI BELGII remind us
that Belgium was intimately connected with
the Netherlands. The circle of wheat that
surrounds the motto suggests the abundance
to be found in the new lands.

substantial structures. The practice of starting in the ground and moving
upward persisted for most of the seventeenth century.

But the Colony of New Netherland lagged behind those that other
countries were establishing in the New World. Since it was in the hands of
men of business, the Dutch West India Company was understandably more
devoted to exploitation than civilization. The directors weren't entirely
greedy, however. Like the great explorer who had worked with inaccurate

and often false maps in his attempt to discover a passage to the East through North America, the directors were trying to find the best way to proceed on the shores of the river that would one day be known as the Hudson.

Four directors-general stand out in the history of the colony, though not always for the best reasons. Each left his mark on the landscape and the culture of the valley.

➤ Peter Minuit, the first and in many ways the best, especially when it came to business, arrived in May 1626 to replace a corrupt commander whom the Nineteen had ordered to be deported. One of his first acts, the purchase of Manhattan Island that year from a group of Canarsie Indian sachems for sixty guilders (about twenty-four dollars) worth of trinkets, established his place in history. More than merely a sound financial deal, Minuit's acquisition lent an air of legitimacy to the Dutch West India Company's presence on the island, and, so the Dutch thought, would enable them to "live amongst the natives."

Minuit's other acts as director-general were equally important to the success of New Netherland. He bought Eghquaous Island across from Manhattan, renaming it Staten Island. At the southern tip of Manhattan, where Dutch builders were busy constructing Fort Amsterdam, he created houses for some of the families from Fort Orange who retreated downriver as the war between the Mohawks and the Mahicans became more violent. Minuit's foreboding was correct, for the Mohawks attacked and killed four of the remaining settlers, including the commander whom, true to their name, they roasted and ate.

The natives at the mouth of the Hudson traded their pelts at Fort Amsterdam. A delegate of the States General reported that the same ship that brought the news of Minuit's purchase of Manhattan was also carrying "samples of summer grain; such as wheat, rye, barley, oats, buckwheat, canary seed, beans and flax," as well as:

7246 Beaver Skins.
853½ Otter skins.
48 Minck skins.
36 Wild cat skins.
33 Mincks.
34 Rat skins.

What use the Dutch had for the rat skins the delegate did not say. The Dutch chronicler Nicolaes van Wassenaer recorded in his November entry that a stone countinghouse had been built within the walls of the fort. By the end of 1628 "two hundred seventy souls" were living on Manhattan Island, most outside the fort.

Although it occupied only a small part of the very tip of Manhattan Island and was crude in every respect, the city of New York had begun. Its people were "rather rough and unrestrained," as Reverend Jonas Michaëlius put it. Sent to minister to the colony in 1628, Dominie (the name the Dutch Reformed Church gave to its pastors) Michaëlius found settlers "beginning to build new houses in place of the hovels and holes in which heretofore they huddled rather than dwelt." The settlers the reverend wrote about began to consider themselves a community in the mid 1620s, calling their settlement New Amsterdam. Workers were "busy building a fort of good quarry stone" and a windmill for sawing lumber. There was a gristmill, and a brick kiln, but the brick was "very poor."

In purchasing Manhattan and establishing Fort Orange, Minuit affirmed an essential fact of the colony: the Hudson was the spine of New Netherland. All, or nearly all, settlements would take place on the river's shores. In the future, control of the river would determine the success of the Dutch West India Company and ultimately of the Netherlands' presence in the New World. Others would regard the Hudson in a similar way, especially those who fought in the French and Indian War and the American Revolution or defended the harbor in the War of 1812. They realized that the fortunes of the colonists and later of the republic were inextricably bound to the river.

To the Nineteen busy counting guilders in Amsterdam, New Netherland's profits were of supreme importance. To keep expenses in check, they sent few animals or implements to help sustain the settlement. Michaëlius complained that "there are no horses, cows, or laborers to be obtained here for the money. . . . Everyone is short in these particulars and wants more." Butter and milk were dear, and the "hard, stale food" the pastor likened to sea rations.

While such a parsimonious stance yielded a short-term gain for the Dutch West India Company, by 1628 signs of the long-term consequences were beginning to show. A good number of the Walloons chose to leave, and the few boats that arrived from Amsterdam brought only the occasional party of settlers. That August, Dominie Michaëlius, himself no innocent in the world of intrigue, sent a letter back to Amsterdam reporting that "the business of furs is dull on account of the new war of the Maechibaeys [Mohawks] against the Mohicans at the upper end of this river." It wasn't long before those who remained began to focus blame for the colony's failings on its director-general, Peter Minuit.

With his every act, Minuit's enemies multiplied. Principal among them were Isaak De Rasière, a secretary who believed he deserved more respect, but who meanwhile skimmed company funds; Jan van Remunde, De Rasière's replacement who took Minuit to court; and Dominie Michaëlius, who complained to the Nineteen, "We have a governor who is most unworthy of his office, a slippery man who under a treacherous mask of honesty is compound of all iniquity and wickedness." As a recent arrival wrote, "Now the director and Jan Romonde [Remunde] are very much embittered against one another. . . . The minister, Jonas Michielsz, is very energetic here stirring up the fire between them; he ought to be a media-tor in God's church and community but seems to me to be the contrary." Gradually, the Nineteen realized they could not ignore the rancor across the Atlantic, so in August 1631 they recalled the three angry men. Early the following year, De Rasière, Michaëlius, and Minuit embarked for Holland on the ship *Eendracht*, the Dutch word for unity.

Although pelts and lumber flowed out of the Hudson Valley at a steady rate (contrary to the dominie's sour report), the financial returns from New Netherland failed to meet the expectations of the directors of the Dutch West India Company. A split emerged among the directors: some wanted to stop all immigration and maintain a few trading posts in the Hudson Valley staffed by their own employees. Each summer, so these directors reasoned, company ships could sail up the river, fill their cargo holds with furs, and return to Amsterdam. There would be few expenses for supplying and defending settlements, and they would maximize their profits. Other directors championed a different policy: In the ship carry-ing news of his purchase of Manhattan Island, Peter Minuit had included "samples of summer grain" to suggest what might be achieved if there were enough people and animals to clear the trees and till the fields. The Hudson Valley could be a rich source of grain as well as furs.

After much conflict and internal strife among themselves, the Nineteen passed a "Charter of Freedoms and Exemptions" in 1628, to "promote the peopling of those fruitful and unsettled parts." Under it, the Dutch West India Company promised to grant large manorial estates outside Manhattan Island to proprietors, or "patroons," who agreed to "plant there a colony of 50 souls." The amount of land, to be located along the banks of a "navigable river," was generous: two leagues on each shore or four leagues on one, "and as far inland as the situation of the occupants will permit." The patroon (the Dutch adapted the English word "patron," that is, a master or protector) would have the power "to administer civil and criminal justice," and "to appoint officers and magistrates." And, most important for the history of the Hudson Valley, the patroon would "forever own and possess and hold" the estate "as a perpetual fief of inheritance." The liberal terms of the charter made it—on paper at least—one of the most important land giveaways in American history. (The following year the directors revised the charter, making the conditions for settlement even more attractive.)

Few stepped forward to take advantage of the charter, however, and those who did faced considerable impediments. The directors of the Dutch West India Company were still very much divided over the proper course for New Netherland, and in Amsterdam new directors opposed to settlements gained control of the Nineteen. They sometimes failed to provide ship passage for emigrants and animals for their land. Many of the few Netherlanders courageous enough to establish a patroonship soon lost heart and abandoned their settlements. Only one patroonship survived, at Rensselaerwyck on the banks of the Hudson 150 miles north of the fort at New Amsterdam. Though there were exceptions, most of the events that took place in the Hudson Valley over the next four decades occurred in these two settlements.

The patroon of Rensselaerwyck was Kiliaen van Rensselaer, a diamond merchant in Amsterdam. He owned and controlled more land than anyone else in New Netherland, at least 700,000 acres at the head of the navigable Hudson, perhaps more, and far in excess of the limits set by the Dutch West India Company. His authority was absolute. Over time he acquired the services of several paid administrative officials: a "commis," who served as his personal agent tending to records, keeping accounts, and following his meticulous instructions for cultivation, sawing lumber, milling grain, brewing beer, and erecting buildings; a "schout," who served as sheriff, enforcing the laws and, when necessary, judging those who broke them; and a parson, or "dominie," who saw to the spiritual welfare of the inhabitants. Even the directors-general of New Netherland, secure in their fort at New Amsterdam more than a hundred miles south, knew they had to reckon with the patroon's power. Yet for all his land and dominion, Kiliaen van Rensselaer, patroon of Rensselaerwyck, never set foot in the New World.

In Amsterdam, where he lived most of his life, Kiliaen van Rensselaer took his place among the city's leading burghers. More than a bourgeois businessman, though van Rensselaer was surely this, he was a burgher who participated in the affairs of civic life, sometimes even risking his money on a speculative enterprise for the greater good of the community. He had once backed a successful scheme to reclaim and cultivate heath lands in Holland. It was a natural step for him to become one of the Amsterdam directors of the Dutch West India Company in 1621 and to stand with the chief promoters of the Charter of Freedoms and Exemptions of 1628 and its revision of 1629. It was natural, too, for van Rensselaer to desire a patroonship in New Netherland, for it squared perfectly with the concept of a burgher in Amsterdam.

Kiliaen van Rensselaer's cleverness enabled him to excel as a merchant. Born about 1580 in Hasselt, a small city in the eastern province of Overijssel, he was apprenticed in his twenties to a diamond and pearl trader in Amsterdam. Van Rensselaer's business acumen extended to his choice of a wife. He married his employer's daughter, who brought a generous dowry into the union. After she died, he married the daughter of another employer who also possessed a sizable dowry. Very possibly it was the fortune van Rensselaer had accrued from his business and marriage dealings that enabled him to finance his most speculative venture.

When it came to his land in the New World, Kiliaen van Rensselaer was not content with half measures. Starting in 1630, when he instructed his agent to "try to buy the lands hereafter named for the said Rensselaer from the Mahijcans, Maquaas or some such other nations as have any claim to them, giving them no occasion for discontent, but treating them with all courtesy and discretion," van Rensselaer began to amass land on both sides of the Hudson. Through such purchases he extended his domain forty-eight miles along both sides of the river, and twenty-four miles inland. In time his lands would extend from the Mohawk River at Cohoes south through Albany, Rensselaer, and part of Columbia counties.

Yet in the actual execution of his plans for Rensselaerwyck, the patroon showed himself to be a curious mixture of small-mindedness and farsightedness. His detailed letters and copious remonstrances reveal him to be petty, argumentative, complaining, and parsimonious, but also sagacious, perceptive, sensible, and shrewd. "You do superfluous work by putting the date both at the top and the bottom of the letter," the patroon grumbled to a schout, "once is enough." He published a lengthy pamphlet, "Redress of the abuses and faults in the colony Rensselaerwyck," berating the colonists for their "licentiousness and wantoness . . . unfaithfulness . . . covetousness." Yet even from Amsterdam, the patroon understood local affairs enough to order his agents to purchase land from the natives "in the presence of them all," and to take the chiefs to New Amsterdam to record the deeds before the director-general. More than anyone else among the colonists and the Nineteen, Kiliaen van Rensselaer understood the folly of basing the New Netherland economy entirely on furs, and he knew that New Netherland would have to develop its farming in order to survive.

Van Rensselaer's plan to populate a land some four thousand miles and a two-month sea voyage away—and at the northernmost spot on the navigable Hudson—was audacious, especially as he did not intend to preside personally over his demesne. But he understood that Fort Orange would give his settlement a modicum of protection from attacks by the natives, and he depended on his commis and schout to keep him informed about the progress of his province.

First, however, the patroon had to establish the colony. Two of his most difficult jobs as patroon were to serve as recruiter of settlers and procurer of animals. He contracted with colonists, usually for three years and for specific purposes. One of the first contracts, and a typical one, went to Andries Christensz. Christensz and two others were to build a sawmill and gristmill beside Mill Creek, which joins the river north of the city of Hudson. The company gave them free passage provided "that they do proper ship duty," but on arrival at New Amsterdam they had to "betake themselves" at their own expense to Fort Orange. They would be entitled to split the fees for grinding and sawing—half for themselves and half for the patroon. The same terms applied to those who farmed—half of the produce sales after expenses went to the farmers; half to van Rensselaer. And, jewel merchant that he was, van Rensselaer demanded in all contracts that if a settler should "discover any mines, minerals, pearl fisheries . . . he shall disclose the same to no one but the patroon."

Recruiting went slowly—just twelve had settled in Rensselaerwyck by 1632, and several of these were slaves or had moved north to Rensselaerwyck from Manhattan Island. Procuring animals—especially horses, cows, and sheep—proved as challenging for the patroon as it was for the rest of New Netherland. (As animals drink copiously and consume extraordinary amounts of fodder, they are difficult to transport.) One journal of a future settler of Rensselaerwyck recorded the animal deaths during his five-month trip across the Atlantic: three calves, two heifers, and a sheep. Of the eight horses that were shipped from Texel, five died along the way, and a sixth as the boat lay at anchor off Manhattan. "Thus the Lord delivered us after much adversity," the colonist wrote, "for which He be praised forever. Amen. The next day a dead horse overboard."

Hoping that van Rensselaer and other patroons would give up on schemes to develop colonies within the colony, some directors of the Dutch West India Company did their best to make the shipment of farm animals even more difficult. On one voyage the company allowed but "a few calves on the upper deck," the patroon complained, "and they were all thrown overboard" after the ship left port. Desperate, van Rensselaer resorted to subterfuge. When one of the farms that Minuit had established for the company on Manhattan Island came up for sale, he instructed his agent to buy it and ship the cattle up river to Rensselaerwyck. This time Bastian Jansz Krol, the director who succeeded Minuit for seven months, stepped in to stop the shipment. "If I cannot get animals," the patroon wrote to his nephew Wouter van Twiller, understanding fully the gravity of his predicament, "I shall not be able to send over 50 persons and . . . then certain partial people will call for action."

Clearly van Rensselaer had very different ideas about the development of his estate in New Netherland than many of the Nineteen did. They still conceived of their territory almost entirely in terms of the fur trade, not settlement or civilization; yet the Freedoms and Exemptions demanded that the patroon populate his land and make it self-sustaining. These often contradictory goals of the directors and the patroon would continue for the duration of the Dutch occupation of New Netherland.

The 150 miles between the two principal settlements meant that they developed separately and, usually, in isolation. Even in fair weather a letter traveling by sloop between New Amsterdam and Fort Orange took about ten days; in winter it was impossible. As Kiliaen van Rensselaer lived in Amsterdam, letters about his patroonship often took at least six months to reach Rensselaerwyck. But in July 1632 an unexpected turn of events in Amsterdam brought the potential for greater communication between the two settlements: the Nineteen named van Rensselaer's twenty-seven-year-old nephew Wouter van Twiller, a minor official in the Dutch West India Company's Amsterdam office, to the post of director-general.

Historians have made Wouter van Twiller the stock comic character in the Dutch drama on the Hudson, sometimes ridiculous, sometimes bombastic, and always foolish. One must wonder why the directors of the Dutch West India Company would entrust the future of New Netherland to an affable but, if we are to believe David Pietersen De Vries, wholly in-experienced and often drunken lout. De Vries was a merchant, sea captain, and owner of Staten Island who wrote numerous remonstrances to the Nineteen about the conduct of their director-general. Perhaps the ap-pointment shows the Nineteen's lack of interest in the colony as anything other than a few trading posts in the wilderness of the New World; perhaps Kiliaen van Rensselaer lobbied for the appointment, though given his relationship with the Nineteen, he had little influence to use. The one incontrovertible fact is Wouter van Twiller's disastrous rule as director-general. Though he occasionally possessed good ideas, he lacked the reso-lution, maturity, and, if we are to believe De Vries, the sobriety to achieve them. His record of four years of folly and failures ranks him among the very worst who have ever governed in the Hudson Valley. Still, for Kiliaen van Rensselaer, the appointment was an extraordinary stroke of luck, one that helped the patroonship at Rensselaerwyck to survive.

Although the patroon appears to have had little faith in his nephew's judgment, he knew that he would be tractable in a way that neither Krol nor the Nineteen had ever been. As van Rensselaer later observed in a letter to van Twiller himself, "one can not accomplish as much by well doing as by having friends in the game."

At that moment, van Rensselaer's friend was his nephew. In his very first letter to van Twiller after the appointment was announced, the patroon asked him to "purchase for me some more animals in New Netherland." Van Twiller appears to have understood the importance of strengthening Rensselaerwyck and Pavonia, a short-lived patroonship on the west side of the Hudson that included present-day Hoboken. Whenever possible he secured farm animals for the patroons, dividing them equally between each colony. Shortly after he arrived at New Amsterdam, he received a request from his uncle to allow the settlers in Rensselaerwyck to exchange "their products of the soil" for furs from the natives. To van Rensselaer that meant turning grain into alcohol, so he announced he was shipping a kettle for distilling brandy. Several years later he persuaded his nephew to pass a resolution authorizing the payment of company furs for grain.

For the most part Wouter van Twiller was preoccupied with the administration of the fort at New Amsterdam. Soon the director-general needed a friend in Amsterdam. Ships returning from New Netherland brought reports of the director-general's bizarre behavior. One letter concerned the belligerence of the English merchant ship the *William,* which in April 1633 decided to test the Netherlanders' control in New Netherland by sailing a ship up the Hudson to barter with the natives. When the captain appeared off Manhattan Island and announced his intentions, van Twiller responded not with his soldiers and marines but with bluster and wine. Realizing that he was facing an inept and witless opponent, the captain of the *William* ignored the director-general's threats, waited a week, and then weighed anchor and sailed north. De Vries remembered that as van Twiller watched the English sails recede in the distance of the river, he "assembled all his forces before his door, had a cask of wine brought out, filled a bumper, and cried out for those who loved the Prince of Orange and him, to do the same as he did, and protect him from the outrage of the Englishman. . . . The people all began to laugh at him; for they understood well how to drink dry a cask of wine, as it was just the thing that suited them, even if there had been six casks, and did not wish to trouble the Englishman, saying they were friends."

After the director-general had sobered up and received stern counsel from several of the wiser colonists, he dispatched a contingent of marines in pursuit of the *William*. They found the captain in a tent south of Fort Orange conducting a booming trade, arrested him and his crew, and sailed the *William* back to New Amsterdam with Dutch sailors. After confiscating the beaver pelts, van Twiller had the ship and sailors escorted from the river. The English left with an empty hull and the substance for a protest to be lodged with the Dutch ambassador in London.

Other tales were circulating, too. When van Twiller sacked his secretary Jan van Remunde, the same man who had earlier quarreled violently with Peter Minuit, Remunde sent a scathing letter to his wife in the Netherlands reporting on the director-general's drunken street brawls with New Amsterdam's new dominie, Everardus Bogardus. No stranger to strong drink himself, Bogardus possessed an erratic temper that rivaled the director-general's. Denouncing van Twiller as a "child of the devil," he threatened to expose him from the pulpit.

Though van Rensselaer knew of his nephew's irresolute character and fondness for the flagon, he realized that it was in his best interests to keep him in command as long as he could. As the "shameful" stories defaming his family's honor swirled about town, van Rensselaer could never quite acknowledge that one of his own blood could act so badly; he covered for his nephew as best he could with the Nineteen.

"Such a shameful pot has been on the fire for you," the patroon wrote to his nephew, "that I in all my life never would have believed that one could find men base enough to plan it." One of the stories circulating through the streets and in the directors' rooms at the Dutch West India Company was "that your honor, being drunk, had run out on the street" after Bogardus "with a naked sword." "Believe me freely," the patroon wrote, "had your honor not had me here they would have summoned you home with an affront," and he adjured him to follow eight moral precepts, including "Be temperate in eating and drinking" and "Be diligent and vigilant in the execution of your official duty." Though he might have been expected to conclude his letter with this stern warning to his nephew, van Rensselaer wrote an additional seven thousand words discussing details of his arrangements at Rensselaerwyck.

In spite of the reports, the directors in the boardroom of the Dutch West India Company did nothing. For a while van Twiller settled down in Fort Amsterdam and actually began to execute his plan to change the rude village on the Hudson, which now counted between four hundred and five hundred people, into a fortified colonial capital. He employed slaves to work on the walls of the fort, and he built barracks for the soldiers who had arrived with him, a small house for a midwife, and a large one for himself. For Dominie Bogardus, he began a church and parsonage on the East River to replace the loft over the mill that Peter Minuit had set aside for worship. The director-general imported a schoolmaster to give instruction to the children. Numerous ships usually lay at anchor in the Hudson, for New Amsterdam was developing into a lively trading port complete with chandlers, grog shops, and prostitutes.

As van Twiller was building up New Amsterdam, he was also accumulating land, and lots of it, for himself. He seemed to love islands. Governors Island, several islands in the East River, portions of Long Island, the Red Hook section of Brooklyn, and a tobacco plantation in Greenwich Village all became his. His motive for these purchases might well have been principled, for he wanted to advance the colony's agriculture, but he appears to have made them without the consent or even the knowledge of the directors in the Netherlands.

Still, van Twiller seemed unable to save himself, especially from his predilection for alcohol. The year 1635 found him reeling from blunder to blunder. Though the contempt of De Vries for the director-general no doubt led him to exaggeration, van Twiller fed his scorn. To end a drinking contest he was having with his friends one night, the director-general fired a cannon that ignited the thatched roof of a nearby house. Too stupefied to act, van Twiller and his companions watched as the building burned to the ground. The fire might have consumed the wooden fort itself had other colonists not formed a bucket brigade to drown the flames.

It was Wouter van Twiller's quarrel with New Netherland's schout Lubbert van Dinclagen over the supplying of horses to his uncle's Rensselaerwyck that finally brought him down. After van Dinclagen sent a protest to Amsterdam outlining van Twiller's feckless leadership, the director-general ordered him to prison, but he eventually escaped to Amsterdam to tell the Nineteen of his ill treatment. The directors ordered that van Twiller be replaced. When he left in 1638, the town of New Amsterdam was a shambles. Just two of its four windmills were in working order; the fort's walls had fallen in so that "people could go in and out . . . on all sides"; the director-general's house, Bogardus's church, and five workshops were all dilapidated; pigs and sheep occupied cabins that once had housed people. No doubt some of those animals had come from the boweries (the Dutch name for farms) north of the town, which now were "vacant and fallen into decay." New Amsterdam was so poor that the cobbler, the mason, the blacksmith, and the carpenters had little work. Even the schoolmaster had to take in washing in order to get by.

As dire as circumstances were at New Amsterdam, they were even more desperate in Rensselaerwyck. Fewer than two hundred people had settled there in its first fourteen years, and a number of them had left after several years. By 1641 the number of settlers had dwindled to a hundred, most of whom lived in or near Fort Orange. Fortunately for the future of the colony, some of them either had brought their wives and children with them or intended to create a family, and these people provided much of the settlement's stability. They were often large families, too. But most who found their way to Rensselaerwyck during those years were young single men seeking adventure and excitement in the New World rather than to make a life there for themselves. Only two were single women, who had come from Holland to join their father who had arrived the previous year.

In spite of the small population, Kiliaen van Rensselaer seemed as determined as ever to make Rensselaerwyck successful. With every ship that arrived from Amsterdam came voluminous letters from the patroon: letters attending to every detail of land management and farm management ("I am very anxious for the increase of the horses but especially of the cows"); or cajoling his commis ("you spend too much time in the woods, that ought not to be"); or fretting with him about financial reports ("I have seen the accounts of Albert Andriesen but cannot understand them"); or complaining about the costs ("I am no child and know very well what profit the farmers can make. . . . You should first find out also who is most faithful toward me. I am far from my property and must therefore pay close attention to prevent losses"); or imploring the commis to advance himself ("Read and reread all my writings"); or adjuring him to have good habits ("guard yourself against bad women, Indian or others, and keep the fear of the Lord before your eyes and He will bless you"). A rough calculation of orders, complaints, and remonstrances in 1640 that have survived finds that the patroon wrote about twenty-seven thousand words. It was an average year.

It was with the hope of imposing some order on his sparsely populated colony on the Hudson that Kiliaen van Rensselaer decided to appoint Adriaen van der Donck to the post of schout, to see to it that the populace adhered to the laws and regulations of the colony and to collect rents and debts owed to the patroon. A true polymath, van der Donck possessed all the qualifications of a Renaissance educated man, as well as all the credentials van Rensselaer could wish for: a famous family of patriots, including his paternal grandfather who had distinguished himself in the defeat of the Spanish at the castle of Breda in 1590, and a doctoral degree in both civil and canon law from the University of Leiden. And as van der Donck was in his twenties, he was, perhaps, tractable and willing to follow the patroon's voluminous instructions.

Surely this was the man to look after van Rensselaer's legal interests and enforce the laws of Rensselaerwyck. As a badge of his office and the advance in civilization it represented, the patroon presented van der Donck with a silver-plated rapier with a radiant baldric to support it and a hat with an ostrich plume to wear as he strode about the land. Yet, as with so many of those in whom he placed great hopes and faith, the patroon ended up being disappointed.

More than most who emigrated to the New World, van der Donck became entranced by all that he saw, smelled, and heard. The land appeared to him very different from the Netherlands. To begin with, it was immense. (The state of New York is about four times larger than Holland, including the Zuider Zee.) Then, it was stable. Unlike the continually shifting and eroding coast of the Netherlands, this mainland, as he observed in his description of New Netherland, was well protected from ocean storms by "forelands," islands, and sand bars that also provided for "sea-havens." The most famous bay, at the mouth of the Hudson, he wrote, "affords a safe and convenient haven from all winds, wherein a thousand ships may ride in safely inland."

The sheer abundance of the river valley struck van der Donck. The great river was filled with fish, "sturgeon, dunns, bass, sheep-heads." The land's great variety of features made a deep impression. "The whole country has a wavering surface, and in some places high hills and protruding mountains." But there were also "fine level land, intersected with brooks, affording pasturage of great length and breadth." Sometimes, he reported, he found himself looking down from the top of a mountain, "arrested in the beautiful landscape." The trees—oak and nut—seemed as great as any in Europe and far greater in number. There were vines and grapes, roses and tulips, herbs and Spanish figs, maize and wheat, and fields of barley six and seven feet high. "I admit," writes van der Donck in defeat, "that I am incompetent to describe the beauties, the grand and sublime works, wherewith Providence has diversified this land."

After van der Donck's arrival the pace of settlement in Rensselaerwyck began to increase. New settlers arrived in the colony each spring and summer, and fewer settlers left. In 1642 twenty-eight emigrants, some with wives and children, sailed up the Hudson. They included a bookkeeper, farm laborers, two carpenters, a brewer, a surgeon, a tailor, a mason, and a clergyman. This last, Johannes Megapolensis, arrived with his wife and four children. Van Rensselaer contracted with him to serve as a pastor for six years and provided him a worship space in the patroon's storehouse near Fort Orange. The dominie chose to live at Greenbush on the east side of the Hudson opposite Fort Orange. Although there were about thirty wooden houses around the fort, most of Rensselaerwyck's inhabitants worked on farms scattered across the vast expanse of the colony's 700,000 acres.

Such a cornucopia of delights caused the new schout's attention to wander. Though van der Donck possessed the requisite qualifications, he lacked the proper temperament. The patroon had hired him to look out for his rights, which van Rensselaer believed were being circumvented and abused by Rensselaerwyck's settlers. The carpenters were idle because farmers were hiring others to work at a cheaper wage. Van Rensselaer was left to support them or they would starve. Van der Donck had to check "such disorder and impertinence"; he had to acquaint other colonies on the Hudson with the patroon's rights; he had to fine and even imprison the dissolute; and all the time he had to tell van Rensselaer of his actions. For the patroon the orders were simple: "If there is any one who injures or wrongs my person or goods," he wrote early in 1643, "investigate who the man is, make him own up, force him to show proof and convict him according to the law." The restless van der Donck, however, quickly found himself consumed by new experiences, the land, the air, the Hudson, the smells, the Wilden. Surely these were more important than searching the length and breadth of Rensselaerwyck for cheats, adulterers, and other miscreants. Since his arrival van der Donck had leased a farm on Castle Island below Fort Orange. But by 1643 he wanted some of the rich land in the Hudson Valley for himself, and he had his eye on some acres in the Catskills adjacent to Rensselaerwyck.

Once the patroon learned of van der Donck's plan to buy land, he became incensed. He alone controlled the upper Hudson—the land, the people, and even, van Rensselaer maintained, the river itself. To enforce his presumed right to the river, the patroon built "Rensselaers Steyn," a fort on Barren Island at the southern boundary of Rensselaerwyck, and attempted to collect a duty on every fur trader who sailed past. To prove this point van Rensselaer immediately bought the land van der Donck wanted for himself and populated it with new colonists beholden only to him. But this purchase turned out to be one of Kiliaen van Rensselaer's last acts. By the end of 1643, the diamond merchant lay dead in Amsterdam, leaving a widow and nine children. Rensselaerwyck passed into the hands of his son Johannes, who was still a minor.

Van der Donck stayed on in Rensselaerwyck for several years after Kiliaen van Rensselaer's death. He took an English bride and lived at Castle Island until his farmhouse burned to the ground. As a reward for help in negotiating a treaty between New Netherland and the Mohawks, the directors of the Dutch West India Company allowed him to buy twenty-four thousand acres on the east bank of the Hudson in what is now Westchester County and the Bronx. He called the land Colen Donck, built a house overlooking the Spuyten Duyvil Creek, used the creek's waters to power a sawmill, and farmed the land of what is today Van Cortlandt Park. It became a small patroonship and attracted settlers of its own. Families in Colen Donck called it "Jonkheer's Landt," or the land of the young squire; the name survives today as Yonkers.

Willem Kieft, who replaced the disgraced Wouter van Twiller, found New Netherland in near chaos when he arrived in the spring of 1638. Few of the predominantly male population living at the edge of civilization paid much attention to the rules of civilized conduct. For many settlers, especially those in New Amsterdam, the most important recreational activities were drinking and whoring. From the beginning the Dutch West India Company had exported liquor to New Netherland, and Peter Minuit even placed a taproom in the countinghouse, the natural place of congregation for fur traders. "Grog-shops or houses where nothing is to be got but tobacco and beer" made up a quarter of the town's buildings, and liquor sales ranked second only to the sale of furs in the Dutch West India Company's revenues. At least one Dutch prostitute settled on Manhattan Island, and tales suggested that she had ample assistance from unmarried and married Dutch bawds as well as some native and slave women.

Slavery had begun to creep into the Hudson Valley as early as the directorship of Peter Minuit. By 1635, van Twiller appointed an overseer who directed the slaves in a variety of jobs in addition to building wooden palisades for the fort: removing dead animals from the streets, tilling fields, and harvesting the crops. Slave women served as domestic servants. They were quartered north of New Amsterdam, on the shore of the East River opposite Roosevelt Island.

Although their lot was hardly pleasant, slaves in the Hudson region nevertheless enjoyed more respect and liberties than they did in other parts of the New World. They were allowed to have their unions solemnized in the Dutch Reformed Church, and after 1644 older slaves were given land on which they could support themselves, though they had to pay an annual rent and their children remained in servitude.

Little is known of Kieft before his arrival, but in his nine years as director-general, he made many enemies and few friends. Proud and inflexible, ill-natured and fractious, and often weak and craven, Kieft brought ignominy and near ruin upon the Dutch colony. "Strange! that the science of government, which seems to be so generally understood," wrote one commentator, "should invariably be denied to the only one called upon to exercise it." Strange, too, that the Nineteen could have been so foolish as to choose one so singularly inept.

Like van Twiller before him, Willem Kieft came to bring order to New Amsterdam, but when he left in disgrace nine years later, New Amsterdam and Rensselaerwyck were the poorer for his tenure. Stained as it is with native blood, Kieft's record is far darker than van Twiller's. From the start, the new director-general demanded that New Amsterdam be a disciplined and virtuous community over which he would have absolute and unchallenged authority. Kieft governed by a council of two—himself and another man—but he weighted the vote so that his counted twice. He took the same tack with the rules he issued about conduct. To end drunkenness he shut down the tapsters, "except those who sold wine at a decent price, and in moderate quantities"; to stop smuggling, he ordered all sailors off the island after sunset; to end licentious behavior he ordered everyone "to abstain from fighting, from carnal intercourse with heathens, blacks, or other persons," and "from rebellion, theft, false swearing, calumny, and all other immoralities." To show that he was in charge of all morality, he imposed a curfew.

At the same time Willem Kieft was striving to establish order, the Dutch West India Company, in yet another policy shift, was taking steps to encourage settlement by liberalizing the terms of ownership. According to a new Charter of Freedoms and Exemptions, "Masters or Colonists" could have a grant of "one hundred morgens" of land provided that they settled five adults there. The new policy had its greatest effect on Manhattan. The company issued deeds for plantations, farms, and houses. Thus on October 19, 1638, Thomas Sanders was issued a "Patent" for a house "and five and twenty morgens of land, adjoining it," provided of course that Sanders "shall submit to all such taxes and levies, as the Company has already imposed . . . and he promises to pay all dues, as other free peoples are obliged to pay under the same condition." As the number of settlers increased, the idea of private ownership gradually took hold in the land.

It was Kieft's foolish and brutal war against the Native Americans that stained his tenure as director-general. The causes were several, but the increasing population and landownership were certainly among them. As more individuals traded directly with the natives, they added more guns, powder, lead, and alcohol to the natives' arsenal. The effects were devastating: resources and energy, not to mention human lives and trust, were squandered in such a way that the development of the Dutch colony in the Hudson Valley never completely recovered.

But Willem Kieft's attitude toward the natives led to his stubborn tactics and sanctioning of treachery. To the director-general the native people were "Wilden" and nothing more, an attitude that allowed him to justify his own "unnatural, barbarous, unnecessary, unjust, and disgraceful" acts. Early in his tenure he attempted to tax the natives' harvest of corn, which caused skirmishes on Staten Island and in Westchester in 1640 and 1641, and again in Newark Bay in 1642. In February 1643 Kieft sanctioned an attack by about eighty soldiers on the Hackensack people at Pavonia that turned into a shameful massacre. "About midnight, I heard a great shrieking," David Pietersen De Vries remembered. De Vries had warned Kieft, "'You wish to break the mouths of the Indians, but you will also murder our own nation.'" But he had cautioned the director-general in vain. "I ran to the ramparts of the fort, and looked over to Pavonia. Saw nothing but firing." De Vries was on hand the next morning when the soldiers returned with pride to report eighty natives dead, "considering they had done a deed of Roman valor, in murdering so many in their sleep."

The natives answered in like fashion. Within a matter of days, eleven bands were roaming the countryside, killing settlers and firing every farmstead that they could. While the Native Americans were wreaking their vengeance on the countryside, Roger Williams happened to be in New Amsterdam, preparing to embark for Europe. The clergyman and leader of Rhode Island witnessed the destruction: "Mine eyes did see ye first breaking forth of ye Indian War. . . . before we waighed Anchor their Boweries were in Flames. . . . Dutch and Eng[lish] slaine[;] mine eyes saw . . . flames at their Townes . . . & ye Flights and Hurries of Men, Women & Children." Even De Vries, who had been careful to maintain peaceful relations with the Hackensacks, lost some settlers as well as his barns.

Though many had prosecuted the war against the natives, none would take responsibility. Kieft tried "by cunning and numerous certificates and petitions" to shift responsibility for the conception of the massacre onto his schout and commis. Another former supporter tried to assassinate him.

The violence subsided with the planting season, when the Native Americans turned their attention toward their crops, but it revived after the harvest. From New Amsterdam, the colonists could look across the Hudson to Pavonia and see boweries in flames. Farmers in Westchester, even those in boweries just north of New Amsterdam's walls, were forced to retreat to Fort Amsterdam, abandoning their houses, land, crops, and cattle.

The seemingly endless pattern of massacres followed by raids continued until April 1645, when natives and settlers concluded a peace in New Amsterdam and later at Fort Orange. By September the land was calm once again. No longer would the natives fire houses and burn crops; no more would the Dutch of New Amsterdam flay their "Wilden" captives, mounting their heads on sticks or kicking them about the street like footballs. But the losses were great: Perhaps a thousand natives had died in the five years and one month of war; in New Amsterdam the population had dwindled to 250 men, women, and children, most of whom had few provisions for the future. There was a greater loss still for the Dutch: Kieft's battles with the natives had left the entire province of New Netherland more vulnerable than ever.

One positive outcome did emerge from the debacle: Early in 1641 the director-general asked the heads of New Amsterdam's white families to choose some men to advise him on what was quickly developing into a war. The very idea of one person or a group of persons acting in a "representative" way was a novel seventeenth-century concept, and almost audacious in a colony that was controlled by a private group of shareholders thousands of miles away. Still, Kieft faced some contentious settlers who wanted blood. "Is it right and proper," the director-general asked, "to punish the scandalous murder lately perpetrated by a savage on Claes Swits; and in case the Indians do not surrender the murderer to our demand is it not right to destroy the whole village to which he belongs?" The Committee of Twelve, as the representatives were known, responded quickly: "The murderer should be punished as the Director proposes."

By January 1642, however, the Twelve turned their attention to other matters, requesting that "taxes may not be imposed on the country in the absence of the Twelve." "As regards the 12 men," Kieft replied, "we are not aware that they received fuller powers from the Commonalty than

simply to give their advice respecting the murder of the late Claes Swits."
With that, the director-general dissolved the Committee of Twelve and
forbade its members to assemble or meet "on pain of being punished as
disobedient subjects."

Kieft found it relatively easy to dissolve the group of twelve men, but
by September 1643, as native bands fired the countryside and threatened
the very survival of the settlements at New Amsterdam, Westchester, and
Staten Island, circumstances again forced him to turn grudgingly to the
commonalty for advice. This time the settlers elected a group known as the
Eight Men. They devised war strategies and wrote complaints and pleas for
relief to the Nineteen. "We, wretched people, must skulk, with wives and
little ones . . . in and around the Fort at the Manhatas where we are not
safe even for an hour; whilst the Indians daily threaten to overwhelm us
with it," they wrote in one remonstrance, which caused Kieft to dismiss
them in 1644. The eight then composed a formal letter of complaint to the
States General about the director-general's failures. "Our fields lie fallow
and waste," they began, "our dwellings and other buildings are burnt," all
because of "a foolish hankering after war." It was the director-general who
had "embittered [the natives] against the Dutch nation," and the result was
their ruin. "We pray," they concluded "that a Governor may be speedily
sent with a beloved peace to us; or, that your Honors will be pleased to
permit us to return . . . to our dear Fatherland. For it is impossible to
settle this country until a different system be introduced here . . . so that
the entire country may not be hereafter, at the whim of one man, again
reduced to similar danger."

Sitting in Amsterdam, the Nineteen faced a great problem of their own:
the Dutch West India Company was on the verge of bankruptcy. By 1645,
New Netherland had cost the company half a million guilders. Privateering
no longer brought vast amounts of Spanish silver, and the cost of garri-
soning soldiers at distant outposts was draining the company's resources.
As part of their retrenchment the directors considered selling company
ships, cannon, and dock yards.

Now the Nineteen had to adjudicate another crisis of leadership in
New Netherland. Although they chose to ignore the plea for "a different
system" of government, the directors decided at the end of July 1646 to
replace Willem Kieft. In one of the first such instances in the history of

the New World, a group of representatives of the populace living on the banks of the Hudson River had petitioned the government for reform, and the government had heard them.

Passions continued to swirl in the breasts of Kieft and his accusers even after he was replaced. After much storm and stress the new director-general shipped Kieft and two of his most virulent accusers to Amsterdam on *The Princess Amalia* to air their suits and countersuits before the Nineteen. Another passenger was Dominie Bogardus, whom Kieft had charged with "scattering abuse during our administration."

It took an act of divine intervention to settle the dispute. Off Bristol, England, *The Princess Amalia* foundered on the rocks. Kieft and Bogardus were drowned, while his two other accusers survived. They reported that, near the moment of his last breath, Kieft was heard to say, "Friends, I have done wrong, can you forgive me?"

As the *Groote Gerret* (Great Crow) sailed into the Upper Bay of the river on May 11, 1647, its most prominent passenger, the new director-general, thirty-seven-year-old Peter Stuyvesant, was no doubt disturbed as he looked out upon the crude, undisciplined "city" of about five hundred souls living behind a flimsy wall on the southern tip of Manhattan Island. He wasn't reassured to learn that, in their effusive welcome, soldiers had consumed the city's entire store of gunpowder firing their cannon from the crumbling walls of Fort Amsterdam, a bastion he would later compare to a "molehill." (Despite Kieft's early efforts at repair, the walls were again in ruins.) Nor would the rest of New Amsterdam reassure him. It was usual for pigs and sheep to wander outside the fences meant to keep them in; residents often placed their outhouses in the dirt streets. Building lots were narrow. The houses themselves were crude rectangular wooden structures with thatched roofs, usually eight feet wide and eighteen feet long, with a door and a window at each end. Those that sheltered families sometimes had a small loft where children slept. Inside was a single room with a fireplace on one of the long walls and a wooden bed in the corner. That May, Stuyvesant might occasionally have seen a small formal garden with the first blossoms of flowers and sprouts of vegetables. In time he would come to know that his citizens ate very well: turkey and partridge, geese and ducks, fish and shellfish, clams and oysters. Only eggs and milk were still scarce.

The new director-general's ears were assaulted, too. Crude as it was, New Amsterdam was also a cosmopolitan, polyglot city where Dutch competed with English, French, German, Swedish, and Polish, among other languages. The sounds on the shore were especially diverse, as New Amsterdam had become an important trading post for merchants who brought goods to sell from the ports of western Europe, and to give passage to those who wanted to return. If we are to believe contemporary accounts, Stuyvesant regularly heard the drunken cries of natives who, contrary to every edict, had been sold their alcohol illegally. These noises competed with the drunken screams of New Amsterdam citizens who patronized the score of tiny smoke-filled taverns, some of which engaged in illegal trade. The disrepair of the primitive buildings on undeveloped streets, and the disorder of citizens and other animals, undoubtedly offended the man charged with New Amsterdam's welfare, Peter Stuyvesant.

Defeat had made Peter Stuyvesant into a hero. An ill-planned charge in 1640 for the Dutch West India Company against the Portuguese forces on the island of St. Martin in the Caribbean had cost him his right leg, but it also earned him a reputation for fearlessness. Stuyvesant happened to be in Amsterdam being fitted for a new wooden leg complete with silver trimmings while the Nineteen were debating the fate of Willem Kieft. Recognizing Stuyvesant's bravery and perhaps his authoritarian ways, the Nineteen looked to him to establish order in their beleaguered province. Remarkable in every way, Stuyvesant possessed a formidable will, shining virtues, and extraordinary flaws; all were reflected in his seventeen-year rule, which saw the population on the Hudson more than double and the civilization advance in order and general decency. But forces beyond Stuyvesant's control would bring about his second defeat.

A three-quarter portrait of the director-general, probably limned when he was about fifty years old, suggests much of his character and temperament. His dress is typical of the time: a broad collar favored by Dutch gentlemen extends partway over small plates of brigandine armor, and a golden sash covers his right shoulder. But the smooth, florid complexion of his face, the sharp-lined furrow at the bridge of his beaked triangular nose, his high forehead and fat chin and jowls distinguish him. His severe eyes lend a sense of humorless surety to the portrait, a surety leading to arrogance.

A slave to ritual, decorum, and the God of John Calvin, Stuyvesant reflected the austere strictness of his father, a dour Dutch Reformed Church pastor in Friesland. In New Amsterdam he demanded to be addressed as "Mijn Heer General," a title never employed by his predecessors, and treated his subjects with a sober paternalism. Aloof and remote, stubborn, at times as great a martinet as his predecessor Kieft, Stuyvesant alone knew what was right for *his* people; he would not suffer those who dared to question his commands or challenge his authority.

To put his stamp of order on the unruly populace on Manhattan Island, the director-general issued edicts and orders as rapidly as Kieft had— decrees about drunkenness, fighting, the building of houses (with chimneys of stone or brick rather than wood), smuggling, and selling liquor and guns to natives—all of which the reckless and intemperate inhabitants did their best to ignore.

But Peter Stuyvesant refused to let them. Animals were to be penned; garbage, including "rubbish, filth, ashes, dead animals, and such like things," as well as human excrement, were no longer to be dumped in the streets. Reflecting his own sober ways, which were something of a novelty in New Amsterdam, taverns were to close at 9 PM on weekdays, and remain closed entirely on Sundays. Imported wines and liquors were to be taxed. Two sermons, rather than one, would be preached on Sunday. Leather fire buckets were to be placed at street corners; fire wardens would direct the fighting of fires. Knives were not to be drawn in tavern fights. A farmers' market was to be built east of the fort where citizens might buy game, fish, and vegetables on market days, whose schedule he set. Shopkeepers were to use standard weights and measures that had to be certified. Before his reign ended, Stuyvesant created the first hospital for the care of sick soldiers and slaves, forbade shooting partridges within the city, and even established the first speed limit: horses leading wagons had to be walked whenever they traveled on Manhattan streets. Only Broadway was the exception.

Stuyvesant's reforms likely induced a more stable group of settlers to emigrate to New Netherland. Families seeking a land where they might put down roots began to take the place of bachelor fur traders in search of adventure. The director-general took steps to ensure their safety. In 1652 when another war in Europe, this one between England and the Netherlands, threatened the tranquillity at home, he decided to fortify the northern border of New Amsterdam. He directed that a ditch be dug from the East River to the North River (one of the early Dutch names for the Hudson), "4 to 5 feet deep and 11 to 12 feet wide at the top sloping in a little at the bottom," and later had it reinforced with planks "5 & 6 feet high"; this rampart became known as Wall Street.

Stuyvesant brought his penchant for order to the task of settling the boundary disputes with the English that had plagued the colony since it first appeared. With remarkably specious reasoning the English had claimed from their arrival that they held title to all the land north of Jamestown in Virginia. More recently settlers from John Winthrop's Massachusetts colony had begun to move to the western shore of Long Island Sound and to eastern Long Island. In 1650, Stuyvesant reached a diplomatic accord with Winthrop and the English, which put the matter to rest for the moment. Five years later he led a successful military expedition against Fort Christina, an outpost of Swedish settlers that had been established by Peter Minuit on the Delaware River where Wilmington is today. (The former director-general of New Netherland had helped the Royal Swedish Trading Company gain a foothold in the New World.) As the Swedes numbered but thirty men, and as Stuyvesant surrounded the fort with three divisions, the Dutch were able to force a surrender without the loss of a single life.

In his own mind, no doubt, Mijn Heer General stood before his people as a benevolent despot (undoubtedly he put the stress on benevolent), but in his convictions he was a despot nonetheless. He demonstrated those convictions whenever he dealt with native peoples, the leaders of Rensselaerwyck, or those professing faiths other than that of the Dutch Reformed Church, and especially whenever he took on those intractable inhabitants who, to his way of thinking, would not submit to his indomitable will.

The Hudson Valley badly needed authority as well. Directors-general before Stuyvesant had spent most of their energy and effort in New Amsterdam, content to maintain a wary relationship with the patroon's domain to the north. The Hudson River still served as the spine between New

Amsterdam and Fort Orange in Rensselaerwyck; the sparse settlements between them were little more than far-off trading posts in a hostile wilderness. If they were to grow, the residents would have to be able to emulate the life they had left behind in Europe, and Stuyvesant would have to ensure their safety. For the entire length of his directorship he sought to do just this with measures that promoted civility and the economy, diplomacy with the natives and foreign powers at his borders, and when necessary, force.

Director-General Stuyvesant found the residents of Rensselaerwyck, the nearly autonomous province 150 miles up the Hudson, to be as fractious as ever. Because all of the late Kiliaen van Rensselaer's children were minors, the family appointed his nephew, the former director-general Wouter van Twiller, to serve as their representative, and they named Brant van Slichtenhorst to be director of the patroon's land. Exercising de facto control over the territory, these plenipotentiaries accorded themselves sovereign and beholden to no one. They represented the "infant patroon," the name they gave to Johannes, the eighteen-year-old son of Kiliaen. Backed by several cannon, they demanded a fee from every captain who approached "Rensselaers Steyn."

Van Slichtenhorst enjoyed and abused his extraordinary power over Rensselaerwyck. Known as a cantankerous character, he relished a fight with anyone who challenged his authority in the slightest way. After taking up residence with his family and servants in a large house near Fort Orange, he quickly established control over every aspect of Rensselaerwyck's society, including its forests, farms, wharf, streets, and the courts, which he filled with numerous trivial cases.

It was inevitable that van Slichtenhorst would clash with Peter Stuyvesant for ultimate authority over Rensselaerwyck. He began with a series of small defiant acts: he refused to post Stuyvesant's numerous edicts, especially one declaring the first Wednesday in May a day of general fasting and public worship; he purchased more land on the Hudson at the site of present-day Claverack and Catskill without giving notice to the director-general; he built settlers' houses up to the perimeter of the Dutch West India Company's Fort Orange; and he even forbade anyone from bringing building materials inside the fort's walls.

Clearly van Slichtenhorst was looking for a fight, and the redoubtable

Stuyvesant did not disappoint him. The director-general stopped the practice of levying tolls at Rensselaers Steyn. In early 1652, he sailed up the Hudson with a company of soldiers and declared the land within the distance of a cannon shot of Fort Orange a separate village, Beverwyck, the district of the beaver. Henceforth, he declared, a garrison of soldiers would maintain the peace. Van Slichtenhorst responded predictably: Beverwyck still belonged to the patroon; he would fly the van Rensselaer flag from his house. And fly it he did, until Dutch soldiers tore it down and shipped him down the river to prison in New Amsterdam. Van Slichtenhorst languished there until 1655, when he returned to Amsterdam.

The one part of New Netherland's life that Stuyvesant failed to control was the exercise of religion. On this subject Mijn Heer General's bigotry was implacable. In his view, to him alone had God ordained the institution of the state and the church. As director-general he served as God's agent. Surely he should not tolerate any who professed another belief. In this regard he differed from the burghers who had made Amsterdam a beacon of tolerance in Europe. In North America Stuyvesant labored hard to make New Amsterdam a citadel of intolerance in the New World. Assured as he was that the God of the Dutch Reformed Church was the only true deity, he suppressed the religions of those who believed differently.

To assist in the suppression he persuaded Reverend Johannes Megapolensis, dominie in Rensselaerwyck, to take the same position in New Amsterdam. In Rensselaerwyck, Megapolensis had shown his Christian goodness and charity when he enabled two Jesuit missionary priests to escape the clutches of the Mohawks who held them captive in the wilderness. But when persons of other faiths wished to practice their religion in the city, he proved as narrow-minded as the director-general. Contrary beliefs were the product of the devil, of course, and Megapolensis and Stuyvesant knew that those of the devil's party were abroad in the land. They would tolerate them only so long as they made no attempt to worship in public. Living in such a diverse city as New Amsterdam had become, the director-general and his dominie were only setting themselves up for frustration and failure. Religious diversity would become a part of the Hudson Valley.

Megapolensis and Stuyvesant persisted on their course. The director-general ordered Lutherans imprisoned for worshiping together. When a Lutheran pastor arrived in Manhattan, Megapolensis declared that "the snake [is] in our bosom," and Stuyvesant ordered him deported. The snake was eventually cast out, but not before slipping into the wilderness of Long Island to preach the message of God for several years.

Stuyvesant ordered a boatload of Quakers that arrived in the harbor to leave immediately for Rhode Island, which Megapolensis declared "the *latrina* of New England"; but five of their number also snuck ashore to preach God's word. The men quickly found their way to Long Island, but the women, Dorothy Waugh and Mary Weatherhead, "as soon as the ship had fairly departed . . . began to quake and go into a frenzy, and cry out in the middle of the street, that men should repent, for the day of judgment was at hand." Megapolensis bemoaned the fact that "the devil is the same everywhere"; Stuyvesant shipped them out to Rhode Island.

Still, Stuyvesant's inflexible stand was countered by the Nineteen's leniency. Word came from Amsterdam that Lutherans were to be treated "quietly and leniently." Of the Quakers, the Nineteen wrote: "Although we heartily desire, that these and other sectarians remained away from there, yet as they do not, we doubt very much whether we can proceed against them rigorously without diminishing the population and stopping immigration which must be favored at so tender a stage of the country's existence. You may therefore, shut your eyes . . . [and] allow everyone to have his own belief."

The challenge that the Lutherans and Quakers presented paled in comparison with the arrival in September 1654 of twenty-three Sephardic Jews from Brazil. The trials these unhappy refugees endured had begun when the Portuguese reclaimed Brazil from the increasingly hapless Dutch West India Company and kicked them out of the country. On their way to Amsterdam, the Jews were captured by Spanish pirates, who themselves were seized by a French privateer. The French captain agreed to carry the Jews to New Amsterdam for a fee. Arriving with no money, the Jews petitioned the director-general to let them stay and begged Megapolensis for money to pay their debts. Though the dominie gave them money, he wanted them gone, complaining to the Nineteen of the "Papists, Mennonites, and Lutherans among the Dutch; also many Puritans or Independents, and many Atheists and various other servants of Baal . . . it would create a still greater confusion, if the obstinate and immovable Jews came to settle here. . . . These people have no other God than the Mammon of unrighteousness and no other aim than to get possession of Christian property." Stuyvesant also protested, but to no avail. "The Jewish race" had "permission to sail and trade in New Netherland and to live and remain there," the Nineteen wrote to Stuyvesant. They had suffered a "considerable loss" in the taking of Brazil, and they had invested a "large amount of capital in shares of this Company." For the merchant princes in Amsterdam pragmatism and perhaps just common sense trumped the Calvinist God of Megapolensis and Stuyvesant.

Adriaen van der Donck posed a different sort of problem to Peter Stuyvesant's conception of order. The former schout of Rensselaerwyck, who was now the squire of Colen Donck on the east bank of the Hudson, collided with the director-general. From the regime of Willem Kieft, Stuyvesant had inherited the committee of eight men, later expanded to nine, selected from a group of eighteen prominent men chosen by the people. In December 1648, Stuyvesant made the mistake of selecting van der Donck to serve on the board. Almost immediately the new adviser rallied his colleagues to complain about the management of the colony. By the following July he had framed a remonstrance outlining his complaints about the governance of New Netherland.

The colony was a land of abundance, van der Donck asserted in his grievance, with countless species of fish, game, and plants for medicines. Its waters were abundant, especially the North River, which is "best as regards trade and population." And yet, van der Donck asserted, it was a land of great decay. The "evil consequences" of Kieft's administration remain; Kieft acted like a sovereign, while Stuyvesant is swayed by pride and refuses to heed advice. His administration bears hard on the inhabitants and no one dares to give counsel.

By August, van der Donck was sailing for Amsterdam to lay his remonstrance at the feet of the States General. Master bureaucrats that they were, the members of the States General referred his complaints to a committee, which heard charge and countercharge without reaching any decision. Caught in a Gordian knot that no doubt had been tied by Stuyvesant and the Nineteen, van der Donck was denied permission to return to his land

and his wife. But he would not give up his dream for New Netherland. It was in Amsterdam that he wrote his narrative of the land he so loved. When he did finally return to his home on the Hudson in December 1653, he arrived broken and dispirited; he lasted another year, until at age thirty-five he died in his house overlooking the Spuyten Duyvil Creek in the valley that had enchanted him from the moment he first saw it scarcely a dozen years earlier. Peter Stuyvesant had triumphed.

Unquestionably, Peter Stuyvesant's seventeen-year reign was the most successful of the Dutch West India Company's directors-general. As he established order the population increased. By 1664 there were roughly nine thousand people in New Netherland, most living in the Hudson Valley. About 40 percent were Dutch; 19 percent German, 15 percent English. Seventy percent of those who had emigrated there were part of a family (the rest were single males and females). Farmers now came in place of adventurers; craftsmen became more common than fur traders.

While the order Stuyvesant brought was most welcome, New Netherland was still inextricably bound to the fortunes of the Dutch West India Company. The sure success of mercantile-minded Dutchmen in 1623 was headed toward collapse by 1645. Stuyvesant's arrival coincided with the ebbing fortunes of the company, which by this time was facing bankruptcy. The company that had thrived on war was incapable of surviving in peace. The Treaty of Westphalia in 1648 not only concluded hostilities between the Dutch and the Spanish, but also ended the company's ability to seize Spanish boats filled with silver. With each passing month, insolvency became more and more the norm. A nasty and costly war with the Portuguese in Brazil had further bled the Dutch West India Company's resources, and English pirates were now harassing Dutch boats.

Yet other events in Europe, this time in London and Amsterdam, over which Stuyvesant had no control doomed him and New Netherland to failure. In London, where King Charles I was dead and Oliver Cromwell's theocratic regicides ruled, Parliament passed a navigation act intended to limit imports of goods to those arriving in English-owned vessels. In Amsterdam, whose riches had largely depended on the Dutch domination of the sea, the States General had no choice but to fight. In New Netherland, where Stuyvesant knew the defenses would never be able to resist an English challenge, he tried his best to maintain "neighborly friendship" while at the same time he braced himself as best he could for a fight. In New England, firebrands in the various colonies raised a militia and prepared to send an armada to the Hudson. Only a merchant ship bringing news of a treaty between England and Holland returned calm to the colonies in North America.

As early as 1649, Adriaen van der Donck had warned the States General, "The country has arrived to that state, that if it be not assisted it will not need any aid hereafter because the English will wholly absorb it." In fact, the English were slowly doing just that. With British colonies on the southwestern and northeastern boundaries of New Netherland, Stuyvesant found himself caught in the jaws of a slowly closing vise. The English were gradually heading westward beyond the Connecticut River and they were building settlements on the eastern end of Long Island. More and more English were emigrating to New Netherland.

In September 1655, a year after the threat of war with New England seemed to abate, Algonquins in the Hudson Valley overran farms on Manhattan and Staten Island. To make matters worse, Stuyvesant was away dealing with the Swedes at Fort Christina. The trouble began at a bowery on Broadway when Hendrick van Dyck, a former schout who loathed the natives, killed a native woman for stealing peaches from his orchard. Soon the conflict escalated; the Algonquins plundered farms and a well-aimed Algonquin arrow pierced van Dyck's breast. When Stuyvesant returned he found the settlements along the Hudson in panic. By the time he managed to restore an uneasy peace through a timely prisoner exchange and a gift of munitions, about fifty colonists and sixty natives had died, and twenty-eight farms on Manhattan, Long Island, and Pavonia had been torched. Worse than the loss of life and crops and property was the damage to the self-assurance of the settlers.

The Peach War, as it came to be known, paled in comparison to the more savage and destructive Esopus wars that followed, starting in 1659. The immediate cause of these conflagrations on the west bank of the Hudson, at present-day Kingston, was the Dutch slaughter of a group of natives whom the Dutch had made drunk with strong liquor; but as always, land and the fruits of the land lay at the heart of the dispute.

Stuyvesant's success in attracting settlers to the Hudson Valley also contributed to the conflict and ultimately helped bring about his demise. As the population and farms increased in the valley in the 1650s, the natives on the Esopus Creek found themselves pushed farther and farther into the interior and away from the Hudson, their chief avenue of communication. True, they sometimes had "sold" their land to the strange Europeans, but their conception of what constituted property and the rights of property owners was very different. For their part, the Europeans could scarcely understand why the fact of their purchases was ever in dispute. After all, the Dutch West India Company controlled this province, and they usually saw to it that a schout or even the director-general himself witnessed the sale. The natives of the Esopus lands understood none of this. They only knew that the Dutch constrained their freedom to do what they wished, and wherever and whenever they pleased. To be sure, they had received a treaty string of wampum, and perhaps some pots, or even guns and powder in exchange; but the perfidious Dutch had taken advantage of them. And as was the case with Henry Hudson's first visit in 1609, the Dutch in the Esopus region frequently took advantage of the natives with alcohol.

After the slaughter and the consequent native attacks, Stuyvesant sailed up the Hudson with a force of armed men, restored order, and demanded that the colonists gather together behind a palisade, which he named Wiltwyck, or Wild Place. His dealings with the natives were equally direct. "It would be best," he told them, "if they were to sell me the whole country of the Esopus and move inland or to some other place; that it was not good, that they lived so near to the . . . Dutch, so that the cattle and hogs . . . could not run any more into the cornfields of the savages and be killed by them." The natives did not yield easily. The land upriver remained dangerous for colonists from the fall of 1659 until Stuyvesant's troops prevailed at Wiltwyck in the spring of 1660. Then the director-general himself gave the natives gifts to conclude a truce.

But the Dutch demand for more land made an enduring peace illusory. From Wiltwyck the Europeans pushed several miles westward to establish Nieuw Dorp, or New Village, on farmland the Esopus people thought of as theirs. Beginning in June 1663 the Esopus natives launched a series of fierce attacks on Nieuw Dorp and Wiltwyck, cutting down entire families with axes, taking numerous prisoners, and plunging the Hudson Valley from Fort Orange to New Amsterdam into panic. Again Stuyvesant sailed up the river, this time with a large force of soldiers. And again, he prevailed, but this time there were no gifts. His men destroyed crops and laid waste to fields, burned native villages, and killed as many as they could. By May 1664, when he declared a day of thanksgiving in New Amsterdam, Stuyvesant had driven the last of the formidable native groups from the Hudson; the Dutch ruled the valley.

Peter Stuyvesant's thanksgiving was short-lived. In London, where the House of Stuart reigned once more, Charles II had given his brother James, the Duke of York and Albany, a royal patent over New Netherland. By summer, residents of New Amsterdam and the Hudson Valley began to hear that the British were planning an invasion, but there was little Stuyvesant could do to prepare. The walls of the fort at New Amsterdam had fallen into disrepair once again and the powder was low; the north wall remained a wooden palisade; the shore of the Hudson had no defenses: Manhattan Island was vulnerable from all sides. Upriver, the fortifications were even more exposed. The bankrupt Nineteen in Amsterdam seemed not to be overly concerned with the reports and rumors, and even had they been, there was little they could do. On September 1, 1664, Colonel Richard Nicolls in command of four British ships and 400 soldiers sailed through the Narrows with a message for the director-general holed up behind the weak walls of Fort Amsterdam with 150 soldiers and less than a day's powder and lead. After several tense days of negotiations, and after New Amsterdam's burghers implored him to submit, Peter Stuyvesant reluctantly turned the Hudson and New Netherland over to the British. Farther north, Nicolls's men secured the peaceable surrender of Fort Orange and concluded a favorable treaty with the Iroquois. Adriaen van der Donck's dark prophecy had come to pass.

Now all of the Atlantic coast lay in British hands. To please his master, Nicolls named these prizes after him: Fort Amsterdam and Fort Orange became Fort James and Fort Albany; Rondout on the western shore south of Albany became King's Town or Kingston in 1679; and the richest prizes of all, New Netherland and New Amsterdam, became New York. The great river that led north into the fur-rich wilderness, the river the Dutch had sometimes called the Nordt and sometimes the Mauritius, would gradually take on the name of its English discoverer, Henry Hudson.

Nine years later events in Europe briefly changed the fortunes of the people on the Hudson. In November 1673, when a third Anglo-Dutch war erupted across the Atlantic, two enterprising Dutch captains arrived with a fleet in the Upper Bay. As the English had done no better job fortifying New York than the Dutch before them, they quickly ceded control of the city and the river. Again under the Dutch flag, New York became New Orange and Albany became Willemstad. What the Dutch had won handily in war, however, they quickly relinquished in peace. The following February, Charles II concluded the Treaty of Westminster, which returned the Hudson to the English. "If it has to be," wrote Jeremias van Rensselaer, the third Patroon of Rensselaerwyck, about the decision made three thousand miles away, "we commend the matter to God, who knows what is best for us." The English controlled the coast of North America again; another century passed before anyone would seriously challenge them.

CHAPTER 4

The Valley Transformed

The Treaty of Westminster had enormous significance for the English monarchy. Since 1497, when John Cabot claimed Newfoundland for Henry VII, British interest in North America had been quietly growing. By 1640 England counted three colonies on the continent: Virginia and Maryland in the south and the Massachusetts Bay Company in New England. Following the treaty in 1674, the British could boast a contiguous coastline between Virginia and present-day Maine, united, albeit loosely, under their military, civil, and commercial authority and aligned against the French, whose presence in the St. Lawrence valley posed a continual threat. The Hudson River valley and the deepwater port at the river's mouth proved to be the greatest prize of all, for the valley led directly north to the French.

To those living in the Hudson Valley the change of government seemed slight at first, especially as the first two governors, Richard Nicolls and Francis Lovelace, imposed English rule in as prudent and wise a manner as possible. Although Nicolls substituted the Duke's Laws modeled on New England legal codes for Dutch laws modeled on the Justinian code, he renewed land titles and called for religious tolerance at the same time. Officers of the new government saluted a different flag and spoke a new language. For the most part these changes were gradual rather than abrupt. Magistrates conducted court cases in English, but for those living in the Hudson Valley the proceedings were translated into Dutch. Dutch remained the language used by people in forests and fields, on sloops and wharves, and in taverns and churches. Other than the prize acquisitions, New York, Albany, and Kingston, Dutch place names in the Hudson Valley—Catskill, Watervliet, Spuyten Duyvil, Claverack, and Peekskill—remained.

Nevertheless, over the next century the transformation brought by British control did take place. The valley became more populous and by virtue of geography allied more closely to England's interest in international relations and wars and treaties. This change was gradual, but it connected the valley's residents to English plans for the development of North America, and it bound them to British foreign policy toward the French. But the most immediate transformation took place on the landscape, where the British continued the tradition of issuing patents for large manors, most on the banks of the Hudson River. It was the lords of these manors, espe-

Overleaf: "Nieu Amsterdam," an engraving that depicts a dour Dutch merchant and his wife standing before the thriving Hudson River port at Manhattan Island. The couple, possibly Frederick Philipse and his wife, Margaret Hardenbroeck de Vries, tower above their slaves, whose labor enables them to hold a basket of fruit and a sheaf of tobacco leaves. (I. N. Phelps Stokes Collection, Miriam and Ira D. Wallach Division of Art, Prints, and Photographs, The New York Public Library, Astor, Lenox, and Tilden Foundations)

cially the ones belonging to the Livingston, Philipse, and van Rensselaer families, who had the greatest effect on the average farmer and carpenter, mason and merchant.

Family legend suggests that Livingston Manor may be said to have begun in 1678 at the bedside of Nicholaes van Rensselaer, who lay dying in the patroon's house in Albany. Nicholaes, the first patroon's eighth child, had a penchant for spendthrift living, mystical visions, and spiritual thoughts. His prodigal ways saddled him with enormous debts in Amsterdam, which led him ultimately to flee to America; his mystical visions gained him the favor of the exiled Charles II, who, he prophesied, would be restored to the English throne; and Nicholaes's spiritual thoughts brought him to his family's manor at Rensselaerwyck. There he set himself up as the "director" of the colony, and after the death of his older brother, Jeremias, he petitioned his family in the Netherlands to declare him the third patroon. Wary of giving him too much power, his family declined, preferring instead to rely on Jeremias's widow, Maria. For her part, Maria contended that the patroonship should pass to Jeremias's eldest son. Far less prudent was the English governor, who at the behest of the Stuarts in England, appointed Nicholaes co-minister to the faithful in Albany.

Shortly after his arrival in the Hudson Valley, the thirty-nine-year-old Nicholaes married an eighteen-year-old daughter of Philip Pieterse Schuyler, named Alida, and moved into the patroon's house in Albany. Alida endured four years of her arranged and childless marriage before her husband fell ill. Now, on his deathbed, Nicholaes asked to dictate his last will and testament. But when his secretary Robert Livingston appeared at his bedside, Nicholaes had his final vision: "No, no, send him away," he exclaimed, raising his head from his pillow, "he's going to marry my widow." With that Nicholaes promptly expired. Eight months later his vision was realized: Alida Schuyler van Rensselaer married Robert Livingston.

In one stroke Robert Livingston had united himself with the van Rensselaers and the Schuylers, the two most important Dutch ruling families of the upper Hudson. By the time Livingston died in 1728, he was proprietor of Livingston Manor, 157,000 acres stretching from the east bank of the Hudson to Massachusetts and Connecticut. Over the years his heirs would expand the Livingston landholdings to more than a million acres on both sides of the Hudson—more land than may be found in the state of Rhode Island or Yosemite National Park.

When making his way in the Hudson Valley, Robert Livingston always coupled his skills and experience with his innate shrewdness and sense of timing. The youngest of fourteen children, he had been born in Scotland to a Presbyterian clergyman and raised in a strict Calvinist household, where it was a given that God predestined some to eternal salvation and others to eternal damnation. In the pastor's case, God had also ordained that he should flee with his family to Rotterdam after he delivered sermons condemning Charles Stuart for restoring the episcopacy to England. In the Netherlands, Robert gained the skills he later needed on the Hudson. He mastered the language and manners of the Dutch traders and observed the business of Dutch countinghouses. At age nineteen, after his father died, Robert decided to resolve his destiny in the vast space of America, first in Puritan Massachusetts, which proved too constricting for his taste, and then in Albany where trading rather than religion ruled. With impeccable timing and good luck, he arrived on the Hudson in December 1674, shortly after word of the Treaty of Westminster reached America.

There was little in the Hudson Valley to impress Livingston when he arrived by sloop at his new home. From the Hudson, Albany appeared as a small palisaded town crowded at the river's edge. Fort Orange, the old outpost of the Dutch West India Company, had fallen victim to spring floods and now was a decayed and abandoned shell. About eighty houses surrounded the fort, many located on the two principal streets, Market and Pearl, running parallel to the Hudson, or on Yonker Street, which ran west from the river and connected with a path that led still farther west beyond the palisade to Schenectady. Certainly the most dominant feature was the Dutch Reformed Church, at Market and Yonker streets, a large hip-roofed structure topped by a tall cupola with a rooster weather vane, while the most prominent residence, situated at the corner of Yonker and Pearl, belonged to the patroon.

Albany's frontier rusticity aside, the town was the perfect place for Robert Livingston. His knowledge of Dutch and English and his understanding of the nuances of business conduct in both cultures became an invaluable asset. He shrewdly insinuated himself into both the English and Dutch societies and soon made himself indispensable. Within a year the governor appointed Livingston to the Board of Indian Commissioners, which had the task of continuing good relations with the natives, Nicholaes van Rensselaer appointed him secretary, and he was also appointed to be secretary to Albany. (Never mind that this last position was really a glorified town clerk; it gave Livingston a valuable entrée to the English government.) Within five years he had married van Rensselaer's widow, Alida, and, with his wife at his side, was maneuvering to gain control of the Rensselaerwyck estate from her former sister-in-law, Maria van Rensselaer.

The daughter of Oloff Stevenzen Van Cortlandt, a wealthy Manhattan brewer, fur trader, merchant, and member of Stuyvesant's Council of Nine Men, Maria knew how to survive the test that Rensselaerwyck faced from Livingston. She was fortunate, too, as were other females in New Netherland, to live under Roman Dutch law, which not only guided civic and business affairs but accorded women a greater status than was given those living under English law. Women frequently took their place in business affairs and sometimes engaged in trade, and those like Maria, who came from a family of privilege and substance, possessed reasonable security, influence, and respect. Jeremias van Rensselaer, in announcing his union with Maria to his mother in the Netherlands, said he had "not much to write" of "her figure and face," but he assured his mother she would be "a good partner." Jeremias recognized that Maria's business abilities were obviously her greatest asset.

It was Roman Dutch law, however, that Robert Livingston chose to exploit against Maria van Rensselaer. The law that bound Nicholaes and Alida in marriage had given the couple joint ownership of their property. As Nicholaes died with neither a will nor children, his property, so Robert Livingston contended, passed entirely into his widow's hands. Under English law, which governed Alida's second marriage, to Livingston, all her property was bound over to her new husband. The 750,000 acres of Rensselaerwyck, Livingston shamelessly argued, belonged to him.

Clearly, the ambiguity of the change from Dutch to English law put any claim Maria had to Rensselaerwyck into question, and Robert Livingston used that ambiguity to harass her at every turn. Almost immediately after the demise of Nicholaes van Rensselaer, Livingston began pestering her for Rensselaerwyck's financial records and sued her for payment of bills he claimed her husband had incurred. He and Alida lived in the van

Rensselaer house in Albany and, particularly galling to Maria, took over the farm that she and her late husband had established across the Hudson at Crailo. "I cannot bear to see him any longer in possession of the patroon's garden, where my husband, my child, and brother deceased, lie buried," Maria lamented in vain to Jeremias's surviving brother in Amsterdam.

Robert Livingston was the first, but far from the last, of his clan to marry into the Schuyler and van Rensselaer families. Indeed, intermarriage among the families that counted in the Hudson Valley—those with wealth and land—was a routine occurrence. In future generations the van Rensselaers, Schuylers, and Livingstons, as well as Van Cortlandts, Beekmans, and other families from New York City, intermarried often and, to the consternation of historians and genealogists, just as frequently recycled first names. Such alliances often led to entangled and strained relations. No doubt Stephanus Van Cortlandt tested the harmony he enjoyed with his sister Maria by marrying Alida Schuyler's sister, Gertrude. Stephanus had supported Maria in her struggle with Nicholaes, but now that Alida had married Robert Livingston, did his allegiance lie with his sister or his wife's family?

Robert Livingston's chief desire was to acquire land, lots of land, the great European symbol of rank and prestige, and even nobility. His marriage to Alida gave him a chance to realize his ambition, so he claimed, yet he was clever enough not to assert his right to Rensselaerwyck too intensely. True, the manor had fallen into Alida's hands, but so had a great pile of debts the prodigal Nicholaes had accrued in the course of his progress through the Netherlands, England, and North America. The courts, too, and various governors of New York were hesitant to accede to Livingston's claim to Rensselaerwyck and reluctant to dismiss Nicholaes's creditors' demands to recover their money. Livingston shrewdly allowed the governor to negotiate a settlement that gave Rensselaerwyck to the van Rensselaer family and freed him from any of the debts left behind by Nicholaes. Of his original claim he retained only the house at the corner of Yonker and Pearl streets. At the same time Livingston quietly negotiated the purchase of two thousand acres south of Albany on the eastern shore of the Hudson. The land boasted a broad stream that could be harnessed for a mill, a safe harbor, and a magnificent view of the Catskill Mountains to the west. The payment for his patent to the land was a pittance:

> three hundred guilders in Zewant, Eight Blankets and two Childs Blankets, five and twenty ells of Duffels and four garments of Strouds, ten large shirts and ten small ditto, Ten pairs of large stockings and ten pairs of Small; Six Guns, fifty pounds of Powder, Fifty staves of Lead, four caps, Ten Kettles, Ten Axes, ten adzes, Two pounds of Paint, Twenty little Scissors, Twenty little looking-glasses, one hundred fish hooks, Awls and Nails of each one hundred, four Rolls of Tobacco, one hundred Pipes, ten Bottles, Three kegs of Rum, one Barrel of Strong Beer and Twenty knives, Four Stroud-Coats and Two duffel-Coats: and four Tin kettles.

The motto of the Livingston family was "Spero meliora" (I hope for better things), but Robert did more than merely hope. He achieved better things for himself and his family, in a spectacular if not quite legitimate way. In November 1684 the English governor of New York issued him his patent; another patent followed in 1685, for six hundred more acres east of his property, "in the territory called by the Indians Tachkanick." In 1686, New York's governor Thomas Dongan issued yet a third patent, this time to the "Manor of Livingston," "for Encouraging the future Settlement." Though he eschewed the title to the end, Robert Livingston became "Lord of the Manor." Those who resided on his land were his tenants and bound to pay him quitrents each year. This third patent proved a positive bonanza. It defined the boundaries loosely: "begining behind Pattkook on a Certaine Creeke that runns into the East side of Hudson's river and is known by the name of Roeloffe Johnsons kill Begining on the North West side of the said kill . . . at a Place Called by Native Minissichtanock where two black Oake Trees are marked with an L." Most important for Livingston, the patent declared the two parcels of land as "*being adjacent,*" ignoring the fact that they were actually separated by more than a hundred thousand acres. The governor's slip of the pen—which Livingston neglected to correct—increased the size of Livingston Manor from 2,600 acres to 160,000 acres, stretching from the east bank of the Hudson to the Massachusetts and Connecticut lines. Every Lady Day, March 25, Livingston, and after him his "Heires and Assignes," collected quitrents from each tenant who

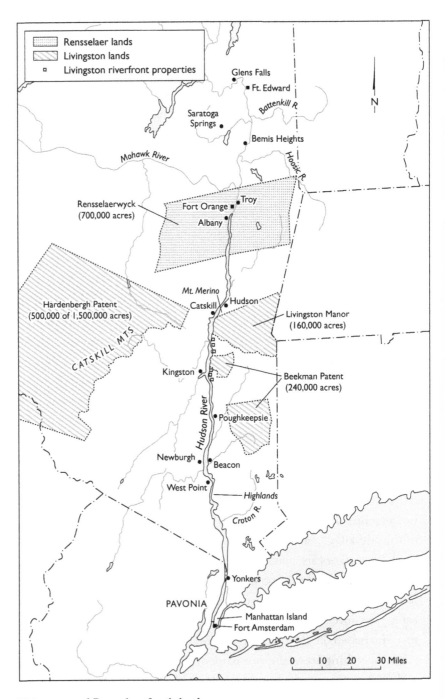

Livingston and Rensselaer family lands

resided on Livingston land. And every year on the same day, Livingston and his heirs paid to the governor their annual quitrent—all of twenty-eight shillings—for the lands of Livingston Manor.

For the next three decades after he received his third patent, on July 22, 1686, Robert Livingston walked a tightrope between the various factions, intrigues, and events that constituted political life in New York and London. A succession of governors (some honest but most corrupt), a rebellion, threats of native attack, charges of piracy, and the formidable challenge of populating his land continually tested him. Over the years he faced certain loss of his property and quite possibly his life. Though he often teetered on the brink of misfortune, he always recovered and ultimately prospered.

Jacob Leisler presented Livingston with his first serious test. A merchant, tobacco, fur, and slave trader, the strict Calvinist Leisler came to prominence as a result of the crisis in London that resulted from the ascension of the Roman Catholic James II to the throne of England. James consolidated New York with the New England colonies, an act that did not sit well with most New Yorkers, who were already worried about the new king's religion. They had tolerated the Duke of York's appointment of Thomas Dongan (whose error handed Robert Livingston the additional 160,000 acres) as their governor, ignoring Dongan's Catholicism and his private chapel and priest. But now they worried, lest King James II's Roman sympathies encourage the Catholic French Canadians and their brutal Iroquois accomplices to attack English and Dutch settlements in the Hudson Valley. Perhaps the king would contract an alliance between New York and Catholic Canada?

When word from London arrived in New York, in March 1689, that prominent members of Parliament had staged a "glorious revolution" and had crowned James's Protestant daughter Mary and her Dutch husband, William of Orange, as their monarchs, the governmental structure of the colony collapsed. The citizens of Boston promptly jailed the royal governor, Edmond Andros, while in Manhattan a group of citizens deposed the lieutenant governor. Into the vacuum of leadership stepped Jacob Leisler, who became commander in chief of the province of New York.

These events had a dramatic effect on the farmers and traders scattered throughout the valley between Albany and New York, especially as Leisler's Calvinism came to the fore. Dissolving the city council, he proposed a proto-democracy, an association for "the preservation of the true Protestant Religion and his Majesties Person and Royall State and our Laws Liberties and Properties." But the association soon changed into a ruthless tyranny. Ever suspicious, Leisler seemed to find demons and popish plotters everywhere he turned in the Hudson Valley, especially when he looked at Stephanus Van Cortlandt and Robert Livingston, merchants like himself but aristocratic in their outlook. Van Cortlandt and others of his class sailed for Albany, where they joined Livingston in a convention to declare their allegiance to William and Mary and their opposition to Leisler. After calling his adversary "Ye vulgar sort" and "a Dutch boor," Livingston thought it prudent to avoid Leisler's warrant for his arrest. He raised troops to defend Albany and Schenectady from the French and natives whose invasion was expected daily. From England came a legitimate governor appointed by the king; Leisler refused to acknowledge the new man and took refuge in the fort at New York. A battle ensued; men on both sides died before Leisler and his son-in-law were captured, tried, convicted of treason, and hanged. Robert Livingston returned to Manhattan in May 1691, in time to watch the Dutch boor swing from the gibbet.

Following Jacob Leisler's execution, Livingston danced attendance before a succession of governors who arrived and departed with alarming frequency. Like the Dutch before them, the English had a knack for appointing governors who were all too often wholly unsuited for the office. Some, appointed by the Tories, would favor the manors and the creation of great estates and aristocrats; others, appointed by the Whigs, would favor a Leislerian form of representation. Some were honest; others were corrupt. Almost all were inept. Livingston sought to gain the favor of them all. At first he succeeded. But the Scotsman's almost palpable charm, smoothness, and persuasiveness soon proved to be evanescent qualities that gave way to his aggressive pride. Governors frequently began their relationship with Livingston expressing admiration for his skills, but more often than not, after other, less attractive aspects of his character came to the fore, especially what they perceived as his arrogance and avarice, they grew exasperated by his methods.

Livingston also suffered from bad luck that tested his skills for survival. Henry Sloughter, the legitimate English governor who defeated Leisler, rewarded Livingston for his loyalty with the lucrative job of victualing the British soldiers at Albany; but then Sloughter died after just four months.

Benjamin Fletcher, the man the Tory government appointed to succeed Sloughter, made public corruption and embezzlement into a high art; perhaps recognizing his competition, Fletcher moved against Robert Livingston. "This man by false insinuations," Fletcher wrote to London, "has made a considerable fortune by his employments in the Government, never disbursing six pence, but with the expectation of twelve pence, his beginning being a little Book keeper, he has screwed himself into one of the most considerable estates in the province. . . . he is known by all men here, to have neither Religion nor morality, his whole thirst being at any rate and by any ways to inrich himself and has said as I am credibly informed by many persons, he had rather be called knave Livingston, than poor Livingston." After displaying his indignation, Fletcher proceeded to divert Livingston's victualing remuneration to his own pockets, knowing that this left "knave Livingston" in a quandary: soldiers without food would abandon Albany and his property to the French and their native allies. Remembering their massacre of sixty people in Schenectady in 1690, which he said "should not pass from our memory," Livingston had no choice but to continue providing the soldiers' rations, plead for payment, and, if it did not come, seek redress from the Crown.

The story of Captain Kidd demonstrates Livingston's penchant for the shading of honesty as well as his extraordinary luck. A fellow Scotsman, William Kidd lived the life of a privateer, roaming the seas with letters of marque from the Crown and preying upon merchant ships of hostile nations. He had helped Sloughter defeat Leisler, and when not attacking the French he lived with his wife in their New York City townhouse. Livingston met Kidd not in New York but in London, where he went in 1696 to seek payment for his victualing. He and the captain joined in a syndicate to outfit a privateer, the *Adventure Galley,* to "take prizes from the Kings enemies and otherwise . . . annoy them." By that time the Whigs had taken control of Parliament and appointed Richard Coote, Earl of Bellomont, to succeed Benjamin Fletcher. Livingston lured Bellomont to become a major partner in the venture, with the agreement that the trio would divide the spoils. But by midyear of 1698, Bellomont, having arrived in the colony, learned that Kidd himself had become a pirate and was harrying English ships in the Atlantic; a year later the governor used the inference of fair treatment to lure Kidd and his crew into Boston harbor. When the *Adventure Galley* let down its anchor, Bellomont ordered the arrest of the pirate whose career as a privateer he had helped to finance.

Kidd's story fast became a scandal to the Whigs in London; Livingston knew that Bellomont might well condemn him along with the pirate in order to protect himself. But there was even more cause for alarm: Despite his abandonment of Kidd, Bellomont was fundamentally honest. Shortly after his arrival he had found that Fletcher had taken bribes in the "intolerable corrupt selling away the lands of this Province" to manor lords downriver like Philipse and Stephanus Van Cortlandt. He had passed a bill to vacate those grants; would he next move on Livingston Manor and Rensselaerwyck? That winter Livingston remained quietly in Albany with Alida tending to his trading business.

In a Boston jail that winter Captain Kidd waited in solitary confinement for a British frigate to carry him to London, where he was to be tried and, in 1701, hanged for piracy and murder. Kidd went to the scaffold maintaining that he had merely been the "tool" of the "Ambition and Avarice" of Lord Bellomont and Robert Livingston. Whatever remorse the governor and Livingston might have felt for William Kidd's fate has not been recorded. Bellomont himself never knew of the pirate's execution, for several months earlier the governor himself had died suddenly in New York City. Livingston remained silent in his new house on Livingston Manor, so silent that rumors spread through the valley of his hiding treasure he had somehow spirited away from the *Adventure Galley* when it made landfall. (The lord, so people said, had buried it around his property.) But no doubt Robert Livingston was contemplating good fortune of another sort: had Kidd survived, he would have continued to implicate the other members of the syndicate in the perfidy; had Bellomont remained governor, he probably would have broken up all the manors in the Hudson Valley. But

Bellomont and Kidd were in their graves. Livingston knew the fates had allowed him to recover once again.

In truth, Livingston Manor was just where Robert Livingston wanted to be. In the beginning, the "manor" had been only an idea, 160,000 acres fronting on the colony's principal highway and trade route, the Hudson River. But for many years that was all; there was no manor house and few quitrents to collect as there were merely a dozen tenants. Indeed, for a few years at least, Livingston saw his land only when he looked eastward from the deck of a sloop plying the waters between Albany and New York. Downriver, he had bought a house in New York City, which doubled as much as a warehouse for his trading. Upriver, he and Alida remained in their house in Albany, which also served as a warehouse and store.

Late in the century, Robert and Alida began to develop the manor. They erected mills for flour and lumber and a brewery. Eventually Livingston added a shipyard where he built his own sloops to carry goods from Albany and the manor to Manhattan Island. In 1699, on a bluff overlooking the harbor at Roeliff Jansen Kill, they began their first "manor house," which was as much a trading post and bakery as a place to live. Still, unlike the houses they had acquired in Albany and New York, the one at Roeliff Jansen Kill was their own creation. It would be their anchorage, the solid foundation for their family's fortunes in America.

Alida remained Robert Livingston's personal anchorage. Industrious, energetic, faithful, and almost always patient beyond all understanding, she endured his increasing absences, the tension of living at the edge of scandal, and precarious finances. Early in their marriage Alida had kept a store in their Albany house, and over the years she gave birth to ten children. While retaining his positions as secretary in Albany and a member of the Board of Indian Commissioners, Robert devoted more and more of his energy to trade. Stacks of beaver pelts, barrels of wheat, and occasionally barrels of lard were loaded onto sloops at Albany for the journey to New York and then England. Alida had tended to the trade and their children when he traveled to London in 1694. From 1703 to 1706, while Robert sojourned again in London seeking money for his work at various positions in the colony, Alida alone supervised affairs at the manor and their Albany house, as well as managing his trading enterprise. She shipped goods to and from New York, and beyond the city to Philadelphia, Boston, and the West Indies.

When Livingston finally was ready to return to the valley in the spring of 1706, he shipped "13 bales of goods, amounting to more than £940 . . . also a box of clothes for my sweetheart." By that time he was over fifty; his enemies had subsided; corrupt governors had come and gone; his political place was secure; and Robert Livingston ranked among the wealthiest men in the Hudson Valley.

Livingston's fortunes prospered under Edward Hyde, Viscount Cornbury, Queen Anne's cousin, who followed the Earl of Bellomont as governor and whose administration matched—and even eclipsed—the corruption of Benjamin Fletcher's. A Tory, Cornbury saved Livingston Manor from confiscation, and saved Robert Livingston from personal embarrassment when he was caught trading illegally with the French. The Leislerians hated Cornbury's unabashed favoring of the aristocracy and exploited allegations that he had a fetish for women's clothing. Rumors spread through the colony that on Sundays the governor liked nothing more than to dress up in "coats and gowns" commandeered from ladies, adorn himself in rouge and pearls, and, sporting a fan in his right hand, prance about the fort. Cornbury's taste in dress aside (a story now generally discredited), his persecution of all who weren't Anglicans, his curtailment of political rights of the people, and his restless craving for bribes made him, as Theodore Roosevelt once wrote, "very nearly an ideal example of what a royal governor should not be." Finally, the Tories determined him to be a liability and ordered his return. But Cornbury had done Livingston a service. His land on the Hudson was more secure than ever.

When Robert Hunter, Cornbury's replacement, arrived in New York in 1710 in a convoy of ships carrying twenty-four hundred German Palatine refugees, Livingston finally saw a chance to make his manor lands pay. The Palatines, refugees from the War of Spanish Succession, were to settle in the pine forests of New York where they would produce tar, pitch, turpentine, and spars for the British Navy. Livingston persuaded Hunter to settle eighteen hundred of the refugees on his lands and the rest on the opposite shore of the Hudson.

In theory the idea promised success for all: It was, Hunter wrote to London, "[a] usefull design of providing England for ever hereafter with Naval Stores." The Crown agreed to pay Livingston 400 pounds (266 pounds in sterling) for "title to the soil," a rich stand of pines. And Livingston's lands lay adjacent to the Hudson at "a place where Ships of 50 foot water may go without difficulty," said Hunter. Alida Livingston, who resided at the manor, took the job of victualing the settlers. The Hudson Valley—and Livingston Manor—would get the population it so desperately needed, and Robert Livingston would get six pence a day (four pence for children) for every Palatine mouth Alida fed. And even better, the Palatines would purchase all their other goods, tools and farm implements, pans and knives, from his store at the manor house.

In reality, however, the scheme quickly turned into a fiasco: The pine trees failed to yield the abundance of pitch, tar, and turpentine Livingston had promised; indeed they were the wrong kind. Alida couldn't procure enough beef and pork to meet the rations the Palatines were promised; there were continual shortages of wheat, butter, and cheese. At one point she had to hide the man in charge of actually distributing the rations, as two Palatines arrived at the manor house intent upon "tearing him apart." In the spring of 1711 soldiers had to come to the manor to keep order. Shipments of goods from New York for which Livingston was responsible seldom came with the right merchandise. "I wish," Alida wrote her husband in July 1711, "the Palatines had never come here." Matters only got worse as there was no money to be had for victualing and consequently no food. At Christmas an armed group of starving Palatines raided the stores at the manor house.

The fiasco ended in the autumn of 1712. The Crown government formally stopped the victualing and, since there was no pine tar to be had, released the Palatines from their obligation to produce it. Instead of the bonanza of population that he expected, Livingston could count just thirty-three families living on the manor in 1713. Most of the families drifted away, some westward to the Schoharie Valley, some to Pennsylvania, where William Penn promised them land; some to Dutchess County. The few bitter souls who remained became tenants of Robert Livingston, who deemed them "worse than northern savages." His attitude toward his tenants descended through many of the generations of Livingstons that followed him, and the bitterness of the Palatines survives to this day in the hearts of some of their descendants who still make their homes in towns and hamlets along the Hudson.

In 1715, when he was in his sixth decade, Robert Livingston received a confirmatory patent from England's newly crowned king, George I. The king's act sanctioned anew his ownership of the land he had acquired under questionable circumstances in 1684 and 1686. Royal governors had issued those patents; this one came with the signature of the king. It insulated Livingston and his manor from the ever shifting politics of Crown governments and the capriciousness of governors. Governors might look with hostile or benign eyes upon the idea of one man being lord over 160,000 acres of land, but it would matter not at all to Livingston and his heirs. In addition, the patent enabled him to send a representative from Livingston Manor to the Colonial Assembly. Naturally he appointed himself, and naturally he used his position to enhance his political power. At the onset of what were to be his final years, Livingston finally achieved all that he had sought for himself and his family.

But Robert's and Alida's heirs who survived childhood were something of a disappointment. In 1720, after a superannuated adolescence that included profligate spending and several amorous disasters, their oldest son, Johannes, died at age forty. Their second child, Philip, prosperous and careful to the point of plodding, had become a merchant in Albany. Their third son, also named Robert, was a spendthrift and a fop, but he possessed all the charm that his surviving older brother lacked.

Alida's health had been in a slow decline for years. Though she suffered from weakening eyesight and poor circulation in her legs, she held on, steadfastly resisting the ministrations of a doctor her husband sent upriver ("it may take a long time before I get rid of the queer fish," she said), and managing the manor's affairs to her end, in May 1727. Robert's death followed in October 1728. He, too, had experienced a gradual deterioration, first suffering from kidney stones and then kidney failure. In his will he left Philip the bulk of the manor lands; but, much to Philip's chagrin, he left his son Robert thirteen thousand acres near the southern boundary, in thanks, so family legend has it, for once rescuing the manor house and his mother from a native attack. And he signed his will "Robert Livingston, Proprietor of Livingston Manor." It was his final testament to all he had achieved.

South of Livingston Manor, on twenty-one miles of the east bank of the Hudson on part of the land where Adriaen van der Donck had created his settlement of Colen Donck, another New World entrepreneur from the Netherlands, Frederick Philipse, was developing a ninety thousand acre demesne of his own. Philipse's life had some significant parallels with Livingston's: each arrived in the valley with little means; each seized every opportunity for advancement and wealth that he could; each acquired land and buildings; each engaged in trade, and not always within the bounds of the law; each used his skills to serve the government and himself in a variety of political posts; and each made advantageous marriages, in Philipse's case, twice.

Philipse arrived in the Hudson Valley earlier than Livingston, possibly with Peter Stuyvesant in 1647, to be a "master builder," a carpenter for the Dutch West India Company in New Amsterdam. But for Philipse building went far beyond the saw and the adze; he was more intent on creating a trading empire. By 1660 he took the modest step of acquiring a "Small Burgher Right," which enabled him to engage in trade in Virginia. His next step proved far more significant and shrewd: in 1662 he married a wealthy and talented widow, Margaret Hardenbroeck de Vries. Her first husband had also been a successful trader, and Philipse was more than happy to take his place. Margaret's dowry included a complement of ships and trading contracts with companies in England and the Netherlands. Through this alliance Frederick Philipse became one of the wealthiest men in New Netherland.

The union was both an emotional and a commercial success. Margaret brought a daughter into her marriage whom Frederick adopted, and they had four more children together. Their commercial enterprise proved an even more successful union of talents. Born into an Amsterdam trading family, Margaret Hardenbroeck understood the nuances of the business. She often directly superintended her commercial ventures by shipping as a supercargo on trading voyages. Enjoying the privileges of a wife married under Dutch law, which changed only gradually under the English, she maintained and frequently executed trading agreements using her maiden name. Trading was a risky business, encumbered by monopolies (which Frederick and Margaret sometimes circumvented), and continually subjected to the disasters of storms and piracy. Yet Margaret and Frederick

Philipse thrived. By the time Captain Nicolls and his four English ships sailed into the harbor in August 1664, Philipse had amassed about 14 percent of all the money in New Amsterdam, thirteen thousand pounds, and "whole hogsheads of Indian wampum."

When they saw the English ships, Frederick and Margaret Philipse prudently urged Stuyvesant to surrender control of the province, and quickly swore their allegiance to the king; as a result they prospered all the more. Governors appointed Frederick to positions in New York: city surveyor, alderman, and, in 1682, member of the Duke of York's Council. Philipse knew just the right words to say—or, whenever necessary, the gifts to give—to curry favor with the English. Rivals alleged that he sometimes managed to avoid inspections of his ships, and thus escape tariffs and even arrest for illegal trading. As the Philipses imported cloth and other manufactured goods from Europe, and cottons and spices from the East, in exchange for raw commodities like furs, whale oil, tobacco, and timber, those tariff charges were considerable.

Philipse was creating a commercial empire, for he understood better than most the importance of controlling the source of the commodity, its manufacture into a finished product, its transportation to a buyer, and its sale. He already owned property on Manhattan Island; next he looked northward for more land farther up the Hudson. In 1672 he purchased a section of Colen Donck known as the Lower Mills, from the Spuyten Duyvil Creek to the Neperhan River; over the next decade he extended his holdings up to the Croton River, including the Upper Mills around the Pocantico River. On the banks of the Hudson he grew grain, ground it into flour in his mills, and then transported the product in his ships to ports near and far. And the money grew. It grew even more after Margaret Hardenbroeck died in 1692. Philipse then made another advantageous marriage, to Catherine Van Cortlandt, sister of Stephanus Van Cortlandt and sister-in-law to Alida Livingston. Catherine brought additional prestige to their union and enabled Philipse to continue his connections with those who could help him in the colony. With Governor Fletcher's assistance, he procured a royal charter from the king for the "Manor of Philipsborough," for which he paid "yearly and every year on the feast of the Annunciation of the Blessed Virgin Mary . . . the annual rent of £4 12s current money of our said Province."

The Manor of Philipsborough became the heart of Philipse's commercial machine, its money generator and its purse. At the southern tip, he erected a toll bridge (the King's Bridge) across the Spuyten Duyvil Creek and collected fees from everyone traveling through his manor on their way to and from Manhattan. He built mills at the Pocantico and Neperhan rivers where he gathered the raw materials and produced lumber, flour, and grain for shipment to the West Indies. He erected a manor house as well as a Dutch church on the Pocantico. And to power his great commercial machine, he brought slaves from Africa.

As slaves and free blacks had been present in the Hudson Valley since the time of Minuit, when the Dutch West India Company brought eleven male Africans to New Amsterdam to build public buildings, roads, and the fort, they were hardly a novelty. Throughout the seventeenth century slaves trickled into the valley. Schuylers, van Rensselaers, Van Cortlandts, and later Livingstons, all kept them as laborers and house servants. Farmers kept them, too, and master and slave often worked together in farm yards and fields. Willem Kieft gave them arms to defend New Amsterdam in his war with the natives. Kiliaen van Rensselaer wrote of using them "almost as brute forces against malevolents [law breakers]" in Rensselaerwyck. There were other blacks in the valley who had earned their freedom and owned property.

Up to 1655, most African slaves came to New Netherland by way of Curaçao in the West Indies. But that September, when the *Witte Paert* anchored in the Hudson off Fort Amsterdam with nearly three hundred slaves "directly from Guinea" aboard, a horrible stench from the vessel permeated the air of the Manhattan waterfront, for, as one writer described conditions on another slaver that plied the waters between Africa and New York, "Bad Food, short Allowance, Want of Water, foul Air, and Bloody Flux were the Attendants on the Passage." The air was but a forewarning of the future. The very concept of slavery in New Netherland changed, for now human flesh had become a commodity to be traded.

Slaves from the *Witte Paert* sold for twelve hundred florins each. Over the next decade more slavers moored in the Hudson, each announcing its arrival with a hideous smell emanating from the human cargo stuffed into its crowded hull. Because they were unskilled, slaves from Africa weren't as desirable as West Indian imports. As a result many were sold to buyers from New England and the South, which pleased the director-general and his council, for there was a 10 percent tax on each head sold outside New Netherland. When the English arrived, they found the slave trade well established. It only awaited their development.

Like others in New York who lived for profit, Frederick Philipse was ready to add the trading in human flesh to his diversified commercial empire. In 1685 Philipse had imported about forty-five slaves directly from the Kongo kingdom of Angola to work the land and mills near the Pocantico River. He favored direct importation over purchase. Why purchase slaves from the Royal African Company, the enterprise that was seeking to control the New York market, when he could finance his own ship to purchase them from pirates in Madagascar and bring them directly to New York? Slaves were to be had for thirty shillings each in Madagascar. No matter that such business deals were illegal. Governor Fletcher had made New York's harbor into a haven for pirates and illegal shipping, skimming off substantial fees for himself in the process. In 1691 Philipse and his son Adolph (by his first wife) began contracting with pirates to carry slaves to New York and to send back products from the manor's mills. A storm would cost him a ship and its cargo, but still the rewards of slave trading outweighed the risks. "For negroes in these times," wrote Philipse to his pirate broker in Madagascar, "will fetch thirty pound and upwards the head."

He traded some slaves to the South and kept others to work in his warehouses in Manhattan and to operate the mills on the manor. Only the arrival of Lord Bellomont in 1698, himself tainted by the scandal of Captain Kidd and desperate to show his rectitude, put an end to such ventures. Bellomont used the English capture of one of Philipse's pirate ships as a way to set an example: he ordered Frederick and Adolph to cease their illegal trading, and he forbade them from holding government office for two years. But Philipse knew that he and his family had survived the caprices and reversals of the various governors, and he expected to continue. As he wrote after totaling the accounts of a particularly successful voyage: "It is by negroes that I find my chievest [chiefest] Profitt. All other trade I only look upon as by the by."

Frederick Philipse died four years after Bellomont put a stop to his slave trading, but his commercial empire on the banks of the Hudson continued. His son Adolph took over the Upper Mills and his orphaned grandson, Frederick II, the Lower Mills. The younger Frederick, who became the second lord, built the Albany Post Road on a footpath long used by natives, which brought even more travelers through the manor and across the toll bridge over the Spuyten Duyvil Creek. His son, yet another Frederick, succeeded his father as the third lord. Each lord followed the founder's practice by marrying well, serving in the government, especially on the Governor's Council, and proclaiming his loyalty to the British Crown. The family continued in the slave trade, too. Consorting with pirates was out of the question, of course, but the Philipses still could act as private slave traders.

Nor were they alone. At one time or another the major families on the river, including Beekmans, Schuylers, Van Zandts, Van Cortlandts, and Livingstons, all imported slaves for their households or manors, or for trade; in London, James, Duke of York, even decided to join the slave trade by taking a controlling interest in the Royal African Company. Over the first quarter of the eighteenth century more than twenty-three hundred slaves arrived from Africa and the West Indies; by 1750, of the sixty thousand people in the province of New York, more than nine thousand were enslaved. The density of slaves living on the five square miles of developed property on Manhattan Island was very likely as great as any place in North America. At the onset of the Revolutionary War, New York City ranked behind only Charleston, South Carolina, in the number of people held in bondage.

Slavery was not confined to manor lords, either, or even just the very wealthy in the Hudson Valley, as an important early landscape painting attests. Late in the seventeenth century, Marten Gerritsen Van Bergen, a clerk in Albany who had lived along the river probably since the 1650s, purchased from Native Americans of the area half of a patent on the west side of the Hudson at the present-day town of Catskill. Like so many Dutch settlers, Van Bergen saw his family's future in land, and the roughly eight-mile circular tract that included the outflow of the Catskill and Kaaterskill creeks, along with about four miles of frontage on the river, gave him real property in the New World. On a hill at Leeds, Van Bergen erected a house; a gristmill near the Kaaterskill Falls and another mill at Leeds followed. And he brought slaves to run the mill and till the fertile lands beside

John Heaten, overmantel painted for the Marten Van Bergen house near Leeds, New York, ca. 1733. The painting, approximately seven feet long, depicts the Van Bergen family in a time of prosperity, with a full granary, livestock, and slaves. (Fenimore Art Museum, Cooperstown, New York)

the Catskill Creek. There the Van Bergens prospered, perhaps none more so than his middle son, whom Marten had named after himself.

In the late 1720s Marten the younger built an impressive farm on the flat lands near Leeds, so impressive that when the itinerant limner John Heaten came through the area in 1733, he had him paint the scene as a decoration for the seven-foot-long mantel over his fireplace. This delightful and primitive painting presents a narrative of rural abundance in the Hudson Valley. The Van Bergen farm stands in a fenced clearing before dense woods and beneath the gray peaks of the Catskill Mountains looming in the background. Smoke curls from the chimneys of the house at the center. The house itself tells a story. It is really two structures, the large red-roofed main building and a smaller addition, perhaps built to shelter the Van Bergens' seven children or their slaves. Marten and his wife, Caterina, herself the daughter of a wealthy Kingston merchant, stand in front. On a bench sit two of their four daughters, while two others are running off to play. On a road that passes through the Van Bergens' farmyard two horses pull a high Dutch wagon filled with sacks of flour (ground, no doubt, in Van Bergen mills). Two of their sons gallop by on horses, while a third son appears to have been thrown from his mount. To the left are the family's farm buildings, a barn and two hexagonal "barracks" for stor-

ing hay. (Guided by six poles at each corner, the roofs of such barracks, which rose and fell with the amount of hay in them, served as a barometer of good fortune, fertile land, and a bounteous harvest. Marten Van Bergen's barometer stands at fair.) One of the barracks has a raised floor to shelter animals in stormy weather. Marten and Caterina are greeting Marten's brother, Gerrit, and his two sons, who are arriving on the road from the right.

It is a bounteous idyll: horses play in a field, there are geese and chickens, cows and sheep, and even birds flying overhead. Two natives in the foreground tell of harmony, or perhaps they have come to trade. There are servants, too. A white laborer totes a bucket of water for the horses. A slave woman with a pail approaches the chickens under the hay barrack to feed them; another shepherds the sheep; a third tends to the cows; and a slave boy throws a ball to a dog.

But how peaceful was it for the slaves and their masters? Slaveholders in New York liked to think they—unlike those in the South, or worse, the West Indies—treated their African slaves with tenderness. And slaveholders up the Hudson believed they were kinder still. As Mrs. Anne Grant, who stayed with the Schuylers in Albany, writes in her memoirs, "even the dark aspect of slavery was softened into a smile," because the relation between master and servant was "better understood here than in any other place." Characterizing slaveholding as an "injustice," she tells us that these colonists thought of neither law nor philosophy, but saw "their code of morality in the Bible," and believed "this hapless race [to be] condemned to perpetual slavery." Despite the softening smile, Mrs. Grant reports, a few slaves in rare instances betrayed their master's trust, took to liquor, "or habitually neglected their duty." These unmanageable and intractable slaves were sold to Jamaica.

And what of miscegenation in the valley—"moral delicacy," as Mrs. Grant put it? There were mulattoes on the Hudson, evidence that masters did engage in "criminal and disgraceful" conduct in "violation" of nature's laws. The British soldiers living in the Hudson Valley during the French and Indian War certainly left evidence of their crimes, but similar behavior took place in more respectable families as well. Indeed, Mrs. Grant tells us that Colonel Schuyler himself had a "weak" relative, an "idle bachelor," who consorted with an African slave woman. To atone for his relative's actions, the colonel had the illegitimate child "carefully educated," and provided him with a farm in the "depth of [the] woods" about two miles away from the Schuyler house at Albany.

Still, for the most part the lot of slaves on the Hudson *was* better than that of their brothers and sisters on the Mississippi. Some were even allowed to negotiate their sale to another master if they were unhappy with their present one. Perhaps more important to the slaves' daily lives, owners permitted them to gather together on the sabbath. They often celebrated holidays with their masters, especially Pinkster, the day of Pentecost when the holy spirit caused Christ's disciples to speak in tongues. This "great Saturnalia of the New York blacks," as James Fenimore Cooper described it, gave slaves and the few free Africans the chance to return to the practices of their pagan religion under the mantle of Christianity, play musical instruments similar to those they had been forced to leave behind in Africa, dance ecstatically, feast abundantly, and drink with abandon.

For about one week of the year Pinkster allowed the slaves to turn the world upside down. They became masters, parodying the acts and rituals of the whites they had witnessed all year. After the English arrived, the slaves elected one of their number to act as King Charles. By the late eighteenth century, Pinkster had evolved into an even greater holiday, especially north of New York City. In Albany the street leading up to the present-day state capitol and near the slave burial grounds became known as "Pinkster Hill."

Their treatment, however kind it may have been, did not mitigate the fact that these Africans and their children were enslaved, and had no rights.

At the same time, white owners were uncomfortable because they realized that they too were vulnerable. Their property might be stolen or destroyed, or worse, they themselves might be attacked by their slaves. Over time they established laws forbidding slaves to congregate in groups of three or more other than at Pinkster time, or to drink liquor, or even to walk outside after dark. But of course the laws were difficult, even impossible, to enforce, as the threat of punishment (usually a whipping) was often no worse for the slaves than their usual lot in life.

The record of rebellions and responses to the threat of them shows how harsh punishments might be. In April 1712, a group of slaves on Manhattan set fire to their master's outhouse and ambushed those who tried to put it out. When the conflagration and killing ended, nine whites lay dead and six rebellious slaves had committed suicide. Twenty more captured slaves were hanged, burned, hung in chains, or broken on the wheel.

The events of 1712 were merely a prelude to the fear that spread among whites nearly three decades later, in 1741. A slave revolt in the colony of South Carolina the previous year certainly fed that fear, as well as the fact that a slave underworld of thieves and thugs had grown up among the two thousand blacks and nine thousand whites on Manhattan. Criminal whites served as fences for slave thieves. When fires broke out in houses (including the governor's), barns, warehouses, and stables throughout the city that March and April, white New Yorkers came to believe they were victims of a slave "plot." Mobs of whites roamed the streets seeking to catch a slave firing a building. As one early chronicler put it, the panic that seized the "people and the courts . . . made them as unreliable as in the days of Salem witchcraft." Whites looked for conspirators; they found Adolph Philipse's houseboy, Cuffee.

Cuffee proved an easy target. His master had continued his father's pattern of acquiring great riches through trade. Cuffee incited jealousy among many whites who believed they did not live as well as the houseboy to the richest man in the colony. A witness said he had seen Cuffee running from a building near a burning warehouse; others said he had refused to fight the fire. Still a third heard him talking with two others about burning the fort, indeed, the whole town. The trial was swift; the verdict harsh. Cuffee was taken just outside the wall of the city and chained to a stake that rose from a pile of faggots and wood. Perhaps hoping for a stay of execution, he made a confession: he had set fire to the warehouse, there had been a plot among the slaves and some willing white accomplices. His admission, especially his naming other conspirators, eventually resulted in the execution of more than thirty slaves. But it did not stay his own death. The mob grew restless; the sheriff ordered the wood to be fired. Cuffee was consumed in the flames.

However well the affairs of those living in the Hudson Valley went, the condition of their lives—the clothes they wore, the money they made, the liquor they drank, the places where they worshiped, the land that they rented or owned—was bound, always, to the words and deeds and caprices of monarchs and ministers in London and Paris. At times the changes in London's policy appeared to be sudden and arbitrary, but those living in the Hudson Valley, especially people of property, Livingston and Schuyler, Philipse and Van Cortlandt among them, had to comply—or at least appear to do so. And more than most in North America, those living in the valley were connected to a larger struggle for control of the New World, a struggle that had been smoldering since the early seventeenth century and would erupt in a series of wars on the northern frontier of the colonies in the eighteenth.

The allegiance of the Iroquois, inhabitants of the wilderness and chief suppliers of pelts, was crucial to the plans of both France and England. Early in their rule the English had agreed to an alliance, called a covenant chain, with the Iroquois. Because the natives found their goods—especially textiles and liquor—so desirable, the English traded and gave presents liberally. The French on the St. Lawrence, who had long coveted the land to the south where beaver pelts fetched a higher price, countered by sowing discord. For years they had sent Jesuit missionaries into the forests to propagate the Gospel among natives; once the natives chose to follow their religion, the French encouraged their support against the Dutch and, later, the English. As a result the English in the early eighteenth century found their control of the land beyond New York City weakened with each mile they traveled up the Hudson. And Albany, their northernmost fortification, was the least secure of all.

After King William's accession to the throne in 1689, relations between England and France soured even more. That May, William brought England and the Netherlands into a Grand Alliance with Spain, Sweden, Bavaria, Saxony, and the Palatinate to thwart Louis XIV's claims to the Rhine. War ensued, and by 1690 it spread to North America. That February about one hundred fifty French joined with about two hundred Algonquins and Christian Iroquois to massacre more than sixty settlers living in Schenectady, just a few miles west of Albany. News of the murders brought panic to the hearts of everyone living on the upper Hudson, who at the time were preoccupied with Jacob Leisler's seizure of the government. Counterattacks from the British proved futile. Fitz-John Winthrop from the neighboring Colony of Connecticut led some troops from Albany on a mission to Canada, but at the foot of Lake Champlain poor planning and inadequate supplies compelled him to retreat. Leisler used the debacle as an opportunity to have Winthrop jailed in Albany for treason, but a group of friendly Mohawks quickly set him free. What became known as King William's War ended in 1697 with the peace of Ryswyck, a stalemate that did little more than halt the conflict temporarily. It was followed in 1701 by ten years of fighting known as Queen Anne's War.

Men like Robert Livingston and his brother-in-law Pieter Schuyler (Alida's brother) understood all that was at stake for the English and especially for themselves in the Hudson Valley. Should the French prevail, their property and future prosperity would be doomed, and England's aspirations for an empire on the continent would end. Shortly after Governor Sloughter dispatched Leisler, Livingston got the chance to put the skills he had honed as a trader and his knowledge of the Iroquois gained as secretary to the Indian commissioners to good use. Armed with one hundred pounds' worth of presents, Sloughter sailed to Albany in late May 1691. He and Livingston met with the Iroquois to pledge England's good will and to plan a preemptive raid against the French. Were it not for the fact that neither the English nor the natives provided enough men or arms to create a potent force, the plan might have succeeded. For his part, Livingston blamed the "heathens." "They are a broken reed to depend upon; but . . . they must be tenderly handled."

It was Pieter Schuyler who bore much of the burden of opposing the French designs on the natives. The eldest son of Philip Pieterse Schuyler, Pieter joined with his father to trade with the Iroquois, gained an intimate knowledge of their language, and earned their respect. (They addressed him as "brotor Quidor," meaning brother Peter.) Like his father, Pieter also became one of Albany's leaders: its first mayor in 1686, an officer of the Dutch Reformed Church, the first man from the city to be appointed to the provincial council, and, with Livingston, a leader of the resistance to Leisler.

Pieter Schuyler's greatest distinction came as a soldier and statesman. As a colonel in the Albany militia, he had joined with his brother Johannes (who later established a plantation at Saratoga) and Fitz-John Winthrop in the march on French Canada in 1690, and again on Quebec in 1709. Although those expeditions failed because the English did not commit enough troops, Schuyler distinguished himself with his patriotic fervor. Far more important than his military exploits was his knowledge of the Iroquois language and culture. He understood better than most how critical the security of Albany and the northern frontier were to the future of the colony. Beginning with Thomas Dongan, a succession of English governors relied on his skills as a negotiator and appointed him to the various Indian commissions.

To drum up support in England for the country's North American interests, Schuyler brought four of the most loyal Iroquois sachems to London in 1710, where they became the exotic novelty of the season. Queen Anne received them at court, dressed them in scarlet, and commissioned their portraits. Since the sachems, too, had been converted to Christianity, the queen gave them a silver communion set for their wilderness chapel, and promised to send more missionaries to spread the Gospel among them. Schuyler counted the trip a triumph, but the success was short lived. London pledged to send troops and ships, and the New York Assembly voted ten thousand pounds for an assault on the French at Quebec, but the plan failed when the English diverted their ships to the Iberian peninsula rather than the St. Lawrence. Stranded without support once more, Pieter Schuyler and his men returned to Albany.

The colonists, especially those in Albany, remained worried, but they had little stomach for a northern adventure that might cost them their lives and would certainly jeopardize their lucrative trade with the natives and the French. For them the safest course was appeasement. To the natives they gave "private presents to Engage [them] to be true to her Majies Interest," wrote Philip Livingston, who had succeeded his father as secretary of the

Indian commission. The gift included "96 Knives, 12 gunns 28 baggs of Powder 25 blanketts 17 faddom of Strouds 27 fadm of Duffels 14 Shirts 22 Stroudwater stockings 3 Kitles 45 hatchetts &c."

For their part the Iroquois were content to have compacts with both England and France, which freed the northern border of New York from fighting. The long-anticipated invasion never came, and while other towns across the northern frontier—Deerfield, Massachusetts, and Winter Harbor, Maine, among them—suffered from massacres, Albany remained relatively secure. When French and English diplomats meeting to negotiate the Treaty of Utrecht brought an end to Queen Anne's War in 1713, residents of the Hudson Valley could count themselves lucky.

For the three decades that the Treaty of Utrecht endured, the Hudson Valley thrived. Partly as a result of the latest English governor, William Burnet, instituting a policy that for a time forbade trade with Montreal and expanded the British presence west of the valley with a fort at Oswego, more furs than ever flooded into Albany. In 1698, Albany County's population stood at just 1,476, including 23 blacks; by 1737 it had jumped to 10,681, including 1,630 blacks. In 1737 Albany's population even eclipsed New York City's, which numbered 10,664, including 1,719 slaves. Between 1698 and 1737 the number of people living in the counties of the river valley rose from 18,000 to 60,000. Many of the inhabitants traded with the Indians, of course, and many more tilled the soil. Farmers in the Hudson Valley provided most of the flour that kept the city's populace in bread; traders like Philipse shipped still more barrels to the Caribbean. While there had been no great migrations since Robert Hunter landed with the Palatines in 1710, a steady stream of men and women, often with families, arrived in the valley from Scotland, France, Germany, and the Netherlands.

But the affairs of monarchs and ministers in London and Paris continued to hold sway over the lives of those dwelling in the valley. A change of government in London usually altered the policy—and the governor—for the Hudson. Whatever the government, the neglect of military fortifications in the valley remained a constant. As early as 1731 the French had established their presence by building Fort St. Frédéric at Crown Point on Lake Champlain, from which they could easily launch a raid on New

York's northern frontier. But as relations with the French in the Hudson-Champlain Valley were relatively peaceful, the English did little to increase their own fortifications on the river. For his forays to Canada during Queen Anne's War, Pieter Schuyler had built forts on the Hudson at Stillwater, Saratoga, and Fort Edward, but in the intervening years neglect had led to their ruin. In 1740, when a complicated web of alliances in Europe brought England into battle once again with France in the War of the Austrian Succession, conflict once again spread to North America. From New York City privateers sailed forth in search of French ships to seize, and often they were successful. A French attack on Port Royal in Nova Scotia, in 1744, gave rise to British fears on the Hudson.

That June New York's latest governor, George Clinton, hastened to Albany with wampum and ceremonial belts, "to renew, strengthen and brighten the Covenant Chain" with the sachems of the Six Nations of the Iroquois. "Be on your guard against the French, who you know by wofull experience to be a false & treacherous People," Clinton warned. "Stay at home, to watch their motions . . . transmit such Intelligence as you shall gett concerning the Enemy, from time to time, to the Commissioners of Indian affairs." For their part the sachems said, "We leave it to you to do with the French that may come into our Country as you shall think proper."

In October of the following year, the governor again met with the Iroquois in Albany; again an exchange of belts and wampum and words took place, but with little effect. Instead, the commissioners urged restraint. As the governor and the assembly in New York City were locked in a struggle for control of the purse, he had no money for supplies or men. New York's northern frontier on the Hudson remained vulnerable.

Late in 1745, the French brought King George's War, as it came to be known in North America, to Albany's doorstep. On the evening of November 27, a party of French and Indians from Crown Point raided Johannes Schuyler's defenseless plantation at Saratoga. The attack was swift and the results were devastating: twelve people, including Johannes's son Philip, were scalped; the mills, barns, and houses were burned; and Schuyler's slaves were captured and sent to Montreal where they were auctioned off. By daybreak the raiders had gone.

The ruins of the Saratoga plantation and its long-neglected fort stood as an example of English ineptitude. Though Governor Clinton had once assigned ten soldiers to make repairs, he received no support from the assembly or the Indian commissioners in Albany. As Sergeant Convers, one of the soldiers whom Clinton had sent, told a court of inquiry called after the raid, "There was neither Well nor Oven in [the] Garrison, the Floors above never laid, except the Floor in one of the Block houses, that the Roofs of none of the Block houses were made tight, and that they, neither could keep themselves or arms ettc. drye when it rained; that their powder was at last damaged notwithstanding they took the greatest care to preserve it." The soldiers had withdrawn to Albany, leaving the small settlement for the French to destroy.

Another European treaty, this one signed at Aix-la-Chapelle in 1748, ended King George's War, but not the conflict. The French continued to erect a string of forts from Canada through the Ohio Valley and south to Louisiana, which would effectively pen the British on the Atlantic coastal plain. By 1753, British control of the northern and western frontiers of their colonies seemed more precarious than ever.

In April 1754 the French showed their strength when their capture of the forks of the Ohio River effectively ended British efforts to settle the Ohio territory. That June orders came from London to hold yet another conference in Albany, this one with the dual purpose to renew the covenant with the Iroquois and to discuss ways all the colonies might cooperate to better defend themselves against the French. Not every colony sent a representative, but one of the delegates from Pennsylvania, Benjamin Franklin, arrived with a proposal, "Short Hints towards a Scheme for Uniting the Northern Colonies," known generally as the Albany Plan. Although the delegates voted to adopt Franklin's proposal, their colonial assemblies rejected it, "and in England," so Franklin said, "it was judged to have too much of the *democratic*." Members of the Albany Congress could agree to cooperate in principle, but whenever they tried to act in concert, they failed. Even a proposal to build two forts in the West stalled because the delegates could not agree on how much each colony would pay.

The meeting with the Iroquois didn't fare much better. The new governor, James De Lancey, proffered the usual gifts of belts, wampum, gunpowder, guns, blankets, and face paint, and he made the usual professions of cooperation, but the Indians were angry.

Hendrick, chief of the Mohawks, spoke for his people. He was the most important sachem, one of the Christian chiefs who had accompanied Pieter Schuyler to London in 1710, and he regularly supplied the English with valuable information about the French. To one observer he appeared "singularly impressive and commanding, . . . as if born to control other men." The delegates, even those who knew him only by reputation, respected his counsel. But now Hendrick spoke with contempt: The English had neglected the Indians, "whereas the French are a subtle and vigilant people, ever using their utmost endeavours to seduce and bring our people over to them." The French had burned the fort at Saratoga, the Mohawk continued, but the English ran away: "Look about your Country & see, you have no Fortifications about you, no, not even to this City, tis but one Step from Canada hither, and the French may easily come and turn you out of your doors." And then, Hendrick concluded by mocking the delegates: "The French, they are Men, they are fortifying everywhere—but, we are ashamed to say it, you are like women bare and open without any fortifications."

Two years later in the French and Indian War, battle after battle proved Hendrick to be right. General Louis-Joseph de Montcalm overran the British at Fort Oswego to gain control of the Mohawk Valley. The enemy now threatened Albany's western doorstep. But the grand sachem of the Mohawks knew nothing of this. Fourteen months after he had addressed the colonial delegates at Albany, Hendrick was ambushed and murdered by the French at Lake George.

The theater of the French and Indian War lay largely to the north of Albany, at Fort Ticonderoga on Lake Champlain and on the St. Lawrence River at Montreal and Quebec. But the lesson of these wars for those on the Hudson was simple: The river valley and all its inhabitants were bound to the policies of the British government three thousand miles away. And, whether they wished it or not, the Hudson River valley was a major part of any British strategy in North America.

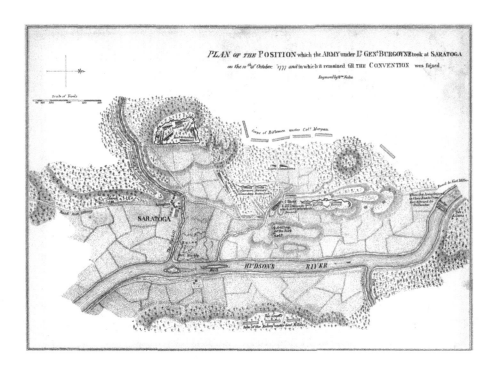

PLAN OF THE POSITION which the ARMY under Lᵗ GENˡ BURGOYNE took at SARATOGA on the 10ᵗʰ of October, 1777 and in which it remained till THE CONVENTION was signed.

CHAPTER 5

The Only Passage

In the long and far-ranging fight over the newly declared United States of America, of all the regions involved, the Hudson River valley posed the greatest concern to the revolutionaries and the greatest opportunity to the British. Both Sir William Howe, their commander in chief, and George Washington knew that the deepwater port at the mouth of the Hudson offered a safe harbor for vessels, good wharfage for unloading matériel, as well as houses and a fort for billeting troops; they recognized that the river neatly divided the four New England states from the eight states south of New York; and they understood that the valley offered a passage to the north and, possibly, a connection with forces in British Canada. Control of the Hudson would decide the destiny of the young nation.

In part it was these facts that led George Washington to spend more time in the Hudson Valley during the Revolution than in any other part of the country. Early in the war, the British had forced his retreat from Manhattan and defeated his troops at the Battle of White Plains in October 1776. Later that fall the British captured Fort Washington on Manhattan Island and Fort Lee on the opposite shore, at about the point of the present-day George Washington Bridge, forcing the general and his men into New Jersey.

Even when Washington was marching his forces through New Jersey he kept a wary eye on the valley, knowing that, as he had written earlier, "passage of the Enemy up the North River, is a point big with many Consequences to the Public Interest." In 1777 he expressed his fears to General Israel Putnam:

> The importance of the North River in the present contest and the necessity of defending it, are subjects which have been so frequently and so fully discussed and are so well understood, that it is unnecessary to enlarge upon them. . . . it is the only passage by which the Enemy from New York or any part of our coast can ever hope to co operate with an Army that may come from Canada. . . . it is indispensably essential to preserve the communication between Eastern—Middle and Southern States. . . . upon its security in a great measure depend our chief supplies of Flour for the subsistence of such forces as we may have occasion for, in the course of the War.

Whatever else might happen, Washington had to hold the Hudson; the general kept as large a force as he could muster at Newburgh so that he could deploy it quickly if needed to the south or New England, and always it was on hand to defend the river.

Washington had another worry: the Hudson River flowed through a

Overleaf: Map showing the position of the British and Brunswickan troops on October 10, 1777. Defeated in the battles of September 27 and October 7, Burgoyne and his men were effectively trapped. On October 17, Burgoyne surrendered, saying, "It is my fortune, sir, and not my fault that I am here." This battle on the Hudson changed the fortunes of the United States in the American Revolution.

land divided between Patriots and Loyalists. Patriots controlled most of Albany and had maintained a secret Committee of Correspondence since the 1760s, but many members of the Anglican Church and most of its ministers, along with disgruntled tenants of the van Rensselaer and Livingston manors, declared their allegiance to England. Farther south, Patriots controlled Orange and Ulster counties on the west bank of the Hudson.

The situation on the east bank of the river was very different, however. Dutchess and Putnam counties had many Loyalist sympathizers, and Westchester had more still. Chief among those who maintained their allegiance to the king were the descendants of Frederick Philipse; their property could be found in Westchester County and New York City. Frederick Philipse III, who inherited the manor but not his forebears' acumen for public affairs or making money, remained content to collect rents from his tenants, whom he treated well, to adorn his manor house at Yonkers, and to add evermore weight to his corpulent body ("there was not room enough for [him and his wife] in the family chariot"). Remaining loyal to George III, he fled first to his house in New York City and then to England.

Frederick's sisters had also married Loyalists: Susannah to Beverly Robinson, a Virginia gentleman, and Polly to Roger Morris. Washington had known them all for several decades. He had stayed with Beverly Robinson and his wife in New York when he had come north in 1756 to court Susannah's younger sister, Polly. Land attracted the young Colonel Washington as much as Polly's grace; she would bring over fifty thousand rich Hudson Valley acres into her marriage. Only a prior claim for Miss Philipse's affections from a fellow soldier, Captain Roger Morris, deterred the colonel from pressing his suit.

Washington was well acquainted with the topography of the lower Hudson, and fortunately he had a general of the northern department of the army who knew the topography of the upper Hudson intimately. Two places, the Highlands and Saratoga, offered a superb natural defense against enemy passage. Washington certainly knew of the choke point at the entrance to the Highlands. Fortunately for his forces and the future of the United States, his general of the northern department knew the river land at Saratoga north of Albany, for he owned much of it. A crucial fortification at the Highlands and a key battle at Saratoga would save the nation.

꩜

The Battle of Saratoga had its origin in the comfort of the waters and gaming tables at Bath in England, where General John Burgoyne was taking leave from his military duties in North America during the winter of 1776–77. A man of fashion, Burgoyne enjoyed a reputation as an aggressive self-promoter, a gambler and high liver. As a military strategist his ambition would exceed his prudence. His plan for defeating the rebels in North America, which he called "Thoughts for Conducting the War from the Side of Canada," was not especially new. Others had made similar proposals as early as 1775. But it was straightforward and simple: an army would sail up the Hudson from New York City and join forces at Albany with an army that Burgoyne would command, heading south from Canada. The colonies would be divided, the revolution would be defeated, and the Hudson would be theirs.

It was to be just a quick trip up the St. Lawrence and the Richelieu rivers into Lake Champlain, a battle for Fort Ticonderoga at the southern end of the lake, a short portage to the Hudson, and then a swift trip to Albany. It all looked so easy as Burgoyne and others considered his route on imperfect maps. He would command eight thousand men (including three thousand troops from Brunswick in Germany and a few hundred natives). Another thousand or so commissaries, transport men, women (wives of the officers), and children would also accompany them. Before embarking for North America in late spring, Burgoyne stopped at his London club to bet a companion fifty pounds he would return victorious by Christmas.

The trip down the St. Lawrence and Richelieu rivers, and then the sail down to the southern tip of Lake Champlain, all went smoothly. Fort Ticonderoga fell easily in 1777, so easily that some believed General Philip Schuyler, then the commander of the Continental Army's northern department, had not wished to hold it. But after this triumph and victories in several minor skirmishes, Burgoyne's troubles began. From Ticonderoga, "Gentleman Johnny," as his troops affectionately called him, proceeded with some thirty wagons of clothing, food, and wine about fifteen miles south of the fort to Skenesborough to enjoy the hospitality of the staunch Loyalist Philip Skene. Distracted by Skene, his two daughters, the gaming table, his mistress, and an abundance of spirits, the general and his staff relaxed for eighteen days, time enough for the Americans to regroup.

Under the direction of Thaddeus Kosciusko, one of Schuyler's engineers, hundreds of rebels made the dirt path between Skenesborough and Fort Edward impassable: they tore up the crude log road that had been laid over three miles of marshland, they felled trees and rolled boulders down hills into the pathway, they destroyed more than forty bridges, and they flooded the road by diverting waters from nearby Wood Creek, which was already high because of an unusually abundant rainfall that July. The result was a morass that overwhelmed all who entered. It took Burgoyne and his troops twenty-four days to travel twenty-three miles from Skenesborough to Fort Edward. On his previous journey to America in 1775, he had confined himself to the streets of Boston. Now he was struggling in impenetrable forests, alien terrain, and wildness.

Then two rough commanders, John Stark from New Hampshire and Seth Warner with his Green Mountain Boys, defeated a group of Brunswickans who had gone east toward Bennington in search of provisions, arms, and horses. They killed two hundred and took seven hundred prisoners. In spite of the "unfortunate affair at Bennington," the British remained confident. Burgoyne and his officers led their three-mile-long procession of men, horses, munitions, stores, wives, and children through the wilderness down the east bank of the Hudson from Fort Edward. As a member of the party observed, everyone was "in very high spirits"; they believed they were close to the "promised land." They crossed to the western shore near the mouth of the Fishkill (present-day Fish Creek), a small tributary that feeds the river at Saratoga. Once across, Burgoyne halted his troops and destroyed the crude bateaux bridge that his army had constructed, declaring, "Britons never retreat."

In the shortening days of mid-September however, Gentleman Johnny realized that his vision of the promised land was fast fading. His dalliance at Skenesborough, along with British arrogance and bad planning, had brought his troops into serious peril. His supply line from Canada was attenuated at best and there was little food to be had. In the Mohawk Valley, Benedict Arnold had defeated a British force that was hastening east to join Howe and Burgoyne in Albany; Howe's troops that Burgoyne had expected to sail north from New York City failed to materialize; and buoyed by their victory at Bennington, the Americans were demonstrating a fresh resolve.

General Horatio Gates, who had replaced Philip Schuyler as commander of the northern department, followed his predecessor's plan. The British were moving through Schuyler's patent, land that he knew intimately. This was the place to stop Burgoyne's advance. On September 12, Gates moved his troops to Bemis Heights on the western shore of the Hudson and, under Kosciusko's direction, built three miles of earthen fortifications. From this high prospect the Continental Army could command all traffic on the water and the narrow road that hugged the river's western shore. At last, using the river and the land, the Americans had taken charge. Bemis Heights and the narrow valley on the Hudson would be the American Thermopylae, but the Americans would hold the pass.

It was now up to the British to overtake the American positions behind Kosciusko's fortifications. In his first attempt to do so, on September 19, Burgoyne learned once again what he had observed at Bunker Hill two years earlier.

> Composed as the American army is, together with the strength of the country, full of woods, swamps, stone walls, and other enclosures and hiding pieces, it may be said of it that every private man will in action be his own general, who will turn every tree and bush into a temporary fortress, from whence, when he hath fired his shot with all the deliberation, coolness, and certaincy which hidden safety inspires, he will skip as it were to the next, and so on for a long time until dislodged either by cannon or by a resolute attack by light infantry.

Dislodging the enemy proved to be a formidable task. As one Brunswickan present at Saratoga learned, "Every inhabitant [of the country] is a born soldier and a good marksman; in addition, the thought of fighting for their country and for freedom made them braver than ever." The British lost 556 men; the Americans 287. It was difficult to recover the wounded and bury all the bodies before dark. One British officer saw "fifteen, sixteen, and twenty being buried in a whole." That night farmers who lived near the field listened with horror to the howling of wolves as they tore the flesh from the limbs of the dying and dead men left in the darkness.

"The army was in a pitiful situation here," wrote a Brunswickan officer in his diary. British soldiers took to bartering for food and supplies with the few farmers who remained. A half pint of brandy was "paid for with 2 ½ shillings or 20 groschen of German money, one bottle of cheap wine with

6 shillings." By early October the day's ration for each man had dwindled to "1 ½ loaves of bread and 20 ounces of salted pork"; no vegetables could be had "for any money." Men took to deserting. Burgoyne had to act.

A second battle for the heights, on October 7, ended forever Burgoyne's chances to capture the Hudson. Another 650 men fell (to the Americans' 150), including his second in command, Brigadier General Simon Fraser, whose final words were, "Oh fatal ambition! Poor General Burgoyne!"

Vain attempts at retreat followed the second defeat, but the Americans kept up the pressure, taking in prisoners and deserters, sinking bateaux on the river, and attacking the British wherever they might be found. "There was no place of safety," the commander of the Brunswickans later wrote. "The soldier could not lay down his arms day or night. . . . The sick and wounded would drag themselves along into a quiet corner of the woods and lie down to die on the damp ground. Nor even here were they longer safe, since every little while a ball would come crashing down among the trees." With Americans closing in on three sides and the Hudson on the other, Burgoyne knew he and his five thousand men were trapped.

On October 13, John Stark, one of the heroes of the battle at Bennington, took control of a steep escarpment of volcanic rock north of Burgoyne's troops camped at Saratoga. Below the gaze and guns of Stark's men lay the passage from Saratoga to the north; beside it was a marshland at the bank of the river. Stark later likened the scene to a narrow-mouth jar, declaring that he had "corked the bottle," and the British couldn't get out. Retreat became impossible for the Britons who never retreated.

"We had enemy on all sides," the Brunswickan army officer wrote in his journal. "The army had the front toward the woods, and the Hudson River in the back. . . . All hope for retreat was now lost." With no forage to sustain them, the horses of the artillery took to "eating the saddles off their bellies, and one horse after another starved to death." Though succor was promised from the south and the west, none came. Even water grew scarce, for rebel batteries on the eastern shore of the Hudson fired on any soldier who approached the opposite shore. "I believe that the Braunschweiger had never been so [taken in]," the officer lamented, "as they were on this evil, mountainous, and watery continent."

At last, on the morning of October 17, the ghastly battle ended with the British general's supplication before Gates. "I am glad to see you," Gates said in greeting his adversary. "I am not glad to see you," Burgoyne replied. "It is my fortune, sir, and not my fault that I am here."

"The Pastures," the pastoral name Philip Schuyler gave to his imposing nine-thousand-square-foot mansion on a promontory overlooking the Hudson at Albany, became a prison house for the defeated British and Brunswickan commanders. Built of rose-colored brick, the house seemed more like a modest English country house than a prison. Burgoyne also arrived at the Pastures with his retinue and, as François-Jean de Beauvoir, the Marquis de Chastellux, recounted, "was lodged in the best apartment," served an excellent supper, and given a fine bed. Only Philip Jeremiah Schuyler, the general's nine-year-old son, disturbed his parents' hospitality, when he burst in on Burgoyne and his officers and shouted, "Ye are all my prisoners." Baron Friedrich Adolph von Riedesel, the commander of the Brunswickan troops, also arrived with his wife and three young daughters. "Mother," exclaimed one of the children on seeing the house, "is this the palace father was to have when he came to America?"

Word of Burgoyne's September defeat at Saratoga gave Washington the first bright news of the summer. Since losing the Battle of White Plains, the general had kept his forces in New Jersey and Pennsylvania, trying to determine Lord Howe's next move. Albany? Philadelphia? He scurried his troops back and forth. But Howe chose Philadelphia, and Gates defeated Burgoyne at Saratoga. To celebrate, the American commander ordered that his troops outside Philadelphia be served "a gill of rum a man" and that "*Thirteen* pieces of artillery be discharged."

The victory at Saratoga changed the fortunes of the United States. Early in December 1777, Major Jonathan Loring Austin arrived from Boston at Benjamin Franklin's house in the village of Passy on the outskirts of Paris. He carried a special dispatch for Franklin. For more than a year the seventy-one-year-old printer, inventor, and diplomat had been on a mission to persuade Louis XVI to conclude a commerce treaty with his new nation. Austin arrived with momentous news. Before he had time to alight from his horse, so the American commissioners told the story, Franklin addressed him: "Sir, *is* Philadelphia taken?" "Yes, sir," Austin replied. "But, sir, I have greater news than that. GENERAL BURGOYNE *and his whole army are prisoners of war!*" Franklin quickly—and with liberal embellishments—spread the word. Burgoyne and 9,203 of his men had been taken prisoner or killed in the Battle of Saratoga; General Gates had sent reinforcements to Washington; and though Howe was in Philadelphia, he had lost communication with his fleet and "would soon be reduced to submit to the same Terms with Burgoyne." Within a few hours Charles Gravier, Comte de Vergennes and Louis XVI's minister of foreign affairs, told Franklin that France would enter into an alliance with the United States of America. That winter and spring Franklin played the British against the French. The British offered reconciliation—and even independence—for her former colonies, while the French, after a year of polite evasion, suddenly wanted an alliance. Franklin's diplomatic triumph in Paris equaled Gates's military victory at Saratoga.

Washington's hopes had dimmed temporarily when he learned that Sir Henry Clinton was belatedly sailing north from New York. Clinton captured Verplanck Point, south of Peekskill, in October 1777, and attacked Fort Montgomery and Fort Clinton (named in honor of New York's governor and Sir Henry's distant relative, General George Clinton) from the rear. Because many of the Americans had gone to help Washington defend Philadelphia, Clinton's forces met with little resistance when they overran the forts. The British captured close to 70 unspiked cannon and killed more than 250 soldiers. Although Washington had ordered a great iron chain to be stretched between the forts to prevent enemy warships from sailing up the Hudson, the British found that this obstacle yielded easily to Sir Henry's hacksaws. (Many of its links sank to the bottom of the river, though Clinton purportedly sent some across the Atlantic to safeguard the British harbor at the rock of Gibraltar.) Alarmed that the enemy was "meditat[ing] a serious blow against our forces in the Highlands," Washington asked William Livingston, the governor of New Jersey, to send his militia without delay.

Trapped as he was at Saratoga, Burgoyne urged General Clinton to "make a push" on Fort Montgomery at the entrance to the Highlands and then move north to Albany. "Do it, my dear Friend, directly," he urged. Clinton, however, demurred: "General Burgoyne could not suppose that Sir Henry Clinton had an idea of penetrating to Albany with the small force he mentioned in his last letter," he wrote back. But fate intervened to prevent Burgoyne from receiving the note. It wasn't until mid-October, while Burgoyne was contemplating his surrender to General Gates, that Clinton sent a small flotilla of ten warships and an equal number of transports up the Hudson. Led by General John Vaughan, commanding a craft incongruously christened the *Friendship*, they arrived at Esopus Landing at Kingston on October 16, where they carried out one of the most vindictive attacks of the American Revolution. The third largest settlement on the Hudson, Kingston paid a dear price for being the capital of New York's state government. John Jay and a "Convention of Representatives" had recently drafted the state constitution there, and that September the senate and assembly and the state supreme court had held their first sessions in Kingston.

In just three hours, Vaughan reported to Henry Clinton, British troops captured six sloops "loaded with provisions," including fourteen cannon, and demolished "1150 Stands of Arms 44 Barrels of Gunpowder 80 Small Vessels 400 Houses, Barns, Mills &ca." He had destroyed the entire town. The rebels were firing on them, wrote Vaughan, which was reason enough for the scourge, and then added, "but I had a much greater Inducement as the Congress and Clinton had taken Refuge there that Morning and its being a Town notorious for harbouring the most rebellious People in that Part of the Country."

In spite of the razing of Kingston, Burgoyne's surrender at Saratoga rendered the British hold on the Hudson above the Highlands tenuous at best. Continental soldiers were regrouping on both the east and west banks and planning a counterattack. George Washington understood this as well. He knew that despite his victory, Howe was already having trouble holding Philadelphia. Surely, now that the question of a rendezvous in Albany was moot, the British would have to yield. "The complete captivity of Burgoigne and his army exceeds our most sanguine expectations," Washington wrote. "I have not yet heard of Sir Henry Clinton's falling down the North River again, but I should hardly imagine he would persist in his operations there, after hearing of Burgogoygne's [*sic*] destruction."

In Philadelphia, Sir William Howe understood, though perhaps only dimly, the significance of Burgoyne's surrender. And he felt acutely his troop's precarious position. Already he had withdrawn from Germantown into the center of the city. He ordered Vaughan to return with his fleet to

New York City, and to dispatch his troops to Philadelphia. On October 26, Vaughan passed West Point. Howe's order marked the turning point in the Revolution. British control of the Highlands had lasted just thirteen days; they would never return.

Before returning to New York, John Vaughan and his troops on the *Friendship* had another score to settle on the eastern side of the Hudson. Landing at Rhinecliff, Vaughan's troops followed the road north, burning and plundering all rebel houses in their path. Their destination was Livingston Manor.

In the nearly half century since Robert Livingston had left the manor to his eldest surviving son, Philip, and thirteen thousand acres to his brother Robert, Livingston Manor and the Livingston landholdings and fortunes in the Hudson Valley had changed dramatically. By offering generous parcels to his tenants, Philip increased the population; his tenants in turn cleared and cultivated more land and made a handsome profit for themselves and the proprietor. Fifteen miles to the east of the Hudson he created an iron works that he hoped would gain him great wealth. Robert, who had never had much success in life prior to his father's death, decided to become a country squire. With money he acquired from privateering, he built a great Georgian mansion of brick, which he named Clermont, and added a cluster of farm buildings and outhouses. He purchased a half million acres of the Hardenburgh patent across the river from Clermont, including much of the Catskill Mountains.

Philip hadn't been happy when he learned that Robert was to receive a share of Livingston Manor. He exercised his right to reject the first two names Robert chose for his mansion; he and Robert engaged in protracted litigation over water rights on the Roeliff Jansen Kill that separated their properties; and he demanded that Robert pay him an annual quitrent for Clermont of eight shillings. Still, the Clermont Livingstons, as they came to be called, continued to prosper. Robert of Clermont's only son, Robert Robert Livingston, a scholarly lawyer and future colonial judge, married Margaret Beekman, heir to another bonanza of 240,000 acres just south of Clermont in Dutchess County. But every time Philip contemplated the landscape to the south of his manor he saw the hand of his brother. Clermont grew steadily, and at dusk as he gazed across the Hudson toward the sun slipping behind the sawtooth outline of the Catskills, he was looking at *Robert's* mountains.

In spite of their business acumen and the wealth of acres of the Clermont and the Manor Livingstons, the family was impoverished in the matter of Christian names. Over the various generations numerous Roberts, Philips, Henrys, and Peters have come to roost in the thick forest of Livingston genealogical charts. Livingstons also had a penchant for doubling names to distinguish sons: Robert [son of] Robert, Philip Philip, even Livingston Livingston. To keep order, historians, genealogists, and sometimes family members distinguish the various Livingstons by their place on the family tree or their works; thus Robert the Founder, Robert the Nephew [of Robert the Founder], Robert of Clermont, Robert the Judge, Robert the Chancellor [of the State of New York], Philip, the First Proprietor, Philip the Signer [of the Declaration of Independence], and Robert Cambridge—after Cambridge University where he was educated. One descendant, who earned a reputation by fathering a number of illegitimate children in the valley, was Henry the Rake.

Divided though Livingstons might be over matters of land and primogeniture, they were united—albeit reluctantly in some cases—by the Revolution; almost all family members decided for the radicals over the Loyalists. On the manor side, Robert the third proprietor's brother Philip signed the Declaration of Independence. Robert's oldest surviving son, Peter Robert, early joined the Sons of Liberty, perhaps too early for his father, who was slow in joining the cause of independence. Philip's brother William became the revolutionary governor of New Jersey, and William's only son, Henry Brockholst Livingston, served with Schuyler and Arnold at Saratoga.

On the other side of the family, Robert of Clermont, who lived until 1775, early declared for independence; his son, Robert Robert, or Robert the Judge, had been chairman of New York's committee of correspondence in opposition to the Stamp Act and was committed to economic independence, though he preferred it to be achieved through conciliation rather than revolution. Robert R., who inherited Clermont on Robert the Judge's death, also in 1775, had delivered a "spirited Oration in praise of Liberty" on his graduation from King's College, and for a time he joined with John Jay in law practice. He had been a member of the Continental Congress, sat as one of five drafters of the Declaration of Independence, and had recently been made chancellor of the State of New York. His brother, the mercurial Henry Beekman Livingston ("the Rake"), who before the Revolution had become so disenchanted with the Crown that he took to wearing his court dress while plowing the fields at Clermont, also fought at Saratoga. And three of Robert's brothers-in-law had distinguished themselves in the battle.

No doubt General John Vaughan believed that in attacking Livingston Manor he was striking a blow at the heart of radicalism in the Hudson Valley. On learning about the scourge at Kingston, Margaret Beekman Livingston, Robert the Judge's widow who still lived at Clermont, ordered the silver buried and bundled herself, her daughters, and her slaves into farm carts and carriages and headed for Connecticut. From a distance they could see smoke rising from Clermont. Vaughan destroyed the house, the barns, and all the outbuildings. He also burned Belvedere, the house Robert the Chancellor had built for himself near Clermont. Robert, who was away at the time, returned to find only the charred walls of Clermont remained standing.

His work done, Vaughan and his troops retreated downriver. Henry Livingston protested Vaughan's "Horrid Barbarity" directly to Sir Henry Clinton: "You have reduced to ashes the Beautiful Village of Kingston and many buildings the Proprietors of which could never have injured you." For his part, Sir Henry couldn't understand why his general had acted with such vengeance, noting that he had ordered Vaughan "to proceed d[i]rect for Burgoyne cooperate with him nay join him if necessary." And then Sir Henry added, "He stopt at Kingston burned it & Esopus fr what reason I am yet to learn." Later that year the chancellor's friend and fellow aristocrat Gouverneur Morris wrote a brief note of commiseration. "I hear you intend to keep your burned home as a monumental ruin," Morris began, and then he proposed an inscription for the monument:

When the King of Great Britain attempted to establish
Tyranny over the extensive regions of America
        The Roof of Hospitality
Sacred to Friendship and Science & to Love
        Was violated by the Hand of War
To perpetuate the Pleasure he received from British
Barbarity this pillar is erected by

Robert R. Livingston
Who would have blushed to be exempted
From the calamities of his country.

It is at the Highlands that the Hudson earns its sobriquet River of Mountains. For about the next fifteen miles to the north the river flows through its narrowest point in the valley. The spectacular steep wooded barrier that in places rises directly from the water's edge lends itself to defense. The narrowest and most treacherous place, "the key to America," George Washington called it, is West Point. He knew that if the continental forces were to succeed, they would have to prevent the British from controlling the Hudson, thereby separating the rebel hotbed of New England from the rest of the new nation. This high crag is the ideal place for fortifications; from its vantage point, guns can dominate all ships passing on the river below. Here the Hudson curves in a narrow S bend that forces all sailing ships to tack. The water currents are swift and hostile, and to the north the river is over two hundred feet deep. As the wind whips through this small gap in the mountains, the air currents challenge even the most seasoned mariner. Across from the point, the gray rocky shore of Constitution Island, which the Dutch had called Martelaer's Island, stands at the southern curve of the hostile S bend so treacherous to ships. No wonder that English sailors corrupted the Dutch name into Martyr's Island.

General Vaughan and his fleet had sailed past West Point in October 1777, when the defenses on the Hudson were weak. Washington determined that it would not happen again. "Seize the present opportunity and employ your whole work force and all means in your power for erecting and completing, as far as possible such works and obstructions as may be necessary to defend and secure the river against any future attempts of the Enemy," he wrote to General Israel Putnam in early December. "By gaining the passage, you know the Enemy have already laid waste and destroyed all the Houses—Mills and Towns accessible to them," he continued, referring to Vaughan's raid. "Unless proper measures are taken, to prevent them," he worried, "they will renew their Ravages in the Spring, or as soon as the Season will admit, and perhaps Albany the only Town in the State of any importance remaining in our Hands, may undergoe a like fate and a general Havoc and devastation take place." And then came the order: "To prevent these Evils therefore, I shall expect that you will exert every Nerve and employ your whole force in future, while and whenever practicable, in constructing and forwarding the proper works and means of defence." The result of Washington's order is the great fortress of West Point.

Not so much a single fort as a series of redoubts and batteries dominated by a polygonal citadel, West Point shows the brilliance of its designer, the Polish engineer Colonel Thaddeus Kosciusko. One of the first Europeans to lend his support to the American cause, Kosciusko arrived shortly after the signing of the Declaration of Independence in 1776. He proved his abilities by designing fortifications on the Delaware below Philadelphia, then at Ticonderoga, and most spectacularly at Bemis Heights. Promoted to colonel after Saratoga, he now directed a force of eighty-five masons, stone cutters, and laborers in the task of creating the new nation's largest fortress. Construction began in the spring of 1778 and was not completed until mid 1780; the cost was $3 million. The men built stone and wood ramparts that clung to the steep hills 180 feet above the water. From them cannon could command all boats great and small that sought to pass around the point. The S bend insured that any hostile ships would suffer withering fire from above. To guard against attack from the land behind West Point, Kosciusko constructed two other fortifications, Fort Arnold, in honor of the commander General Benedict Arnold, and Fort Putnam, named for General Israel Putnam, as well as a number of smaller batteries and redoubts.

On a narrow terrace reached by a steep path down the nearly vertical cliff that drops to the river, Kosciusko found a small spring bubbling from the rock face. Shaded by a weeping willow, it is said to have become the colonel's hermitage, an ideal spot for him to reflect on his accomplishments. To it he repaired in quiet moments to meditate and take in the view of the Hudson below, Constitution Island to the northeast, and the Philipses' land on the opposite shore. On the cliffs above him stood the batteries and redoubts that would ensure no enemy could disturb his peace or destroy the nation's new democracy by sailing up the Hudson. The success of Kosciusko's creation lay in the fact that no enemy tried. Short of an act of treason, the fortifications at West Point formed an impregnable bulwark that would delay the British, whether on ship or on foot, for weeks.

But Washington decided he needed more protection. He ordered

Kosciusko to have another great chain constructed that would block the passage upriver, to replace the one the British had broken through in October 1777 five miles downstream. The new chain was massive, five hundred yards long, made of twelve hundred links forged from two-and-a-quarter-inch square stock, weighing sixty-five tons in all. It took forty men four days in April 1778 to fasten the chain to the rocks at Gees Point, a spit of land below the ramparts, and float it across the river on great wooden pontoons to Fort Constitution on Constitution Island. Kosciusko even installed a log boom to protect the chain. Sixty cannon looked down on the river from the ramparts at West Point and Fort Constitution. No wooden-hulled ship, the rebels believed, even one sailing in the dead of night, could hope to breach the defense. A fusillade from above would certainly destroy it.

The British knew better than to test the chain and the cannon at West Point. But two centuries later a group of enterprising cadets devised a computer model to test the chain's strength. Far from being able to withstand the force of a frigate ramming it, the links most likely would have snapped easily had they been struck by a sloop.

Only corruption from within could destroy the impregnable barrier to the Hudson that the Americans had erected at West Point. But, as every school child knows, corruption did come in 1780. A tale worthy of Sophocles or Shakespeare, a story of good and evil, faithfulness and treason, honor and falsity, it included an amoral villain, a pretty and flirtatious seductress, a man of decency who acted with folly, and three stock country swains who in the face of temptation showed their simple integrity. And on this tale's outcome rested the future course of Britain's empire and the United States.

The amoral villain of the tale, Benedict Arnold from Norwich, Connecticut, had been a bookseller, a druggist, a West Indies trader, a war hero, a gambler, and a spendthrift. Endowed with courage, resourcefulness, and a quick temper as well as the attributes of a great warrior, he also possessed a towering ego and was quick to take offense when he believed his qualities were not recognized. He excelled at fighting but failed miserably at regimental politics. He became bitter when he was passed over for promotion from the rank of brigadier to major general. He quarreled frequently with his superiors, Gates among them, but on October 7, 1777, fortified by "a dipperful of . . . rum" and shouting "Victory or death," he defied Gates's orders and proved himself a hero at the battle for Bemis Heights. The price Arnold paid for his valor was a crippled leg that he injured when his own horse fell on him at the end of the battle.

The following year, Washington gave the infirm Arnold command of Philadelphia after the Americans had recaptured the city. The post proved a cold comfort. Gates gave him little credit for the victory at Saratoga; Congress, he believed, slighted his valor; and Philadelphia proved expensive. Thinking that his command obligated him to lavish great sums on various social entertainments, Arnold quickly fell into debt. He was ripe for treason, and Philadelphia, whose belles had only recently entertained British officers, proved the best place to hatch a plot. An aristocratic eighteen-year-old from a Loyalist family, Peggy Shippen, had ranked among the most flirtatious of the young ladies in the city, especially with one young officer named John André. After the British left, Shippen looked to the American officers; soon she was smitten with the general whose prominent nose, high forehead, and gray eyes gave him an air of distinction. Once they were married, in April 1779, Arnold began to correspond with the enemy, feeding information about troop movements and supplies and the strength of the French forces. The information went through Sir Henry Clinton and his chief aide, John André. From the start, Peggy Shippen collaborated with her husband at every turn.

In April 1780, Arnold importuned Philip Schuyler, whom he had championed over Gates at Saratoga, to use his influence with Washington to help get Arnold posted to West Point. In August, Washington made the appointment; Arnold now held the key to America in his hand. In the meantime Arnold was negotiating for his "most essential services," delivery of the fortress, three thousand soldiers, and even George Washington himself. The price was twenty thousand pounds if he should succeed, and ten thousand pounds if he should fail. As the new commander of the fortress, Arnold made his residence at the Beverly Robinson house on the east bank of the Hudson. By mid-August he began quietly to decimate the troop strength; by mid-September he had winnowed the number of men at West Point to about fifteen hundred. Nor did Arnold stop with the men. He ordered hams, rum, barrels of pork, and sacks of grain shipped across to the Robinson house, where he locked them in his private storehouse.

On the night of September 21, off Teller's Point, fifteen miles south of West Point where the Croton River joins the Hudson, Major John André was rowed from the British sloop *Vulture* at anchor in the river to the western shore for an assignation with Benedict Arnold. The commander passed the major papers detailing the weaknesses of the fortress, troop strength, and Washington's plans for war.

After their meeting broke at four o'clock in the morning, the plan went terribly wrong. The two farmers who had rowed André ashore refused to return to the *Vulture;* the next morning the American battery at Teller's Point, commanded by Colonel John Livingston (Robert the Nephew's grandson, who also had distinguished himself at Saratoga), began firing on the *Vulture,* forcing it to withdraw downstream and ride at anchor off Sing Sing. André was left with no choice but to disguise himself as an American and, with a pass from Arnold, cross the Hudson at Stony Point under the assumed name of John Anderson. Once ashore, he planned to ride down the eastern shore to the British lines at White Plains.

He almost made it. On Saturday morning, September 23, as André rode through the dangerous no-man's land of the Hudson Valley known as the "neutral ground," where Loyalist "Cowboys" and rebel "Skinners" preyed on travelers for their money, three militia men, probably with robbery in mind, ordered him to halt. One of them, John Paulding, was a giant of a man dressed in a tattered red Hessian coat who towered over the slight André. Seeing the coat, André revealed himself to be an officer in the king's service. His captors brought him to a thicket, stripped him, and found the damning papers. Paulding alone of the three rebels could read, but with halting comprehension. Still, after mouthing a few words of Arnold's report, he could understand enough: "This," he declared, "is a spy!"

At the Beverly Robinson house two mornings later, Benedict Arnold awaited the arrival of George Washington and General Marie-Joseph Lafayette and their aides. They were due to arrive at any moment for a late but leisurely breakfast with Arnold and his enticing wife. A lieutenant appeared with a message from Colonel John Jameson, the commander of a small outpost at North Castle in Westchester County downstream. "A certain John Anderson," carrying a pass "signed with your name," had been apprehended. "He had a parcel of papers taken from under his stockings,

Thomas Sully, *The Capture of Major André*, 1812. In the nineteenth century André's capture
and execution became a subject for numerous artists. (Even André, who was an artist,
sketched a self-portrait on the morning of his execution.) Here Sully records the
moment when John Paulding makes the discovery of the papers revealing André to be
a spy. (Worcester Art Museum, Worcester, Massachusetts; gift of Andrew J. Bates II)

which I think of a very dangerous tendency." Jameson concluded with a
sentence that told Arnold all was lost: "The papers I have sent to General
Washington." Arnold rushed upstairs to Peggy, told her that their treason-
ous plot was out, and left her in a swoon. He escaped the house, passing
Washington's party on the way, and ordered his bargemen to row him to
the *Vulture*, which he met in Haverstraw Bay off Stony Point.

Peggy Shippen Arnold put on a brilliant performance of hysterical passion that fooled all. General Arnold was gone forever, she screamed; they
had put hot irons on his head; General Washington wanted to kill her
infant child. "I saw an amiable woman frantic with distress for the loss of
a husband she tenderly loved—a traitor to his country and to his fame,"

Alexander Hamilton wrote to his fiancée, Elizabeth Schuyler. "She for a considerable time intirely lost her senses." Washington himself went up to console her. At that moment, Hamilton reported, "All the sweetness of beauty, all the loveliness of innocence, all the tenderness of a wife and all the fondness of a mother showed themselves in her appearance and conduct." Hamilton and his commander were completely taken in.

In the old Dutch church at Tappan, a village situated west of Piermont on the Hudson about twenty miles south of West Point, fourteen generals, including John Stark and the Marquis de Lafayette, met to decide the fate of John André. He was a spy, they decided, and he should be hanged. It was the final ignominy to be suffered in a life that had begun with much promise. In England the handsome and delicately featured lad had fancied himself a poet and an artist; a thwarted romance moved the hopeless romantic to join the British army and go to America. But soon he was a prisoner, sent to board with a Quaker family in Pennsylvania before being exchanged. He joined the British in Philadelphia. There he amused the young beauty Peggy Shippen with his drawings, including several of her. When the British withdrew to New York under the command of Sir Henry Clinton, the general made André his most trusted aide. It was André's acquaintance with Shippen that enabled the treacherous correspondence with Arnold to proceed.

Had Arnold's scheme not been foiled it likely would have helped save the American colonies for the British, and André would have received his measure of glory for his daring ride. But it was not to be. He was to die not as a soldier, but as a spy, disgraced. He was a "man of honor," he told Washington in a letter. "Let me hope, sir, that if aught in my character impresses you with esteem toward you . . . I shall experience the operation of these feelings in your breast by being informed that I am not to die on the gibbet." André considered himself a British gentleman; gentlemen did not die on the gallows.

From Washington, who had moved his own headquarters to Tappan, came no reply. The general plotted unsuccessfully to kidnap the traitor Arnold from the New York City house in which he had taken refuge. He tried also to arrange an exchange of Arnold for André, but that plan, too, failed. From New York came the traitor's threat: Should André die, he would be bound "by duty . . . and honor to retaliate on such unhappy persons of your army as may fall in my power." Washington would not relent, but André knew none of this. He only wanted to die with honor.

Late in the morning of October 2, guards put their prisoner into a wagon and drove it to the tree prepared for his execution. When the gibbet came into view, André "started backward." But later he regained his composure and slipped the noose over his own head, adjusting it "without the assistance of the awkward executioner." "I pray you to bear me witness that I meet my fate like a brave man." At noon the wagon was ordered forward. Guards cut down the lifeless body dressed in its royal uniform, including the boots that had once held the traitorous papers, placed it in a crude coffin, and buried the box beneath the gallows.

Benedict Arnold fared better, but forever he wore a mantle of infamy that made his new British comrades uncomfortable. From his safe haven in New York City, he threatened a "torrent of blood" if André was hanged, published a vindication of his actions, and unsuccessfully urged others in New York to desert to his side. Clinton appointed him a brigadier general but cut his reward to six thousand pounds (from the promised ten thousand) and sent him on several nasty marauding expeditions. At New London, Connecticut, Arnold oversaw a massacre and watched as the town was consumed in flames. Few were sad when the general, his future glories behind him, sailed for England in 1782. Business ventures in New Brunswick, Canada, and the West Indies yielded little more than disappointment. Embarrassed by his treason, impoverished by his bad judgment, he fell into despondency, dying finally in 1801 of what his faithful wife, Peggy Shippen, described as a "perturbed mind." Peggy's own death from cancer followed in 1804. Together, the couple lie in a crypt at St. Mary's Church in Battersea, London. Arnold is said to be dressed in the uniform of a Continental soldier.

Early in 1783, as the war wound down, Washington faced a final challenge on the Hudson; this time it came not from British troops or conspirators but from the men in his own army. Since April of the previous year the general had made his headquarters in a handsome stone house overlooking the river at Newburgh; that October he established his winter quarters at New Windsor, just south of his headquarters. Worried about the British who still clung to their position in New York City, the general wanted to have his men close at hand should the enemy attempt to take the river. In Europe, peace negotiations were proceeding "very limpingly."

The British never came; the men remained idle and largely unpaid. The situation grew dangerous. Congress had assured them in 1780 that on their discharge they would receive a life pension of half pay. But the United States was near bankruptcy; the states had refused to levy the taxes that would enable Congress to pay the men. "The Army, as usual, are without pay," Washington wrote in January 1783, "and a great part of the Soldiery without Shirts." People began to murmur that even if peace did come, the army should remain active and force state legislatures to grant them their pay and pensions. Only the commander in chief stood in their way. Earlier Washington had rejected, "with abhorrence," a proposal to make him king of the new nation, regarding the idea as "one of the greatest mischiefs that can befall my country." Still, the threat remained that the soldiers intended to resort to violence, as Hamilton wrote, "to procure justice for itself."

In March 1783, unsigned papers, known as the Newburgh addresses, began to circulate through the camp. The anonymous author argued eloquently that the soldiers should "suspect the man who would advise to more moderation and further forbearance," stating that only direct action would coerce justice from Congress, and he called for a meeting of the officers. Just at its moment of victory, the revolution that had begun on the highest principle—that all possessed "inalienable rights of Life, Liberty and the pursuit of Happiness"—and the men who had resisted since 1775 against improbable odds the assault from one of the greatest powers on earth, now stood after seven years of struggle on the precipice of tyranny.

Washington forbade the meeting; instead he called for a meeting of his own to be held on March 15. For most of his remarks he showed carefully controlled indignation at the very reason for the convocation.

"How inconsistent with the rules of propriety!—how unmilitary!—and how subversive of all order and discipline" the anonymous summons and the anonymous letters were to the commander in chief. Though the author of the letter deserved credit for "the goodness of his pen," the general wished he "had as much credit for the rectitude of his heart." The author had suggested that the army simply withdraw into the unsettled territory, leaving the "ungrateful country to fend for itself." To this Washington asked, "My God! What can this writer have in view, by recommending such measures? Can he be a friend to the army?—Can he be a friend to this country?—Rather is he not an insidious foe?" He had reason to believe that Congress would act justly, but "like all other large bodies, where there is a variety of different interests to reconcile, their deliberations are slow." To distrust that body would "tarnish the reputation of an army" that had earned respect throughout "all Europe." After pledging himself to do whatever he could to get the men their pay and pensions, he concluded with an appeal to their honor: "And you will, by the dignity of your conduct, afford occasion for posterity to say, when speaking of the glorious example you have exhibited to mankind, had this day been wanting, the world has never seen the last stage of perfection to which human nature is capable of attaining."

And then the austere general made one of the most effective gestures of his career. He began to read a congressman's letter, one that assured him the deliberations over pay and pensions in that democratic body were going forward, when he was forced to reach in a pocket for his eyeglasses. "You will permit me to put on my spectacles," he said, "for I have not only grown gray but almost blind in the service of my country." With those simple words, George Washington added a human dimension to the cold reason of his appeal. No officer who had been with him at Harlem Heights or West Point, Fort Lee or Morristown, Long Island or Trenton, could fail to be affected. The assembled unanimously disavowed "the infamous propositions in a late anonymous address" and affirmed their patriotism. That afternoon at Newburgh reason and emotion saved the nascent democracy.

The following month, Congress ratified the Peace of Paris, and as many as ten thousand dispirited Loyalists, including Beverly Robinson and his sons, embarked from New York harbor for a free passage to Canada and Europe. By June, thousands of continental soldiers, many of whom had made the Hudson Highlands their home since April 1782, left for their farms and families across the colonies. Only a skeleton force remained with the commander in chief when, on November 25, he returned to New York, the city he had yielded to the enemy in 1776.

Abandoned after seven years of British occupation, much of New York

"Evacuation of New York by the British, November 25, 1783." New Yorkers continued to celebrate evacuation day for more than a century. This image commemorates the one hundredth anniversary of the moment when the British soldiers sailed from the last stronghold in their former colonies. As Washington leads his army into the city, one of his men returns the United States flag to fly over the Battery.

resembled a hollow shell. Two fires had left many blocks in rubble; other houses were crumbling; churches had been converted into stables and barracks; and wharves were derelict. Washington's triumphal procession was delayed when an advance party found that, in a final empty gesture of nastiness, a British soldier had cut the halyards and greased the flagpole at Fort George, leaving the Union Jack flying over the Battery. But no matter. After a short pause the stars and stripes flew over the fort once again, and the general arrived. New York, the last British stronghold in their former colonies, and the entire Hudson River belonged to the United States.

The cost was atrocious. Redoubts, bunkers, fortresses, and defenses had been built and destroyed. About 3,400 New Yorkers, many living along the Hudson, gave six or seven years of their lives to the service of the Continental Army; thousands more were "levies," militia men from different regiments who fought outside the state; and tens of thousands served at one time or another in the militia. About 550 men were taken prisoner, thousands were wounded, untold numbers died. Some, like Lieutenant Tobias Van Vechten of the First New York Regimentals, were scalped by Indians in the employ of Burgoyne in 1777; others, like Captain Van Wyck, died in August 1776 when lightning struck his tent on Manhattan Island. The rolls of soldiers read like a who's who of Dutch and English names in the valley: two Broncks and five Ingersolls, twenty-four van Rensselaers and twenty-six Livingstons, twenty-three Schuylers and nineteen Hudsons. About 450 citizens with names like Livingston, Schuyler, Hardenbrook, and Van Cortlandt stripped the lead from their windows to make bullets for the soldiers. Vast amounts of property from the Battery through Manhattan, the Highlands, Newburgh, Kingston, Saratoga, and into the north country had been destroyed by rebels and redcoats; huge tracts of Loyalist land belonging to families like Robinson, Colden, and Philipse were confiscated. Through all the changes and violence in the valley, only the river remained constant.

LANDING OF GEN. LA FAYETTE
At Castle Garden, New York,
16th August 1824.

Entered According to Act of Congress the 27th Day of October 1824 by Samuel Maverick of the State of New York

CHAPTER 6

The Democratic River

At nine o'clock on the morning of August 15, 1824, the packet ship *Cadmus*, thirty-one days out of Le Havre, passed into the Narrows of New York harbor. From Fort Lafayette on the Brooklyn side of the water came the report of thirteen guns fired in salute of the ship's famous passenger, Marie-Joseph-Paul-Yves-Roch-Gilbert du Motier de Lafayette, the last surviving major general of the American Revolution. After an absence of forty-two years, the man whose personal valor, integrity, and idealism had made him an abiding symbol of the good will and spiritual solidarity of America and France, was returning to tour the nation whose democracy he had helped to secure. Over the next thirteen months, Lafayette would visit each of the twenty-three states of the union, meet old comrades, and make sentimental pilgrimages to those places he knew from the Revolution. But despite the many months it had to prepare, New York City's welcoming committee wasn't ready for the general's arrival; Lafayette was forced to spend the night at the house of Vice President Daniel Tompkins on Staten Island. The next morning he boarded the great steamboat *Chancellor Livingston*, which led a flotilla of steamboats across the harbor to the Battery. There Lafayette heard "the unceasing shouts and the congratulations of 50,000 freemen." It was said that on Greenwich Street that afternoon, seats in the upper windows of houses the general's grand parade passed by sold for as much as four dollars.

A month later the general boarded another boat, the *James Kent*, for a journey up the Hudson that was scarcely inferior in pomp and circumstance to a royal procession. It was a nostalgic trip for Lafayette and the thousands whom he saw and met along the way. Except for a few hours the first day, when the *James Kent* became stranded on the bed of oyster shells at the mouth of the Croton River, and the inevitable delays caused by huge crowds, the trip went smoothly. Though the steamboat had more than a hundred berths, so many women were aboard that many men were obliged to sleep on deck.

Opposite: The landing of General Lafayette at Castle Garden, August 1824. This engraving depicts Lafayette's arrival in New York City for the first time since the end of the Revolutionary War. The general was aboard the steamboat *Chancellor Livingston*, identified by the tall smokestack and side paddlewheel. When he arrived at the Battery, Lafayette was greeted by enormous crowds that came out to honor the French hero of the Revolution. (I. N. Phelps Stokes Collection, Miriam and Ira D. Wallach Division of Art, Prints, and Photographs, The New York Public Library, Astor, Lenox, and Tilden Foundations)

Many times during the Revolution Lafayette had been in the Hudson Valley and crossed the river, but he had never sailed up its reaches to Albany and Troy. At West Point the cadets and generals feted him with a great dinner in the mess; at Newburgh "at least 10,000 persons" greeted him; at Poughkeepsie, where the New York legislature had decided by a margin of three votes to ratify the federal Constitution, the town's leading citizen, Colonel Henry A. Livingston, greeted the "country's benefactor and friend"; at Catskill and Hudson, Kingston and Greenbush, Albany and Troy, there were similar parades, memorial arches, and speeches. Day and night, in rain and fog, cloud or sunshine, citizens lined both banks of the river for the thrill of seeing Lafayette's boat pass by. Some had been with him at West Point when Arnold proved himself a traitor; some had been encamped at New Windsor when he was there with Washington; some had been in the Virginia campaign and fought alongside him at Yorktown in his victory over General Charles Cornwallis. When the thick smoke from the stack of the *James Kent* appeared on the horizon, they raised the guns they had brought, muskets and long rifles many of them had carried in the Revolution, and fired a lusty salute.

Indeed the journey was a nostalgic one for Lafayette, too. The general recalled his learning of Arnold's defection ("gloom and distrust seemed to pervade every mind"); he exchanged memories with a soldier who had been wounded at Monmouth, and to whom he had given two guineas so that he might have a nurse ("to you, sir . . . I owe my life," the man told Lafayette); and he told the story of the hapless major who had slipped through the ice on the river off Newburgh when on an outing with some local girls ("an eccentric, but an excellent man"). Near Kingston, Colonel Henry Livingston boarded the *James Kent* to reminisce with Lafayette about the war. Henry the Rake had fought courageously, if recklessly, at Saratoga; he had braved the fierce winter at Valley Forge; and he had been with the general at Newport. Later that day Lafayette made a special stop at Clermont, where he was met by Robert L. Livingston (the Manor Livingston who had married the chancellor's daughter Margaret), hundreds of family members, guests, and veterans, a regiment of troops, and a large delegation of Masons.

Lafayette's return to the Hudson River valley was more than an occasion to indulge his memories. He had left the fledgling democracy at the end of the Revolution to advance his republican ideals, support the cause of liberty, and promulgate American political principles. His return in 1824 enabled him to observe the course democracy had taken in North America.

No doubt the changes the general saw in the valley were impressive. The population of New York City had soared since he had last been there in 1784. Between 1786 and 1820 the number of people living on Manhattan Island had jumped from 23,000 to 123,000, making New York nearly twice the size of Philadelphia and almost three times larger than Boston. New York's commerce concentrated the wealthiest men in the nation on the shores of the Hudson. After the peace of 1815, immigration soared, especially after January 1818, when the Black Ball packet line began regular service with four ships sailing between New York and Liverpool. Each vessel returned from Europe with a fresh load of immigrants. Mayor Cadwallader D. Colden, son of the Tory lieutenant governor and brother of Jane Colden, estimated that between March 1818 and November 1819, close to nineteen thousand immigrants had registered at his office. Many decided to stay in New York or in the valley.

Although the nation's political center had moved to Washington on the shore of the Potomac, its financial center remained in New York on the shore of the Hudson. The city was the home of the New York Stock Exchange, the Bank of New York, a branch of the Bank of the United States, and the Manhattan Company. The last was actually a water company that Aaron Burr had organized. Burr cleverly inserted a clause in the state charter that gave the company the right to engage in "monied transactions or operations." The directors proved themselves better bankers than hydrologists, too. While the Manhattan Company bank thrived, they failed to provide New Yorkers with safe drinking water; disease and epidemics became common as a consequence.

In the midst of wealth, however, there was poverty. New York City had a large alms population. Buildings in the once prosperous Five Points area, built on the unstable landfill of a former pond, were becoming squalid and foul smelling as they settled into the earth. The result was a giant slum that became a home for Irish immigrants and free blacks. But by 1824 New York also had several orphanages, a Deaf and Dumb Asylum, a New York Asylum for Lying-In Women, and, north of the city, at what is now Columbia University, Bloomingdale Insane Asylum.

One of the chief reasons for New York's prosperity was its deepwater port, which by the turn of the century had surpassed Philadelphia, Boston, Charleston, Savannah, and New Orleans in importance. Cotton accounted for much of its success, as New York became the third leg in what planters and shippers called the cotton triangle. Ships laden with cotton would sail from New Orleans to Liverpool and then return to New York with immigrants and European cargo. Later, however, southern shippers found it easier to send their cotton to New York and transfer it to an eastbound ship. In either case, New York's port handled not only the cargo but the insurance, interest, commissions, and freight charges. By 1822, cotton accounted for 40 percent—nearly $4 million—of New York's domestic imports. Flour was a distant second at nearly $800,000; furs, the commodity that had sparked the Dutch interest in New Netherland two centuries before, accounted for less than $300,000.

Up the Hudson, Albany and Troy proved equally impressive. When Lafayette had last occupied his military headquarters on North Pearl Street, Albany's populace numbered about thirty-five hundred; it was now close to thirteen thousand. Nearly a mile of wharves lined the river. As the city had become the state capital in 1797, the legislators erected a capitol building, and the governor made his residence on State Street. Nearby were parks and rows of trees. Albany boasted three banks—the Bank of New York, the New York State National Bank, and the Mechanics and Farmers Bank—each backed by good Albany names like Van Rensselaer and Van Zandt, Ten Broeck and Ten Eyck. In 1813, Mayor Philip Van Rensselaer began the Albany Academy for boys; a year later a local lawyer, Ebenezer Foote and his wife, Betsy, began the Albany Academy for Girls, the first school in America for females.

Across the Hudson at Troy, Lafayette found a thriving town that embodied the spirit of democracy. Henry Burden, an immigrant from Edinburgh, was expanding an iron works that he had recently acquired. The meat packer Samuel Wilson still enjoyed fame as "Uncle Sam," the name he had acquired in 1812 when he provided the American army with barrels of pork. Stephen Van Rensselaer, the eighth patroon, had established the Rensselaer School (later renamed Rensselaer Polytechnic Institute), with Amos Eaton as its head of academics. Undoubtedly one of the highlights of the general's tour was his visit to the Troy Female Seminary, where Emma Hart Willard and a delegation of her students serenaded him with a song Mrs. Willard had composed herself:

> And art thou, then, dear Hero come?
> And do our eyes behold the man
>> Who nerved his arm and bared his breast
> For us, ere yet our life began?
>> For us and for our native land,
> And youthful valor dared the war;
>> And now, in winter of thy age
> Thou'st come and left thy lov'd ones far.

The *James Kent* that brought Lafayette up the river in 1824 was itself a testament to America's progress. Steam was changing the nation. The latest and best steamboat to ply the waters of the river, it measured 140 feet long and 48 feet wide, and was built by the New York shipbuilding firm of Blossom, Smith, and Dimon. It belonged to a company begun by the two pioneers of steam navigation in the United States, Chancellor Robert R. Livingston and Robert Fulton. Though their backgrounds and circumstances couldn't have been more different, Fulton and Livingston shared the fervor of the Enlightenment's interest in science and invention.

Fulton was no stranger to financial adversity. Born in Lancaster, Pennsylvania, in 1765 to a failed hardscrabble farmer, he had spent his early years on the edge of poverty. He longed for fame and fortune. First he thought his modest artistic talent would bring him success, so in 1787 he went to London to study at the feet of his fellow Pennsylvanian, the famous artist Benjamin West. But after several desperate years in which he learned just how meager his talent really was, he turned to mechanics. He dabbled in designs and schemes for any number of machines: submarines, a mill for cutting marble, and a boat propelled by a rear fin that imitated the movement of a salmon. Canals might make him his fortune. In 1796 he published a *Treatise on Canal Navigation*, and tried in vain to interest George Washington and an English lord in his schemes. Thinking Napoleon would take notice of his designs, he sailed for Paris. There, in 1802, he met a man of means who was intrigued, America's minister to France, Robert R. Livingston.

Livingston's progress through the political heavens of New York and the nation had left a luminous meteoric trail. He had taken part in the Revolution as a delegate to the Continental Congress and a member of the committee that drafted the Declaration of Independence. As chancellor of the state, he had administered the presidential oath of office to George Washington on the steps of the new Federal Hall in New York City, concluding the ceremony by shouting, "Long live George Washington, President of the United States!" But the evanescent blaze was swiftly consumed in the atmosphere of democratic realities. In his time on the committee drafting the Declaration, he contributed nothing, and wasn't able to be in Philadelphia to sign it. (Perhaps even more irritating to him was the fact that his cousin Philip Livingston, from the Manor side of the family, did add his signature.) He expected the president would appoint him as the first secretary of the treasury, or, failing that, the first chief justice of the Supreme Court; Washington passed over him for Hamilton and Jay. Switching his allegiance from the Federalists to the Republicans hadn't helped either, as in 1798 he lost the race for governor to Jay by the largest margin ever recorded.

Jefferson appointed Livingston minister to France with the task of negotiating the purchase of Louisiana, but the conclusion of the deal in 1803 brought the final extinction of his political star. The negotiations had been moving so slowly that Jefferson dispatched James Monroe to spur them on. Two days after Monroe's arrival, Napoleon offered to sell the entire Louisiana territory, and the Americans quickly accepted. Robert the Chancellor would have returned a hero and probably would have been elected governor of New York, the position he coveted, had he not antedated Napoleon's offer to make it appear that he alone had been responsible for completing the negotiations. Soon his fraud was exposed, and he was forced to resign. But he didn't return to the United States until the summer of 1805, and then he confined himself to Clermont.

For much of his life Livingston had played the role of gentleman farmer, inventor, and scientific investigator. He founded the New York Society for the Promotion of Agriculture, Manufactures, and the Useful Arts, serving as its president. He published an article in the society's *Transactions* on the use of gypsum as manure. At Clermont he created a model farm. His ideas could be—and often were—fantastic. "Frog's spit," the name locals gave to a weed growing in the shallow waters of the Hudson, looked like paper. Though the plant's leaves were brittle when dried, might they not be ground to a powder and reconstituted into actual paper, he wondered? Paper was expensive, composed of rags and usually made by hand. Surely his weed pulp would be better and more economical, "a cheap substitute for rags." A recent émigré, a French romantic who was creating Tivoli, a utopian community upriver from Clermont, joined him in the venture and conducted most of the experiments. The weed was indigenous to the Hudson Valley; it would bring him riches, for he would "undersell the world in paper." The government issued him a patent for his invention. But alas, the paper he produced proved as brittle as the plant's leaves.

Such setbacks never discouraged Robert the Chancellor. "Mechanicks is my hobby horse," he once told Joseph Priestley. And so his meeting with Fulton simply fed his own interest. Over the years he had tried his hand at designing a steamboat, but he had produced only impractical ones that challenged the laws of the natural world. In anticipation of his success, Livingston persuaded the New York state legislature in 1798 to give him the exclusive right to operate steamboats on the Hudson, provided he produced one of twenty tons that could move against an ordinary river current with a speed of at least four miles an hour, and he had renewed it several times. Laughing at his idea and thinking nothing practical would come of it, the legislators were happy to grant the monopoly. In October 1806, the aristocrat and the penurious designer entered a compact to pro-duce steamboats, a partnership that combined Livingston's robust bankroll and political control of the river with Fulton's mechanical expertise and engineering skills. As long as Livingston provided the money and stayed away from the design table, they had a chance of succeeding.

By 1807, when both men had returned to the United States, Fulton began work on the steamboat. It would be stronger than the one he had tested on the Seine, in Paris, which a small storm had sent to the bottom of the river. As expenses at Fulton's Hudson slip rose, straining his part-ner's finances, Livingston asked his wealthy brother-in-law John Stevens, himself an engineer who was also experimenting with steamboats, if he would like to join in the venture. No, came the reply: a craft like Fulton's, long, narrow, straight-sided, and flat-bottomed, would surely sink; its paddlewheel would surely break under the stress of the current. But Fulton persevered; several investors came forward to give small amounts of money on the condition of anonymity.

Although he hadn't even completed its outfitting, by June 1807 Fulton began to worry that the rivermen would sabotage and destroy his new boat. A captain had purposely run his vessel against her at the Paulus Hook Ferry slip on the Hudson near the Newgate State Prison. As he labored to finish his new craft, he hired guards to watch over it day and night. Money was tight. Nevertheless Fulton was forced to spend more: "$20.00 to pay to the men who guard the boat," he wrote in his expense book on June 13. The rivermen kept their distance, but they knew the strange craft with its immense copper boiler and center chimney threatened their futures.

On August 9, Fulton conducted his first test on the Hudson. "She will, when in complete order, run up to my full calculations," Fulton told Livingston afterward. He had beaten all the sloops. Command of the Hudson was his. He was ready for the maiden voyage to Albany, with only one stop scheduled, at Clermont.

Encouraged by Fulton's reports, Livingston invited his family and some of his patrician friends to make the trip. "Cousin Chancellor has a wonderful new boat, which is to make the voyage up the Hudson some day soon," wrote Helen Livingston, one of Livingston's Poughkeepsie relatives, to her mother, adding "he has, with his usual kindness, invited us to be of the party." Helen made the trip with two of her cousins, Harriet, the daughter of Walter Livingston of the Manor side of the family, and Robert's younger brother John. Rounding out the group were Samuel Latham Mitchill, the physician, scholar, and legislator who had sponsored the bill giving Livingston his steam monopoly, and his wife, as well as the Anglican dean of Ripon Cathedral. For their pleasure, Fulton provided an ample store of food and spirits, including wine, brandy, and sugar.

At one o'clock on the afternoon of August 17, all was ready. Black smoke pouring from the stack drew a crowd to the shore. The party on board grew silent as the boat slowly left its slip; but then it stopped abruptly for no apparent reason in the middle of the stream. "To the silence of the preceding moment, now succeeded murmurs of discontent and agitations, whispers, and shrugs." Fulton begged their indulgence for half an hour, went below and made some adjustments. *The Steamboat,* as he called it, began to move again. "We left the fair city of New York; we passed through the romantic and ever varying scenery of the highlands."

As the day lengthened into shadows and the party joined in a song by Robert Burns, "Ye banks and braes o' bonny doon," people looked with awe from the riverbanks and the decks of sloops. All the while on board men stoked the fire with fat pine logs that sent glowing sparks up the stack to be consumed in the darkness. As the ladies settled down to sleep in the cabin and the men slept fitfully on deck, the fiery vessel plied northward.

Early in the afternoon of August 18, 1807, Chancellor Robert R. Livingston looked downriver from his landing at Clermont for the smoke of *The Steamboat.* Now sixty years old, Livingston had retired almost entirely from public life to the rustication of his estate.

At one o'clock, as he watched *The Steamboat* tie up at his dock, the chancellor no doubt understood that this was his moment of triumph. Even though his own designs had not been successful, he had been able to join with a man who succeeded despite the scorn and disparagement of people like his brother-in-law. And he had the steamboat monopoly on the Hudson. How wise he had been to renew his monopoly with the legislature, even when he had been away in Paris. He knew that many of his friends and all of his rivals, even members of his family, had thought his schemes misguided; at last he would prove them wrong. *The Steamboat* might enable him to salvage the reputation that had been tarnished in the Louisiana Purchase debacle, and also make him money.

After stopping at Clermont for the night, the party—with the chancellor aboard—embarked for Albany at 9:13 the next morning. "Our Steamboat has succeeded wonderfully well," Robert Livingston wrote to his son-in-law Robert L. Livingston; it had "reached Albany . . . in 8 hours." The following month Fulton and Livingston outfitted *The Steamboat* with two dozen sleeping berths and commenced regular service between Albany and New York. Still more passengers, as many as forty, sat up on the deck through the night. By November the chancellor reported that he and Fulton had cleared thirty-five hundred dollars each on their venture. Though neither man appears to have understood it completely, the effect of the steamboat went far beyond fattening their wallets. It began a revolution, the first of several that would take place on the Hudson in the nineteenth century.

The rivermen were upset. Their crafts had ruled the Hudson since the seventeenth century. The name "sloop" had come from the old Dutch word *sloep;* the settlers of New Netherland had adapted their Hudson River boats from the small, single-masted, fore-and-aft rigged vessels they had sailed in Holland. Half the length of Fulton's ungainly boat, they were much easier to maneuver, and their retractable keels made them ideal for sailing in the narrow shoals of the river. They boasted comfortable cabin accommodations for their passengers, and their decks were suitable for dancing. They carried packages and mail with such addresses as "care of Capt. A. Davids, Sloop *Caroline* with Box & Basket." They carried passengers from western New England who found it easier to get to New York on a sloop from Poughkeepsie or Hudson than to trek over the Berkshire Mountains to Boston. And their captains gave them evocative names rich with romance and history: the *Belvedere* and the *John Jay,* the *Mohican* and the *Commodore Jones,* the *Victory* and the *General Putnam.*

Against the most fervent hopes that the rivermen held on that August day, *The Steamboat,* which Fulton later renamed the *Clermont,* had succeeded. Once the boat began its scheduled trips between Albany and New York, they made sure that their crafts "accidentally" rammed it whenever they could; occasionally they smashed one of the paddleboards that whirled on the great wheel in the stern. But the damage was minimal. Fulton's boat survived.

The transition from wind to steam was gradual. Passenger sloops continued for many years, but they no longer dominated the waterway once Fulton's ship arrived. Schooners that carried cargoes of grain and vegetables for New York City lasted until the end of the nineteenth century. Only the introduction of great scows and barges towed by steam tugboats changed the river scene. The schooners were no match for the sheer size of these vessels that were capable of hauling cement or marble or iron.

When it came to passengers, however, the sloops could not compete with people's altered conception of time. With propitious winds, favorable currents, and an expert pilot, a sloop might sail from New York to Albany in the same time—or faster than—it took a steamboat, though this was rarely the case. But the sloop's progress was organic. Good captains knew the

Hudson intimately and understood just how far a flood or ebb tide would take their craft through one of the river's reaches. On embarking, passengers understood that their trip might take several days, or even a week. As James Fenimore Cooper remembered, the sloop's leisurely progress enabled them to enjoy "the beautiful scenery of the river."

The vessel usually ran aground, once at least, and frequently several times in a trip, and often a day or two was thus delightfully lost and gave the stranger an opportunity of visiting the surrounding countryside. A foul wind coupled with an opposing tide forced captains to lie at anchor, thus lending to the excursion something of the character of an exploring expedition.

With the advent of the *Clermont* time changed, if only because this new way of travel followed a schedule of commerce. A person boarding the boat at Albany could expect to dine in New York City the following evening. Fulton's boat signaled an important advance in the mechanization of modern culture for an individual's daily life, something that did not escape Cooper's notice: "How different, too, was the passage, from one in a steam-boat! There was no jostling of each other, no scrambling for places at table, no bolting of food, no impertinence manifested, no swearing about missing the eastern or southern boats, or Schenectady, or Saratoga, or Boston trains, on account of a screw being loose." Screws did come loose, of course, just as sloops had been becalmed or gone aground in the past. No longer was time a sequence of experiences for the traveler; the steamboat made saving time sacred. Speed of passage on the Hudson, rather than the river's beauty, became paramount in every traveler's mind.

Time was ascendant, and passengers were willing to pay Fulton expensive fees for the privilege of saving it. The least one could spend was a dollar—the equivalent of more than $15 today—for a one-way trip up to twenty miles. The journey from New York City to West Point cost $2.50; to Poughkeepsie, which took seventeen hours, was $3.50; to Hudson, thirty hours, $5; and to Albany, thirty-six hours, $7, which would be about $108 today. Meals were half a dollar; freight was three cents a pound.

That winter, 1807–8, when ice blocked the river's passage, Robert Fulton brought the *Clermont* to Red Hook, a few miles south of Robert Livingston's Clermont, for rebuilding. He made it wider, longer, and stiffer; and he changed its name to *North River*. The new craft could take "a much greater quantity of sail" to supplement the engines, had berths, a kitchen, and a steward's room below deck and a "permanent awning" above. The "strong boat" would make 120 trips a year, Fulton believed, and would enable each partner to clear $12,000 a year (about $185,000 today). That sum did not include the money the pair expected to make from their new steamboat, *The Car of Neptune,* due to be launched in May.

Clearly, in his forty-second year Robert Fulton had emerged from the privations of his early life in Pennsylvania and his failed schemes in Europe to find his destiny on the Hudson River. His association with the chancellor had elevated his social standing enough to enable him to court his partner's cousin, Harriet, the twenty-four-year-old granddaughter of the third lord of the manor who lived with her father, Walter Livingston, at Teviotdale. (She had accompanied him on the maiden voyage of *The Steamboat* to Clermont.) Fulton was celebrated in New York City as the "inventor" of the steamboat, although the acclaim was exaggerated, as he really had combined and adapted the technologies of others. Successful at last, he married Harriet in January 1808. That spring the legislature renewed Livingston and Fulton's monopoly "to use steam navigation on all the waters of New York for thirty years." With such a lock on all of New York's waters, how could they fail?

The returns from the steamboat were so great that a challenge to the monopoly was all but inevitable. It came from a family member, John Stevens, Robert Livingston's brother-in-law, who had declined to invest in Fulton's first steamboat venture. A "mechanicks" inventor himself, who held several patents for improvements to steam boilers, Stevens had joined with Livingston and another partner in a brief but ill-fated steamboat venture in 1798. As Livingston had invested most of the money, he insisted that the partners build a steamboat to his specifications. When it was launched in the Hudson, steam pressure built in the boiler and the paddlewheel turned, but the boat didn't move. Livingston and Stevens dissolved their partnership, but the chancellor was careful to keep the monopoly on the Hudson for himself. Stevens decided to build a steamboat of his own in Perth Amboy, and he threatened to sail it in the Hudson.

Incensed, Livingston threatened legal action. But Stevens was just as adamant: Fulton had appropriated some of his inventions and infringed on *his* patents, and, anyway, the monopoly given by the state of New York violated the federal Constitution, which declared, "Congress shall have the power to regulate commerce . . . among the several states." Stevens kept building. That spring he defied the monopoly and piloted his steamship *Phoenix* across the Hudson to Paulus Hook.

It was a standoff. Whenever Livingston or Fulton threatened to take Stevens to court for infringing on their steamboat designs or for operating on the Hudson, which he occasionally did, he replied that he would challenge the constitutionality of their monopoly. The deep stream of acrimony flowed on until the end of 1809. That year the trio agreed to share all patent rights on steamboats; Livingston and Fulton would retain their monopoly in New York; Stevens gained the right to run steamboats on the Connecticut, the Delaware, and several rivers in the South. The agreement saved the monopoly on the Hudson, but the challenges were far from over.

Livingston and Fulton launched the *Car of Neptune* in 1809, and the *Paragon* the following year, but it seemed that the more boats the monopolists put into the Hudson the more challenges they faced. The chancellor's dyspeptic brother John (who had once derided the steamboat by saying, "Bob has had many a bee in his bonnet before now, but this steam folly will prove the worst yet") bought the right to operate the *Raritan* between New Brunswick and New York, and proceeded to criticize every action of the monopoly. Passengers protested the steep fares, valley residents complained that the wood the boats were consuming had caused a shortage; rival entrepreneurs launched costly lawsuits that ate into the profits; and despite the cast-iron covers Fulton had placed over the paddles, rivermen still rammed the steamboats. Even the bedbugs attacked. "We have taken all the Beding out and scalded it," reported the captain of the *North River* steamboat to Livingston, but he added "I do not believe they can be got rid of without burning the Boat to Ashes."

As lawsuits and aggravations multiplied, Livingston expended much of his energy in Albany using his name and exercising his political influence to save the monopoly. But in his mind at least, the chancellor had moved on. Perhaps sensing he had little time left on earth, and recognizing that the steamboat enterprise would not yield the riches in his lifetime that he had once envisioned, he turned his thoughts to his estate on the Hudson.

His mother had rebuilt Clermont from the ashes General Vaughn left in 1777. Clermont became his sanctuary. He rose each morning at five, walked his property, inspected his animals, surveyed his gardens, and returned to breakfast served by his slaves dressed in green apparel with red piping. Sheep shearing became his hobby, which he pursued with avidity. In one of his last acts he published a lengthy treatise on domestic sheep. In a letter he addressed to "a brother agriculturist," Thomas Jefferson termed it "excellent."

By December of 1812, the chancellor was failing. "Apoplectic and paralytic seizures," his doctor told him, had left him unable to write. His doctor proceeded to treat him with bloodlettings and purgings, until he died three months later of a massive stroke. The erudite, cultured eighteenth-century squire of the Hudson had helped to found a democracy he never really trusted, and to usher in the technology that changed the landscape of his valley forever.

Learning the news of his partner's demise left Robert Fulton in shock. An even greater shock awaited him: the chancellor's will antedated even his ministry in Paris. He had made no provision for the disposition of his steamboat enterprise, and had kept irregular financial accounts. The Livingston heirs turned on Fulton, who had no means to fight them, and took over as much control of the monopoly as they could.

Fulton faced other obstacles. Rivals persisted in challenging the monopoly and his patents. He didn't advance his cause when, in January 1815, he forged a document that he claimed proved the precedence of his steam patents. The watermark on the paper proved him a fraud. The following month he contracted pneumonia after protracted exposure while supervising the outfitting of his new steam frigate *Fulton I* in Jersey City. The great doctor David Hosack hurried to his mansion in New York City, but it was too late. His pulse grew "feeble," his respiration "labored," his countenance "anxious." The next morning, at the age of forty-nine, Robert Fulton, the man who had created a transportation revolution, lay dead.

After their deaths the challenges to the Fulton and Livingston monopoly, which the chancellor's executor, John Livingston, inherited, grew intense. The steamboat might have made the Hudson River accessible to more people than ever, but travel still remained in the hands of a monopoly that determined the price for a trip, the time when a passenger might travel, and even the places along the river where the boats would land. The enterprise of river travel was still far from democratic, and other entrepreneurs wanted a change. It came with one who was rough and crude in speech and manner, who could scarcely read and write, Cornelius Vanderbilt.

From the age of sixteen Cornelius Vanderbilt showed that he knew better than anyone how to add sums of money and understand the future of commerce in the Hudson River valley. His black eyes, huge frame, and massive hands made him an intimidating presence on the deck of a schooner or a steamboat, or in a courtroom. His masterful sense of timing told him just the right moment to invest, and when to sell. He hated monopolies, except those he controlled. And through his ventures on the Hudson River he became one of the richest men in the world.

Cornelius Van Derbilt, as he preferred to call himself, grew up on a Staten Island farm overlooking the bay. He hated learning and farming, loved swimming and sailing, and from an early age dreamed of owning a boat of his own. By the spring of 1810, when Cornelius was in his sixteenth year, he made a pact with his mother: in exchange for turning eight acres of stony land into tillable soil, she would advance him one hundred dollars to buy a periauger, an open, flat-bottomed, schooner-rigged vessel that was common to the lower Hudson. In a month the land was clear; Vanderbilt bought his periauger and began regular ferry and freight service between Staten Island and the southern tip of Manhattan. By the time the ice blocked the river that winter, he had paid back his hundred-dollar loan and given his mother a thousand dollars, which represented all of his daytime and half of his nighttime earnings. He had also purchased an interest in two other periaugers.

The War of 1812 only added to Vanderbilt's fortunes, as he received a government contract to supply the fortifications on Bedloe's Island, Governors Island, and islands in the East River at night. By day he still ran his ferry. It was said that Cornelius Vanderbilt was the most reliable of all the rivermen. He now had an interest in a fleet of boats and was on the water night and day in fair weather or foul. One of his schooners, a coastal vessel named the *Charlotte*, made trips to Charleston. Somehow he found time on December 19, 1813, to come ashore and marry Sophia Johnson, his young neighbor and first cousin. Even the nuptials did not deter him from his duty. At dawn the next day Vanderbilt was at the tiller of his ferry headed to Manhattan.

He continued to prosper after the war. When Vanderbilt added up his assets at the end of 1817, he could count an interest in several periaugers and schooners and nine thousand dollars in cash, no insignificant sum for a man of twenty-three years.

But Vanderbilt realized that changes were coming on the river, and that his future was far from assured. That year Daniel Tompkins, the former governor of New York and now vice president of the United States, under James Monroe, had taken out a license to operate a steamboat line between Manhattan and Staten Island. On a rare break from his work that summer, Vanderbilt had booked a return passage to Albany on a Livingston boat. He had studied the "b'ilrs," the paddlewheels, the accommodations, the pilot house, and the decks, and he saw that the future lay with steam rather than sail. Early in 1818, Vanderbilt made his move. He sold all his boats, save several periaugers that his father now sailed on the ferry run to Manhattan, and took a job as captain on a steamboat line owned by Thomas Gibbons. The pay was $720 a year, thousands less than he had made before. The often obstinate and contentious Gibbons had a reputation for being crooked and shady, but Vanderbilt knew that Gibbons was beginning a war against his old business partner Aaron Ogden, who had recently joined the Livingston monopoly. Should his new employer break the monopoly, the Hudson River would be open to steamboats that he would build and pilot. Cornelius Vanderbilt wanted to serve as Thomas Gibbons's major general.

The fight on the Hudson flared for six years, between 1818 and 1824, and the chief weapon was the *Bellona*, a sidewheel steamboat built to Gibbons's specifications. Gibbons acquired a federal coasting license, which he maintained allowed the *Bellona* to travel between New Jersey and New York. The Livingston-Ogden monopoly, however, held the view that New York controlled the *entire* Hudson River up to the New Jersey shore, and a court in New York issued an injunction against Gibbons. Should the *Bellona* enter the Hudson, it was liable to seizure and its captain would be put under arrest. Of course, the ruling angered the state of New Jersey, for it denied its citizens the right to operate on the river. New Jersey officials made a threat of their own: they would arrest any New York lawmen who interfered in their state's commerce.

Late in 1818, Vanderbilt and Gibbons devised a mischievous strategy of playing mouse to the Livingston-Ogden cat. Invariably the mouse proved swifter. Flying a flag that proclaimed "New Jersey Must Be Free," the *Bellona* began to make runs between New Brunswick and the Battery. For twelve weeks Vanderbilt landed at Manhattan, sometimes at one dock, sometimes at another. Whenever a deputy arrived to arrest him, he would allow the man to come aboard and then pull the boat away from the dock. The official had the choice of jumping ashore or riding to an awaiting jail in New Jersey. When the Livingston-Ogden interests swore out a warrant for Vanderbilt's arrest, he hid in a secret compartment he had built below the pilot house, and directed the vessel with a series of discreet taps that he transmitted to another person in the pilot house. One time when Vanderbilt stepped ashore on Manhattan, he was promptly arrested, taken to Albany, and brought before the chancellor of the state. Only in Albany did he produce a document showing that the *Bellona* had been leased for that day to Daniel Tompkins, who had a license from the monopoly to operate on the river.

Gibbons rewarded his resourceful captain with a salary of two thousand dollars and offered him the chance to operate a derelict inn near the ferry slip at New Brunswick. Vanderbilt moved his family there. Sophia renamed it Bellona Hall and added a tavern; within a year so many travelers were stopping there that Gibbons had to build a large addition and an even larger tavern. Sophia now brought in as much money as her husband did. John Livingston tried to buy off his crafty rival with an offer of five thousand dollars and command of his largest steamboat, but Vanderbilt declined. "I don't care half so much about making money as I do about making my point and coming out ahead."

While Cornelius Vanderbilt and the New York deputies were skirmishing on the Hudson, Thomas Gibbons was not content to sit idly on the shore. At the end of 1819, after a summer of cat and mouse on the river, he sent a letter to Daniel Webster, the brilliant lawyer, orator, and congressman. He had a case before the court in New York challenging the steamboat monopoly, Gibbons wrote. "If that Court should decide against me . . . I shall carry it before the Supreme Court . . . where I shall wish your services." After Webster accepted the invitation, Gibbons dispatched Vanderbilt to Washington with the retainer, five hundred dollars in cash, for Webster.

As it had in every prior case, New York's court found in favor of the Livingston-Ogden interest. After numerous delays, Webster finally argued the case of *Gibbons v. Ogden* before the Supreme Court on the morning of February 4, 1824. The decision would define the scope of Article 1, Section 8 of the U.S. Constitution, which gave "Congress . . . the power . . . to regulate the commerce with foreign nations, and among the several States."

Webster's arguments before the bench lasted two and a half hours. He anchored his thesis on the commerce clause of the Constitution. Although New York's law gave Livingston and Fulton the exclusive right to use the steamboat in New York waters, he conceded at the outset, "the right set . . . is a monopoly . . . [and] the people of New York have the right to be protected against this monopoly." Indeed, the framers of the Constitution transferred "from the several states to a general government" the power to regulate commerce in order to "maintain an uniform and general system" of regulations. In this instance the welfare of the United States took precedence over the narrow interest of New York, and Gibbons's federal coasting license gave him the right to operate his steamboat on the Hudson.

A month later, Chief Justice John Marshall delivered the court's unanimous ninety-five-hundred-word opinion in "a low feeble voice." Nevertheless he warmed to his task of defining with greater precision the various words of the commerce clause. Commerce is the "commercial intercourse between nations, and parts of nations," he wrote. To this he added, "The mind can scarcely conceive a system for regulating commerce . . . which shall exclude all laws concerning navigation." "What is this power?" Marshall asked. "It is . . . to regulate . . . to prescribe the rule by which commerce is to be governed." The Constitution, "the supreme law," empowered Congress to regulate the coasting trade. And since, the chief justice concluded, Thomas Gibbons operated the *Bellona* under that federal regulation, the New York monopoly law as it applied to interstate commerce "is hereby reversed and annulled."

The importance of the court's decision went far beyond the Hudson in 1824; indeed, it granted Congress broad powers to pass laws that favor the interests of the national government over the states. Time and again Congress and the courts have based legislation and law on Marshall's opinion in the *Gibbons* decision. Congress had the interstate commerce clause in mind when it enacted antitrust legislation at the turn of the twentieth century. The Supreme Court referred to it frequently in labor cases in the 1930s and '40s, and it decided that Congress was correct in using the interstate commerce clause as the basis for its passage of the Civil Rights Act in 1964.

Ogden and John Livingston, who controlled the Livingston-Ogden interests, were of course devastated. They suffered yet another blow the following spring when the New York Court of Errors annulled the monopoly's exclusive right to operate on waters within the state. Aaron Ogden went to debtors' prison, lost his house, and only briefly recovered when, a year before his death in 1830, President Andrew Jackson appointed him collector of customs in Jersey City in 1829. Thomas Gibbons died a millionaire in 1826. Scrappy to the end, he divorced his wife, fought with his daughter and her husband, whom he once challenged to a duel, and cut them both from his will. Cornelius Vanderbilt, who in 1824 was just thirty years old, prospered.

In June 1825, Lafayette's great circular tour of the nation was drawing to a close. Most of the time he had ridden in carriages and stagecoaches over bad roads, or on steamboats that were by that time commonplace on the Mississippi and the Ohio, as well as the Hudson. On June 4, however, Lafayette set out from Buffalo for Albany on the grand canal of New York, the Erie. The general's trip over many of the canal's completed sections marked one of his final blessings upon the nation whose democracy he had helped to secure. New York's citizens celebrated the man and the moment: at Lockport, canal workers set off hundreds of small explosions in salute; at Rochester crowds lined both banks; at Syracuse, the reception committee served him a sumptuous breakfast; from every bridge children showered the general's boat with flowers.

The canal Lafayette saw is a testament to impassioned amateurs who overcame resistance from many who thought the idea of a shallow ditch connecting the Hudson River with the rest of the nation to the west impractical and foolish. There had been proposals for a canal across New York since the eighteenth century when Cadwallader Colden wrote that the colony offered "such a Scene of inland Navigation as cannot be parallel'd in any other Part of the World." After touring the state in 1783, George Washington envisioned "vast inland navigation of these United States" as an aid to trade and commerce. Since 1810, DeWitt Clinton had led a group of prominent New Yorkers in a vain quest to secure funding from the federal government for the canal's construction, claiming that it would benefit the nation. Though he failed at the federal level, he ran for governor in 1817 promising to build the canal. On Independence Day that year, three days after his inauguration, Governor Clinton turned the first spade of earth to begin his canal.

The Erie Canal's designers were polymaths. They had little or no engineering experience, and none professed any skills or formal training in canal building. Clinton himself set the example. An outstanding naturalist, historian, and politician, Clinton was equally comfortable writing scientific papers on pigeons, swallows, rice, wheat, or a new species of fish he had discovered at the same time he was governing the state. Other amateurs assisted him. James Geddes, a wealthy salt-mine owner, surveyed the land and established the canal's route, though he had no formal technical training; before his work on the canal he had used a level but once. Nathan Roberts, a schoolteacher from Oriskany, designed and superintended the construction of five of the canal's great locks that raise boats five hundred feet to the level of Lake Erie. Luke Hitchcock, a farmer from central New York, supervised construction of many of the waterway's locks. At the end of his life, Hitchcock also designed his own tombstone—a two-foot cube of marble on which he carved a bas-relief of a canal boat floating across a stone aqueduct on the Erie Canal.

The Erie Canal is also a testament to hundreds of European immigrants accustomed to working with stone. Primarily German and Irish, they worked ten and twelve hours daily for eighty cents a day. They shaped millions of cubic yards of earth into hundreds of miles of embankments and towpaths. They erected scores of bridges, dozens of waste weirs, and, most important of all, eighteen stone aqueducts and eighty-three locks. All this was done with primitive hand tools, carts, and teams of oxen. In just eight years they constructed a 363-mile ribbon of water, 40 feet wide and 4 feet deep, that rises over 550 feet to carry boats from the Hudson River to Lake Erie.

By Wednesday, October 26, 1825, all was ready. At ten that morning, the canal boat *Seneca Chief* left its slip at Buffalo for the trip to the Atlantic. On board were Governor DeWitt Clinton and a group of dignitaries, along with symbols of the western lands: cedar and bird's-eye maple boards from Ohio, whitefish from the Great Lakes, a Native American canoe from Lake Superior, and a small wooden barrel decorated with an American eagle and the words "WATER" and "Lake Erie" inscribed in gold. Other boats followed, forming a grand flotilla headed to Albany, where the travelers were treated to a banquet for six hundred at the city's boat basin. Seven days and dozens of speeches, parades, and grand feasts later, the *Seneca Chief* arrived at the Hudson, where a squadron of eight steamboats accompanied the craft to New York harbor.

On Friday, November 4, as the *Seneca Chief* and a fleet of barges, sloops, steamboats, and warships floated off New York's Battery, Clinton ceremonially hoisted the water barrel and poured its contents steadily into the Atlantic Ocean, save the last few ounces, which the governor proclaimed would be sent to General Lafayette, who had returned to France. It was "the Wedding of the Waters," said Clinton. Two days later a steamship towed the *Seneca Chief* back up the Hudson to Albany, where it entered the canal for its return trip to Buffalo. On board was yet another gold keg, this one filled with water from the Atlantic. Inscribed in green letters was "Neptune's Return to Pan."

The Erie Canal was more than a mere "water highway, crowded with the commerce of two worlds, till then inaccessible to each other," as Nathaniel Hawthorne once called it. By uniting the eastern and western slopes of the Appalachians, this water highway transformed the nation. It conquered the distance of the vast land and brought a flood of settlers into the West. Thousands of people from the eastern states, including recent immigrants from Europe, traveled over the Erie Canal to settle in the northern regions of Ohio, Indiana, and Illinois, as well as in the territories of Wisconsin and Iowa. And the canal boats that floated west with immigrants returned with cheap grain. By the end of the decade, the governor of Georgia was complaining that in Savannah it was cheaper to buy wheat from central

New York than from central Georgia. That grain traveled south down the Hudson to waiting ships in New York, the busiest of all ports in the United States. After 1826, a traveler who wanted the cheapest and fastest route from Philadelphia to Pittsburgh, instead of traveling west across Pennsylvania, sailed north to New York, then up the Hudson, through the canal to Lake Erie, and then followed the wagon road south to Pittsburgh.

The Erie Canal spawned yet more waterways: Ohio built a canal to link the Great Lakes with the Mississippi Valley; Pennsylvania built nearly a thousand miles of canals and inclined planes over the Alleghenies. New York had already opened the Champlain Canal connecting the Hudson with commerce on Lake Champlain and in Canada. The Delaware and Hudson Canal followed in 1828. It connected the port of Kingston with Pennsylvania's anthracite mines, thereby enabling boats to bring coal to Kingston and ultimately to the furnaces and stoves of New York City. Alexis de Tocqueville saw these waterways as a means of "bringing the achievements of industry and thought quickly from one place to another."

The consequences of the Erie Canal were both material and spiritual. After a boat trip across the state, Nathaniel Hawthorne reflected: "Surely the water of this canal must be the most fertilizing of all fluids, for it causes towns with their masses of brick and stone, their churches and theatres, their business . . . to spring up." The novelist imagined the surprise of the sleepy Dutchmen when the "new river" brought them cash and foreign commodities for "their hitherto unmarketable produce," and looked to the time when "the wondrous stream" would "flow between two continuous lines of building . . . from Buffalo to Albany." His prediction wasn't far off. The canal did create towns along its path, some of the first edge cities in America.

"We delight in the promised sunshine of the future," proclaimed one of the orators at the canal's opening. He was, of course, thinking of America's future ordained by God. The engineering triumph of the great waterway signaled to all that the divinely ordained completion of "God's work" was a testament to the creative powers of America's democracy.

The canal changed the economy of the Hudson Valley. Even by the time of Lafayette's visit in 1824, the finished sections were generating more than $300,000 in tolls annually; a quarter century later they were taking in more than $3 million. Troy became one of the nation's most important industrial centers, most famous before the Civil War for its production of iron. Hundreds of thousands of tons of cargo passed through Albany each year. In 1823 the city commenced building a four-thousand-foot-long basin in the Hudson to accommodate the shipping traffic. "The pier, which encloses the basin on the river side," Theodore Dwight reported in his guidebook *The Northern Traveller,* "is built of logs, and wide enough for a spacious street. It is a place of deposit for vast quantities of lumber." He went on to note that in 1825 "there were 9594 arrivals and departures of canal boats at Albany, with 165,000 barrels of flour, and near 16 million feet of plank and boards. 23,292 tons of merchandise also, went north and west."

The increasing number of ships and steamboats on the river brought about by the opening of the Erie Canal, as well as population increases and the abundance of sloops, made dredging and dike building between the city of Hudson and Albany imperative. Dominated by marshlands or "flats," the reaches on this part of the river had challenged navigators since 1609 when Robert Juet reported "we borrowed so here the shaore, that we grounded," and after heaving off "we borrowed on the banke in the channell, and came aground againe." The Upper and Lower Overslaugh, the narrow sand flats just south of Albany, proved to be especially tricky for captains. In October 1800, John Maude, a visitor from Britain traveling from Albany to New York City, kept a precise log of his adventure: "5:00 PM. Embarked. . . . 5:30 PM Grounded on the Upper Overslaugh. . . . 7:00 PM Grounded on the Lower Overslaugh. . . . there was no prospect of our getting over this shoal till the tide had attained its highest point." Maude concluded, "The remedy is easy: block up all the channels except one, and the water will accumulate there and keep it ever free.

DeWitt Clinton proposed just such a series of parallel dikes to straighten the passage. Constructed with rocks and pilings, the dikes constricted the river's flow and prevented the banks from eroding, and the increased turbulence in the narrow channel helped to keep the silt from settling to the bottom. Dredging, something Clinton also championed, became more common by midcentury. Steam engines powered huge buckets that scoured the river bottom and deposited the fill between the dikes and the shore. Over time the Hudson was reshaped into a straighter, narrower, and deeper waterway.

Farmers in the valley worried that the Erie Canal would be far from an unalloyed blessing for their own fields, and their fears were confirmed even before the line of water reached Lake Erie. As early as 1822 mills in Rochester began grinding wheat from the Genesee Valley, and two decades later the city ranked as the most important flour-milling center in the nation. Hudson Valley farmers had long considered their fields the breadbasket of New York City, but now Manhattan bakers looked to the west for cheaper flour. Gristmills on the banks of the larger creeks that fed the river went idle.

The steamboat and the Erie Canal served as bellwethers of the democratic change that was slowly taking hold across the valley. Though the costs for passage were initially high, steamboats gave more people access to the river than ever before. (After the Supreme Court's decision in *Gibbons v. Ogden,* people enjoyed more steamboats and cheaper fares.) The Erie Canal brought more goods than ever before to those with limited means. The population in the valley began to grow. And both the steamboats and the canal helped redefine the idea of wealth. Before this time one acquired wealth in the valley by accumulating land and trade. Now men were making vast sums of money in great new enterprises, including shipping goods and people, banking, and providing vast tenements for immigrants. The smooth mold of social relations as the Livingstons and Van Rensselaers knew it was shattering.

While men like Vanderbilt prospered with their newly minted wealth, the older families, Livingstons and Van Rensselaers especially, were facing a series of challenges from within and without, but the most important were money and proprietorship of the land. Of the wealthiest Americans in 1800 (individuals who had $10,000 or more), Stephen Van Rensselaer, eighth Patroon of Rensselaerwyck, was the wealthiest, with $3.5 million. Margaret Beekman Livingston, wife of Robert the Judge, ranked second with $1 million. Twenty-six other Livingstons and one Van Rensselaer also had places on the list. Other venerable New York names appeared as well, people like Peter Stuyvesant III, who had made $750,000 in real estate, and Thomas Buchanan, whose $500,000 came from trade. The source of the Livingston and Van Rensselaer wealth was primarily inheritance and rents from inherited land, and the value of the land itself. The lands that Robert Livingston and Kiliaen van Rensselaer had acquired in the seventeenth century now passed to a new generation of family members who clustered primarily on Manhattan Island and on the east bank of the Hudson.

But the Livingstons, along with the Dutch patroons the Van Rensselaers to the north, faced an even greater challenge than loss of status. For more than a century they had been engaged in a protracted and smoldering war with their tenants, who had the temerity to challenge the foundation of manorial society, the payment of rent.

Even by 1840 few of the residents living on Van Rensselaer lands in Rensselaer County and Livingston lands in Columbia County owned their property outright; instead, they leased their land. The eighth patroon, Stephen Van Rensselaer, had rented his land on a "durable lease" that lasted as long as the family survived. His freeholders had paid an annual rent of about ten bushels of wheat per hundred acres, "four fat fowl," and a day's work with a team of horses or oxen and a wagon. Livingston leases were similar but lasted only for two generations before the land reverted to the manor lord. Freeholders could sell their improvements to another family, but they generally had to pay a quarter of their value to their master.

In the minds of the manor lords the system had worked well since its inception in the seventeenth century. Grateful farmers, so the thinking went, brought their grain and fat fowl to the manor and happily gave a day of their labor with a team and wagon to their master; Livingstons and Van Rensselaers, Van Cortlandts and Philipses, all accepted the same logic with aristocratic and patronizing kindness. Agents and sheriffs were sent to collect from those ungrateful louts who failed to pay homage.

In theory the system worked, but the reality was altogether another matter. The freehold system had always been an anomaly on American soil. From time to time, the tenants had been known to revolt. "Robert Livingston, Kiss his Ass," shouted a rebellious eighteenth-century farmer over his shoulder as he fled one of the third proprietor's agents who had been sent to quell an early land uprising. From time to time farmers threatened their lord, but as officials in Albany sided with the landowners, these minor skirmishes came to naught. Over the years the resentment grew. Many had escaped aristocratic domination in Europe only to find themselves living in the Hudson Valley where archaic laws prevented them from owning land and obligated them to pay rent to a manor lord. Many chose default over payment.

By the nineteenth century the system had begun to break down. The procrustean arrangement did not account for economic realities like the condition of the land, the price of wheat, changes in the weather, or the health and age of the farmer. Still the same number of fowls and bushels of wheat, the same day's labor, came due each year. After fighting a Revolution to throw off the yoke of a European master, the freeholders were quick to see that they were still not entirely free. Every Fourth of July they gathered in the river villages and towns to celebrate their independence from tyranny, only to return that evening to their houses and fields knowing that they were still held in the thrall of their master on the Hudson River.

On January 26, 1839, Stephen Van Rensselaer III, graduate of Harvard College, founder of Rensselaer Polytechnic Institute, former state assemblyman, state senator, and lieutenant governor, member of the United States House of Representatives, and major general in the New York state militia; chancellor of the State University of New York and president of the Erie Canal Commission; husband of Margaret Schuyler, the daughter of General Philip Schuyler, and following her death, of Cornelia Patterson, the daughter of William Patterson, governor of New Jersey and associate justice of the Supreme Court of the United States; and eighth and last Patroon of Rensselaerwyck, died at the age of seventy-five at his house on Manor Street in Albany. Van Rensselaer had been the most modern and forward-thinking of the Hudson River aristocrats, and sometimes he suffered from the unintended consequences of his endeavors. He had promoted agriculture in the valley and welcomed farmers who headed west from New England into Rensselaerwyck. For two decades between 1790 and 1810, Rensselaerwyck actually grew faster than New York City. But the eighth patroon had also championed the construction of the Erie Canal, the very enterprise that brought financial ruin to many of his tenants.

It was Stephen Van Rensselaer's death that helped precipitate the latest and the last battle of the rent wars that had begun in the seventeenth century. Starting about 1818, the year of the first serious financial crisis that brought about the closing of banks and foreclosures on property, Van Rensselaer had allowed his tenants to reduce or even defer altogether payment of their rents if they could not afford to make them. The nation recovered by 1822, but farmers in the Hudson Valley, including those in Rensselaerwyck, suffered from the cheap wheat produced in the west. The general financial panic of 1837 only made their condition more precarious. By 1839, Van Rensselaer's tenants stood about $400,000 in arrears on their rent; nevertheless, since their patroon had been so lenient during his lifetime, they felt sure their debts would be forgiven after his death.

It was not to be. The executors found that Van Rensselaer himself had piled up more than $300,000 of debt, and his will directed his two sons, Stephen and William, to collect the back rents to pay it off. When Stephen Van Rensselaer IV, who inherited the Rensselaerwyck lands on the west side of the Hudson, demanded immediate payment from his tenants, he set off the Helderberg War, so named for the steep hills twenty miles west of the river where Van Rensselaer's agents met with the greatest resistance. The young Van Rensselaer dispatched sheriffs with writs to evict the tenants from their land, but whenever they approached, the farmers blew on tin horns to summon their fellow anti-renters. Often wearing calico dresses (hemmed at the knee) and covering their heads with sheepskins, arming themselves with guns and alcohol, these "Indians," as they called themselves, burned the writs, threatened violence, and sometimes employed tar and feathers to drive off the lawmen.

By 1844 the anti-rent sentiment had become a movement throughout the valley. Anti-renters began a newspaper, *The Freeholder*. They organized themselves into small cells, ready to don their dresses and sheepskins whenever they heard the call of the tin horn. It was now a matter of their independence. Even if they had the means to pay, the tenants were on strike:

Strike till the last armed foe expires,
Strike for your altars and your fires—
Strike for the green graves of your sires,
God and your happy homes!

COMPLAINTS OF THE RENTERS OF VAN RENSSELAER'S MANOR, read one anti-rent pamphlet: "*Unequal* ratio of taxation"; the landlords "reserve all water powers, all mines, ores and mineral beds, of every name and nature"; "this system of things, as practised on the renters of the Rensselaer and Livingston manors, has an improper bearing on the freedom of the Elective Franchises, through *fear* of oppression." These were, so the complaints maintained, "figments of the old *feudal* system of Baronial law in Europe."

The tin-horn rebellion jumped from the west to the east bank of the river into the lands owned by William Van Rensselaer and the Livingstons. Chief provocateur and leader was Smith A. Boughton, a Middlebury-educated medical doctor who practiced in the tiny Rensselaerwyck village of Alps, about twelve miles inland from the Hudson. When he wasn't pulling teeth, setting broken bones, or delivering babies, Boughton worked to incite his fellow tenants against William Van Rensselaer. "I could not stand idle," he wrote later in life, "and see thousands deprived of their natural and, as I conceived, social and legal rights." By 1844 the doctor enlarged his sphere to include the Livingston tenants in Columbia County. Crowds of angry tenants listened. The mood grew violent. In Claverack a man was murdered for refusing to shout "Down with the Rent"; Boughton was soon arrested and hauled off to the city of Hudson to stand trial; the governor called out troops to maintain order. At the trial, lawyers for the defense and the prosecution had a fistfight before Boughton was convicted for the crime of seizing and destroying the sheriff's eviction notices. The judge sentenced the doctor to life in state prison.

Justice, so the Livingstons and Van Rensselaers believed, had been served. Few others agreed. Dr. Boughton might languish in prison, but his conviction only served to solidify the opposition. Tenants still refused to pay their annual rents and "Indian" raids continued up and down the Hudson and to the west. If payments weren't forthcoming, the lords sent a sheriff along with a posse to evict the tenants. When sheriffs tried to auction off property, they often had no bidders. At other times property, especially livestock, would "disappear" just before it went on the block. Winning bidders for farmsteads and barns found their new property in flames.

In 1846 New York ratified a new state constitution that abolished manorial tenure. Still, lawsuits over ownership lingered in the valley, where the landholders remained intransigent. On February 1, 1847, the state's new governor, who had been elected with anti-rent support, pardoned Dr. Boughton and other anti-renters. Lawsuits continued until late 1852, when the chief justice of New York's Court of Appeals decided that the Van Rensselaers actually were no longer landlords and had no power to collect rents. Stephen Van Rensselaer IV immediately put his family's land up for sale.

It might be presumed that after successive generations of dealing with threats from sullen tenants, foreclosures, attacks on property and persons, fires, and occasional shootings, the Van Rensselaer and Livingston families would be only too happy to divest themselves of the burden of being liege lords on the Hudson. Yet the opposite was the case. Since the days of Kiliaen and Robert the Founder, land and a quiet lordship had defined their being. No matter the headaches that came with the land, their vast holdings gave them a sense of entitlement as well as status in Albany, New York City, and the nation. In times past their land had brought them considerable wealth as well. But by this time Livingston money was diminishing, and the eighth patroon had left his sons with huge debts. The extension of universal suffrage to white males diluted their family's power at the ballot box, as evidenced by the change in New York's laws governing their rent system. Livingston and Van Rensselaer family dominance in the Hudson Valley was on the wane, but family pride was increasing in inverse proportion to family fortunes.

Yet another sign of the decline of the manor lords and the fragmentation of society was the advent of the railroad. Though Alexis de Tocqueville recognized that Americans are quick to embrace advances in the speed of communication, the French observer had failed to consider the Hudson Valley. Just four years after Governor Clinton officiated over the marriage of the waters, the Delaware and Hudson Canal Company began the first steam-powered railroad in the United States. By 1831, Tocqueville would remark that the young republic "already has more railways than France." But it wasn't until midcentury that a railroad line had been built to follow the natural corridor of the Hudson River.

The dream of a railroad along the course of the river began in the 1830s. Chief dreamer was the English-born brewer, whaling ship owner, and, later, women's college founder Matthew Vassar from Poughkeepsie. Along with others, Vassar was unhappy that his city of nearly thirteen thousand people was being passed by as New York and Albany grew. Steamboats had taken to bypassing the city too, preferring the wharves at Kingston and

Newburgh on the west bank of the river. When they did stop, the boats provided only limited service, and for ninety to a hundred days during the winter months when ice clogged the river Poughkeepsie was entirely isolated. If a rail line were to connect Poughkeepsie with New York and Albany, Vassar reasoned, it would cut the travel time in half to those cities and Poughkeepsie would prosper. In 1842 a group of engineers Vassar had hired reported that it would be cheapest to site the tracks along the river's eastern shore about five feet above the water.

Although the report was entirely favorable, Vassar had not counted on the opposition of steamboat owners who viewed the railroad as a threat to their monopoly on transportation through the valley. The number of boats carrying passengers had grown from sixteen in 1826, two years after the *Gibbons v. Ogden* decision, to about one hundred. As many as seven steamboats ran between New York and Albany each day. Though the dozen steam companies that operated boats on the river were bitter rivals, they agreed to join together to stop the railroad. They used their influence to have the state legislature deny the brewer the charter he needed for construction. Like the sloop owners before them, they resisted the inevitable.

The idea of a railroad up the Hudson, however, could not be stopped. In 1846, James Boorman, an English-born merchant from New York, put together a syndicate of directors that raised $3 million to build the line, and sold another $3 million in stock to the public. He called it the Hudson River Railroad and, over the protests of steamboat owners, procured a charter from the legislature. All that Boorman needed was a competent engineer to build his railroad.

The directors turned to John Bloomfield Jervis. Regarded by many as the foremost engineer in America, Jervis had learned engineering on the Erie Canal. He began in 1817 as an axman, clearing trees along the route of the waterway, but soon was promoted to a rodman on the surveyor team. When he wasn't working on the canal he was studying surveying and engineering, and he soon took charge of seventeen miles of the canal. Later he took on more and more demanding assignments, and by 1825 he was supervising the engineering and construction of about fifty miles of the entire route. Jervis had led other engineering projects: he designed the entire Delaware and Hudson Canal that enabled boats to bring anthracite coal from Pennsylvania's mines to the city of Kingston, and ultimately to the furnaces and stoves of New York City; he had built the Croton Aqueduct that supplied New York with its drinking water; and he had served as chief engineer of the Mohawk and Hudson Railway, the first railroad in the state. A major port on the Delaware and Hudson Canal, Port Jervis, was named in his honor. Jervis warmed to the task of building a rail line up the Hudson. Not only did he determine the best route but in newspaper articles and official reports he tirelessly promoted the advantages of trains over steamboats. A train, Jervis declared, would run year round, be more convenient, and take just five hours to travel between New York and Albany, half the time of a steamboat.

The river route Jervis chose for the railroad is the exact one that can be seen today, hugging the eastern shore of the Hudson, sometimes just a few feet from the water. The route allowed Jervis to build without concern for significant grade changes and, except in places in the Highlands, without the necessity of building tunnels. It is more or less straight, too, for across most bays Jervis constructed causeways for the tracks. Though he did have difficulties drilling some of the tunnels, and had to halt work because of an outbreak of cholera among the laborers, he was able to prevail. By the end of 1849, the first Hudson River Railroad engine steamed into the station at Poughkeepsie; two years later the line reached East Albany. The railroad ran eight trains a day each way between New York City and Albany and cut travel time to just four hours. A new era in travel through the valley had begun.

"It was a happy thought to build the Hudson river railroad right along the shore," Walt Whitman wrote in his autobiographical memoir *Specimen Days*. "The grade is already made by nature; you are sure of ventilation one side—and you are in nobody's way." Of course, Whitman's sensibilities of the mid nineteenth century, when land seemed unlimited, were not those of the valley dweller in the mid twentieth whose small parcel of space along the Hudson was dear, or the city dweller who saw the tracks as a despoiling barrier to the water. Moved by the excitement and force of steam locomotion, Whitman believed that the rails would bind America. The railroad on the shore of the Hudson was part of a greater, divine mission:

Lo, soul, seest thou not God's purpose from the first?
The earth to be spann'd, connected by network,

The races, neighbors, to marry and be given in marriage,
The oceans to be cross'd, the distant brought near,
The lands to be welded together.

For Whitman, the railroad was also part of the greater scene of progress. "I see, hear, the locomotives and cars, rumbling, roaring, flaming, smoking, constantly," he wrote in his enumerative style. The sounds moved him; express trains "thundered and lightened" along. And at night, "far down you see the headlight approaching, coming steadily on like a meteor." The engines added to the "twinkling" scene on the river, "the husky panting of the steamers" and the "sloops' and schooners' shadowy forms, like phantoms, white, silent, indefinite, out there. Then the Hudson of a clear moonlight night."

Not everyone considered the advent of the trains a blessing, however. As the railroad began to cut into the profits of the steamboat companies, they responded with a rate war. The steamboat *Hendrick Hudson* cut its fare for passage between Albany and New York City to fifty cents; the *Kosciusko* to six and a quarter cents. Still, the steamboat lines held on. They would not begin to collapse until later in the century when Commodore Vanderbilt, who by then had turned his attention to railroads, decided to acquire the Hudson River Railroad and take on his former colleagues the way he had the Livingston-Ogden monopoly nearly four decades earlier.

Nor were landowners along the eastern shore of the river happy with the railroad. They had fought against giving easements for the tracks that would cut them off from their river. The Livingstons felt the intrusion of the tracks as much as any other family. The trains passing Clermont rattled the china, and the coal-burning engines sometimes left a wake of sparks that threatened to ignite the brush. Shortly after the railroad was finished, one of Chancellor Livingston's nieces, Margaret, who lived at Barrytown in a Greek Revival house she had built at the river's edge in 1820, declared the railroad a monstrous intrusion, left for Belgium, and never returned.

But most landowners resigned themselves to the inevitable encroachment of civilization upon their rural landscape. "If the Garden of Eden were now on earth," Washington Irving wearily grumbled from Sunnyside, his house near Tarrytown on the banks of the Hudson, "they would not hesitate to run a railroad through it." Like many, Irving was ambivalent.

Outing on the Hudson, by an unknown artist, ca. 1850. In addition to the merry scene
the painting portrays, the city, the steamboat, the bridge, and even the tree stump
in the foreground show some of the effects humans have had on the river's landscape.
(Abby Aldrich Rockefeller Art Museum, Colonial Williamsburg Foundation,
Williamsburg, Virginia)

He prized "the sweet quiet" of Sunnyside, which he called his "little rural nest"; but he cheerfully accepted the thirty-five hundred dollars the
railroad company paid him for the easement. He complained bitterly to
one of the Hudson River Railroad's directors about the "diabolical blasts"
from the engine's whistle that "left me in a deplorable state of nervous
agitation for upward of an hour"; but from 1846 until his death at Sunnyside in 1859, Washington Irving always took the train when he went to
New York City.

Outing on the Hudson, a delightfully primitive painting by an unknown artist of about 1850, depicts a group of people on the shore beside the river

and a small, sheltered bay. It is a gay scene: adults and children and dogs gambol on the shore in the foreground beside the bay. Some of the adults are courting while the children play with their dogs; one flies a red balloon. And the scene reveals, too, that humans have helped to shape the landscape. A tree stump appears in the center and a couple crosses a bridge that spans a rude declivity. Steamboats and sloops ply the water, while across the river, at the foot of mountain peaks, a small town nestles on the shore. Smoke rises from its red brick buildings, telling us of industry and prosperity within. All is peaceful, for directly and indirectly, the steamboat, the railroad, the rising tide of population in New York, the port, the Palisades, the Highlands, the Catskills, the cities great and small that were strung along the east and west riverbanks between New York and Albany, all helped make the Hudson River into an icon of America's nineteenth-century sensibilities.

Steam made the possibility of excursion accessible to all. For Ralph Waldo Emerson, who traveled by train through the valley after the Civil War, the Hudson was *the* river. He thought "that Nature had marked the site of New York with such a rare combination of advantages, as she now and then furnishes a man or woman to a perfection in all parts, and in all details, as if to know the luxuriant type of the race; finishing in one what is attempted or only begun in a thousand individuals." Surely, he thought, "the length and volume of the river; the gentle beauty of the banks; the country rising immediately behind the bank on either side; the noble outlines of the Catskills; the breadth of the bays at Croton and Tarrytown; then, West Point; then as you approach New York, the sculpted Palisades;—then, at the city itself, the meeting of the waters, the river like Sound; and the Ocean at once,—instead of the weary Chesapeake and Delaware Bays."

Nor were the beauties of the Hudson exclusively for the enjoyment of Americans. During the nineteenth century a multitude of Europeans descended on the river. "However widely European travelers have differed about other things in America," wrote the English social reformer Harriet Martineau, "all seem to agree in their love of the Hudson." Martineau recalled meeting a gentleman on her visit in 1835 who booked passage on a steamboat between Albany and New York for the entire summer. From the deck he stood "gazing at the shores all day long with apparently undiminished delight." While she was in America, Martineau herself took three trips up the river. As she looked out upon the water at Hyde Park one morning, she had a transcendental vision that rivaled those of her American friends Emerson or Hawthorne:

> I experienced a sensation which I had often heard of, but never quite believed in; the certainty that one has awakened in another world. . . . This night I left my window open close to my head, so that I could see the stars reflected on the river. When I woke the scene was in the light of the sunrise, and as still as death. Its ineffable beauty was all; I remarked no individual objects; but my heart stood still with an emotion which I should be glad to think I may feel again whenever I really do enter a new scene of existence.

Until roughly the late nineteenth century it was a halcyon time on the Hudson, a time when steam seemed to make all things possible. Steamboats and steam engines brought businessmen from Albany to New York; steamboats brought young beauties to West Point for dances with their cadets; steamboats brought the Prince of Wales to review the battalions and watch artillery fire from the battlements across the river; and steam power brought the actress Fanny Kemble who, looking out from the Highlands, believed she had been carried into the "immediate presence of God." For Kemble, the Hudson had brought her to the sublime.

CHAPTER 7

Definers of the Landscape

Since 1609, when Henry Hudson's first mate Robert Juet remarked in his journal that "this is a very good Land to fall with and a very pleasant Land to see," travelers have looked upon the Hudson River valley in wonder and delight. About two hundred years after Juet sailed into the river, artists and entrepreneurs began to shape their impressions of the valley in a conscious way. The result was the first American literature that gained the attention of readers in Europe, the first indigenous school of art, and one of the first outlines of architectural precepts that sought to shape American taste. Although the aesthetic began in one region of the nation, it was national and even international in its importance.

Yet at the same time that American artists were creating their aesthetic, others were exploiting the landscape for financial gain. Some sought to capitalize on its beauty by bringing visitors into the valley so that they might take pleasure from all they saw, and not incidentally spend their money doing so. These entrepreneurs offered amusements and recreation for people of leisure. Still other entrepreneurs chose to ignore aesthetic considerations altogether. For them the valley's abundant resources were a means to an end.

The effect of the Hudson Valley on Washington Irving's aesthetic sensibilities began in the spring of 1800, when he took his first trip up the river. As was the case with so much of what he wrote, his memory embellished the actual experience. His spirit had been so dulled by continual slogging through legal documents in his reluctant preparation for a career in the law, Irving remembered, that he decided to visit his sisters upstate. A relative engaged a sloop captain "of the old Dutch stocks" and his crew of slaves, to whom he spoke Dutch; after a delay waiting for cargo, the vessel slipped slowly from its dock into the Hudson. It was from the deck of the sloop that Irving first experienced "with intense delight" the Highlands and the Catskill Mountains.

As the craft "slowly floated along" at the foot of the "stern" mountains that challenge the river at the entrance to the Highlands, Irving looked up with awe at the cliffs. Eagles were "sailing and screaming" around him; he heard an "unseen stream dashing down precipices" and beheld rocks and trees, cloud and sky, reflected in the "glassy stream of the river." At dusk, when the captain anchored his sloop at the foot of the mountains, and

Opposite: Thomas Cole, *View of Round-Top in the Catskill Mountains,* 1827. "The mist below the mountain began first to be lighted up," Cole wrote of this sunrise scene looking southeast from his vantage point in the Catskills across the Hudson Valley, "and the trees on the tops of the lower hills, cast their shadows over the misty surface." The artist often depicted the wildness of nature, as in the storm-blasted rock and withered tree of the foreground. (Museum of Fine Arts, Boston; gift of Martha C. Karolik for the M. and M. Karolik Collection of American Paintings, 1815–1865; photograph © 2005 Museum of Fine Arts, Boston)

"every thing grew dark and mysterious," Irving heard the "plaintive note of the whip-poor-will" and "was startled now and then by the sudden leap and heavy splash of the sturgeon."

The next day he saw the Catskills for the first time, the mountains that were to have "the most witching effect upon his boyish imagination."

> Never shall I forget . . . them predominating over a wide extent of the country, part wild, woody, and rugged; part softened away into all the graces of cultivation. As we slowly floated along, I lay on the deck and watched them through a long summer's day; undergoing a thousand mutations under the magical effects of atmosphere; sometimes seeming to approach; at other times to recede; now almost melting into hazy distance, now burnished by the setting sun, until, in the evening, they printed themselves against the glowing sky in deep purple of an Italian landscape.

Although the landscape had no associations with a European past of castles, ancient villages, and myths, he strove to connect the quality of light to an Italian sunset. The valley's atmosphere altered Irving's imagination forever. The spell of the Hudson landscape was upon him.

Irving began his writing career as a merry prankster and wearer of masks; it was a fictional pose he could never quite abandon. Living in New York City, he found much in current politics, fashion, and intellectual endeavor to satirize. In 1805 "Jonathan Oldstyle" wrote letters about contemporary manners to the editor of *The Morning Chronicle*. Several years later, Irving and some like-minded juvenile friends created a satirical magazine called *Salmagundi*. Satire came naturally to one who was instinctively a Federalist follower of Alexander Hamilton and naturally distrusted Thomas Jefferson's democratic mob. Irreverent and disrespectful, audacious and fresh, *Salmagundi* was New York City's cultural graffiti.

His first book, *A History of New York*, was published in 1809, and it made Washington Irving famous. It began as a spoof on Samuel Latham Mitchill's *The Picture of New-York; or The Traveller's Guide through the Commercial Metropolis of the United States*, a book that purported to present a history of the state from the time of the natives to the present in just fifty pages. Behind the mask of the pen name Diedrich Knickerbocker, Irving presented a satirical history of Dutch New York. As was the case with *Salmagundi*, he treated Jefferson and the Republicans savagely, but the humor, mystery, and insight that he found at the heart of the people who had settled the Hudson Valley proved to be more enduring. Through his pen Irving gives historical figures new life as comedic characters. Thus Wouter van Twiller, the early director-general of New Netherland, becomes Walter the Doubter, a man of vacant face and "two small gray eyes" that twinkle "feebly . . . like two stars of lesser magnitude in a hazy firmament"; his successor Willem Kieft becomes William the Testy, with "a temperament as hot as an old radish, and a mind subject to perpetual whirlwinds and tornadoes"; and Stuyvesant becomes Peter the Headstrong, whose noble virtues were "stowed away in a corner of his heart . . . where they flourished . . . like so many sweet wild flowers, shooting forth and thriving with redundant luxuriance among stubborn rocks."

Knickerbocker's nonsensical and edge-of-madness accounts lend a vividness to the land and people of New Amsterdam and the Hudson Valley. The river is never far from the story, though the Dutch seem oblivious to the magic that had so stirred Irving on his first voyage. Of Stuyvesant's boat trip up the Hudson, Irving spent a chapter describing the spell of the scenery. At sunset, the "vast bosom" of the Tappan Zee appeared "like an unruffled mirror, reflecting the golden splendor of the heavens." The twilight seems to ignite the imagination. The rocks appear as "lofty towers," the trees as "mighty giants." Irving describes the "vast prison" of the Highlands that held the waters of the river in "admantine chains" until at last "the lordly Hudson, in his irresistible career toward the ocean, burst open their prison house." But the description is lost on Peter the Headstrong and the "vacant" minds of his crewmen. They remain oblivious to the enchantment about them.

After the *History* appeared in early December 1809, readers, at least those who weren't Dutch, declared their love for Diedrich Knickerbocker and asked for more. Some with Dutch forebears took offense, and several families "never forgave" him for the ridicule. "It took with the public, and gave me celebrity, as an original work was something remarkable and uncommon in America," Irving wrote. "I was . . . caressed." But by 1810, mourning the death of his fiancée, Matilda Hoffman, his first and only love, Irving had grown profoundly bored with his Dutch persona. Matilda had succumbed to consumption the previous April; work on the *History* had sustained him in the initial stages of his grief. Now that the book was launched, he sought solace in travel; to Peekskill in the Highlands he went, notebook in hand, for a drowsy visit: "29 Morning—5 o'clock sky perfectly clear," he entered in his notebook. "Sun not up yet a soft below yellowish light over the landscape—perfectly calm—river like a glass. In some places almost black from the dark shadows of the mountains, in others the colour of the heavens long sheets of mist suspended in mid air halfway up the mountains. . . . Sound of the cattle bells from opposite shore cocks crowing—roll of a drum from West Point." Notebook entries like this reveal the impact that the mystery of the Hudson had on Irving, a mystery that he would draw upon in his two greatest tales from the "Posthumous Writing" of Diedrich Knickerbocker, "Rip Van Winkle" and "The Legend of Sleepy Hollow."

We have grown up with these tales: Rip, who falls asleep high in the Catskill Mountains where he has climbed with his gun and faithful hound to escape the nagging of his termagant wife, and who meets with Henry Hudson and his men resembling "figures in an old Flemish painting," only to learn when he awakens two decades later that a revolution has passed him by; the story of Ichabod Crane, the hapless Yankee schoolmaster "of small shrewdness and simple credulity," from farther down the Hudson at Tarry-town on the Tappan Zee, who woos Katrina Van Tassel, the daughter of a prosperous Dutch farmer, only to be scared off by his rival Brom Bones and the fantastically conceived, chimerical Headless Horseman.

With "Rip Van Winkle" and "The Legend of Sleepy Hollow," Irving creates a literary version of the Hudson. It is the Hudson—river and valley—that threads its way through both tales. After he climbs into the Catskills, Rip surveys "the lordly Hudson, far, far below him, moving on its silent but majestic course, with the reflection of a purple cloud, or the sail of a lagging bark here and there sleeping on its glassy bosom, and at last losing itself in the blue highlands."

It is the mountains that hold the greatest mystery. They "have always been a region full of fable," Irving tells us in the postscript to his story. They were home to the great Manitou. Just before he falls into his sleep, Rip sees "a deep mountain glen, wild, lonely, and shagged, . . . scarcely lighted by the rays of the setting sun." Just as he thinks he must descend to "the terrors of Dame Van Winkle," he hears the repetitive siren call of his name urging him into the wild, where he meets "the short, square-built old fellow" carrying a stout keg filled with the liquorous release from care. In the Catskills, Irving finds a gentler region of the spirit free of ordinary cares.

Of course, the mystery lives first in Irving's mind before he plants it in ours. When Irving writes that the place, "under the sway of some witching power," causes people "to walk in a continual reverie," we cannot help but think that he is remembering his own past and rendering his own infatuation with the land in his tale. For Irving it is in such "little retired Dutch valleys, found here and there embosomed in the great State of New York, that population, manners, and customs remain fixed, while the great torrent of migration and improvement, which is making such incessant changes in other parts of this restless country, sweeps by them unobserved."

In the landscape of Tarrytown on the shore of the Tappan Zee, the Connecticut native Ichabod Crane also finds an enchanted region. This is the land of Major André's capture. "In this by place of nature," as Irving called it, "a drowsy, dreamy influence" seems to "pervade the very atmosphere." Naturally skeptical of schooling, the people of the hollow resist the gaunt man who reads to them extracts from Cotton Mather and dreams of winning "the blooming" Katrina Van Tassel. For Crane, Sleepy Hollow is but a place to "tarry" in his larger quest to migrate to the West. With Katrina, "a whole family of children," and "a wagon loaded with household trumpery," he will set out "for Kentucky, Tennessee,—or the Lord knows where." The "Sleepy Hollow Boys" will have none of the vain Connecticut Yankee whose name is an omen of his frame, so they contrive to have the terrified Crane confront the headless ghost of the Hessian trooper. The schoolmaster himself becomes a part of the mythic landscape; "old country wives maintain to this day that Ichabod was spirited away by supernatural means." The Dutch dreamers of the Hudson Valley defeat the Yankee interloper; the schoolhouse falls into decay; isolation and superstition reign supreme.

These are distinctly democratic and American tales as well. Rip's twenty-year sleep enables him to escape not only "the clamour of wife" but the entire American Revolution. On awakening, he finds all has changed. The flag is now "a singular assemblage of stars and stripes"; the inn is gone, replaced by "The Union Hotel"; even the sign with its "ruby face of King George" holding a scepter has been transformed into an image of a man in blue holding a sword; underneath are the words GENERAL WASHINGTON. When Rip asks about his friend Brom Dutcher, he learns that he was killed in the war; some say he died when storming Stony Point, others that he drowned off Anthony's Nose. Van Bummel the schoolmaster became a "great militia General and is now in Congress."

Rejected by Katrina and scared from the banks of the Hudson, the schoolmaster from Connecticut also makes his way in the new democratic republic. Ichabod moves to a distant part of the country and, though he still keeps a school, he studies law. Once admitted to the bar, it was only natural for him to turn to politics, electioneering, and writing for newspapers. And finally, writes Irving, the dandy schoolmaster is made a justice of the Ten Pound Court.

Earnings from his writings enabled Irving to give up the law. Most of the royalties from *A History of New York* came from American readers. The work went through numerous printings in his lifetime, and it became even more popular after he muted the intensity of some of his acerbic comments about the Dutch. His next book, *The Sketch Book of Geoffrey Crayon, Gent.,* broadened his fame across England and Europe. By 1820 Irving had established himself as the first writer of note that the pioneering and still unusual democracy in North America had yet produced. Irving also became the first literary celebrity, not only in America, but also in England and on the continent, where he lived for many years. "Our sides," wrote Sir Walter Scott of the *History,* "are absolutely sore with laughing." Later Sir Walter found the *Sketch Book* "Beautiful." Adoring women sent him locks of their hair, and Mary Wollstonecraft Shelley became smitten with him. When he returned to New York in 1836, after an absence of nearly twenty years, he purchased a colonial farmhouse on the eastern shore of the Hudson near Tarrytown, and named it Sunnyside. There he would write a five-volume biography of his namesake, George Washington, which gained him even more fame. Writers from Europe and America who were visiting the Hudson Valley made it a habit to call at Sunnyside and pay their respects. At a large dinner party in New York, Charles Dickens rose, laid his hand on Irving's round shoulder, and declared to the rapt audience that he made it a point to read Washington Irving two nights a week.

Sunnyside itself stands as one of Washington Irving's most important creations, almost as great and enduring as Rip or Ichabod. The house and grounds reflect both Irving's personality and the spirit of the valley. Not content with the colonial structure he had purchased, he added stepped gables at each end to emulate the Dutch city dwellings he remembered from his New York City childhood. He borrowed the idea for a stepped gable portico at Sunnyside's entrance, the steeply pitched roofs, and the distinctive chimney pots from Abbotsford, Walter Scott's house on the River Tweed. He looked to Spain when he built a small tower patterned on a monastery to the east side of his house, and to Italy when he added a delicately columned piazza on the west and north. The thirty-five hundred dollars Irving received from the Hudson River Railroad for its easement across his property helped to finance their construction. At the foundations he planted wisteria and ivy cuttings said to have been clipped from Abbotsford. On the grounds he created ponds and streams. Away from the house he built farm buildings, repaired barns and henhouses, and fenced fields for cattle. From the perspective of the hill that rises behind the property, the whole assemblage suggests a small village set on the bank of a great river. House and grounds are pure romantic whimsy, pure Washington Irving.

Never really recovering from the loss of Matilda Hoffman, Irving spent much of his life as a restless vagabond. A sojourn in Scotland, or England or Paris or Granada, kept him busy and distant from all but the most intimate friends. When in America, Sunnyside became an anchorage, a place where he finally might settle and continue writing. Writing was essential, for it brought the money he needed to maintain his home. His elder brother Ebenezer and Ebenezer's three unmarried daughters took up residence with him. The daughters kept the house, welcomed and controlled the steady stream of visitors, and helped him run the farm.

Irving made Sunnyside into a house for the Hudson. He chose an east room for his study, away from the river, but with two bright windows overlooking his verdant grounds. The dining and drawing rooms on the river side offer dramatic views of the water. Mirrors over the mantelpieces in each room reflect the light and the river itself. French doors lead from the drawing room to the piazza. "I have made more openings by pruning and cutting down trees," he wrote a friend in August 1847, "so that from the piazza I have several charming views of the Tappan Zee and the hills

Sunnyside from the Hudson, by an unknown artist, ca. 1860–80. This painting of Washington Irving's house shows the tracks of the Hudson River Railroad as they pass between the river and the house. They cut off a small cove at the right, which has since dried up. In addition to a train and a steamboat, the painting shows people in quieter pursuits, including rowing, fishing, and strolling along the embankment. (Historic Hudson Valley, Tarrytown, New York)

beyond; all set as it were in verdant frames, and I am never tired of sitting there in my old Voltaire chair, on a long summer morning, with a book in my hand, sometimes reading, sometimes musing on the landscape, and sometimes dozing and mixing up all in a pleasant dream." Upstairs, he slept in a bedroom on the river side, until noise from the nearby train tracks forced him to move to a room across the hall.

Irving was seventy-seven and in "feeble health" when the illustrator and author Benson Lossing paid him a visit in November 1859. While Lossing sketched the author in his study, they spoke of his work. The final volume of his life of Washington had recently appeared. Irving declared it would be his last. "I have laid aside my pen for ever . . . My work is finished and now

I intend to rest." At the end of the month, he collapsed in his bedroom and soon died. On the table by his bed was a gold-framed miniature of Matilda Hoffman and a small Bible inscribed in her hand. These he kept with him, always, to the end.

In 1825, a quarter century after Washington Irving's transformative experience on the Hudson, Thomas Cole, a young Englishman who had been schooled on Wordsworth and Coleridge, tramped through the valley, sketchbook in hand, in search of the sublime. As a child in England he had shown a talent for drawing. When he arrived in America in 1820, he apprenticed himself briefly to a Philadelphia engraver, then roamed through western Pennsylvania and Ohio painting portraits and landscapes, before returning to Philadelphia to study painting at the Pennsylvania Academy of Fine Arts. Early in 1825, he moved to New York and declared that he would devote himself to landscapes, poetry, and an occasional prose sketch. In the late summer of that year the Hudson Valley in all its atmospheres and lights and weathers beckoned.

In his sketchbook he recorded nature directly. Even in this small way, he broke with the more traditional practice then common among artists to remain in their studios making up nature from their own minds, rather than making up their minds from nature. With graphite and pen Cole had already made elaborate individual studies of trees and rocks in western Pennsylvania, each weathered and skeletal, spare and bleak. This time he followed the river north past West Point and Cold Spring to Cohoes; then on his return he stopped to make sketches of Fort Putnam looming over West Point, the source of the Kaaterskill Creek, and its falls.

The landscape Cole found in the Catskills overwhelmed his sensibilities. Surely this was the sublime that he had sought. The overwhelming grandeur and power of the scene, its beauty and vastness, inspired intense emotion and awe. It infused his poetry:

> I saw
> The idle River slowly roll along,
> And on its gentle glassy surface dwelt
> Reflected objects beautifully soft
> E'en the little stars that spring like flowers, . . .
> Did twinkle there as bright as in the sky.

Thomas Cole, *Lake with Dead Trees (Catskill),* 1825. The antlers on the stags in the foreground of Cole's famous canvas echo the branches of the dead trees around the lake, emphasizing the evanescence of all life beneath the divine light of heaven. (Allen Memorial Art Museum, Oberlin, Ohio)

In New York, Cole's pale drawings of the Catskill scenes that he had carefully annotated served as "luminous remembrancers" of the essence of nature, the essence that Cole captured in three landscapes that he completed early in the fall of 1825: *A View of Fort Putnam, Lake with Dead Trees,* and *Kaaterskill Upper Fall Catskill Mountain.*

The three Catskill paintings brought Cole fame. That October, almost at the very moment DeWitt Clinton was officiating at the "marriage of the waters," Colonel John Trumbull, the one-eyed artist known for his portraits of the heroes of the American Revolution, spotted the paintings in the window of William Coleman's book and art supply shop at 80

Broadway in Manhattan. As president of the American Academy of Fine Arts, Trumbull regarded himself as the chief arbiter of taste in America, the one who set the standards for others to follow. Heretofore he had favored paintings of biblical scenes, portraits of patriots, and, of course, great historical tableaus such as his own canvases *The Signing of the Declaration of Independence* and the *Surrender of General Burgoyne at Saratoga*. Now Trumbull recognized that Cole presented a fresh vision of the landscape. For inspiration and subject this unknown artist had looked not across the Atlantic to some classical ruin in an Italian countryside or a scene in the Netherlands, but instead had turned his gaze to the immense and wild forests and mountains of the Hudson River valley.

Trumbull bought the painting of Kaaterskill Falls and told two fellow artists, Asher B. Durand and William Dunlap, of his find. Durand quickly purchased the canvas of Fort Putnam, and Dunlap, the lake. Each artist paid twenty-five dollars, and they eventually put the paintings on view at New York's American Academy of Fine Arts. It is said that when they invited Cole to meet with them, Trumbull, Durand, and Dunlap were surprised to find he was just twenty-four. The sixty-nine-year-old Trumbull was heard to lament, "You have already done what I, with all my years and experience, am yet unable to do." The trio showed the paintings to friends, including New York City's mayor and diarist Philip Hone, who immediately bought *Lake with Dead Trees* for fifty dollars. Such a tacit endorsement started Thomas Cole's career and gave sanction and support to the genre of landscape painting in America.

Thomas Cole had discovered a distinctly American landscape, invested with an untamed and an often savage natural order. "The painter of American scenery," he wrote later, "has . . . Privileges superior to any other. All nature here is new to art." To Cole's thinking the nature revealed in American scenery made him a witness to the power of God. He was always attentive to light, which he equated with God's radiance that had brought him to the sublime. "The woods are dark," he began a poem about twilight, "but yet the lingering light / Spreads its last beauty o'er the sunset sky." On a voyage up the Hudson on a moonlit night, the poet meditated, "Midnight hath loosed the chain that bound / The spirit to its earthly round." Once, from the sheltering cave of an overhanging rock, he recorded the progress of a storm "in its majesty." As lightning "kindled the gloom" and the sound of thunder echoed "from crag to crag," Cole counted the moment as one of "sublime expectation." His imagination transported him "far from the earth" into a region of primeval chaos. He awakened from his reverie feeling "the weakness of humanity." To Cole a greater divine power stood behind the visible natural world; he would attempt to capture the power in his landscapes.

"The scenery is not grand," Cole wrote of the Catskills in an essay on nature, "but it has a wild sort of beauty that approaches it: quietness—solitude—the untamed—the unchanged aspect of nature—an aspect which the scene has worn thousands of years, affected only by the seasons, the sunshine and the tempest. We stand on the border of a cultivated plain, and look into the heart of nature."

Lake with Dead Trees shows just how penetrating Cole's gaze was. The edenic Hudson Valley scene that he captures is free of human corruption. A wild stillness has overtaken the landscape. From the shore we look across a small lake to a mountain peak framed against the pale rose of the sky. A stand of dead trees, their gnarled trunks highlighted by the sunset, shows the process of death in the natural world. Two male deer in the foreground suggest life in the presence of death. Yet they also appear mindful of the human intrusion. One cocks his head and looks inquisitively at the viewer, while the other is bounding off. Most important for Cole is the light, which inspires surprise, awe, even terror. It suggests that the hand of God above has ordained the natural cycle before us.

"The great struggle for freedom," Cole wrote in an essay on American scenery, "has sanctified many a spot." *A View of Fort Putnam* records the historical and legendary associations. The crumbling stone walls of the fort stand like an abandoned sentinel on the hill behind West Point. Below is a house and a verdant field with sheep grazing, and in the foreground beside a dead tree an old man wearing a brown hat, red vest, and long coat leans upon a walking staff. Caught between life and death, he appears to be looking across the vale, contemplating the fort and the pale sky above. Of all the images Cole presents, trees, man, vale, sheep, hills, fort, and sky, surely only the changeless and yet ever-changing force of nature is all powerful.

Although the canvas from 1825 is lost, we know from his sketchbook and a copy Cole made the following year that *The Falls of the Kaaterskill* shows the

Thomas Cole, *A View of Fort Putnam*, 1825, one of the three paintings that secured Cole's reputation and may be said to have begun the Hudson River school of painting. By the summer of 1825, the nation had begun to lose the generation of people directly associated with the American Revolution. The aged man in the foreground before the ruins of Fort Putnam suggests that Cole was attempting to evoke a connection with the past. Although this work was long thought to be lost, it has recently gone on view at the Philadelphia Museum of Art. (Philadelphia Museum of Art)

three stages of the waters' descent. His notes show the color of the rocks, the location of limbs, and the place of moss and trees. Cole also sketched the millhouse that had been erected beside the upper falls, something he eliminated from his painting. No need to introduce a human intrusion into his composition; better to suggest instead the restorative powers of nature. The falls present "a singular, a wonderful scene," he remembered nearly two decades later, "whether viewed from above, where [the water] leaps into the tremendous gulf scooped into the very heart of the huge

Thomas Cole, *The Falls of the Kaaterskill,* 1826. Although the famous falls appear pristine and unspoiled by humans in this painting, they had in fact already been changed dramatically. When Cole visited the scene in 1825, there was a millhouse on the right bank of the upper falls, but he chose to ignore such intrusions into the landscape. Instead he depicted a lone, and no doubt imaginary, native standing on the rocky precipice overlooking the middle falls. (The Warner Collection of Gulf States Corporation; on view in the Westervelt-Warner Museum of Art, Tuscaloosa, Alabama)

mountain," or viewed from the cavern below the second fall where the water is "broken into fleecy forms." To Cole falling water demonstrated nature's "fixedness and motion . . . Unceasing change and everlasting duration." As he would write a decade later, the Kaaterskill stream, though "diminutive," throws "itself headlong over a fearful precipice into a deep gorge of densely wooded mountains." The only sign of human activity the artist tolerates is the organic one of a lone Indian, bow and arrow in hand, standing on a rock outcropping.

In the Hudson Valley Thomas Cole found the uniqueness and power of the American landscape, an originality all the more dear because the Hudson in 1825 was in the vanguard of America's transformation. Robert Fulton and Robert Livingston had brought steam to the river; DeWitt Clinton had wedded the Atlantic to the Great Lakes. The heroic relics of the Revolution were passing rapidly. Washington and Franklin had gone before the end of the previous century; Jefferson and his longtime antagonist Adams had just a year to live. What was left of the landscape that so many had experienced firsthand in the Revolution and on journeys upriver? In his Hudson Valley landscapes of sublimity and hope Cole recorded a moment of veneration of the past, and a recognition of the nation's promising future.

As Cole's star rose in the firmament, he began to receive the attention of prominent art patrons. Commissions for landscapes—and copies of landscapes he had previously executed—came in. He spent the summer of 1827 in the Catskills searching for unknown tarns and waterfalls, tramping up mountains seeking just the right spot where he would bring out his pad and make a draftsman-like sketch of the scene.

Cole also wrote poems and recorded his observations in nature journals. "The mists were resting on the vale of the Hudson like drifted snow," he said of a sunrise he saw over Catskill, his favorite place on the river, and "tops of distant mountains in the east were visible—things of another world." In 1827 he depicted just such a scene, the view from Round-Top Mountain in the Catskills looking east across the Hudson. From this vantage point the artist gazes down across the low-lying mists of the valley. A dark sugarloaf hillock occupies the left middle ground, while in the foreground stand the eroded layers of a small sedimentary rock outcropping and a storm-blasted stand of trees. From our vantage point we sense an energy, a wildness in the air as the wisps of cloud swirl above and below. "The mist below the mountain began first to be lighted up," Cole had written, "and the trees on the tops of the lower hills, cast their shadows over the misty surface." In the distance across a plain flows the Hudson, the river whose "natural magnificence," he once said, "is unsurpassed." Unlike the intensity of the atmosphere in the distant mountains and sky, the river appears peaceful; just a few ghostly sails break its placid surface. Above the scene glows the eastern light, for in the Hudson Valley Cole always reveals the hand of his creator.

> When the morning lights the sky
> Our own simple songs should rise
> Unto God who dwells on high.

With the help of a patron, Cole journeyed to Europe in 1829. The journalist and fellow poet William Cullen Bryant, who had also come to New York City in 1825, adjured his friend in a sonnet to be faithful to his American vision of nature:

> Thine eyes shall see the light of distant skies:
> Yet, COLE! thy heart shall bear to Europe's strand
> A living image of thy native land,
> Such as on thy own glorious canvas lies.
> Lone lakes—savannas where the bison roves—
> Rocks rich with summer garlands—solemn streams—
> Skies, where the desert eagle wheels and screams—
> Spring bloom and autumn blaze of boundless groves.
> Fair scenes shall greet thee where thou goest—fair,
> But different—everywhere the trace of men,
> Paths, homes, graves, ruins, from the lowest glen
> To where life shrinks from the fierce Alpine air.
> Gaze on them, till the tears shall dim thy sight,
> But keep that earlier, wilder image bright.

And before sailing Cole himself said, "I wish to take a 'last, lingering look' at our wild scenery . . . That, in the midst of the fine scenery of other countries, their grand and beautiful peculiarities shall not be erased." After Cole returned to the Hudson Valley, he rented a room and studio space in 1834 at Cedar Grove, a large Federal-style house built on a promontory overlooking the village of Catskill by a wealthy merchant. The house offered him a superb view of the "varied, undulating, and exceedingly beautiful outlines" of his beloved Catskills, which, he once declared, "heave from the valley of the Hudson like the subsiding billows of the ocean after a storm." And there was another reason for Cole's settling at Cedar Grove. Late that year, in the west parlor that looks onto the Catskills, the artist married Maria Bartow, the owner's youngest niece.

From Cedar Grove the artist would set forth on rambles, often with a companion, and always with a sketchbook, "after," one companion said, "the picturesque." Cole and his friends would sketch the Hudson or Catskill Creek, and occasionally venture farther for a climb to the Catskill Mountain House. He developed an interest in architecture, designing an Episcopal Church for the village of Catskill, a small studio for a barn at Cedar Grove, and even a beautiful outhouse for the property. On Christmas day 1846, he moved into a large Italianate-style studio of his own design close by the main house at Cedar Grove. Lit by tall windows on three sides, the graceful building became the place where Cole could withdraw from his growing family of three children—and Maria's extended family of unmarried sisters—to the world of the spirit.

In the autumn of 1847 Cole climbed South Peak in the Catskills with several friends. He looked to the east across the valley to the Hudson River and the mountains beyond. It was the last hike into the Catskills that Thomas Cole made. Just after his forty-seventh birthday the following February he succumbed to a lung infection. An Episcopal priest gave him communion at his bedside. After the last prayer, Cole said "I want to be quiet," lay back on his pillow, and died.

After his death, Cole's influence on other artists and writers increased. Asher B. Durand captured it in his large canvas *Kindred Spirits,* a painting that depicts Cole and his friend William Cullen Bryant standing on the edge of a rock outcrop in the Kaaterskill Clove, overlooking the famous falls. Sketchbook in hand, Cole stands authoritatively, pointing to the falling water that he had made so famous—and which had in turn made him famous—with his paintings in 1825 and 1826. Bryant listens attentively to the discourse. Overhead birds float on thermals. No matter that the scene does not exist in nature. Following Cole's precept, Durand has chosen to

Asher B. Durand, *Kindred Spirits*, 1849. Following in Thomas Cole's footsteps, Durand also chose to create an ideal scene. Here he depicts Cole gesturing to William Cullen Bryant about the beauties of the ideal landscape in the Kaaterskill Clove before them. Durand was not above gentle humor, either. In the painting, the names "Bryant" and "Cole" are carved into the trunk of the birch tree in the left foreground. (The New York Public Library, Astor, Lenox, and Tilden Foundations)

borrow signature emblems of the Hudson River valley and combine them in a single view. The image speaks of the artist's and the poet's affinity for the power of nature.

The Hudson River had brought Cole, Bryant, and Durand together. Cole had met Durand through Jonathan Trumbull; he had introduced Bryant to the valley and the Catskills. For the *New York Evening Post,* the newspaper he edited, Bryant wrote a lyrical description of a storm in the mountains ("dark summits of the distant mountains penetrated the sky until the whole seemed like one continuous wall of black"). From these walks as well as others in New England, he produced a preface to a book of landscapes to which Cole and Durand contributed. In it Bryant spoke of the "peculiarities" of the American landscape, "the absence of tamings and softenings of cultivation." Foreigners who visited American mountains "have spoken of a far-spread wildness, a look as if the new world was fresher from the hand of Him who made it." The scenery suggested to these visitors from the old world, so Bryant reported, "the idea of unity and immensity" and transported the mind "to the idea of a mightier power, and to the great mystery of the origin of things."

Bryant's language might be mistaken for Cole's. Indeed, while the painter was creating landscapes of the Hudson Valley and the Catskills, Bryant was creating poems that possessed a "landscape of mood." In one such landscape, "A Scene on the Banks of the Hudson," Bryant contemplates the transience of life as he looks over the calm water.

> All, save this little nook of land,
> Circled with trees, on which I stand;
> All, save that line of hills which lie
> Suspended in the mimic sky-
> Seems a blue void, above, below,
> Through which the white clouds come and go;
> And from the green world's farthest steep . . .
> I gaze into the airy deep.
> Loveliest of lovely things are they,
> On earth, that soonest pass away.

Concluding,

River! In this still hour thou hast
Too much of heaven on earth to last;
Nor long may thy still waters lie,
An image of the glorious sky.

After Cole's death, Bryant made sure that the *Evening Post* anointed Asher Durand as "the head of American landscape art," the one who would carry on his friend's ideals. It was a logical choice. Durand had known Cole since October 1825, when he met him at John Trumbull's studio. At that time Durand earned his living by engraving banknotes, college diplomas, and business cards, but he gained his reputation by engraving Trumbull's historical painting *The Signing of the Declaration of Independence,* a three-thousand-dollar commission that he completed in 1823, and portraits of popular patriots of the new republic like Washington, Hamilton, and DeWitt Clinton. By the late 1830s, competition from other engravers soured him on the enterprise so much that he traded his incising tools for paintbrushes.

Cole had encouraged Durand to paint, and he followed his progress with reassuring letters: "I am pleased that you have attacked a landscape, and have no doubt that you will succeed to the satisfaction of all except yourself," he wrote from Catskill in the summer of 1836. Durand must turn away from the city, Cole urged; he must breathe the "pure air of heaven" of the country, where "nature," he said, "is a sovereign remedy." They went together on sketching trips and talked of painting in the field.

With Cole's passing Durand seemed to flourish. His canvases are far more pastoral than Cole's, but still the subject is nature. The brushwork of his Hudson River landscapes, like *River Scene* or *Hudson River Looking Towards the Catskills,* shows a softer rendering than Cole's more vigorous strokes. He seems to be living out the dictum of one of his letters on American landscape painting that "a landscape becomes companionable, holding silent converse" when it touches a "chord that vibrates to the inmost recesses of the heart." He populates the scenes with cattle and, in the latter work, two couples embarking on a skiff. The light is pale, the atmosphere hazy, the Hudson still.

It was Cole who first encouraged Durand to paint plein-air sketches, those first drafts of nature, in the field, but it was Durand who made the practice popular. He devoted several months of every year to travel,

Asher B. Durand, *Hudson River Looking Toward the Catskills*, 1847. Believing that a "landscape becomes companionable, holding silent converse," Durand sought tranquillity in his depiction. Here he set the scene on a quiet cove near Rhinecliff looking northwest to the Catskills beyond. The two couples alighting from their skiff appear in perfect harmony with the sheep and cattle in the foreground. (Fenimore Art Museum, Cooperstown, New York)

packing small bladders of paint (and after 1842 collapsible tin tubes), a sketch box filled with boards or paper, sometimes an easel and a folding stool, and almost always an umbrella. In all, the equipment weighed about twenty-five to thirty pounds. Sometimes bugs landing in the fresh paint would damage the sketch; sometimes the wet papers and boards would jostle together in the sketch box; and sometimes the paints would leak. Still, he and other artists believed plein-air offered the best way to capture the intensity of nature.

In part because of Durand's painting, Cole's influence on American taste seemed to increase after his death. Artists like John Frederick Kensett, Jasper Cropsey, and Sanford Gifford had already walked through the valley on sketching trips. After 1855, when Durand began publishing a series of "Letters on Landscape Painting" for his son's new art journal, the *Crayon*, letters that made studio sketches strictly taboo, another younger generation of landscape painters headed up the Hudson.

By 1860, a tour of the valley seemed almost obligatory for every budding artist. "He may be regarded as the art-devotee who studies Nature most," wrote a critic in the *Cosmopolitan Art Journal*, "and when the *stampede* to the country for study is made one of the *requisites* of [the artist's] profession, then we shall see an American school of art assuming a clearly defined shape." So intense was the stampede that Thomas Nast made it the subject of a humorous woodcut for *Harper's Weekly* in 1866. Armed with their easels and pads, and sometimes sheltered by parasols, no fewer than seven artists sit sketching a waterfall not unlike the Kaaterskill. In the foreground a couple peer over the shoulder of one artist. She wears a summer dress; he sports a stovepipe hat; beside them their little girl looks on. Another courting couple similarly dressed rest on a nearby ledge. A photographer, his camera mounted on a tripod and his head concealed beneath the hood, stands on another rock outcrop over the falls to capture the scene.

Of course the Hudson River artists didn't confine their sketching and painting trips to the Hudson Valley. They usually extended their range to paint landscapes in the White Mountains, the mountains and sea of Mount Desert Island in Maine, and the surging water at Niagara Falls, among other places in the east. Frederic Edwin Church, a pupil of Thomas Cole's at Catskill, went to South America and Persia where he completed his most popular and dramatic canvases; Albert Bierstadt went west to capture the drama of the Sierra Nevadas and the Rocky Mountains. Indeed, the Hudson was more a beginning than an end, the landscape that produced the first autochthonous art that belonged naturally to American soil.

Toward the end of the century the numerous artists that had followed Thomas Cole into the Hudson Valley passed from the scene. John Frederick Kensett, who had painted Storm King Mountain and the view from West Point, died in 1872; Asher Durand in 1886; Jasper Cropsey, who often captured sunsets and autumn scenes on the river, in 1900; Frederic

Thomas Nast, "The Artist in the Mountains," 1866, one
of twenty-seven panels of a large cartoon about life in the
Catskills that Nast drew for *Harper's Weekly*. Other panels
depicted children in peril of falling off the cliff in front
of the Catskill Mountain House, summer visitors pushing
their wagon up the steep ascent to the hotel, and a visitor
leaving the hotel, his pockets turned inside out, unable to
tip the expectant staff lined up at the door.

Edwin Church, who painted the scene from his house overlooking the river
in every season and dozens of different lights, died the same year.

The art scene they created was passing, too. Impressionists and the
French Barbizon school of artists were in ascendance. The public grew
tired of landscapes whose theme seemed all too repetitious and whose style
critics described as academic. As American aesthetics changed, prices for

these artists' canvases slipped dramatically; discerning collectors quietly moved their works from parlors and formal rooms to attics or cellars, barns or rubbish piles. Cole, Church, and Durand—the entire group who had captured the valley's dramatic landscape were passé. Dismissive critics called such artists and their work the "Hudson River school."

Though little remembered today beyond a small circle of architectural and landscape historians, his name was once synonymous with taste across the nation, a taste to which many Americans believed they should aspire. Through his articles and books, he taught Americans how to cultivate their gardens and design their houses in a way that put them into harmony with nature and their landscape. Wealthy landowners, especially those in the Hudson Valley, looked to Andrew Jackson Downing of Newburgh to design their dwellings and landscapes, and Downing obliged them.

Named for the victorious general at the Battle of New Orleans in 1815, the year of his birth, Andrew Jackson Downing lived his life at Newburgh with the sounds and the sights of the Hudson always in his consciousness. Early in his life, his father died, leaving the task of running the family business, the "Botanic Gardens and Nurseries," to his eldest son, Charles. Once he had finished school, Downing joined his brother.

As men who had made their wealth in New York City decided they needed summer "cottages" around Newburgh, the Downing brothers' nursery business prospered. Soon Downing could add the title "Esq."—gentleman—after his name. Local gentlemen sought out the opinion of the tall, slim, dark-eyed man of dignified manner and refinement on how to design their new estates—and they followed it.

When he wasn't attending to the trees and rendering his opinions on design, Downing searched the valley—much as Amos Eaton had at Catskill—for mineralogical and botanical specimens. Swimming became his primary recreation; with a favorable tide and good weather he could swim a mile and a half across the great river to Fishkill Landing on the opposite shore. It was at Fishkill Landing, in 1838, that he married Caroline DeWindt, a grandniece of John Quincy Adams and the daughter of a local Hudson baron.

As the revenues from the nursery increased, Andrew Jackson Downing turned to improving what he called "rural taste" in America. First he laid out his ideas for the landscape in *A Treatise on the Theory and Practice of Landscape Gardening, Adapted to North America.* Downing favored the "Picturesque," or "Natural," style over the well-ordered geometric parterre gardens Americans so often copied from European models. With the picturesque, the landscape gardener could present "a richness and variety never to be found in any one portion of nature." The result was the ordered disorder, the tamed wildness, of a "spirited irregularity," with "growth of a somewhat wild and bold character," a domesticated sublime. In pictures that Downing provided, rural farmhouses, cottages, and villas appear amid seemingly primitive clearings with crooked paths and savage mountains in the background. The *Treatise* proved an immediate success, not only in the Hudson Valley but also throughout the eastern United States and western Europe.

Two more books, *Cottage Residences* and *The Architecture of Country Houses,* followed. Each proved as popular as the first. It was time, Downing said, for America to recover from "the Greek temple disease" that had guided the nation's architecture since the founding of the republic. "Our houses are mostly either of the plainest and most meagre description," he wrote, "or, if of a more ambitious, they are frequently of a more objectionable character." Romantic that he was, Downing believed that architecture had a moral as well as a practical purpose. The lowliest farmhouse, along with the grandest villa, needed a "spirit and grace" to elevate the "state of mind" of its occupants. "There is no reason why the dwelling-houses of our respectable farmers," he wrote, "should not display some evidences of taste, as well as those of professional men, or persons in more affluent circumstances." Each book presented detailed plans for residences as diverse as "A Suburban Cottage," "An Ornamental Farmhouse," "A Villa in the Italian Style," and "A Cottage for a Country Clergyman." And he put his ideas into practice, building Highland Gardens, a new home for his bride, with views of the Hudson and the mountains. It was startlingly different from any house in Newburgh—indeed, from almost any in America. Downing looked to English Gothic designs to produce his structure with lancet windows, twin towers, and great chimney pots.

The ordered disorder that Downing favored mirrored the experience of the American scenery that Bryant had expressed in his "landscape moods," and Cole had captured in his paintings and poetry. Downing

Andrew Jackson Downing, plans for a "Rural Gothic Villa," from *The Architecture of Country Houses*, 1850. Through a series of plans that he presented in his book Downing sought to cure Americans of their reliance on Greek models for their architectural inspiration. In his careful renderings of buildings, he showed humans in harmony with their landscape, and their dwellings as organic extensions of their surroundings. (Collection of John De Marco)

offered people, especially those in the Hudson Valley, the chance not only to absorb the natural world around them but actually to create dwellings and gardens in organic harmony with it. Downing-designed houses, and other buildings that Downing's books inspired, began to dot the valley in places like Fishkill and Kingston, Yonkers and New Windsor, Rhinebeck and Cold Spring. Still others could be found in New York City, Newport, Rhode Island, Orange, New Jersey, and Washington, D.C.

By 1845, people throughout the east, and especially in the valley, followed Downing's strictures as they designed their houses and landscaped their properties. He took on a partner, Calvert Vaux, a young Englishman from London who would later work with Frederick Law Olmsted to plan New York's Central Park. (Both Vaux and Olmsted acknowledged Downing as the one who had exerted the greatest influence on their designs for urban parks throughout America, and in 1899, in homage to their master, they created a park in his name for his city of Newburgh.) To have a house or garden designed by the recognized master was a rich plum. Downing especially liked commissions for houses and grounds along the Hudson, as the land afforded, he said, "accessible perfect seclusion" for those fortunate enough to own them. William Findley, a Newburgh neighbor, had him design his house and gardens; Matthew Vassar commissioned buildings and landscape drawings for Springside, his estate at Poughkeepsie; and Warren Delano, Franklin Delano Roosevelt's great-grandfather, employed him to create Algonac, a huge villa facing Newburgh Bay. But the greatest commission of all came from President Millard Fillmore, who hired the architect to plan the grounds around Washington's Capitol, the new Smithsonian Institution, and the executive mansion. At thirty-six, Andrew Jackson Downing was the acknowledged judge of the beautiful, whose word was taken as the epitome of good taste, not only in the Hudson Valley but for the entire nation.

It was to oversee the work in Washington that the architect embarked with his wife on the *Henry Clay* on the last Sunday of July 1852. When a fire broke out on the ship, survivors reported, Downing behaved with great courage. As flames engulfed the boat, he stayed at the railing, calmly helping passengers into the water, and throwing wooden deck chairs for them to cling to. Once in the water, he struggled to stay afloat while other victims clung to his neck and arms. Caroline Downing was saved, but her husband was lost. The following afternoon, Caroline and a small party of friends returned to Highland Gardens. She ordered her husband's body placed in the library where for the past decade he had written his books and worked on his designs. A fierce thunderstorm rolled over the hills of Newburgh in what one of the party called "the wild sympathy of nature."

The artists and writers who made their way up the river to experience the sublime were part of a larger shift in America's cultural landscape. After the Supreme Court decision in *Gibbons v. Ogden,* the number of steamboats increased substantially. The Erie Canal brought still more river traffic and commerce to the towns and cities in the valley. Over the first three decades of the nineteenth century America's population had more than doubled to 13 million; Manhattan Island inhabitants now numbered 123,000. The city was fulfilling the prophecy of the London *Times*, that it would become "the London of the New World." There were more travelers in the valley, too. By the time Thomas Cole began his tramp into the Catskills in 1825, the artist found that others had preceded him, not artists but businessmen. Their mission was to lure tourists to nature.

Capitalizing on the same ineffable beauty, mystery, and spirituality of the Hudson Valley that so moved artists and writers, these entrepreneurs built hotels high in the mountains for travelers who sought refuge from the fever and heat of the city, cool breezes, and views of all creation. They built roads and railroads, stage lines and steamship docks for easier access to their earthly paradises; they placed discreet advertisements in New York papers advising patrons of rooms. "HOTEL Kaaterskill, LARGEST MOUNTAIN HOTEL IN THE WORLD"; "CATSKILL MOUNTAIN HOUSE *Elevation 2500 feet No malaria*"; "PROSPECT PARK HOTEL, Mountain air, scenery unsurpassed in the world"; and they made sure that eager reporters received the names of their most select guests. "I was kindly allowed to look at the register," wrote one reporter, who proceeded to give a list of prominent, though now forgotten, New Yorkers.

The Catskill Mountain House, the first significant hotel in the region, opened several years before Cole arrived in the valley. It was created by a group of Catskill businessmen who purchased a large flat outcropping of rock high on South Mountain, commanding a magnificent view of the Hudson. Known as Pine Orchard for the pitch pines that grew there, the ledge was likely the place where Natty Bumppo, and therefore James Fenimore Cooper, stood to survey the valley; and it is very likely that Cole was close by when he painted *View of Round-Top in the Catskill Mountains*. After receiving a charter from the state to build "a large and commodious hotel" at Pine Orchard, the association erected a structure 140 feet long and four stories high.

Those standing on the ledge of the Catskill Mountain House could take in about a sixty-mile stretch of the Hudson, "winding, twisting, here wide, there only a little silver wire, but ever smooth as glass and bright as a diamond." And the great Greek Revival structure standing prominently on the mountainside became a focal point for all captains and their pas-

Advertisement for the Catskill Mountain House, 1878, appearing in Wallace Bruce's *The Hudson River by Daylight*. Bruce, who wrote under the pseudonym Thursty McQuill at this time, published numerous maps and guidebooks to the Hudson Valley and the Lake Champlain region. From the hotel one could see about a sixty-mile stretch of the Hudson River. (Collection of John De Marco)

sengers sailing on the river. On his return to America in 1824, Lafayette saw it "situated 2500 feet above the level of the Hudson." August Levasseur, who accompanied the general, declared it "an object of curiosity for the traveller; and of pleasure excursions to the inhabitants of the vicinity." Levasseur might also have mentioned the pleasure it brought to travelers from abroad, for in the 1820s and 1830s the Catskill Mountain House became a destination for foreign visitors.

For Harriet Martineau, who made the four-hour carriage trip to the hotel from Catskill landing in July 1835, it was "an illuminated fairy palace perched among the clouds in opera scenery." She arrived as storm clouds gathered to obscure the valley below. From the edge of the rock shelf she watched as "gashes of red lightning . . . Revealed not merely the horizon, but the course of the river in all its windings." To her the Hudson looked as though it too was "a flash of lightning . . . Laid along in the valley." She found the "dazzling, bewildering alternation of glare and blackness, of vast reality and nothingness," so mesmerizing and frightening that she was glad to withdraw from the precipice to "the candlelight within."

The mountain air, the views of the Hudson and the valley, and the experience of the seemingly wild landscape attracted more and more visitors to the Catskills. Other hotels, including the Laurel, the Prospect, and the Rip Van Winkle, drew the wealthy from New York and Philadelphia into the mountains; and then in 1881 the Hotel Kaaterskill became the largest and most fashionable of all. "It shows beautifully from the Hudson River, 10 or 12 miles away," wrote a reporter for the *New York Times*. The Baedeker guide of 1899 declared that the view it commanded was "little, if at all, inferior to that from the Mountain House."

Changes in the valley, however, compromised the views that visitors had come to praise. Across the hillsides travelers saw great barren tracts where once hemlocks had stood. The trees fell victim to the ancient art of tanning animal hides into leather for boots and shoes, belts and gloves, and saddles and harnesses. A stinking, dirty, and environmentally destructive process, tanning requires washing the hides in a vat of pure water to remove the blood and dirt; soaking them in another vat for as long as a year to loosen the hair; scraping the hair away; and then soaking them in a series of vats, each with an increasingly more astringent solution of tannin to give the hides strength; and finally, after many months, finishing the hides as leather.

The crushed bark of hemlock trees provided the best source of tannin in the northeast. New York City tanners, who concentrated their vats near the Collect Pond in an area aptly named "The Swamp," first cut stands of the trees on the northern end of the island; once they had exhausted those, they moved their operations upriver to the Catskills. Initially the tanners located their vats on the banks of streams that fed the Hudson, but as the supply of trees was depleted, they moved westward to creeks that drained into the Mohawk, whose waters ultimately join the Hudson at Cohoes.

Tanning wrought havoc upon the landscape. The axes began to swing in the spring when the flowing sap made it easy for peelers to remove wide strips of bark from the hemlock trunks. After the first snowfall tanners collected the bark on sleds, brought it to a grinding mill where the fibers were pulverized, then mixed the ground bark with water to make "liquor" for their hides.

"Tanneries are not only carried on as a regular business," secretary of the treasury Alexander Hamilton wrote in his report on manufacturing in 1791, "but they constitute, in some places, a valuable item of incidental family manufacture." Hudson Valley tanneries were usually small operations run by a farmer and his family. The damage to the environment was minimal, if only because farmers tanned their own hides. Although the stripped tree trunks were left to rot where they fell, and the tanners discharged their toxic liquor directly into the Hudson or into nearby streams that fed the river, these operations were small. The forest could afford to lose a few hemlocks, and the streams and the river could absorb the waste.

By the 1820s, however, the size of tanning operations began to increase, and the destruction became visible everywhere. Tanneries in the Swamp gave way to leather merchants who were happy to procure their tanned hides from the Catskills. Across the country, the demand for leather increased with the population. In the valley, grinding mills had to pulverize enormous amounts of hemlock bark to make sufficient tannin for the process, and loggers had to fell about five trees to produce a cord of bark. Each acre in the Catskills yielded about seventy-five trees, to produce fifteen cords. Most tanners cut their hemlocks in a ten-square-mile radius around the tannery, which meant that over the two or three decades of operation they would fell about ninety-six thousand trees. The remaining trunks served as fuel for forest fires. Once the nearby hills were depleted, tanners moved their operations to greener acres, and the barren soil they left behind eroded into nearby streams, which over time deposited their silt into the Hudson.

Principal among the Catskill tanners were William Edwards and Zadock Pratt. In 1817 Edwards arrived from Massachusetts, his pockets filled with sixty-three thousand dollars, given him by six investors, to begin the New York Tannery on twelve hundred acres of land near the Schoharie Creek. Initially Edwards processed five thousand hides a year. Soon he had six men and nine apprentices in his operation and had created a small village, which he named Edwardsville. As was the case with most tanners, Edwards viewed hemlock trees and all his employees merely as a means to acquiring money. There were many like him in the valley, men that Cole characterized as being consumed "in the low pursuits of avarice . . . Unconscious of the harmony of creation." Edwards's low pursuits came to an end after his tannery burned to the ground in 1830. He lingered on for about a decade, and even tried to rebuild his operation, before he decided to move to New York City. He left behind a malevolent legacy.

Zadock Pratt's operation was larger than that of Edwards, and Pratt himself left an indelible mark on the Catskills. Unlike Edwards, he possessed a genuine simpleness in his attitude toward nature, and he particularly loved the hemlocks. The trees' boughs made wonderful bedding for weary forest travelers, he thought; their scent was a restorative, and perhaps it even had medicinal uses. Removing the hemlocks, so Pratt convinced himself, would actually help the land. The treeless fields would serve as pastures for dairy farmers. But it is said that he was often heard to beg the hemlock's forgiveness before he swung his ax into the trunk to bring it down. As his operation expanded, Zadock Pratt had to beg forgiveness many times over.

The nearly illiterate son of a Rensselaer County tanner and shoemaker, Pratt had a natural talent for the trade, making improvements to his father's operation at an early age and perfecting a pump used to move tanning liquor from vat to vat. In 1824 he purchased land at Schohariekill on the former Hardenburgh patent in the Catskills, with the intention of building the largest tannery in the world. The building was indeed huge—530 feet in length, 43 feet in breadth, and two stories high—and filled with 300 liquor vats and sophisticated equipment, some of Pratt's own invention, to transform hides into leather in the shortest possible time. He built two sheds for bark and a dozen houses for his workmen close by. Sloops sailed up the Hudson laden with thousands of hides from California, Venezuela, Uruguay, Mexico, and Argentina destined for Pratt's tannery. And, saying that he came "to live *with* and not *on* his neighbors," he changed the name of Schohariekill to Prattsville.

"Do well and doubt not" was Zadock Pratt's chief motto, and he did well indeed. He married five times; the first three marriages ended in the death of his wives, the fourth in divorce, and the last came late in Pratt's eighth decade, when he had but a few years left, to a secretary of twenty. Unlike most tanners, who were content to house their workers in simple wooden shacks, Pratt built his employees complete houses; churches sprang up in Prattsville, along with a three-story school, an India rubber factory, a hat shop, a foundry, a model dairy farm, even a photographer's studio. Pratt reasoned that these enterprises would enable his village to continue prospering after all the hemlocks had been felled and the tannery closed.

Pratt maintained meticulous records of all he created and accomplished. He tanned over 60,000 hides a year and consumed "more than 6000 cords of bark." Through "judicious use of strong liquors" he was able to increase the thickness of hides "nearly 50 per cent." Pratt boasted to the author of *The Arts of Tanning, Currying, and Leatherdressing* that in twenty years he had produced "about 1,000,000 sides of sole leather," and given his workers "1,000 years of labor at $14 per month."

In 1845, the day arrived that Pratt had foreseen two decades earlier: the last of the hemlocks yielded to the ax, and the tannery shut down. By that time Pratt himself had moved on to other ventures. He was elected to two terms in the United States Congress, where he championed the erection of the Washington monument, the establishment of the Bureau of Standards, a transcontinental railroad, and cheap postage. He then retired from public life and returned to Prattsville to indulge his eccentricities, embellish the legend of his life, which he published in the *Shoe and Leather Reporter,* and earn the affection of all who knew him. He had a passion for pyrotechnics, which he satisfied by executing full-scale assaults on the barns of obliging farmers. After he blew up one of these structures, Pratt always compensated the owner for the privilege. On the fourth of July he wrapped himself in winter blankets and rode about his village in a sleigh. On a rock outcrop on the outskirts of Prattsville, he had an itinerant sculptor carve images of himself and his deeds. Today one can still see bas-reliefs of the great tannery, hemlock branches, and a memorial to his son who died in the first Battle of Manassas. On a ledge above the reliefs, a great bust of the tanner himself looks down. Nearby is the inscription heralding what he considered his greatest achievement: "One million sides of sole leather tanned with hemlock bark, in twenty years, by Zadock Pratt."

In spite of Pratt's respect for the tree that gave him his fortune, the devastation he and his fellow tanners wrought upon the land was visible everywhere.

The Schoharie Creek that fed the Mohawk, which in turn flowed into the Hudson, was filled with the effluent from tanneries. Thousands of acres of land were left barren. A writer for *Harper's Monthly* visiting the Catskills found that a tannery "is not at all calculated to win the love of the hunter of the picturesque. It destroys the beauty of many a fair landscape—discolors the once pure waters—and, what is worse than all, drives the fish from the streams! Think of the sacrilege! The bright-tinted trout offered up upon the ignoble altar of calf-skin, sheepskin, and cow-skin!" The romantic representation of the scenery rendered by artists and writers notwithstanding, much of the landscape Thomas Cole and his followers had so revered was fast disappearing from the valley. "The ravages of the axe are daily increasing," Cole found in 1836, when Pratt and Edwards had consumed about ten thousand acres of hemlock between them. "The most noble scenes are made desolate, and oftentimes with a wantonness and barbarism scarcely credible in a civilized nation. The wayside is becoming shadeless, and another generation will behold spots, now rife with beauty, desecrated by what is called improvement; which, as yet, generally destroys Nature's beauty without substituting Art."

In May of 1825, Captain Elam Lynds, a former hatter from Troy and a veteran of the War of 1812, and a party of one hundred shackled prisoners and thirty armed guards left Auburn Prison in upstate New York in a convoy of wagons and headed up the North Road. At Weedsport, a small village that thrived on business from the newly opened Erie Canal, they boarded two boats for the trip east to the Hudson River. At the Hudson they transferred to a waiting steamer for the final leg of their journey.

Elam Lynds was an impressive man with sinister features. Six feet one inch tall, lean and muscular in build, he liked to dress in a dark coat and tails, topped by a high beaver hat. He had a round, puglike face, small, deep-set eyes, a high forehead, and black wavy hair. But Lynds's most striking feature was a deep red scar that began at his left eye socket and followed a crescent-shaped path ending at the side of his mouth.

The following morning Lynds and his prisoners reached Mount Pleasant, a spot on the east bank of the Hudson thirty-three miles north of New York City. Immediately the captain ordered the prisoners unshackled and put to work. By nightfall they had erected their temporary barracks; a mess hall, blacksmith and carpentry shops, and a wharf on the riverbank soon followed. Then Lynds ordered the men to build their own prison to his pitiless specifications.

So well known was Mount Pleasant for its rich veins of white marble that Indians in the area had long called it Sing Sing, a phrase Europeans translated to mean "stone on stone." But the mountain was hardly pleasant for Lynds's prisoners. They had to blast the marble from the mountain, haul the rough stones to the site, dress them into rectangular blocks, and, stone on stone, erect their stark narrow building. In the blacksmith shop prisoners made the iron doors and beds for their cells; one clever prisoner even invented a lever lock that enabled a guard to open and close fifty doors at a time. In seven months, they completed fifty Lilliputian cells, each six feet seven inches high, seven feet long, and three feet three inches wide, just enough to accommodate a prisoner, a night bucket, and a steel bed. Nine hundred and fifty more cells followed.

Even more impressive than the prison was the hush of the men building it. As the warden at Auburn prison, Lynds had ordered complete silence. "They are not to exchange a word under any pretense whatever," the captain wrote, "nor to communicate any intelligence in writing." Lynds's system—which the guards rigidly enforced with a cat-o'-nine-tails—insured as much as possible a prisoner's isolation from any human contact.

A scandal—the pregnancy of a female prisoner—forced Lynds to retire, but his system remained in place. The eerie quiet stunned two young French aristocrats who were visiting the United States to study the prison system in the young democracy. When Gustave de Beaumont and Alexis de Tocqueville arrived at Sing Sing in May 1831, they saw a prison without walls and just thirty guards watching over "900 [men] whose isolation makes them weak." Lynds had been dismissed by then. The guards, they noted, meted out punishments swiftly and brutally. It was what one prisoner called a "Catocracy." On the shores of the Hudson at Mount Pleasant the only sounds to be heard were the rhythmic pounding of stone hammers, the screech of gulls, and the cries of men being whipped.

After Lynds's departure, reform-minded wardens periodically attempted modest changes at Sing Sing, but by 1865, the prison had become a disgrace and an embarrassment to many in the state. Along with fires, deaths from dysentery, scurvy, and cholera became common. In 1861 the governor had

"Sing Sing Prison and Tappan Sea," an engraving from 1839 after a sketch by W. H. Bartlett depicting the prison as Elam Lynds built it, without walls. "One cannot see the prison of Sing Sing," Alexis de Tocqueville wrote after a visit in 1831, "without being struck by astonishment and fear." Tocqueville likened the system to a steamboat. "Nothing is more comfortable, more swift, more perfect . . . in the normal course of things," he wrote. "But if some part of the machinery happens to go wrong, the vessel, the passengers and the cargo jump in the air." For the Frenchman a prison without walls held the promise of catastrophe.

to call in the army to put down a riot. Walls were erected and the guards began to carry guns. Punishments—cold showers, dark cells, yokes and iron caps—became even more severe. Still, prisoners did try to escape; some succeeded.

At the time it was built, however, Sing Sing was a model prison built at the ideal location. Lynds had achieved more on the shores of the Hudson than any other warden in the nation; Sing Sing was not only self-sufficient but actually earned money for the state. By the time of Tocqueville and Beaumont's visit prison authorities had leased the workshops to entrepreneurs who equipped them with raw materials and tools. Prison laborers turned leather into shoes and boots, wood into chairs and barrels, iron into tools and locks—and loaded the goods onto waiting ships. Everything worked efficiently at Sing Sing. Even the prison sewage went directly into the river.

By far the most important Sing Sing product—and the greatest revenue producer—was marble. Long after they had finished building their cells and workshops, the prisoners continued to mine the mountain in silence, dressing the rough stones in the prison yard and loading them onto waiting ships. Customers knew they could depend on Sing Sing marble for its purity and on the prisoners for their enforced attention to exacting specifications. Today we can see their stones in New York City's Grace Church, New York University, and the United States Treasury Building, as well as Albany's City Hall and State Education building.

Even more than Alcatraz on the West Coast, Elam Lynds's Sing Sing has become an icon of the American prison. It's the "Big House." Hardened felons are sent "up the river." On June 19, 1953, much of the world focused on Sing Sing as its electric chair took the lives of Ethel and Julius Rosenberg for conspiracy to commit espionage. The prison yard is the subject of scores of *New Yorker* and *Saturday Evening Post* cartoons showing men in stripes breaking rocks. Its walled grimness appears in countless films with titles like *Mutiny in the Big House* and *Twenty Thousand Years in Sing Sing.* In *Angels with Dirty Faces,* James Cagney's character went to Sing Sing's famous electric chair, as did Clark Gable's in *Manhattan Melodrama.* In that film's final scene, the lights dim throughout the cell blocks at Sing Sing as one convict says to his friends: "Dey gave 'im da juice." Even Ogden Nash has played with the prison's mellifluous name:

> Pronounce the Nightingale in Persian
> It comes out Bulbul in their version
> Thus every convict in Iran
> Feels kinship with some Ossining man,
> For be it summer-sing or spring-sing
> He loves to hear the Bulbul sing sing.

In many ways Washington Irving's, Thomas Cole's, and Andrew Jackson Downing's Hudson Valley was a fantasy that was belied by the work of men like Zadock Pratt and Elam Lynds. Every artist and writer who gazed on the valley wearing blinders was matched by an entrepreneur who looked on the same scene with the thought of capitalizing on its economic possibilities.

At no place was this more evident than at Kaaterskill Falls. Few who visited the valley in the mid and late nineteenth century left without making a pilgrimage to the site that Thomas Cole and his fellow artists had made famous. Here, so travelers believed, they might experience firsthand the primitive force of nature. Cole's arrival in the forested mountains, however, was simultaneous with that of commerce. Above the Kaaterskill Falls a miller had dammed the stream. Later enterprising locals had built a flight of steps beside the escarpment and charged visitors twenty-five cents to climb them. The owners of the Laurel House, which succeeded the millhouse, found their business declining when the summer heat diminished the flow over the stepped cliffs to a trickle. They maintained the dam and opened the sluice only on payment of twenty-five cents. "How to live without waterfalls but not without guests," asked one writer. "They meet the situation triumphantly by turning off the one and keeping the other. They save up the waterfalls by doing without them at night and at other times when they are not of much use, and are thus able to provide a life-size cataract at certain hours when somebody happens along who can afford one." But another visitor saw the sham of it all: "Catskillians . . . Have found out how to fence in a cataract so that nobody can see it without paying an admission fee," the writer grumbled, adding that the toll taker had said after the visitor paid the fee: "'I don't know as I can get any water just now, for I've just had a party through.'" Even by 1825, the Kaaterskill Falls presented merely a simulacrum of the sublime wilderness; the untamed landscape had vanished.

CHAPTER 8

River of Fortunes

A great cannon was fired at exactly 2:20 on the afternoon of Monday, February 18, 1861, when the flag-draped train bearing Abraham Lincoln and his family came to a halt on Broadway in downtown Albany. Lincoln was en route from Springfield, Illinois, to Washington to take the oath of office. "Show us the Rail-splitter," and "Trot out old ABE," shouted the crowd waiting for the president-elect to appear. After some delay, he emerged dressed in a "shocking bad hat, and a very thin old overcoat," to receive the welcome of Albany's mayor and the governor. Speaking before the New York legislators later that afternoon, Lincoln told the assembled, "It is true that while I hold myself without mock modesty, the humblest of all individuals that have ever been elevated to the Presidency, I have a more difficult task to perform than any of them."

Many in the crowd standing before Lincoln feared for their country's future. Just six weeks earlier, South Carolina had seceded from the Union. Mississippi, Florida, Alabama, Georgia, Louisiana, and Texas soon followed. At Fort Moultrie on the shore of Charleston harbor, Major Robert Anderson had ordered the men of his small garrison to spike the guns and destroy the carriages, before transferring his troops to the larger and more defensible Fort Sumter farther out in the harbor. Secessionist troops had overrun federal forts and arsenals. In Washington a peace conference, convened by former president John Tyler in a desperate effort to save the nation, was foundering. At ports and military posts throughout the land, officers were deciding their allegiance.

It was fitting for Lincoln's train to stop at Albany, the capital of what was the most populous state in the Union. The valley was thriving with commerce and people. Since the opening of the Erie Canal, Albany's population had quadrupled to more than sixty-two thousand, nearly half of whom were foreign born. The city was the eastern terminus of the New York Central Railroad, the home of Albany's—and the nation's—wealthiest men. The New York Central had settled its headquarters, repair shops, and extensive cattle yards there in 1853. The four-thousand-foot pier in the Albany boat basin handled hundreds of sloops, steamboats, and canal boats each day, though at the moment it was recovering from a spring freshet that had left the docks submerged under several feet of water. Since Market Street, the closest parallel street to the Hudson, sometimes flooded in the spring, many merchants had moved their shops inland to the higher ground of Pearl Street, where they sometimes displaced the residences of old Albany families like Van Rensselaers and Schuylers.

At 11 PM, after a dinner with Governor Edwin D. Morgan at the Delavan House, a temperance hotel on Broadway, the president-elect and his fam-

Overleaf: Thomas Rossiter, *A Picnic on the Hudson*, 1863, showing a group of the artist's friends and neighbors enjoying an outing on Constitution Island. They include Robert Parrott, designer of the Parrott gun, seated in front on the right. (Julia L. Butterfield Memorial Library, Cold Spring, New York)

ily retired to their rooms upstairs. Three blocks south, another visitor to Albany, an actor, also retired for the night in his hotel, the Stanwix House. Earlier that evening he had starred at Albany's nearby Gayety Theatre in *The Apostate*, a melodramatic tragedy of the Spanish Inquisition. His role as the villainous Duke Pescara brought him great acclaim. The following morning the *Albany Journal* ran a story on its first page that declared John Wilkes Booth "one of the finest actors this country has ever produced."

The trip through the Hudson River valley from Troy to New York City offered Lincoln a view of the divisions in the Union. Albany and New York, the great cities at the head of navigation and the mouth of the Hudson, had supported the Democrat, Stephen A. Douglas, in the presidential election of 1860; but the cities of Troy, Hudson, Kingston, Newburgh, Poughkeepsie, and Yonkers had all gone for Lincoln. In most cities, Hudson, Troy, and Poughkeepsie especially, abolitionist sentiment was strong. In 1852 a dramatic production of *Uncle Tom's Cabin* had played to packed audiences in Troy for more than a hundred nights. Farmers in Columbia, Dutchess, Putnam, and Westchester counties on the eastern side of the river supported the new president, as did those of Ulster and Greene counties on the west.

Fugitive slaves lived throughout the valley, where there was a network of numerous stations on the Underground Railroad and vigilance committees flourished. A riot in Troy in 1860 had demonstrated just how powerful those committees could be. On April 27 a U.S. marshal and a slave catcher arrested Charles Nalle, a fugitive from Stevensburg, Virginia, and placed him in a slave pen at the federal customs house. Harriet Tubman, the fugitive slave and abolitionist, happened to be in Troy visiting relatives; she led the vigilance committee in a march on the building. In the riot that ensued, Tubman and the committee freed Nalle and spirited him across the river to a railroad station in Niskayuna. After the defeated slave catcher had left Troy, Nalle slipped back into the city to resume his job as a baker.

Nor was abolitionist sentiment a recent development. In 1847, John Bolding escaped from a South Carolina plantation and established himself as a tailor in Poughkeepsie. Recaptured in 1852, Bolding was brought to New York, where a judge decided he should be returned to his owner. Before the exchange took place, however, Matthew Vassar and a committee of Poughkeepsie's leading citizens stepped forward to purchase John A. Bolding's freedom for fifteen hundred dollars.

The morning that Lincoln arrived at Troy, fifteen thousand people greeted him with "a deafening roar of cheers and shouts." In the years since Lafayette had visited in 1825, the city had continued to prosper as a manufacturing center and its population had grown to forty thousand. Owing to the influence of the late Stephen Van Rensselaer, the city combined culture with commerce. His Rensselaer Polytechnic Institute and Emma Willard's female seminary were thriving. The institute had produced some of the best-trained engineers in the nation, men who had built railroads and canals and other civil works projects in the antebellum period. Many graduates, including Washington A. Roebling, the future builder of the Brooklyn Bridge, would use their skills for the Union cause in the coming war. A Troy housewife's invention of a detachable collar for her husband's shirts had made the city the center of the collar industry, which employed hundreds of young Irish women. (One of them, Kate Mullaney, would organize the Collar Workers Union in 1865, the first all-female union in the nation.) Another manufacturer, Titus Eddy, supplied the United States Treasury with all the inks (created from his own secret formulas) that made the nation's currency nearly impossible to counterfeit.

Iron manufacturing accounted for Troy's prosperity. Seven foundries employed nearly seven hundred men to produce over a million dollars' worth of stoves each year. In the fall of 1861 the Albany and Rensselaer Iron Works rolled the Bessemer steel plates for the first ironclad Northern ship, the *Monitor*. Also in Troy, a Scottish emigrant named Henry Burden had built the largest waterwheel in the country to run his foundry on the Wynantskill Creek. Fully sixty feet in diameter and twenty-two feet wide, it provided power for all his machines, including one of his own invention that supplied more railroad spikes than any other in America. Another, his most famous invention, produced thirty-six hundred horseshoes an hour. The Union Army came to rely on Burden to produce enough shoes to keep all its horses shod, and Confederate spies repeatedly tried to duplicate his machinery.

As Lincoln looked through the windows of his special car furnished with chairs, a sofa, and plush carpet, he saw crowds assembled at the river towns of Greenbush, Stuyvesant, and Castleton. When the train stopped at the city of Hudson to switch engines, a crowd of five thousand was waiting. They had come from farms and villages in Columbia County, places like Chatham and Claverack and Ghent; they had crossed the river on the horse ferry that connected the city of Hudson with the town of Athens on the opposite shore—all for a chance to glimpse their next president. "I do not appear before you for the purpose of making a speech," said Lincoln from the train platform; "I come only to see you, and to give you the opportunity to see me; and to say to you . . . I have decidedly the best of the bargain." As the train pulled out of the station, the crowd joined in a lusty "old Columbia Cheer."

The founders of the city of Hudson, families from Nantucket and Martha's Vineyard who settled there in 1783, thought of it as a seaport on the Atlantic coast where they could create a whale oil center. The deep water of the Hudson provided them with an inland shelter for their vessels and safety from Atlantic storms. For two decades their community thrived. The first federal census of 1790 counted 2,584 people (including 193 slaves), making Hudson the twenty-fourth largest city in the United States. New York's legislators came within a single vote of naming Hudson the permanent capital of New York. At the time more vessels were registered in its port than in New York City's. Oceangoing and coastal ships had embarked from Hudson's docks for whaling and sealing ventures in the Atlantic and Pacific as well as for Southern ports like Charleston and Savannah. Understanding that as many as fifteen vessels were arriving and embarking from its wharves each day, the federal government declared Hudson a port of delivery and export.

Though by 1861 shipping had declined and Hudson's good fortune had passed, the city remained an anchorage for commerce in Columbia County and thus retained vestiges of its glory. Its seven thousand citizens worked in the ironworks and stove foundries located there, and in a factory manufacturing ready-to-wear clothing. From its wharves one could travel on the steamboat *Advocate* to Albany or the *Legislator* to New York City.

Poughkeepsie, where Lincoln's train next stopped, and where thousands were on hand to greet him, was now a thriving city of fifteen thousand. Ever since the seventeenth century, when the Dutch had found the spot on the eastern shore halfway between New York and Albany, Poughkeepsie had been an important harbor on the Hudson. The Dutch adapted the name the Indians had given to the area (meaning "reed-covered lodge by the little-water place") and, as one wag suggested, "contrived over twenty ways to spell it, ultimately choosing the most difficult."

Until the opening of the Erie Canal in 1825, farmers from the valley brought their grain to waiting sloops in the harbor, which then transported it to mills and markets downriver. Stage wagons plying the Albany Post Road connecting New York and the state capital made the village a major stop. After the British burned Kingston in 1777, the governors and legislators moved New York's capital to Poughkeepsie. It was there in 1789 that the state's legislators, by a single-vote plurality, voted to adopt the Constitution of the United States.

By 1861, Poughkeepsie had adapted well to the economic changes that the Erie Canal forced upon the valley. The city had sustained itself through retail trade, manufacturing, commerce, and education. Poughkeepsie's citizens worked in the Vassar Brothers' brewery and manufactured carpets, chairs, locomotives, soap, candles, or farm machinery in the city's factories. Though an early whaling venture failed, farmers still used Poughkeepsie's port for their shipments of milk and produce to New York City. In the winters they sent their goods by train. Then they stopped off at nearby stores and saloons to spend their earnings.

It was education, however, that made Poughkeepsie unique among cities on the Hudson. Poughkeepsie was one of the first in the valley to start a lyceum of literature, science, and mechanic arts, and it was bustling with schools, academies, seminaries, and colleges. By the end of the Civil War they numbered fifteen, including Eastman's National Business College and the soon to be created Vassar Female College.

Without question Harvey Gridley Eastman's National Business College ranked among the most financially successful educational institutions anywhere. The college taught "the practical and useful arts of life" (Eastman's words for accounting and business), Eastman's first advertisement declared. As much a triumph of marketing as of pedagogy, the college, which began in 1859 with just one faculty member (Eastman) and three enrolled students, now had sixty-four teachers, seventeen hundred students, and five buildings. Eastman hired the faculty, built classrooms and arranged housing for the students, taught courses, and continually wrote, printed, and shipped bundles of catalogs and circulars promoting his institution across the land. Full-page advertisements regularly appeared in Horace Greeley's *Weekly Tribune,* so often that the popular editor and politician happily accepted Eastman's invitations to speak to the college's alumni at their frequent reunions. Most important, Eastman marshaled all his musically talented students into a huge brass band that he made available for civic and patriotic events, such as the arrival of Lincoln's train.

The educational enterprise that Matthew Vassar was creating was very different. Vassar believed that women were the intellectual equals of men. Having secured his fortune in brewing, he decided it was time to turn his attention to cultural pursuits. He engaged Andrew Jackson Downing to design Springside, a self-sufficient, forty-four-acre rural estate south of the city. Complete with a barn, carriage house, icehouse, dairy room, greenhouse, gardener's cottage, log cabin, even a deer shelter, set among woodland carriage drives, ponds, streams, and rustic bridges, Springside led one newspaper man to compare it with Eden. "Paradise," declared the reporter with authority, "could scarcely have been lovelier."

Springside may have made him into Squire Eastern on the Hudson, but, as a widower with no children, Vassar wanted a monument that would ensure that his name would be remembered for all time. He considered building a huge statue to Hudson on Pollepel Island, but rejected the idea because it celebrated the explorer and not himself. Finally, with thoughts of his late niece who had founded a female seminary in Poughkeepsie, and with some prodding by her successor who promised the brewer "a monument more lasting than the pyramids," he settled on a unique institution bearing his name, one that would continue Poughkeepsie's association with education: Vassar Female College.

"A college for young women which shall be to them what Yale and Harvard are to young men," Vassar proclaimed. Whenever possible, women would administer the college and serve as instructors. By 1861 Vassar had assembled a board of trustees (including Samuel F. B. Morse, the artist and inventor of the telegraph, who lived nearby), purchased the land, and hired James Renwick, architect of the Smithsonian Institution's castle in Washington as well as Grace Church and St. Patrick's Cathedral in New York, to design a great building for instruction. The four-story brick structure, complete with gas lighting, soft water, steam heat, classrooms, a dining hall, and a "separate sleeping room" for each student, would take four years to erect; the first class of 353 women would not arrive until September 1865. Want of money would not deter Vassar. Nor would want of a dramatic gesture, one that would live forever, a reporter for *Harper's Weekly* said, in the "annals of philanthropy and benevolence." To the first meeting of the trustees, a few days after Lincoln's train had passed through Poughkeepsie, the brewer brought a tin box with $408,000 for the college's endowment.

Matthew Vassar was on the platform when Lincoln left his car to tell the crowd, "I must rely upon . . . the people of the whole country . . . and with their sustaining aid, even I, humble as I am, cannot fail to carry the ship of State safely through the storm."

South of Poughkeepsie the Hudson River Railroad tracks hug the eastern bank. The train carrying Lincoln passed New Hamburg and crossed Wappinger's Creek. As it went by Fishkill Landing, the president-elect could look west across the river to Newburgh and the revolutionary headquarters of George Washington, and shortly afterward he could look southwest to the promontory of West Point.

Since 1802 the fortress had been "a military school for young gentlemen," America's elite training ground for its army. Graduates of the United States Military Academy at West Point served as commanders in every important encounter of the Civil War. Nearly every great general, North and South, learned his military tactics in classrooms there and perfected his horsemanship on Cavalry Flats, the academy's drill field on the edge of the river. Less than two months after Lincoln's journey by train, Major Robert Anderson, fifteenth in his class of 1825, would surrender Union control of Fort Sumter in Charleston harbor to the Confederate brigadier general Pierre Gustave Toutant Beauregard, second in his class of 1838 and former superintendent of West Point. And on April 9, 1865, at Appomattox Courthouse, Virginia, General Robert E. Lee, second in his class of 1829 and also a former superintendent of West Point, surrendered the Army of Northern Virginia to Lieutenant General Ulysses Simpson Grant, twenty-first in his class of 1843. Even the president of the

"West Point and the Highlands," an engraving from 1869 by S. V. Hunt after a painting by Henry Fenn, showing soldiers loading cannon at the point with the Hudson to the north, including Constitution Island, Cold Spring, Storm King Mountain, and Pollepel Island in the distance.

Confederacy, Jefferson Davis, had graduated from the academy, twenty-third in the class of 1828.

At Cold Spring the train passed the West Point Foundry, one of the nation's most productive ironworks, which like the Burden Iron Works in Troy would play a significant role in the coming conflict. It was created earlier in the century by Gouverneur Kemble, a prankster friend of Washington Irving's, who decided in 1816 to become a Highlands industrial baron and, as Irving put it, "turned Vulcan." Kemble built a foundry that was, for its time, a model of manufacturing efficiency, since all the essentials for making and distributing iron were in one place. The area around Cold Spring was rich in iron ore and trees to make charcoal for the blast furnaces; a brook provided water power; West Point offered military protection; and a long wharf built at Foundry Cove on the Hudson River provided easy access for ships. Kemble brought artisans from Europe and hired laborers from Cold Spring, Peekskill, and Fishkill, and he built houses for his new workers. For nearly a century Kemble's West Point Foundry would produce steam engines and locomotives, machinery for cotton and sugar mills, kettles and water pipes for New York City, hat racks and umbrella stands, and iron benches for Irving's Sunnyside. In the coming months the West Point Foundry would produce cannons that would serve the Union side well in the Civil War.

An artillery man and West Point graduate, Robert Parker Parrott, since 1836 had directed Kemble's foundry (he also married Kemble's daughter). With his army background, he took a greater interest in developing superior guns and military hardware than ornamental hat racks and benches. At West Point and at the Greenwood Iron Works in Orange County he experimented with rifled cannon barrels that would improve the range and accuracy of the guns. For his test range, Parrott fired the guns from the foundry grounds into the side of Storm King Mountain across the Hudson. In the coming war, the West Point Foundry would produce ten-, twenty-, and thirty-pound field guns, as well as larger two-hundred- and three-hundred-pound cannon for shore defenses. Other gunmakers in Pennsylvania and Massachusetts would follow with better ordnance, but it was Parrott who brought the first modern cannons to American battlefields.

In June 1862, President Lincoln returned to the Hudson Valley to speak with General Winfield Scott, who had retired to West Point, and to inspect the foundry at Cold Spring. He found eleven hundred workers turning out gun carriages, cannons, and thousands of shells and projectiles. The foundry operated twenty-four hours a day in three shifts. The landscape had been transformed with grime and odors from the furnaces. Stacks belched smoke nonstop. Woodsmen felled trees for miles around, and charcoal fires smoldered in the hills east of the river. The war alone mattered. Lincoln stood by as Robert Parrott himself fired a shell from one of his great guns across the Hudson into the side of Storm King. But he failed to impress the president. "I'm confident you can hit that mountain over there," Lincoln is reported to have said after the rumbling boom of the cannon subsided, "so suppose we get something to eat. I'm hungry."

At exactly 3:00 PM the *Constitution*, the engine pulling Lincoln's special train, arrived at the flag-draped Hudson River Railroad depot at Thirtieth Street and Ninth Avenue in New York City. Thirty-five carriages, a host of Republican representatives, and a phalanx of mounted policemen waited to take the president-elect and his family to the Astor House on Broadway. Yet Lincoln's greeting in New York was far less enthusiastic than it had been in any other city or town. Flags were flying from most of the buildings, the procession passed beneath a huge banner inscribed "Fear not, Abraham, I am thy shield and thy exceeding great reward," and the publisher George Putnam had hung a sign on the outside of his Broadway office, "Right makes Might," quoting from a speech that Lincoln himself had given a year earlier at New York's Cooper Union. But the people who lined the streets were subdued.

Walt Whitman happened to be among the crowd as the president-elect's carriage arrived at the Astor House. He remembered witnessing the cheers that had greeted Lafayette, Louis Kossuth, Andrew Jackson, Daniel Webster, and the Prince of Wales, among others, "but on this occasion, not a voice—not a sound," he wrote. On alighting from his carriage, Lincoln "look'd with curiosity upon that immense sea of faces, and the sea of faces returned the look with similar curiosity. In both there was a dash of comedy, almost farce, such as Shakespeare puts in his blackest tragedies." But then, Whitman remembered, after an uncomfortable moment, "the tall figure . . . with moderate pace, and accompanied by a few unknown looking persons, ascended the portico-steps of the Astor House, disappear'd through its broad entrance—and the dumb-show ended."

The lukewarm reception testified to the strained relations between New York City and the rest of the state, and indeed the entire North. Nothing more clearly reveals the mindset of the bourgeois merchant class that had helped to determine the city's character since 1626. New Yorkers cared less about the question of the morality of slavery than they did about slavery's chief product, cotton. At the same time that Philadelphians were cultivating good works and Bostonians were professing abolitionist ideals, New Yorkers busied themselves with commerce without much concern for conscience.

Although slavery had been outlawed in New York state for all blacks born after July 4, 1799, and on July 4, 1827, for all remaining blacks, the city's merchant princes still depended on cotton, the product of slavery, for much of their prosperity. The Southern planters depended on New York, too. Most planters harbored few scruples about making slaves pick cotton, but all found the activities of the countinghouse distasteful. Business and the work of the merchant class was beneath Southern dignity; business and the merchant class constituted New York's dignity. Southerners were happy to send their ships laden with cotton bales from Charleston, Savannah, Mobile, and New Orleans up the east coast to the port of New York. New Yorkers were only too happy to transfer those bales onto their packets bound for Liverpool or Le Havre.

By 1850 forty cents of every dollar paid for Southern cotton went to the merchants of New York City. New York merchants owned the ships that carried the cotton from the South to New York and Europe; New York agents insured the cargoes; and New York bankers loaned Southern planters the money they needed to sow their crops. Occasionally, when a Southern planter went bankrupt, a New York banker ended up becoming a slaveowner. Everyone seemed to prosper from the comfortable arrangement. The same ships that carried bales of cotton from the South to New York returned laden with products from Europe and the North. Bolts of cotton cloth needed for women's clothing were chief among the goods. Changing fashion demanded more fabric, too. Between 1800 and 1855 the number of yards of material needed to make a lady's dress increased from five to twenty, while the yardage required for her underclothes jumped from seven and a half to sixty-three.

As shipping increased in the nineteenth century, the port expanded its wharves to both sides of Manhattan Island, as well as to Staten Island, Brooklyn, and the New Jersey shore—771 miles of wharfage in all. The day Lincoln arrived, steamships from Le Havre, Liverpool, Hamburg, Baltimore, Savannah, and Havana docked in New York; other ships embarked for Glasgow, Marseilles, Liverpool, Hong Kong, and Barbados. Smaller steamers carrying various manufactures landed from Atlantic coastal cities. Each of these boats carried textiles, iron, fruit, silks, and cloth, among other goods, and returned with products made chiefly in New York City. Still more boats laden with goods from the West came down the river from the Erie Canal. And countless ferries shuttled passengers between docks in Brooklyn and New Jersey. "Your insular city of the Manhattoes," Melville described the port in the opening of *Moby Dick*, "belted round with wharves as Indian isles by coral reefs—commerce surrounds it with her surf."

The development of shipping and trade went together with the rise of New York City's economic importance. By 1860, there were more than 800,000 people living on Manhattan Island, and the combined population of the boroughs that now constitute the city was more than a million. Of the other Atlantic coast cities only Philadelphia, with 565,000 people, came close to being a rival. All other port cities lagged far behind.

In the summer of 1860, many in New York City believed that the Republican Party's nomination of Lincoln threatened not only a way of life in the South but their own economic life as well. Should the war between the states actually happen, bankers and merchants would be out millions of dollars in uncollected loans made to Southern planters. Financiers estimated that Southerners owed as much as $200 million. A group of the city's wealthiest financial barons, including August Belmont and William Backhouse Astor and the sugar-refining prince Frederick Christian Havemeyer, coerced the hopelessly split Democratic candidates into uniting behind Stephen A. Douglas as the "Union" candidate to defeat Lincoln for the presidency, "to save this glorious republic from the horrors of disunion and anarchy." Although their plan failed, as Lincoln carried the state, almost three of every four New York City voters supported Douglas.

Most politicians from Tammany Hall, the center of the Democratic Party in the city, had joined with the merchants to back Douglas. Mayor Fernando Wood, who had forged an alliance of support from many of the city's merchants and bankers as well as its mechanics, immigrants, and longshoremen, regularly demonstrated his pro-Southern sentiments whenever it was expedient to do so. Just a month before Lincoln's arrival, Wood even proposed that New York City separate from the union and become a republic.

Although Fernando Wood's proposal went nowhere, it made for a cold meeting on the morning of Wednesday, February 20, when the president-elect met the mayor in the Governor's Room at New York's City Hall. Haughty, vain, impeccably dressed in a black coat, Wood stood before Lincoln, every dyed and combed-out black curl of hair at his temples in place, and delivered a lecture that bordered at times on rudeness. New York was "sorely afflicted" by the discord between the North and the South. "All her material interests are paralyzed. Her commercial greatness is endangered." Should the Union die, he continued, "the present supremacy of New York may perish with it. To you, therefore, chosen under the forms of the Constitution as the head of the Confederacy, we look for a restoration of fraternal relations between the States—only to be accomplished by peaceful and conciliatory means." The words were easy to understand: the nation should not fight to preserve the Union. No doubt Wood intended the word "Confederacy" to rankle the president: in Montgomery, Alabama, just two days earlier, Jefferson Davis had been inaugurated as president of the Confederate States of America.

Lincoln was said to listen with "a sort of dreamy expression of the eye" before drawing himself up to his "fullest height" and replying. "There is nothing that could ever bring me to consent . . . to the destruction of this Union, (in which not only the great City of New York, but the whole country has acquired its greatness)." He would preserve the Union, he concluded, so long as it was possible to preserve "the prosperity and liberties" of the people. The ambiguity of Lincoln's slight remarks saved the moment.

After April 12, 1861, when the Confederates fired on Fort Sumter in Charleston harbor, merchants, politicians, and ordinary citizens united for a time behind the Union cause. New York's Seventh Regiment marched down Broadway in a tumultuous parade. Even Fernando Wood proposed that New York appropriate a million dollars to raise more regiments. As the war dragged on, however, New York became a hotbed for "Copperheads," Northern supporters of the Southern cause, and Wood was the most famous. Poised on the edge of treason, he and his supporters denounced Lincoln's Emancipation Proclamation, and they encouraged talk of black racial inferiority and white supremacy.

No doubt such talk helped fuel New York's infamous draft riot of July 1863, still considered one of the worst riots in the nation's history. What began as a protest by laborers against the first federal conscription act, especially the provision that allowed people of wealth to buy their way out of military service, quickly devolved into a race riot and general chaos. For almost a week mobs roamed the city looting and setting fire to the homes of wealthy Republicans, attacking the police, and destroying saloons and brothels patronized by black sailors. Seven hundred African-Americans took refuge in police stations, and hundreds more found shelter in the private homes of whites. Others were not so lucky: mobs burned the orphan asylum for blacks on Fifth Avenue and Forty-second Street to the ground and murdered and mutilated eleven black men. Abraham Lincoln had to send five units of the Union Army, exhausted from their victory at Gettysburg, north to restore order.

Still, the Belmonts, Astors, and Havemeyers—and Fernando Wood—should not have feared for the supremacy of New York City. By 1861 the city had become more than a mere transfer station for goods and the products of Southern plantations. Without question its deepwater port had no rival in America. In the decade before Lincoln's meeting with Wood, the port had shipped great quantities not only of cotton but also of wheat and corn. Two-thirds of all imports to the United States, and a third of the nation's exports, went through New York.

The city was awash in money, so much money that New York was able to withstand the panic of 1857 and prosper during the war that followed. The streams of California and the soil of Pike's Peak in Colorado had yielded hundreds of millions of dollars of gold bullion; the Comstock Lode in Nevada produced millions more in silver; the minerals and the money they brought often ended up in New York banks. In turn, banks and bankers proliferated. On his death in 1848, John Jacob Astor had left his son William Backhouse Astor thousands of tenement buildings, and these, too, proliferated. By 1864 there were fifteen thousand tenements on Manhattan, and Astor collected rents from most of them. Fourteen sugar-refining plants in New York and Brooklyn, owned by the Havemeyer family, turned out sugar cones and, later, sugar lumps. August Belmont, who had arrived in New York during the financial panic of 1837 and established a private banking firm on Wall Street, worked as a War Democrat to divert foreign investments from the Confederacy to the Union, all the while profiting enormously from foreign exchange transactions, real estate, and railroad investments. By 1865 the city ranked among the greatest meat producers in the nation. Trains from the West daily brought beef cattle to terminals in New Jersey and from there to slaughterhouses on both shores. The location proved especially advantageous for the abattoirs, as the slaughterhouses could discharge the animals' blood directly into the river.

In the four decades between 1860 and 1900 the Hudson River valley continued the development that had begun with the advent of steam. Old Hudson River families, Livingstons and Van Rensselaers especially, saw their wealth continue to decline in relation to the newly minted fortunes that were rapidly accumulating on Manhattan Island. In 1875, nine of the ten wealthiest men in America lived in New York City. Commodore Vanderbilt, the oldest among them at age eighty-one, was also the richest. He had accumulated $75 million from his shipping and railroad ventures. Though he still controlled the largest fleet of steamboats in the United States, the Commodore had made most of his money in railroad lines that dominated much of the nation's transportation. His Hudson River and New York Central lines, as well as others in the West, brought him enormous wealth and power. The second wealthiest man in the nation, A. T. Stewart, made most of his $50 million in his New York City department store. Real estate had formed the basis of the fortunes of others, William Backhouse Astor (who was worth $47 million), John Jacob Astor III ($30 million), and William Rhinelander ($23 million). Bankers and financiers, too, had made their money in Manhattan, often by providing the capital for railroads and manufacturing. Russell Sage ($37 million) invested in western railroads. Moses Taylor, whose father had been an agent and confidant to John Jacob Astor, left the importing business to become president of Manhattan's City Bank. When he died in 1882, he left an estate of $40 million.

During the second half of the century, steam continued to develop and even dominate the valley's life. Beginning in 1881, steam engines pulled freight and passenger cars on the western shore of the river, between Jersey City and Albany. Engineers used steam engines to power the machines in factories at the river's edge, and captains piloted their oceangoing steamships from Europe through the Narrows to Hudson River docks at Manhattan and Hoboken. Steam boilers began to displace wood stoves in houses and buildings throughout the valley. By 1860 coal had replaced wood as the fuel for the steam boilers. Again valley residents depended on the Hudson. Each year at Kingston, the eastern terminus of the Delaware and Hudson Canal, hundreds of boats filled with Pennsylvania coal entered the river. Most headed downstream to furnaces and manufacturing plants in New York City.

Between 1860 and 1900 the population of the valley doubled, to 3 million. Ships carrying millions of immigrants arrived at the port of New York; while most moved on to other parts of the nation, many stayed to find work in New York City's factories. Census enumerators found 214,000 Irish living in New York and Brooklyn in 1860, far more than any other group; their number increased to 275,000 by 1900, but that year the German population of 322,000 eclipsed the Irish. In 1900 two other groups, Russians at 155,000 and Italians at 145,000, had seen their populations grow by more than 200 percent in the previous decade.

Because of its port, the river that led the way to the interior, and the railroad that connected the Hudson Valley with the rest of the nation, New York City's prosperity and population only expanded after the war. The 1870 census found that one of every thirty-three factories in the United States was located on Manhattan Island; factories employed thousands of immigrants, who made up 44 percent of Manhattan's population. By the turn of the century, 1.5 million people were crowded into forty-seven thousand tenements that extended as far north as 110th Street. The wealthy migrated north up Fifth Avenue; Mrs. William Astor put down roots in a mansion at the northeast corner of Sixty-fifth Street. In 1871 the New York Elevated Railroad Company opened its rapid-transit line on Ninth Avenue up to Thirtieth Street; nine years later it finished its last station at 155th Street. Central Park, which was constructed between 1857 and 1860, added a zoo in 1871, and in the 1880s, over the objections of many members of the clergy, offered Sunday concerts for the refreshment of "working men and their families."

Fed by the steady stream of foreigners, Manhattan's population continued to climb: to nearly a million by 1870 and to more than 1.4 million by 1890. In 1855 the city converted Castle Garden, the former stone fort off the southern tip of Manhattan built to protect New York harbor, into a processing center for immigrants. A labor exchange inside the Castle Garden placed thousands of male and female newcomers from abroad, even children, in jobs throughout the city. Wealthy New York housewives came regularly to the exchange to select their domestic servants from the throng of Irish, Swedish, and German girls who arrived daily. At the beginning, the immigrants were mostly northern Europeans. In the late 1880s boatloads of Russian and Polish Jews, along with others from southern and eastern Europe, began arriving. Their numbers would increase dramatically by the turn of the century. Castle Garden served as the nation's immigration gateway until 1892, when the federal government opened Ellis Island in the Hudson's Upper Bay.

The ever increasing numbers of people, as well as the thriving port and manufacturing industry at the mouth of the Hudson River, brought changes to the North. Not only did the valley serve as the vast supply route for grain and goods from the West and coal from Pennsylvania, it also provided New York City with bricks, stone, and cement, materials it needed to sustain its building expansion, and ice, great chunks of frozen river water needed to sustain its health.

Ever since the Dutch arrived in the seventeenth century, the Hudson Valley was noted for its clays. "The country has . . . several sorts of fine clay, such as white, yellow, red, and black, which is fat and tough, suitable for pots, dishes, plates, tobacco—and like wares," wrote Adriaen van der Donck in his *Description of the New Netherlands.* About this time the Dutch began using Hudson River clay to make bricks for their houses and public buildings. By the mid nineteenth century, brick making was an important industry in places like Haverstraw, Mechanicville, Castleton, Schodack, Beacon, Verplanck, and Saugerties.

Because of its close proximity to New York City and the rich glacial deposit of blue clay that lay about thirty feet below the sandy surface, Haverstraw became the richest and best-known brick-making site on the river. Its industry thrived after 1852 when Richard Ver Valen, a local resident, invented a machine that packed the clay firmly into a series of molds. With Ver Valen's molding machine, Haverstraw's factories increased their production from a few thousand bricks a year to more than a million. Haverstraw factory owners prided themselves on using just the right proportions of clay, coal dust, and sand, and firing their bricks at just the right temperature. By the end of the nineteenth century more than forty-one factories lined the shore, producing as many as 325 million bricks a year. A third of all the bricks used in New York City came from Haverstraw.

The brick-making industry came with a cost, however. Owners sometimes demanded more hours and cut wages. Strikes ensued in Haverstraw in 1853 and 1870, and the state militia had to be called in to keep order. The greatest price was exacted in 1906, when improper excavation of one of the clay pits caused a landslide that swallowed up five blocks of houses and about twenty people. Still, Haverstraw's mayor looked at the bright side of the disaster: he estimated that the landslide had exposed another $200,000 worth of clay.

After the Civil War, stone quarrying became a big business along the Hudson. "Crystal, like that of Muscovy, is found there," van der Donck wrote. "Also grey flagging, slate, grit or grinding-stone . . . much quarry stone . . . [and] a kind of stone like alabaster and marble." By the nineteenth century the exploitation of these mineral riches was in full swing. Hook Mountain, south of Haverstraw, yielded countless boatloads of red sandstone. Peekskill Granite became the foundation stones for the Cathedral of St. John the Divine in New York City. Anthony's Nose, five miles south of Peekskill, held more than twenty different minerals. Starting in the nineteenth century miners carved out a wealth of abrasive minerals, created by chemical reactions between the igneous rocks that had intruded into the metamorphic strata. These include the only deposits of emery in the Western Hemisphere. Around Rosendale, southwest of Kingston, the land yielded a natural limestone hydraulic cement, capable of hardening under water to a stonelike mass. Hudson River factories turned out ten thousand barrels of cement each day for New York's monumental nineteenth-century building projects, like the anchorages and towers of the Brooklyn Bridge and the five-pointed pedestal of the Statue of Liberty.

It was Hudson River ice however, that proved most important to New York City's crowded residents in the late nineteenth century. "It is fast becoming a necessary of life in every well-regulated household during hot weather," a *New York Times* reporter wrote of ice in 1857. Of course ice had been cooling food since the Chinese used it sometime before the first millennium. But it was not until 1827, when an enterprising Bostonian named Nathaniel Wyeth used horses pulling saws to cut grooves across the frozen surface of a pond in a checkerboard pattern of two-foot squares that mass production came to the operation. Workers walked behind the horses, guiding the saws to cut out blocks from a lake or a river; still more workers took the neatly cut blocks to icehouses at the water's bank. The equipment was inexpensive but the rewards were great. From the mid nineteenth century until mechanical refrigeration became common in the twentieth, every farmer for miles around the Hudson River could find steady work for three weeks in the late winter before the ice let out. Wyeth's invention brought a revolution to the frozen ponds and rivers of New England, but even more so to the Hudson Valley.

The Hudson provided more ice than any other single operation, and most of the product went to New York City. By 1880, when Manhattan's demand for ice reached 1.5 million tons a year, the 74 icehouses along the river had a capacity of more than 2 million tons; fifteen years later the number had increased to 145 houses with a capacity of more than 3 million tons. The Knickerbocker Ice Company cut blocks from Rockland Lake and sent them down an inclined plane to a huge icehouse at Rockland Landing, on the western shore of the river opposite Ossining, and it established similar operations at Fort Clinton and Verplanck Point. Farther upriver, icehouses dotted the landscape north of Poughkeepsie—16 at Castleton, 10 at Stuyvesant, 9 at Catskill, and still others at Troy, Rhinecliff, Rondout, Athens, and Coxsackie. For about three weeks, usually between mid-January and mid-February, as many as 25,000 men labored to cut blocks weighing 250 to 300 pounds out of the river, float them along a channel they had cut in the ice to a storehouse at the river's bank, and, with the aid of steam-driven conveyor belts, hoist them into the icehouse for storage before their eventual trip by boat to the city.

"No man sows, yet many men reap a harvest from the Hudson," wrote the naturalist John Burroughs of the ice harvest. From the windows of his house, he was able "to look down upon the busy scene, as from a hilltop upon a river meadow in haying time; only here the figures stand out much more sharply than they do from a summer meadow. . . . Sometimes nearly two hundred men and boys with numerous horses, are at work at once, marking, ploughing, planing, scraping, sawing, hauling, chiseling . . . while knots and straggling lines of idlers here and there look on in cold discontent, unable to get a job." By 1875 the harvest had become an important part of many farmers' incomes. "Ice or no ice," Burroughs wrote, "sometimes means bread or no bread to scores of families."

Burroughs looked out on the Knickerbocker Ice Company's storehouse, which held fifty thousand tons. Close by was a large brick building that housed a steam generator to run the machinery, including the inclined elevators. Burroughs marveled at the "unbroken procession" of crystal blocks that ascended on the elevator to a platform at the top of the house. There an inspector with "a sharp eye in his head, and a sharp ice-hook in his hand" picked out the impure blocks while allowing the rest to slide down gentle inclines to their resting place in the cool, sawdust-filled interior.

Whitewashed to reflect the sun's rays, the great rectangular icehouses stood several stories high and measured up to three hundred feet in length. Inside, they were divided into compartments separated by thick wooden walls. During the harvest, workers carefully filled the compartments with layers of ice cakes, each separated by straw or sawdust. When shrouded in mist rising from the water on an autumn dawn, the icehouses that dotted the banks and many of the islands of the river presented a ghostly cast of tombs—massive, solid, immovable.

From the beginning, entrepreneurs quickly understood the vast amounts of money to be made selling Hudson ice. Early on the Knickerbocker Ice Company, one of the largest on the river, along with its smaller rivals, began to act as a monopoly. When the Hygeia Company in Manhattan began to manufacture ice in the 1890s, it too joined with the other companies to set prices and raise them without fear of competition. Although newspapers often railed against the "ice extortionists," the prices rose in the last two decades of the nineteenth century as much as 100 percent. New York's sanitary officials feared that price gouging would mean death for many of the thousands of people crowded into New York's tenements.

Their greed far from slaked, the ice potentates manipulated prices to accumulate even more money. In 1895 the ice companies on the Kennebec River in Maine joined with companies in New York, Baltimore, and Philadelphia to form an ice trust. "The object," one of the trust members said, "is to regulate prices and the amount [of ice] harvested, and hold down competition." By the following July the trust was in full control, and prices were rising.

It took a minor but unscrupulous robber baron from Bath, Maine, and the underhanded intrigues of New York's legendarily corrupt Tammany political machine to achieve full control of every chip of ice sold in New York City. The robber baron was Charles W. Morse, an infamous banker, financier, stock manipulator, and "Ice King," who operated the trust. Before he had even graduated from Bowdoin College in 1877, Morse had made a half million dollars selling Kennebec river ice. By the 1890s, he was

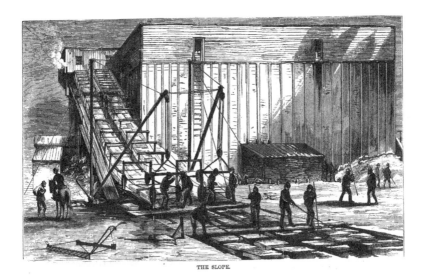

THE SLOPE.

Theodore Russell Davis, "The Ice Crop on the Hudson," 1874, a series of illustrations from *Harper's Weekly*. Readers of *Harper's* were captivated by the industry that systematically cut frozen water into neat rectangular blocks and stored them in huge icehouses for

CUTTING THE ICE—WE

THE RUN.

STOWING THE ICE.

use in the summer. Although horses and men performed much of the labor, they were assisted by steam engines that raised the blocks into the icehouses. (Collection of John De Marco)

VER, ABOVE RONDOUT.

looking southward to the abundance of ice on the Hudson. In 1900 New York's mayor, Robert A. Van Wyck, helped make the trust's stranglehold over the frozen commodity complete.

His ancestors had emigrated from Wyck in Holland to New Amsterdam in 1650; he graduated from Columbia Law School at the head of his class in 1872; he was elected judge of New York's City Court in 1889; he was a founder and later president of the Holland Society, a group of people of Dutch heritage dedicated to perpetuating the history of New Netherland; but in 1900, at the end of his mayoral term, Robert A. Van Wyck proved a willing and well-rewarded accomplice in the ice trust. Van Wyck was a man of few words. In the newly consolidated city's first mayoral campaign, in 1897, he did not speak. He delivered what must be the shortest inaugural address on record, two sentences ("Mr. Mayor, the people have chosen me to be mayor. I shall say whatever I have to say to them"), and then remained silent for the rest of his term. But what Van Wyck lacked in oratorical skill he made up for in greed. Early in his administration he and his Tammany-appointed government gave the American Ice Corporation favorable rates for docking privileges on the Hudson and vetoed a bill to allow other ice companies to compete in the city. Later Van Wyck made more than a half million dollars speculating in American Ice stock.

In May 1900 the avarice of the ice trust exceeded all bounds when it pushed the price from twenty-five cents to sixty cents per hundred pounds of ice. William Randolph Hearst's *New York Journal* revealed that Van Wyck owned eight thousand shares of American Ice, and that his Tammany cronies—even office boys—had made a killing on the trust. Once exposed, Morse quickly lost interest in ice; instead he created a monopoly that controlled all coastal shipping in the East. Van Wyck left office in disgrace; his exit was, said the *New York Times* in an editorial, "an occasion for public thankfulness." In 1906 the newly married Robert A. Van Wyck packed a trunk with three and a half million dollars, and shipped off with his bride to Paris, where he would spend the rest of his life in quiet luxury. Two years later, prosecutors shipped Charles W. Morse off to the federal penitentiary in Atlanta for bank fraud.

Although it still charged exorbitant prices whenever it could, the ice trust was never as strong after the revelations of 1900. As ice manufacturers proliferated in New York, and more affluent New Yorkers bought electric and gas refrigerators, the demand for Hudson River ice began to diminish, until it died out altogether in the 1940s. One by one the great ghostly tombs were dismantled, converted to mushroom houses, or left derelict on the riverbank. For the most part they have become a memory. But even today walkers on the Hotaling-Schodack Island, south of Albany, may come across a foundation wall. Or a casual visitor to Coxsackie may look across the water to Nutten Hook, where stand the remains of one of the last great icehouses, silent reminders of an industry that for half a century brought thousands of men and horses to harvest the frozen river water.

As the nineteenth century progressed, railroads and steamboats opened the Hudson Valley to a new breed of aggressively rich men and their families. These were not "the mellow fruit of society," as the novelist Henry James put it after a visit to the valley in 1870; rather, they were the "hard nuts, which have grown, ripened as they could." These newly rich had amassed great wealth in the factories of Manhattan; they had bought up great tracts of the island's real estate and divided it into lots, which they rented at a handsome profit; they had prospered in the countinghouses, ruthlessly building and financing railroads, speculating in the gold market, financing shipping, and lending money to others. Now, in the Hudson Valley they decided to display their opulent, rough elegance, in ways that the Van Rensselaers, Schuylers, Van Cortlandts, and Livingstons never had.

North of Manhattan, on the eastern shore of the Hudson, the newly wealthy acquired and built sumptuous country retreats. Near Tarrytown, Jay Gould, the speculator known for his immense railroad holdings and his infamous attempt to corner the nation's gold market, purchased Lyndhurst, a great Gothic mansion designed by the architect Alexander Jackson Davis. At Hyde Park, Frederick William Vanderbilt, Commodore Vanderbilt's grandson, ordered the architect Charles F. McKim to design a house "like the Trianon, only larger." Farther north, on Stattsburgh Bay opposite Kingston, Stanford White, society's favorite architect of the 1890s, transformed a modest house belonging to Ruth Livingston (a direct descendant of Robert the Founder) and her husband, Darius Ogden Mills, into a seventy-nine-room Beaux-Arts mansion. For its construction, and to help prop up the Livingston family fortunes, Mills used money he had made in the California gold rush, railroad speculation, and Manhattan real estate ventures in which he had succeeded handsomely. The Mills mansion on the Hudson became "Bellomont," the scene of a memorable house party in Edith Wharton's novel of Gilded Age manners, *The House of Mirth.*

Farther north still, and ten miles west of the river, the village of Saratoga Springs also felt the impact of changes in nineteenth-century transportation. Travelers had long known of the area's mineral-laden waters and the carbonic acid gas that forces them to the earth's surface. Inspired by a visit to the famous waters of Bath, England, a local entrepreneur decided to create his own mineral spa in Saratoga. Visitors to Saratoga Springs marveled at the town's great hotels with long piazzas, public gardens with broad promenades, and a wide main street, Broadway, lined with shops. The waters of Saratoga provided a reason for the fashionable to come and see everyone, and in turn to be seen themselves. Every afternoon marriageable young women dressed in their summer finery and, usually walking in pairs, strolled down Broadway or passed through the tree-shaded inner court of the Grand Union Hotel, or perhaps ambled in Congress Spring Park, where a band presented concerts thrice daily.

Since the 1830s wealthy families, seeking a summer escape from the pestilence and frequent threats of cholera in New York and other eastern cities, took steamers to Albany and overland carriages to the numerous hotels at the spa. "Fifteen hundred people have been known to arrive in a week," wrote the English traveler James Stuart of his visit. "They come from all parts of the States, even from New Orleans . . . to avoid the heat and unhealthy weather . . . and to enjoy the very wholesome and pleasant mineral waters." In 1832 the Saratoga and Schenectady Railroad (followed in 1835 by the Rensselaer and Saratoga line) helped to make the journey even easier. It was after the Civil War, when a former heavyweight boxing champion from New York built a racecourse and a large casino in Congress Spring Park, that greed joined geology to lure some of the nation's wealthiest people to the spa for sporting entertainments. The hotels expanded to truly gargantuan proportions, with vast ballrooms, dining rooms that could accommodate many hundreds, and beds for as many as twenty thousand visitors.

Edith Wharton opens her last novel, *The Buccaneers,* with a depiction of life in Saratoga Springs during the 1870s. By then New York's aristocrats had abandoned the spa resort in favor of the more refined seaside pleasures of Newport, Rhode Island, and bustles had replaced crinolines, but in Saratoga "everybody wore what they pleased." Mrs. St. George, the mother of two eligible daughters, sits on the piazza of the Grand Union Hotel lamenting that Saratoga's society "had grown as mixed and confusing as the fashions." Yet Mrs. St. George endures her stay, for Mr. St. George enjoys his afternoons at the racetrack and his evenings at the poker table.

On his visit to the town in 1870, Henry James acknowledged that a "democratic, vulgar Saratoga" was supplanting the grace of the past, mourned that "old times" were slipping away, and said that he frequently heard people complain "the company is dreadfully mixed." James understood that the change in women's dress and manners reflected the "wholesale equalization of the various social atoms which is the distinctive feature of the collective Saratoga." Here at this inland corner of the Hudson Valley, he found "the democratization of elegance," a leveling of class and status that had begun with the rent wars decades earlier. At last, transportation and industrialization, as well as the democratic forces abroad in the land, had penetrated the isolated and exclusive Hudson Valley.

At the end of August 1904, after an absence of more than two decades while he was in Europe, Henry James returned to America. He wanted to see American life, he said, to taste American air, to see old friends, and he knew that at sixty-one, overweight and suffering from occasional bouts of gout, it would likely be his last trip to his birthplace, New York City. The westward passage from Cherbourg had taken just five and a half days. As he surveyed the skyline of New York from the deck of the *Kaiser Wilhelm II* at its pier at Hoboken, James saw a metropolis transformed. He had left a city of 2 million people and returned to one of 3.6 million, of whom about 1.3 million were foreign born.

Had he looked from the dock at Hoboken two decades earlier, when he was last in the United States, James would have been able to see across Manhattan Island to the towers of the Brooklyn Bridge. Only a few other tall structures, including the spare spire of Trinity Church and the lofty Western Union and New York Tribune buildings, would have been within his sight then. But now, as he looked first from the dock and later from the deck of a ferry, James could no longer see the Brooklyn Bridge. The changed skyline forced him to mix the metaphors he used to describe the "dauntless power" of the city. "Multitudinous sky-scrapers" stood "like extravagant pins in a cushion already overplanted, and stuck as in the dark, anywhere and anyhow. You see the pincushion in profile, so to speak, on passing between Jersey City and Twenty-third Street, but you get it broadside on, this loose nosegay of architectural flowers, if you skirt the Battery, well out, and embrace the whole plantation." In the shadows of the skyscrapers he found a "swarming city, . . . compressed communities, throbbing, through its myriad arteries and pores," that "testified over-whelmingly to the character of New York." And, James noted, there was "a growing invisibility of churches." Trinity had been "mercilessly deprived of its visibility." Across the urban landscape the towers of commerce reigned supreme as New Yorkers celebrated their wealth.

Uptown, James found, the topography of New York City had also changed. The "townside," he said, was "making after the countryside fast." James saw Riverside Drive and Columbia University, which had recently relocated from Madison Avenue and Forty-ninth Street to its new cam-pus on upper Broadway. ("It has taken New York to invent," said James, "the 'moving' university.") He saw the hundred-foot-tall memorial to the Soldiers and Sailors of the Civil War that graced a broad esplanade in the recently completed Riverside Park at Eighty-ninth Street. And "on a bleak winter morning" he beheld at 122nd Street the imposing tomb of Ulysses Grant and his wife, Julia. New York City, the "sordid city" James concluded, sat at the "Beautiful Gate" and commanded "the great per-spective of the River."

Toward the end of his visit to the United States, in April 1905, the novelist returned from the West through the Mohawk Valley and along the shore of the Hudson River. As the train moved eastward, history, James felt, "appeared to meet" him. He likened it to the presence of a "rich-voiced gentlewoman" at "antique Albany," and the gentlewoman of his mind's eye stood at a gabled Dutch window.

The window was one that James remembered from his youth, for his own associations with antique Albany were rich. His father had been raised there and his grandfather had made his money through trade on the Erie Canal and in Albany's banks. As a youth he and his brother William spent several summers in the state capital, and James once thought of attending Union College in Schenectady. Ralph Tobias finds Isabel Archer, the spontaneous young heroine of *The Portrait of a Lady*, "in an old house at Albany, sitting in a dreary room on a rainy day, reading a heavy book and boring herself to death." Albany is the provincial city of the New World, isolated from the worldly life Isabel encounters in Europe. As James surveyed the scene of the city and the river, he looked through a glaze "of all-but filial tears."

As his train proceeded southward through the valley, James found his view of the "perpetually interesting" Hudson to be a bonus of the trip. He responded most intensely to the light on the water that set the mood for his experience. "Its face was veiled, for the most part," he wrote, "in a mist of premature spring heat, an atmosphere draping it indeed in luminous mystery."

The view did not come without guilt, however, for after his journey, James "reflected with acrimony on the obtrusion of track and stations to the Riverside view." He recognized the "ugly presence" of the railroad and that the scenery he so enjoyed came at a price. Perhaps, said James, respectful travelers should confine themselves to a boat. Steamers offered "a peculiar romance," but the rows of steel snaking along the Hudson's shore had all but banished the idea of the contemplative journey.

On a "wet and windy day" a fortnight later, James ventured up the Hudson to West Point. He saw the landscape of the fort as a vast stage, the setting for a "whole procession of storm-effects . . . the weather playing over it all day as with some great watercolor brush." The "cluster of high promontories" looming over the river transcended its location to become part of the "geography of the ideal." For James, the landscape of the Hudson Valley epitomized the best of America.

Twentieth-Century Waters

It was the greatest and longest celebration in the history of the Hudson Valley, a two-week festival commencing on September 25, 1909, to celebrate the achievements of Henry Hudson in 1609 and Robert Fulton in 1807. From New York City to Troy the organizers scheduled parades, flotillas, light shows, art and scientific exhibitions, and long-winded speeches. The people of Holland sent a full-scale reproduction of the *Half Moon;* a descendant of Chancellor Livingston helped to launch an exact replica of Fulton's first steamboat. The navies of England, Germany, France, and the Netherlands each sent a squadron of battleships, submarines, and torpedo boats, which joined the American fleet of more than fifteen hundred military boats and yachts. A million schoolchildren marched in parades that included historical floats depicting, among others, the first sachem of the Iroquois, Minuit's purchase of Manhattan Island, the reception of Peter Stuyvesant, the capture of Major André, Washington's farewell to his officers, Rip Van Winkle, the legend of Sleepy Hollow, an Erie Canal boat, and the Statue of Liberty. The nonagenarian Julia Ward Howe, whose "Battle Hymn of the Republic" had stirred the Union cause in the Civil War, read a new poem about Fulton's accomplishment: "Where fire and water closest blend / There find a servant and a friend." The aeronaut Wilbur Wright demonstrated the possibilities of flight by piloting his plane from Governors Island to Grant's Tomb and back, an astounding distance of twenty miles. On September 25 a great electrical and pyrotechnic display bathed the Hudson River in light from New York City's Battery to Spuyten Duyvil. And on October 9, a chain of fiery beacons flashed up the valley from the river's mouth to the city of Troy. The blazes signaled the end of the Hudson-Fulton Celebration.

The organizers of the celebration had invested it with national and even international significance, but the blazes that shined through the valley that autumn also marked a watershed moment in the Hudson's history. The nineteenth century had seen the advent of the steamboat and the railroad and the end of isolation for the river towns. The new century would see the advent of the automobile and high-speed roads that would supplant both the steamboat and the train. Engineers would span the Hudson's waters with some of the longest bridges in the world. They would dam the river and some of the streams in its watershed to regulate its flow and generate electricity. New industries and people, many of them commuters, would fill older cities and towns and create new ones. A scion of one of the Hudson Valley's oldest families would surpass the Livingstons and Van

Opposite: Poster advertising the Hudson-Fulton Celebration, 1909. Henry Hudson, on the left, and Robert Fulton on the right stand behind the female embodiment of liberty holding two ships, the *Half Moon* and *The Steamboat.*

Rensselaers to become the state's governor and the nation's president. And concern about the spawning ground of striped bass would not only check the expansion of electrical generators on the river, but would also help to change the way Americans thought about their environment and their history.

On the morning before Thanksgiving Day, 1924, a thousand people drove in a parade of automobiles from Peekskill, on the eastern side of the Hudson, up a newly constructed mountain road north of the town. Their destination was an escarpment four hundred feet above the river known as Anthony's Nose. The band from the Military Academy at West Point, playing John Philip Sousa, awaited them. After the cadets finished "The Star-Spangled Banner," Mary Averell Harriman, widow of the rail-road baron Edward Henry Harriman, unveiled a bronze tablet inscribed to "all who with labor and loyalty contributed to the construction of . . . the Bear Mountain Bridge, first highway to span the Hudson south of Albany." The honor rested with Mrs. Harriman because her late husband had long contemplated the span; her family's investment company W. A. Harriman and Company, started by her son Averell, had bankrolled the bridge's $4.5-million construction cost; and her youngest child, Edward Roland Noel Harriman, headed the company that built it. After the un-veiling, Edward Harriman led a party of directors and reporters across the four-lane, 1,624-foot-long suspension bridge—then the longest in the world—to the Bear Mountain House where he treated them to lunch and more speeches.

Probably few attending the ceremony and luncheon realized the full significance of the new bridge. In the seventeenth and eighteenth centuries the valley had served as a threshold into the New World; in the nineteenth it became the industrial and aesthetic heart of the new democracy. Now, in the third decade of the twentieth century, it was poised to enter a new era, one that would see, after a period of extraordinary pollution, an em-phasis on recreation, conservation, preservation, the environment, and, for many, a transformation of the old order. With these changes in the landscape, the Hudson River and valley became more than ever the center of the nation's cultural geography.

The Harrimans' bridge at Bear Mountain brought what Walt Whitman

Bear Mountain Bridge. When it opened in 1924 this was the longest suspension
bridge in the world, and the first to span the Hudson south of Albany. This undated
image from the 1920s is part of a large collection of scenic views of the span.
It suggests the way the bridge, which connects Peekskill with the towns on the western
shore of the river, has made it possible for automobiles to enter the Hudson Valley.

called "the strong light works of engineers" to the Hudson. The river had
always posed a challenge to those wishing to cross it. From colonial times it
had cleaved much of New York and the Middle Atlantic region from New
England. The increased mobility that the railroad and the automobile
brought, coupled with the population explosion in New York City, made
the river seem an even greater challenge. Ferryboats kept cars and trains
waiting in the summer months and were unreliable at best in the winter.
Engineers, too, found that the river's width stretched the capabilities of their
technology. It was no accident that the Harrimans located the new bridge at
Bear Mountain, the Hudson's narrowest point south of Troy and close to
the place where the Continental Army had stretched the first chain across
the river during the Revolution. Nevertheless, human achievement backed
by prodigious amounts of money was able to compress time and space.

Before 1924, railroads had successfully moved trains over and under the river. At Poughkeepsie in 1888, entrepreneurs opened a 3,000-foot cantilever bridge made of steel manufactured by the Bessemer process. It could carry two trains 212 feet above the water. Tunnels from Manhattan to New Jersey had a more troubled history. Since the 1870s, engineers had been thwarted in their attempts to create a railroad passage beneath the river. Though work began on a tunnel between Manhattan and Hoboken in 1874, the construction was plagued by "blowouts," which occurred when the pressurized air escaped through the roof of the shaft and allowed river water to flow in. (One such blowout in 1880 killed twenty men and ultimately brought ruin to the financial backers.) It wasn't until February 1908 that engineers succeeded in tunneling under the Hudson. The Pennsylvania Railroad followed with a tunnel of its own connecting its new station on Thirty-fourth Street in Manhattan to New Jersey. These were the first practical links between Manhattan and the mainland.

But the Bear Mountain Bridge was different. It carried four lanes of automobile traffic and, even though it was built by the Harrimans, no trains. The bridge proved a bellwether of future crossings that would transform the valley. Over the next four decades engineers built ten more automobile bridges, along with two automobile tunnels, to cross the river between New York City and Albany. Most of these crossings came in the 1920s and '30s: the Holland Tunnel in 1927, and the Lincoln Tunnel ten years later; the Mid-Hudson Bridge at Poughkeepsie in 1930, the George Washington Bridge in 1931, and the Rip Van Winkle Bridge at Catskill in 1935. The Tappan Zee Bridge in 1955 and the Verrazano Narrows Bridge in 1964 completed the transformation.

The Hudson crossings and the valley roads that led to them accelerated the rate of change in the daily life and culture of formerly disparate communities like Newburgh and Beacon, Rhinebeck and Kingston, Westchester and Nyack. Unprecedented numbers of people and industries settled in the valley. In the two decades after the Tappan Zee Bridge was opened to automobiles, the population density of the formerly isolated Rockland County on the west bank of the Hudson increased from 500 to 1,300 people per square mile. A similar population surge took place on Staten Island in the wake of the opening of the Verrazano Narrows Bridge. By 1965, the number of people living in the New York metropolitan area stood at 10.5 million.

Among those serving on the Hudson-Fulton Celebration's Public Health and Convenience Committee, "to promote . . . the health, comfort and convenience of the out-of-door public," was a twenty-seven-year-old New York City lawyer, Franklin D. Roosevelt. Roosevelt was born and had grown up at Springwood, his parents' house, which featured a piazza across the rear of the house overlooking Crum Elbow, a bend in the river at Hyde Park. Springwood and the Hudson Valley would serve as his shelter and refuge throughout his life.

From an early age Roosevelt looked with pride on his deep roots in the valley, reaching back to the mid seventeenth century, when Claes Martenszen Roosevelt arrived in New Amsterdam. At Harvard, young Franklin drew from information recorded in his family's Dutch Bible for his history thesis, "The Roosevelts of New Amsterdam." Later he joined the Holland Society and, with Helen Wilkinson Reynolds, a historian at Vassar College, helped to found the Dutchess County Historical Society. In an introduction he wrote for a book on the Dutch houses in the Hudson Valley that Reynolds published, Roosevelt regretted "the march of modern civilization" that spelled the almost certain destruction of the structures and the way of life they embodied. "In these days of good roads, of motors and, soon, common travel by air," he lamented, "the valley of the Hudson river is becoming more accessible to the vast population of the cities."

To Franklin Roosevelt, Springwood provided peace and security as well as an enduring continuity in the face of the "vast population" and turbulence of the outside world. Although he had a house in New York City in the early years of the century, it was to Springwood that he would always retreat. With his mother he enlarged the original farmhouse, raising the roof, building a portico, adding a tower, and replacing the clapboard exterior with brick. The architect for the work based his designs on careful sketches and a detailed model that Roosevelt himself provided. Franklin turned Springwood's grounds into his own forestry preserve, planting seedlings of unusual trees, 300,000 in all, often with indifferent success. (His experiments with redwood seeds from California were a singular failure.) Before polio severely hampered his mobility, he liked to swim in a small pond on the property; later he taught his children how to swim there. In winters he would go ice boating on the frozen Hudson and take his children sledding on the sloping lawn that led down to the river. After he was paralyzed he delighted in spending "historical afternoons" with Helen Wilkinson Reynolds. The pair would sit on the lawn, watch the steamboats and sailboats making their passage around Crum Elbow, and drink punch. They discussed the role of the Hudson in the American Revolution, or the great patent holders in the valley, or the threat posed by encroaching modernization.

Roosevelt's interest in the vanishing architecture of Dutchess County led him to design a cottage for his wife, Eleanor, and a library in Hyde Park named in memory of his father. He chose a spot on the edge of the Fall Kill, where he and Eleanor and her friends often picnicked, and he named it Val-Kill. A low rectangular Dutch-colonial style structure of fieldstone recycled from old walls, Val-Kill featured a typical Dutch roof with a wide overhang. He chose the same fieldstone for the library.

After he became president, Roosevelt wielded his power and his pen to supervise the designs for other buildings in the valley, including post offices, schools, and the reconstruction of Philip Schuyler's house at Saratoga that the British had burned in 1777. At the president's direction compliant architects designed the post offices at Poughkeepsie, Wappingers Falls, Hyde Park, and Rhinebeck in his beloved fieldstone. The last was built next to the Beekman Arms Hotel and copied an eighteenth-century house owned by a Roosevelt ancestor, Henry Beekman. Inside were murals created by the Works Progress Administration depicting the region's history. "We are seeking . . . to adapt the design to the historical background of the locality and to use, insofar as possible, the materials which are indigenous to the locality itself. Hence, fieldstone for Dutchess County. Hence the efforts during the past few years in Federal buildings in the Hudson River Valley to use fieldstone and to copy the early Dutch architecture which was so essentially sound besides being very attractive to the eye."

Many of Roosevelt's designs sprang from an impulse to control the world he knew in the Hudson Valley, but he did not stop with architecture and landscape. The name Springwood did not suit his fancy; his father had chosen it in a misguided attempt to emulate an English estate. Better that it should have a title with good Dutch roots, like Crum Elbow, the name early settlers had given the crooked bend in the river immediately below his house. A distant relative whose house lay on the west bank protested. He had called *his* house Crum Elbow for generations. Anyone on either side of the river may call their property Crum Elbow, Roosevelt replied, but his family on his side of the river claimed the original title. To add the force of law behind his point, President Roosevelt requested the Board of Geographical Names in the Interior Department to support his opinion. The board agreed. Henceforth, Crum Elbow was known as "a point on the *east* side bank of the Hudson River about 4½ miles above Poughkeepsie, Dutchess County, New York."

On a cool and brilliant June day in 1939, King George VI and Queen Elizabeth of England arrived at Hyde Park for a weekend visit. Roosevelt and the king drank cocktails in the library, spent an afternoon chatting on the lawn overlooking the Hudson, and the following morning attended services in St. James' Episcopal Church. Afterward Roosevelt escorted the royal couple up to Top Cottage, a new fieldstone structure he had designed. There everyone feasted on American luncheon favorites, Virginia ham, turkey, and hot dogs. It was said that George—for by this time the president had abolished formalities between them completely—ate two. Later, Anglophile critics said that hot dogs were not the dish to serve a king and queen, and certainly no one should address the royal couple the way the president had. But Roosevelt brushed the criticism aside. After all, he said, his family had lived in New York for centuries longer than the royal family had lived in England. In the Hudson Valley, where his great-grandfather had settled until 1813, he counted himself (through his wife) a descendant of Robert Livingston. Compared with the Roosevelts, the Windsors were mere arrivistes.

"All that is in me goes back to the Hudson," Roosevelt was fond of saying. As a child, his parents had headed the family stationery "Hyde Park on the Hudson." It was to Hyde Park and the Hudson that the president planned to return once he had completed his fourth term. He would live at Top Cottage and spend his days in the fieldstone library he had constructed on the grounds of his Crum Elbow estate, the first presidential library in the nation. He never realized his plans.

On a clear and sunny Sunday morning in mid-April 1945, a special seventeen-car funeral train came to a stop at a siding on the New York Central Railroad tracks that ran below the Roosevelt house. Eight military pallbearers carried the coffin of Franklin Roosevelt up a winding gravel path, which the president had always called "the river road," to a fresh grave plot in the garden. A stiff wind from the west rippled the river water, and scattered the petals of the hundreds of flowers that attendants carried from the train to the grave. The scent of pine and apple blossoms could be detected in the air. A hedge surrounded the grave on three sides, but the west side of the site was open, the better to afford a view across the lawn to the slow-moving waters of the Hudson beyond.

As Franklin Roosevelt had foretold, more bridges and roads, more factories and people, more automobiles and, after 1940, airplanes, all had their way with his beloved valley. Each one enhanced communication and circulation, but each also brought more pollution to the valley. One by one, species of birds like osprey and bald eagles, plants like wild celery and wild rice, aquatic creatures like mussels and crabs, fish like shad and bass, died back or moved away from the polluted waters and compromised land.

By midcentury the pollution was horrendous: at Hastings, Anaconda Wire and Cable dumped millions of gallons of polluted water it had used to pickle and rinse its copper wire; at Fort Edward, General Electric discharged millions of pounds of polychlorinated biphenyls, or PCBs, it had used to manufacture silicones; at the Croton Harmon railroad yards, the Penn Central (successor to the New York Central) pumped waste diesel oil and solvents directly into the river. At Tarrytown, residents knew each day what color General Motors was painting its production of trucks by the color of the Hudson. By 1960 Manhattan was pumping 165 million gallons of raw sewage a day into the river. People avoided fish from Manhattan's waters; many even avoided walking beside it, as the stench on a summer's day made a bankside stroll in Riverside Park almost unbearable. Raw sewage dumped by Troy, Albany, Watervliet, and Rensselaer into what engineers euphemistically call the "Albany pool" made this section of the Hudson the most polluted. Each summer the high level of bacteria and the low level of oxygen made the Albany pool incapable of sustaining any aquatic life. From Albany to New York the river was off-limits to swimmers.

By the 1960s industries and most people regarded the Hudson as an open trough of toxic water that they could use as they saw fit. Mowton Le Compte Waring, of the Consolidated Edison Company, was no exception. Waring had the job of creating generators that would feed electricity to New York City. He had helped to complete Con Edison's nuclear steam-electric generating plant at Indian Point on the east bank of the Hudson a few miles south of Peekskill. Con Ed and Waring were proud of this achievement, for the utility completed the $90-million project ("the most modern nuclear reactor in the world," said Con Ed's advertisements) with private financing. No one seemed to mind that the plant might be deleterious to the environment. What matter if the intake pipes that drew river water to cool the reactors sucked in thousands of fish each hour? What matter if the heat the plant gave off significantly raised the temperature of the water and disturbed the river's aquatic life? Few people dared eat the fish anyway, and fewer still knew or cared about the effects of thermal pollution.

Once he had completed his work on Con Edison's nuclear reactor, Waring turned his attention to another means of generating electricity that had long been his dream: a pumped storage reservoir at Storm King Mountain. The concept was simple and elegant: in the evening, when the demand for electricity was low, the plant would pump 8 billion gallons of river water through a huge pipe to a reservoir at the top of the mountain. In the daytime, when demand for electricity was high, operators would pull the plug on the reservoir, allowing the water to flow down the mountain through huge electrical generators, and then back into the Hudson. With Storm King on line, Waring knew, Con Ed would be able to satisfy New York's voracious appetite for electricity.

Located just north of West Point at the entrance to the Hudson Highlands, Storm King was the perfect site. Viewed from the Hudson, the mountain looks like a steep cliff, a swelling lump jutting into the water. The height of its summit, 1,350 feet above the river (eight times higher than Niagara Falls), would give the 8 billion gallons of water the force they needed to turn the great fins of the generators. Behind the mountain's broad dome there was an ideal spot for the huge earthen reservoir that would be needed to store the water.

Mowton Le Compte Waring came from a family of distinguished engineers. In the nineteenth century his Mowton ancestors had installed gas lighting for Baltimore, the first gas system of any city in the nation. His father was a partner in Waring and Chase, an electrical engineering firm that designed electrical systems for New York office towers. Like his father and grandfather before him, Mowton Le Compte Waring had studied engineering at Virginia Military Institute. After his graduation, he worked

Samuel Colman, *Storm King on the Hudson*, 1866. Located just north of West Point, the mountain appears as a steep cliff, a swelling lump jutting from the water. With its steamboats, fishing boats, and sloops, Colman's Hudson is a working river of utility and commerce, which was how Consolidated Edison saw it a hundred years later when it proposed building an electrical generating plant on the mountain. (Smithsonian American Art Museum, Washington, D.C.; gift of John Gellatly)

in the electrical generator department at General Electric in Schenectady and continued his engineering studies at Union College. In 1933 he married the daughter of his father's partner, and took a job with Consolidated Edison. Now in his fifty-third year, as vice president in charge of power plant construction, Waring believed this pumped storage project at Storm King would be his last and greatest engineering achievement and continue the engineering achievements of his family.

Waring figured it would take about three years to obtain the necessary approvals, and about seven more to build the power plant. Then he could retire to his vacation house in Virginia and indulge his hobbies of cabinet-making, bird watching, and building elaborate bird feeders.

Waring did not anticipate any serious opposition. Con Edison had brought Indian Point on line with little opposition, and New York needed electric power. After Con Ed announced the project in 1963, the mayor of Cornwall, the small river village north of the mountain, gave his approval in exchange for guarantees of ample tax revenues—and declared to all that he had been the one to lure the utility to the site. Seeing a cornucopia of jobs for the valley, the heads of the construction trade unions declared their enthusiastic support. More important was the reaction of the Rockefeller brothers. Laurance Rockefeller, who as chairman of the New York State Parks Council had credentials as an environmentalist and preservationist, gave his blessing; and Nelson A. Rockefeller, who sat in the governor's office, pronounced it an excellent plan. All that was needed before construction could begin, Waring knew, was the approval of the Federal Power Commission. And that was virtually assured, as the commission had never before stopped Con Ed from building anything.

But no one among the planners or boosters of the pumped storage project considered the river, the mountain, or their place in American history and consciousness. They had ignored the ineffable mystery that Irving and Cooper had lent to the landscape. They neglected the sublime canvases that artists like Cole and Church and Durand had produced of the landscape around Storm King Mountain. They forgot the associations the region had with the American Revolution, with Washington and Lafayette, and with Arnold and André. They were ignorant of writers like Fanny Kemble and Harriet Martineau who had been moved by their excursions into the Highlands.

While Waring and his colleagues at Con Ed envisioned a steady flow of kilowatts from riverside generators feeding energy-starved New Yorkers, others saw one of the most scenic views in the East destroyed; they saw an eight-hundred-foot-long generator plant taking a huge bite from the north side of the great domed mountain; and they saw a row of gigantic pylons with transmission lines suspended from their arms crossing to the east side of the river and marching down the valley toward the city. In the American Revolution, Storm King stood at a pivotal spot in the defense of the colonies, close to West Point and the chain the continental forces used to block the British ships. In 1963 a new revolution was about to begin. Its outcome would change the course of the nation's attitude toward the environment and aesthetics.

Those who were opposed to the project joined together as the Scenic Hudson Preservation Conference. Scenic Hudson included an antiques dealer, an avid hiker, the director of the Nature Conservancy, a few Manhattanites who had weekend houses high on the mountain above

A drawing of Consolidated Edison's proposal for Storm King Mountain, 1963. Presented by Con Ed as a marvel of modern technology, the pumped storage facility would have destroyed the landscape and seriously compromised the Hudson's fragile environment. (Scenic Hudson)

Cornwall, the historian of the river Carl Carmer, and the journalist Robert Boyle. Though Con Ed dismissed the group as nothing more than "misinformed bird watchers, nature fakers, land grabbers, and militant adversaries of progress," it seriously underestimated the determination and talents of its members. The antiques dealer had recently raised more than a million dollars to save Boscobel, a great Hudson River mansion, from demolition; the hiker was a prominent attorney; and the wealthy Manhattanites had the resources to hire a public relations firm and support at least the initial stages of a legal challenge.

James Cope, the New York public relations executive whom Scenic Hudson hired, knew he had a perfect David and Goliath case to present to the public, and he relished the chance to make trouble for Con Ed. Soon articles appeared in newspapers and magazines like the *Reader's Digest* about the small group of determined citizens battling the huge, polluting public utility that sought to despoil the scenic beauty of the river. Other articles reminded readers of the Johnstown flood, and raised questions about the safety of storing 8 billion gallons of water in an earthen reservoir thirteen hundred feet above the Cornwall villagers. In 1964, to demonstrate that ordinary citizens were opposed to the bullying Goliath, Cope quietly organized a flotilla of small sailboats and motorboats to converge at the base of Storm King. They were there, they proclaimed, to save the river and the mountain, even civilization itself. And Cope made sure that the New York and national press saw the spectacle. The day after the event, articles appeared comparing the boats at Storm King with those at Dunkirk.

Con Ed made itself an easy target, too. The utility had a penchant for arrogance that rankled nearly everyone. Its urban power plants were known to be some of the greatest polluters in New York. Its electric rates ranked among the highest in the nation. Practices at its Indian Point power plant had begun to raise questions, too, especially after the author and avid sport fisherman Robert Boyle published a dramatic photograph in *Sports Illustrated* of a worker standing in a huge dump of dead fish that had been killed at the screens protecting the plant's cooling water intake pipe. Still, Con Ed executives seemed oblivious to their bad image. On their lapels they proudly wore large, ugly, and imperious pins emblazoned with the utility's advertising slogan, "Dig We Must."

In spite of these public relations coups, Scenic Hudson's lawyer knew that he had little hope of persuading the Federal Power Commission to deny the project. The group's best chance for success lay in a legal challenge. The commission's hearings proceeded as expected. It disregarded arguments about the region's scenic beauty and historical significance. It refused to consider the testimony of experts who demonstrated that Storm King sat in the center of the spawning ground for striped bass, which live in the shelter of the Hudson for several years before swimming into the Atlantic and along the coast from New Jersey to Rhode Island. When the commission gave its approval in March 1965, Scenic Hudson sued in the federal circuit court of appeals to have the decision reversed. But the chances of this happening were slim. Federal courts rarely intruded upon the cozy relationship between the Federal Power Commission and public utilities —and never on environmental grounds. If the court did now, it would be a landmark decision.

This time, Scenic Hudson won. The Federal Power Commission had not considered "the preservation of natural beauty and of national historic shrines," the court declared. It ordered the commission to reconsider the application, including "the fisheries question before deciding whether Storm King is to be licensed." For the first time in U.S. history a group of citizens had used the power of the courts to thwart the will of two bureaucracies that had always had their way.

The denouement of the Storm King story played out over the next fifteen years. Con Edison appealed the decision to the Supreme Court, but the justices refused to hear the case. The Federal Power Commission did reconsider Con Ed's proposal for a pumped storage plant, and after a series of contentious hearings, approved it once again. But by then Congress, acting in part with the Storm King decision in mind, had created the National Environmental Policy Act of 1969 and the Clean Water Act of 1970; each placed more hurdles in the path of Con Ed, including the requirement of an environmental impact study before projects like power plants could be built. In 1973, the court of appeals again ordered the Federal Power Commission to hold further hearings on the question of fisheries.

Con Ed decided it was time to change its style. The company repainted its orange trucks a trendy gray. Crisp designer blue letters replaced its "Dig We Must" advertising slogan with the more up-to-date "Clean Energy." Its board of directors fired the president of the company and hired Charles Luce, a former undersecretary of the interior, to replace him. Mowton Le Compte Waring went too. In one of his first acts as president, Luce requested that his vice president retire.

Ultimately, it was the fish kills at Indian Point that forced Con Ed to cancel its plans for the plant at Storm King Mountain. Millions of bass were dying at the nuclear plant's water intake pipes each year. Goaded by Scenic Hudson, the new federal Environmental Protection Agency threatened to have Indian Point shut down if the company didn't either recirculate the cooling water in giant towers, which would cost several hundred million dollars, or find "other suitable methods of fish protection." Con Ed decided to negotiate a peace with the Hudson environmentalists. In December 1980, seventeen years after the utility had announced its plans to build a pumped storage plant at Storm King Mountain, Luce signed the "Hudson River Compact." In exchange for Scenic Hudson's agreement to drop all suits against the company, Con Ed agreed to install new devices at Indian Point that would reduce the fish kills, to shut down the plant completely during spawning season, to establish fish hatcheries that would stock the river annually, and to study the impact of its power plants on the Hudson's aquatic life. It also gave $12 million to establish a foundation devoted to studying the river's fish. It abandoned the Storm King project forever, and even donated all the property it held there, which led to the creation of Storm King State Park. Charles Luce said when signing the compact, "We lost the Fight."

Mowton Le Compte Waring lost, too. His career had been devoted to electric generation, and the Storm King project was to have been his crowning achievement. But, along with the rest of Con Edison's thinking, he was about a decade behind. For the past three decades Waring had lived at Ardsley-on-Hudson. He could see the river from his porch, until construction closer to the shore blocked his view. It was said that he loved the river scenery and he took pleasure in watching and feeding birds, but he could never make a connection between his work and the way it would affect the world around him. Crushed by his failure, Waring moved from the Hudson to the shore of another river, the Rappahannock in Virginia. There he lived quietly until his death in 1990, building exact replicas of early American furniture in his woodshop and watching birds as they congregated at his backyard feeders.

But the Hudson won. In the seventh decade of the twentieth century, the river became central to a new chapter in America's history, one that emphasized the importance of the environment. The battle at Storm King helped to bring about the restoration of the Hudson. Before the controversy, few studied the way the river functions as a giant tidal estuary and how different it is from the other, wider estuaries on the Atlantic coast. Few understood its fragile ecology, more fragile, biologists say, than that of other rivers. Because of Storm King and the emphasis the controversy placed on the environment, fishermen have banded together; cities, villages, and industries no longer dump raw sewage and pollutants directly into the water; an estuary research institute flourishes at Tivoli Bay; and the sloop *Clearwater* sails the waters of the Hudson regularly, a floating laboratory classroom educating people about the value of their river.

The *Clearwater*, that great symbol of all that the Hudson had been and yet can be again, was the brainchild of the idealist, socialist, and, in this case at least, eminently practical folksinger Pete Seeger. In the 1960s Seeger happened to read a history of the sloops that had once plied the river. He suggested to a friend that they gather "a few hundred families" together to build a "life-size Hudson River Sloop." The idea took wing. The boat would have a cause, to bring people to the river and to inspire them to clean it. "Until people start to love their river," said Seeger, "it's going to be a sewer." As silly as the proposal might have sounded at first, it worked admirably. People came to Seeger's benefit concerts, and they gave handsomely. In the fall of 1969, the *Clearwater* arrived in the Hudson River.

Now in its fourth decade, the *Clearwater* functions as one of the best ways to educate valley residents about appreciating the river. It directs many of its programs toward children—a "classroom of the waves," a tideline discovery program, a Hudson River school, and each June, at Croton Point Park, a Clearwater Music and Environmental Festival. Though the education would take time, Seeger had created a powerful movement to assure the future of the Hudson River. Throughout the valley people began to cherish *their* Hudson. Pollution was declining; the fish were returning. To be sure, it would take time for the river to cleanse itself, to purge a century's worth of toxicity from its estuaries. But for the first time in many years, residents and state and federal agencies began to think of the Hudson as a river, not a sewer.

The future, however, was far from assured. In 1973 the Niagara Mohawk Power Company received permission from the State of New York to remove a small dam on the river at Fort Edward that had been erected for electrical generation earlier in the century. The dam had outlived its usefulness, so Niagara Mohawk maintained; the power plant was outdated. No one realized it at the time, but the dam was holding back far more than water, for collected in the sediment at its base lay hundreds of tons of PCBs.

In the 1970s few people other than chemists and electrical engineers knew what PCBs were, much less the harmful effects they might have on the environment. Those who were aware also knew that the oily fluid possessed remarkable insulating qualities and was just the compound to use for insulating heat-generating transformers and capacitors. Every manufacturer of such electrical components used them, including the General Electric Company, which had factories at Hudson Falls and Fort Edward. GE had received a permit from the federal government to discharge PCBs into the Hudson in 1930, and it had been doing so ever since. For more than four decades GE's effluent pipes released the compound into the water. These chemicals would flow downstream for a short while before sinking to the bottom. The trip to the bottom was relatively short, because the material was about twice as dense as water. Many tons came to rest at the base of Niagara Mohawk's dam. When workers removed the dam, they stirred up the sediment and released the substance once again into the river.

By 1975, New York's environmental commissioner, Ogden Reid, grew alarmed by the increased levels of PCBs being found in fish and eels caught in the river. His scientists had determined that the PCBs in one serving of eel caught at Stillwater "would contaminate an adult with over 50 percent of the Food and Drug Administration's estimated lifetime limit, and a child with 200 percent." Increasingly, scientists were linking the compounds with human birth defects and developmental disorders, as well as life-threatening diseases like cancer. Reid ordered General Electric to stop its discharge into the river. But money trumped health. General Electric balked, threatened to close its manufacturing plants, and pressured New York's governor, Hugh Carey, to overrule Reid. Declaring that economic considerations had to be weighed when making environmental policy, Carey rescinded Reid's order and, questioning the science behind it, declared he would drink a glass of water laden with PCBs. It was a promise the governor never fulfilled.

Stopping the discharge was one matter; remediating four decades of contamination was another. After Niagara Mohawk removed the dam and stirred up the sediment, concentrations of PCBs rose downstream at forty "hot spots," including Stillwater and Thompson Island, north of Schuylerville. In 1980 Congress passed the Comprehensive Environmental Response, Compensation, and Liability Act, known as Superfund, which gave the federal Environmental Protection Agency the power to find the parties responsible for an unsafe release of a toxic substance into the environment and require them to clean it up. In 1984 the agency added the upper Hudson between Fort Edward and the dam at Troy to its Superfund list. General Electric would have to pay to clean the river.

Understanding that the financial implications of the agency's decision for General Electric were serious, its president Jack Welch decided to fight. He created a strategy of stall, question, and misrepresent: More study was needed. The links between PCBs and cancer were tenuous. The substances might degrade naturally. The river was cleaning itself through its natural processes. The remediation would stir up the river bottom once again. Cleaning plants on the Hudson's banks (where the PCBs were to be removed) would actually cause more pollution. The impediments General Electric raised seemed endless. It ran slick television commercials that declared the river safe, the problem without consequence, and the government's remediation something that would only destroy the environment. Because GE owned NBC television, it was able to ensure that few stories about the controversy were aired, and it even enlisted the president of the network to lobby members of New York's City Council to rescind a resolution they had passed supporting the cleanup. General Electric gave heavily to the reelection campaigns of Representative Gerald Solomon, chairman of the House Rules Committee in Congress. Solomon managed to attach riders to bills demanding more study. After Solomon retired from Congress, in 1999, he took a job with General Electric to lobby his former colleagues to block the cleanup. For more than a decade, through Republican and Democratic administrations in Washington, the tactics worked. But the scientific studies that Representative Solomon demanded went forward, and the conclusions largely affirmed the Environmental Protection Agency's decision: the PCBs should be removed. In late 2000 the agency issued a final determination: dredges would remove 2.7 million cubic yards of sediment; plants on the shore would filter the water from the sludge and return it to the river; and trucks would haul the dried toxic sediment to a safe landfill out of state. Christine Todd Whitman, President George W. Bush's new administrator of the agency, affirmed the decision. The Hudson would be cleaned.

Or would it? Welch and General Electric decided to challenge the constitutionality of the Superfund law itself, claiming that it violates due process by giving the government unchecked authority to order a cleanup with no chance for a review by the courts. In early 2004, the circuit court of appeals in Washington ruled in favor of General Electric. The fight will continue in the courts. Meanwhile, General Electric is attempting to attach more riders to legislation that would order yet more study.

In spite of the presence of PCBs, the Hudson was cleaner at the end of the century than it had been at any time in the previous seventy-five years. Swimming below Albany had long been a risky and foolish pleasure, but now some people were actually venturing into the water. John Cronin, a commercial fisherman from Garrison, took it upon himself to become the Hudson Riverkeeper. Financed by concerned citizens, Cronin cruised the waters looking for hazardous waste, gathering information about polluters from civic-minded informers, and initiating lawsuits against powerful corporations who still thought of the river as a dumping ground.

By the end of the century the culture of the Hudson River and its valley had changed considerably. The Livingston genetic web spread over the east bank of the Hudson across more than forty estates and countless houses from Hyde Park to Rhinebeck. Successive generations of Livingstons intermarried with Hudson River families—with Delanos, Beekmans, Schuylers, Van Rensselaers, and Astors, and more often than is wise, with themselves. As the web grew ever wider, it became decidedly thinner and more delicate. Perhaps as a consequence of the rent wars in the nineteenth century, Livingstons who inherited the manor declared themselves "Lord," a title that Robert the Founder had always eschewed. But inevitably, the acres and revenues dwindled, and successive generations of Livingstons divided and subdivided the lands. In the twentieth century, Livingstons eventually found themselves desperately clinging to great manor houses with few resources to maintain them. The imposition of the federal income tax and estate tax early in the century only made their hold more tenuous.

Clermont showed the strain. Cracks in the dining-room ceiling widened and the beams sagged dangerously; roofs leaked; windows and sills rotted from the dampness; stucco on the exterior walls crumbled. As the servants dwindled in number, the house became impossible to maintain. Finally, at the start of World War II, the latest occupant of Clermont, Alice Delafield Livingston, widow of John Henry Livingston, decided to move into the small gardener's cottage on the grounds. She never returned to the manor house.

The Livingston family also clung desperately to its name, its traditions, and the illusion of its position in the valley. Livingstons liked nothing more than to gather at one another's property for clan parties. In the fall young Livingston ladies and gentlemen attended private dancing classes at one of the family houses, returning to their homes on a New York Central train that made a special stop at each of their estates along the river. In September 1931, they gathered at St. Paul's church in Tivoli for the marriage of Honoria Alice Livingston to Reginald Leopold Moore McVitty of Ireland. Ten little girls, all descendants of Robert of Clermont, including Franklin and Eleanor Roosevelt's grandchild Eleanor Dall, attended the bride. Each wore a dress whose design was copied from one of the old family portraits. After the ceremony the guests adjourned to Clermont to celebrate the nuptials and the two hundredth anniversary of the building of the family seat.

In the twentieth century it was clear that those with the Livingston name —even those who called themselves "Lord" or "Robert"—could not withstand the assault from the forces of change. In 1924, the same year that the Bear Mountain Bridge opened, the federal government designated Route 9 on the east side of the river and Route 9W on the west as part of the new national highway system. Henceforth, federal dollars gathered from income and estate taxes paid for improvements to the roads and helped make the valley accessible to all. A few years later Franklin Roosevelt—another member of the Livingston clan, albeit a distant one—headed the commission building the Taconic State Parkway. In 1956, the New York State Thruway opened on the western bank of the Hudson, and the federal government announced that the valley would be laced with a new system of high-speed interstate highways. The roads, along with the bridges, made the valley an attractive place in which to live for many more people than ever before. The new residents took jobs assembling Chevrolets at Tarrytown or typewriters and computers at IBM plants in Poughkeepsie and Kingston.

Some Livingstons tried to remain oblivious to the change that came to the valley. At times they seemed to fight it with a peculiar arrogance that few could match, and learned the lesson of the altered social landscape only through harsh experience. In the late 1950s one of them decided to give a party on the grounds of her estate. She sent invitations to the burghers of the nearby community of Rhinebeck as well as to the usual family members.

But when the good citizens arrived, they found the grounds divided by a rope. On one side, Livingstons frolicked among themselves, while on the other the villagers glowered. Two centuries earlier, in an annual ceremony, their ancestors had brought their quitrents—chickens, geese, vegetables, and an occasional cow—to the proprietor of Livingston Manor. But on this day there were few farmers among them. They owned their land and many had done so for more than a century. Many of their children ranked first and second academically, if not socially, in their classes at college and were preparing for careers in the new corporations that were settling in the valley. They did not belong on the other side of the rope. Only after the locals walked out did the hostess realize her mistake. To her credit, she made a public apology, which the residents graciously accepted.

Better than most in the family, Honoria Livingston McVitty and her mother, Alice Delafield Livingston, recognized the realities of the new age, and they sought to embrace them with a measure of grace. In 1962, Alice made over Clermont, by then in terrible disrepair, to the State of New York. After restoration it would become a public historic site. On Alice's death, her daughter Honoria deeded over additional grounds. Now that Clermont was open to the public, said Alice's husband, Reginald McVitty, "everyone [can] enjoy the privilege of a Hudson River estate without having to pay the taxes."

"Everyone" seemed in attendance at the "first annual" croquet tournament held on Clermont's east lawn in 1984. Clermont had changed since the State of New York took possession. The roof and rafters were sound; the stucco and trim were being repaired. On this afternoon no rope separated Livingstons from the hundreds of valley families who came from towns like Beacon and Tivoli, Germantown and Red Hook, Hyde Park and Wappingers Falls, to enjoy a day of fun on the grounds. Seventy-five-year-old Honoria competed on a team with a young IBM employee who was new to the valley. They proved a formidable pair and won the tournament handily. Together Honoria and her partner raised their hands in a gesture that acknowledged victory and an understanding of the new order in the valley.

As people began to appreciate the river's ecology in the last half of the twentieth century, they came to realize that in large measure the future well-being of the Hudson belonged to its rich past. From the Tappan Zee to Troy, many turned their attention to saving the great houses and estates that lined the shore. By this time many houses and their grounds had fallen to developers and indifferent local officials, but a good number of important structures remained. Some, like the Vanderbilt and Roosevelt mansions, were relatively safe in the hands of the federal government. Others, like the Mills mansion and Clermont, fell under the less certain control of New York State, which, after several false bureaucratic starts and considerable prodding from vocal and well-connected citizens, began to take its responsibility seriously.

The plight of other houses, especially those in private hands, was less certain still. Time and taxes had combined with rising maintenance and restoration costs and declining fortunes to threaten the future of these properties. Often the rescuers of these structures belonged to a new generation of residents who stepped in to save what cash-strapped older families no longer had the energy or the will to do. Often these preservation efforts succeeded because someone with a passion for a particular place was able to find a wealthy person with a civic conscience who was willing to take care of the financing. And often the person with money was able to win support from state and federal officials to make the effort successful.

At one such estate, Boscobel, sensible preservation joined with immense wealth to save a superb Federal-style mansion that was on the verge of being taken apart as salvage. Built between 1795 and 1804 at Crugers Point, south of West Point, Boscobel features delicate carved wooden swags that adorn its facade, with gracious proportions and details in its interior. But after World War II the federal government decided to acquire the land where the mansion stood for a veterans hospital. Boscobel would have to be razed; the Veterans Administration sold the house at auction for thirty-five dollars.

Benjamin West Frazier, an antiques dealer from Garrison and head of the local historical society, joined with Carl Carmer, author of a book on the Hudson published in 1939, to approach Lila Acheson Wallace, a cofounder of the *Reader's Digest*. Wallace funded the purchase of a magnificent tract of land in Garrison, fifteen miles north of the original site, commanding a view of Constitution Island, West Point, and the Bear Mountain Bridge, and she paid to have Boscobel dismantled and moved, piece by piece, to the new location north of Garrison and rebuilt there. (She even rescued portions of the facade that had already been removed from the house and were about to be installed at a Long Island mansion.)

Boscobel's public opening, in 1961, was only the beginning. When new information about the original furnishings and interior of the house came to light in the 1970s, Wallace purchased Federal-style pieces that matched them as closely as possible, and then had the rooms reconstructed. The result is an interior that complements the house's elegant architecture. Boscobel takes its place as one of the finest examples of Federal architecture in America.

On Mount Merino, a hill just south of the city of Hudson that rises about five hundred feet directly from the eastern shore of the river, stands one of the most exotic Hudson River houses. It belonged to the artist Frederic Edwin Church, Thomas Cole's pupil who gained his fame painting dramatic landscape scenes set in the Arctic, Europe, Jamaica, South America, Syria, and the Holy Land, as well as North America. In 1867, the artist returned to the Hudson Valley, where he had begun his career, to create Olana, named after a fortress treasure house in Persia. The house would be his greatest work. His orientalist paradise—"Persian adapted to the occident," in his description—took shape in 1870. "About an hour this side of Albany is the Center of the World," Church wrote to a friend. "I own it."

For a visitor to Olana, the experience begins on the carriage road that leads up the mountain from the Hudson. Church constructed seven and a half miles of roads that follow the contours of the topography, and at each turn he created a different vista of the steep slopes that fall away into the river, the valley, and the Catskill Mountains beyond. "I can make more and better landscapes in this way than by tampering with canvas and paint in the studio," he said. The artist took advantage of a spring to create a fifteen-acre lake, whose outline when viewed from the summit mirrors the topography of the Hudson that flows just a few yards away. He planted thousands of trees around the lake and on the grounds. As in his most dramatic landscapes, Church's design offered viewers a continual and vivid surprise. The last of these is the delightful and breathtaking mansion that converses so amicably with Greek, Italian, French, and Persian buildings of the past.

Frederic Edwin Church's house, Olana. From the windows and porches on Olana's south facade, shown in this photograph, Church and his family could look sixty miles down the Hudson Valley. (Peter Aaron, Esto Photographics)

The south facade appears to a visitor as a rare and exotic specimen of the East that has somehow been transported to the Hudson Valley. As is the case with the grounds, the house at Olana offers wonderful, unexpected visual treats. A sweeping concave polychromed cornice relieves the great mass of its walls, Moorish arches frame its doors and most of the windows, and a brightly patterned slate mansard roof tops its main tower.

The principal feature of Olana's public rooms is a great central "court hall," an idea Church probably borrowed from Persia, from which all rooms and stairs to the second floor radiate. An eclectic gatherer, Church decorated every wall, door, mantle, and window with landscape paintings, Islamic and Indian designs, bas-reliefs, cameos, and portraits. In the corners stand great vases and vessels from ancient Japan and China. These decorations surround the family's Duncan Phyfe chairs, Chippendale sofas, and Sheridan tables. At Olana, Church paid homage to all the great civilizations of the past.

He paid his respect to the Hudson River valley as well. The south windows frame his greatest composition, a view sixty miles down the river. "They are always looking out the windows," wrote an intimate friend. She was right; all public rooms look south into the valley. From his vantage point on Mount Merino, Church took care to capture the scene in paintings and drawings done in every season and light. He felt a compulsion to record the various atmospheres, sometimes sketching one condition of the sky and the air, and then making yet another one as the mist and the hue of the sky changed. He often executed these plein-air scenes quickly, and usually on thin boards or paper. For Church, a sketching trip in the field meant stepping out the door of Olana for a walk about his property.

After Church died, in early 1900, Olana passed to his son and eventually to his son's widow. Following her death in 1964, her nephew began preparations to sell Olana, its contents, and its 327 acres to a developer; the house was to be razed and its extensive collection of art and furnishings sold at auction. Preservationists grew alarmed at the prospect; the *New York Times* decried the loss of the "Xanadu on the Hudson." If not for the efforts of David Huntington, a Smith College art history professor who appreciated the uniqueness of Frederic Edwin Church's creation, along with the cooperation of the bankers handling the estate and the support of Nelson Rockefeller, New York's governor, it is likely that Olana would

The view looking south from the piazza at Olana, taking in the Catskill Mountains on the right and Kingston in the far distance. This was one of several vistas of the river that Church captured in all seasons and atmospheres in his paintings. (Peter Aaron, Esto Photographics)

have been lost. Huntington recruited a cadre of powerful people, including Mrs. Averell Harriman, Mrs. John F. Kennedy, Nelson Rockefeller's cousin Alexander Aldrich, and Livingston descendant Winthrop Aldrich, to support Olana Preservation, an organization created to purchase the house and keep it intact. Olana Preservation held bake sales and art auctions throughout the valley. As it gathered money, the bankers relented and allowed more time for fund-raising. At Governor Rockefeller's behest, the legislature appropriated $477,000 to contribute to the purchase of Olana, and these combined efforts eventually saved the estate from dismantling. In the summer of 1967, the house, grounds, and sublime view of the Hudson were opened to the public. By the end of the century the center of Frederic Church's world had become one of the most popular historic sites in New York state.

A boat trip on the Hudson, an Amtrak ride along the eastern shore, a stroll in New York City's Riverside Park, or even a drive through the dozens of river communities in the valley is a very different experience today than it was a half century ago. Sewage treatment plants now take the place of great pipes that used to dump raw waste into the river. The state has linked the Hudson River communities in a "Greenway" to encourage the creation of parks, preservation of open spaces, and the building of a walking trail between the Battery at the tip of Manhattan Island in New York City and Waterford in Saratoga. On a summer day one may spot the *Clearwater* in the Highlands or the Riverkeeper watching over tankers and tugboats in the Tappan Zee. The Anaconda and General Motors plants have closed, and General Electric is reluctantly facing its massive cleanup of PCBs. Nevertheless, the river is threatened by continued challenges: an electrical generating plant at Athens will compromise the view from Olana; until recently a cement plant threatened the city of Hudson; new housing developments on the western shore, especially south of Newburgh, have stripped the landscape of much of its beauty; the nuclear power plant at Indian Point still generates electricity despite its dubious safety record, breaches in security, and its proximity to millions of inhabitants as well as the cadets at West Point. Such threats notwithstanding, the future of the Hudson holds great promise.

The Hudson has survived and even thrived because individuals and communities have worked to balance its utility with the recognition that it has never been just a river. Thomas Cole and Asher B. Durand realized this, as did Washington Irving and James Fenimore Cooper. And countless individuals who have beheld the Hudson's waters from the deck of a boat off Troy, from Bemis Heights at Saratoga, from the grounds at Clermont, or from an apartment window overlooking Riverside Drive in New York City have realized it as well. It's the spirit of the Hudson River that infuses the acts of all who experience its atmospheres, its lights, its roiling waters, its mountains, and its sublime beauty. This is the symbolic Hudson that lives forever in our conscious and unconscious souls. It is the spirit that the poet and social critic Paul Goodman captured so well in "The Lordly Hudson":

> "Driver, what stream is it?" I asked, well knowing
> it was our lordly Hudson hardly flowing,
> "It is our lordly Hudson hardly flowing,"
> he said, "under the green-grown cliffs."

> Be still, heart! no one needs your passionate
> suffrage to select this glory,
> this is our lordly Hudson hardly flowing
> under the green-grown cliffs.

> "Driver! has this a peer in Europe or the East?"
> "No no!" he said. Home! home!
> be quiet, heart! this is our lordly Hudson
> and has no peer in Europe or the East,

> this is our lordly Hudson hardly flowing
> under the green-grown cliffs
> and has no peer in Europe or the East.
> Be quiet, heart! home! home!

Notes

Text is identified by page number and the first few words of the passage referred to in the note.

Introduction

1   Francis Bannerman: For information about Bannerman Island, see various pamphlets published by the Bannerman Castle Trust and Bannerman's obituary in the *New York Times,* January 16, 1918, 17. I have also profited from conversations with Neil Caplan of the Trust and Alan Wheelock.

2   Queen of England: See the illustrator Benson J. Lossing's *The Hudson: From the Wilderness to the Sea* (Hensonville, New York, 2000), 215. Originally published in 1866, the book describes the house that the fisherman and his wife inhabited as "like a wren's cage in size."

4   the valley's community and culture: The impact of Bannerman's Castle continues into the twenty-first century. In 1993 Neil Caplan, an enterprising local real estate broker and theater director, began the Bannerman Castle Trust with the mission of stabilizing and preserving the ruins. Money began to flow from citizens in Hudson River cities and towns, New York State, and private foundations. Eleven years later, in the summer of 2004, the Trust began its first guided tours of the arsenal.

4   Natty Bumppo: Bumppo speaks about the Hudson in chapter 26 of *The Pioneers* (New York, 1964), 279.

Chapter 1. The River and the Land

12   water supports no fish: In *The Hudson River: A Natural and Unnatural History* (New York, 1969), Robert Boyle confirms that neither Lake Tear of the Clouds nor the Feldspar Brook support any fish; nor did the Opalescent River until it was stocked with brook trout. It is likely that this condition is not the result of acid rain or lack of oxygen in the water, but is rather a matter of colonization. Fish would find it difficult, if not impossible, to swim up Feldspar Brook to the lake. In making these observations I have profited from conversations with Professor Karen A. Kellogg.

12   its first fifty miles: Of the numerous sketches of the Hudson's course

from Mount Marcy to the sea, I have drawn especially from Arthur G. Adams's invaluable resource, *The Hudson River Guidebook* (New York, 1996); Paul Wilstach, *Hudson River Landings* (New York, 1933), 17–18; Boyle, *The Hudson,* 15–25, 68–87; the *Encyclopaedia Britannica,* 11th edition; and my own observations.

14   The geological forces: I am indebted to Professor Kenneth G. Johnson for his careful reading of this chapter. I have drawn much of my information from Bradford T. Van Driver's *Roadside Geology of New York* (Missoula, Montana, 1985), especially chapters 1, 2, 4, and 11.

17   A species of tilefish, lancet fish: Boyle, *The Hudson,* 268–69.

17–18   vast web of natural life: Much of the information for this section comes from Stephen P. Stanne, Roger G. Panetta, and Brian E. Forist, *The Hudson: An Illustrated Guide to the Living River* (New Brunswick, New Jersey, 1996); see especially 19–39.

18   species in the Hudson estuary: C. Lavett Smith, *The Inland Fishes of New York State* (Albany, 1985), 11, 16.

18   sheer number of fish: Smith, *Inland Fishes of New York,* 69–71, 284–85, 381–82; Boyle, *The Hudson,* chapter 7. Both works are excellent resources for the river's ichthyology.

18   "almost any species": Smith, *Inland Fishes of New York,* 381.

19   "oily for three weeks": Adriaen van der Donck, *A Description of the New Netherlands,* ed. Thomas F. O'Donnell (Syracuse, New York, 1968), 11.

19   royal charter of 1693: See "New Museum Unearths Old New York's Heritage," *New York Times,* October 1, 1982, C13.

19   "porpoises played and tumbled": Peter Kalm, *Peter Kalm's Travels in North America* (New York, 1966), 326.

19   a school of dolphins: Alec Wilkinson, "The Riverkeeper," *New Yorker,* May 11, 1987, 50.

19   The rich diversity: Much of this information comes from personal observation. See also *Constitution Island* (West Point, New York, 1936), a pamphlet published by the Constitution Island Association for a meeting of the Garden Club of America; Tom Lake, ed., *Hudson River Almanac* (Fleischmanns, New York, 1996).

19   "We estimate that eighty thousand": Van der Donck, *A Description of the New Netherlands,* 97–98.

20   "The whole country is covered": Van der Donck, *A Description of the New Netherlands,* 19–20.

20   "When the woods are burning": Van der Donck, *A Description of the New Netherlands,* 21.

21   "in all North America": Kalm, *Peter Kalm's Travels in North America,* 334–35.

21   Jane Colden: Information for this section comes from H. W. Rickett, ed., *Botanic Manuscript of Jane Colden, 1724–1766* (New York, 1963); Mary

Harrison, "Jane Colden: Colonial American Botanist," *Arnoldia* 55, no. 2, 19–26; Virginia S. Eifert, *Tall Trees and Far Horizons: Adventure and Discoveries of Early Botanists in America* (New York, 1965), 49–62; Sara Stidstone Gronim, "The Androgynous Daughter: Jane Colden and Her Flora of New York" (unpublished article). I also profited from a long conversation with Ms. Gronim about Jane Colden's life and work.

21   "a small spot of the world": Gronim, "The Androgynous Daughter."

22   "humor in philosophical amusements": Cadwallader Colden to Peter Kalm, c. 1759, in Asa Gray, "Selections from the Scientific Correspondence of Cadwallader Colden with Grovinius, Linnaeus, Collison, and other naturalists," *American Journal of Science and Arts* 44 (1842–43), 109.

22   "Plantæ Coldenghamiæ": The full title is C. Linnæus, "Plantae Coldenghamiae in Provincia Noveboracensi Americes sponte crescentes, quas ad methodum Cl. Linnæi sexualem, anno 1742, &c. observavit & descripsit," *Acta societatis regiae scientiarum Upsaliensis* 4 (1743), 81–136, and 5 (1744–50), 47–82.

22   "bear the fatigue": Colden to Gronovius, October 1, 1755, in Gray, "Selections from the Scientific Correspondence of Cadwallader Colden," 103.

23   "a Long Tube": Quotations in this paragraph come from Rickett, ed., *Botanic Manuscript of Jane Colden*, 30, 80, 184.

23   "a Papilionatious Flower": Rickett, ed., *Botanic Manuscript of Jane Colden*, 53.

23   "She has already": Colden to Gronovius, October 1, 1755, in Gray, "Selections from the Scientific Correspondence of Cadwallader Colden," 103. "She deserves to be celebrated," Collinson wrote of Colden in a letter to Linnaeus, as "perhaps the first lady that has perfectly studied Linnæus' system." This, Collinson considered praise.

24–25   Amos Eaton: For information about Eaton I have relied heavily on Ethel M. McAllister, *Amos Eaton, Scientist and Inventor* (Philadelphia, 1941), John Grasso Rodgers, *Boston to Buffalo, in the Footsteps of Amos Eaton and Edward Hitchcock* (Field Trip Guidebook T169 of the 28th International Geological Congress, 1989), Thomas Phelan and D. Michael Ross, "Amos Eaton and the Magnificent Experiment," *Rensselaer Magazine*, December 1998, and the *Catalog of Rensselaer Institute, 1841–1842*, Folsom Library, Rensselaer Polytechnic Institute. I am also indebted to Kenneth G. Johnson for comments on Eaton's life and importance.

25   Samuel Latham Mitchill: Mitchill also served in the United States House of Representatives and the Senate. He sponsored the resolution authorizing Lewis and Clark's expedition, voted against declaring war against England in 1812, and, anticipating the Marx Brothers by close to two centuries, sought to change the name of the country to Fredonia. He will return later in this tale.

25 "Fortune seemed to smile": McAllister, *Amos Eaton*, 137.

26 "to make practical Botanists": McAllister, *Amos Eaton*, 212.

26 "frighten [Eaton] to New Orleans": McAllister, *Amos Eaton*, 118.

26 "hard labor for and during": McAllister, *Amos Eaton*, 132.

27 Governor Daniel Tompkins: For Tompkins's pardon language see McAllister, *Amos Eaton*, 152–53.

27 the "state sachems": McAllister, *Amos Eaton*, 191.

27 "I have learned to act": McAllister, *Amos Eaton*, 191.

27 "I tell you I am": McAllister, *Amos Eaton*, 284.

28 *An Index to the Geology:* McAllister, *Amos Eaton*, 286.

28 "geological facts": McAllister, *Amos Eaton*, 298.

28 "application of science": Phelan and Ross, "Amos Eaton and the Magnificent Experiment."

28 Rensselaer alumni: Phelan and Ross, "Amos Eaton and the Magnificent Experiment."

28 "professor of chemistry": McAllister, *Amos Eaton*, 371–83.

29 open Rensselaer to women students: Eaton did deliver lectures to "the ladies" from Emma Willard's School in Troy, and arranged for them to be examined by the same committee that examined the male students, but for the most part he did not succeed. McAllister, *Amos Eaton*, 428–29.

29 "If I am to be remembered": McAllister, *Amos Eaton*, 251.

29 the Eatonian Era: Kenneth G. Johnson, "Hudson River Landscape Paintings: A Serendipitous Opportunity to Introduce Students to the Creative Process in the Arts and the Natural Sciences," *Northeastern Geology* 17, no. 3 (1995), 295–305.

30 "He is a young man": Colvin's biography, which he wrote for *The Public Service of the State of New York*, is reprinted in *Adirondack Explorations: Nature Writings of Verplanck Colvin*, ed. Paul Schaefer (Syracuse, New York, 1997), 4–6. Most of my information for this sketch comes from Colvin's *Report on the Topographical Survey of the Adirondack Wilderness of New York for the Year 1873* (Albany, 1874), N. M. Webb, *Footsteps Through the Adirondacks: The Verplanck Colvin Story* (Utica, New York, 1996), and Norman J. Van Valkenburgh, ed., *On the Adirondack Survey with Verplanck Colvin: The Diaries of Percy Reese Morgan* (Fleischmanns, New York, 1991).

31 a Stan Helio: Colvin, *Report on the Topographical Survey of the Adirondack Wilderness*, 10 and illustration.

33 Hendrick Spring: In the summer of 1859, the Indian guide Sabattis took the author and illustrator Benson J. Lossing to Hendrick Spring and told him it was the river's source. Lossing reported this in *The Hudson: From the Wilderness to the Sea* (Hensonville, New York, 2000), 14–15.

33 The *"Summit Water":* Quoted from Colvin, *Adirondack Explorations*, 117–55.

33–34 Nathaniel Pendleton: Lossing, *The Hudson*, 20.

34	Lumbering destroyed the forests: "The Trees Almost Gone; Results of a Winter's Work in the Adirondacks," *New York Times*, March 13, 1890, 9.
35	"forest slaughter": Colvin, *Report on the Topographical Survey of the Adirondack Wilderness*, 116–18.
35–36	legislature abolished the survey: "Verplanck Colvin's Office: The Senate Passes Bill to Abolish the Land Survey Department," *New York Times*, April 5, 1900, 1. Colvin later filed a claim for unremunerated expenses and the state's seizing of files that he maintained belonged to him; "Says State Has Not Been Fair: Superintendent Colvin Files a Claim for $375,241 for Services," *New York Times*, November 9, 1901, 2.
36	rail link to Ottawa: "Railroad Rivalry in the Adirondacks," *New York Times*, September 14, 1902, 3.
36	"most interesting river in America": Lossing, *The Hudson*, 2.

Chapter 2. Explorers and Traders

37–38	a single passion: Henry Hudson is a shadowy figure of whom little is known. Information for this account of his arrival in the river comes from Roland Van Zandt's excellent *Chronicles of the Hudson* (Hensonville, New York, 1992), particularly Robert Juet's journal, 3–15; Henri Van der Zee and Barbara Van der Zee, *A Sweet and Alien Land: The Story of the Dutch in New York* (New York, 1978), 2–5; and the *Dictionary of National Biography*. Llewellyn Powys, *Henry Hudson* (New York, 1928), though fanciful, has also been useful.
39	Thorne drew his own crude map: *The Oxford English Dictionary* lists Thorne's letter of 1527 (as quoted in Richard Hakluyt, *Voyages of 1589*) as the first use of the word "map" in English, "To Make A Bigger And a better mappe." By 1601, Maria, the attendant to Olivia in Shakespeare's *Twelfth Night*, tells Sir Toby Belch that the "affectioned ass" Malvolio "does smile his face into more lynes, then is in the new Map with the augmentation of the Indies" (3.2.84). Thorne might also have been inspired by the tomb of Christopher Columbus, who at the time was buried at the Carthusian monastery of Santa Maria de las Cuevas, in Seville.
39	"From the Navill": Quoted from the article on Hudson in the *Dictionary of National Biography*.
40	Twelve Years' Truce: We cannot link the Twelve Years' Truce directly to Hudson's voyage, however, for it was not signed until June 17, 1609.
40	some of the sailors "behave[d] badly": I have used Robert Juet's journals (which are reprinted in Van Zandt's *Chronicles of the Hudson*) throughout this chapter. Juet recorded the full brutality of the event: "Then we manned our boat and scute with twelve men and muskets, and two stone pieces or murderers, and drave the savages from their houses, and took spoyle of them as they would have done of us." It would not be the last time that a crew of Henry Hudson's ran amok. Van Meteren wrote that Indians

came out to barter "good skins and furs . . . at a very low price." But soon, trouble broke out, "the crew towards the people of the country, taking their property by force, out of which arose quarrels among themselves." J. Franklin Jameson, *Narratives of New Netherland* (New York, 1909), 6–9.

41   "where the sea widens": John Gottlieb Ernestus Heckewelder, an English-born Moravian missionary who prosyletized among a Munsee-speaking branch of the Lenape Indians in Ohio, recorded this story about 1760. The Munsees shared kinship with the Algonquian tribes of the lower Hudson River. Heckewelder's transcription of the story may be found in the New-York Historical Society's *Collections*, 2nd ser., vol. I (1841): 71–74.

42   "a very agreeable place": Lawrence C. Wroth, *The Voyages of Giovanni da Verrazzano, 1524–1528* (New Haven, 1970), 138.

44   at least eight dead: Still, the encounter between the Indians and the crew of the *Half Moon* did not go as badly for the natives as some of their confrontations with Europeans. On their voyages to the East Coast of North America, Verrazano and Gomez had kidnapped natives to bring home as ethnographic souvenirs of their trip.

45   Verrazano kidnapped a child: Verrazano reported the kidnapping to the French king. What happened to the child is not known. His men also tried "to take the young woman (which was very beautiful and of tall stature), they could not possibly, because of the great outcries that she made." Samuel Eliot Morison, *The European Discovery of America* (New York, 1971), 297–98.

45–46   Sir Walter Raleigh: The story of the two natives, Manteo and Wanches, appears in Michael L. Oberg, "Between 'Savage Man' and 'Most Faithful Englishman': Manteo and the Early Anglo-Indian Exchange, 1584–1590," *Itinerario, European Journal of Overseas History* 24, no. 2 (2000).

46   "wild men": Quoted from Adriaen van der Donck, *A Description of the New Netherlands*, ed. Thomas F. O'Donnell (Syracuse, New York, 1968), 71–73.

47   "great and tall Oakes": These quotations come from Van Zandt, *Chronicles of the Hudson*, 9–19.

49   mutiny of the starving crew: Edmund Bailey O'Callaghan, ed., *Documents Relating to the Colonial History of the State of New York* (Albany, 1856), 1:11–13.

49   Robert Juet's body: Ramusio recorded Juet's death ("infelice fine") in his *Navigationi et Viaggi* of 1556. The explorer and six of his crew landed at a seemingly deserted island in the Caribbean. Once on shore, however, they were set upon by cannibals. "They were killed," said the "Storia poetica di Giulio Giovio Vescova di Nocera," "laid on the ground, cut into pieces and eaten down to the smallest bone. . . . Such a sad death had the seeker of new lands." Wroth, *The Voyages of Giovanni da Verrazzano*, 315, and Morison, *The European Discovery of America*, 315.

49   New World a virtual bestiary: Isaack de Rasieres reported in 1628 that
the "savages say that far in the interior there are certain beasts of the size
of oxen, having but one horn, which are very fierce"; Jameson, *Narratives
of New Netherland*, 114.

50   "good skin and furs": Quoted from Emanuel van Meteren's account, in
Jameson, *Narratives of New Netherland*, 7.

51   The van Tweenhuysen syndicate: For much of the information about the
van Tweenhuysen syndicate and its trading in the Hudson Valley, I have
drawn from the excellent account in Oliver A. Rink, *Holland on the Hudson*
(Ithaca, New York, 1986), 33ff., and Simon Hart, *The Prehistory of the New
Netherland Company* (Amsterdam, 1959). Hart, whose work is a principal
source for Rink's work, gathered his facts from the notorial archives of
the City of Amsterdam which recorded the various trading ventures. See
especially pages 18–33 and 48–53.

52   the *Tijger* accidentally caught fire: The nineteenth-century historian of
New York John Romeyn Brodhead described the fire as "accidental," and
quoted a number of sources as evidence. He also gave evidence from the
"Breeden Raedt aen de Vereeinghde Nederlandsche Provintien" that the
natives proved to be especially helpful: "when our people (the Dutch) had
lost a certain ship there, and were building another new ship, they (the
savages) assisted our people with food and all kinds of necessaries, and
provided for them, through two winters, until the ship was finished."
John Romeyn Brodhead, *History of the State of New York* (New York, 1853),
1:48.

52   he aptly named the *Onrust*: The historian Jerry E. Patterson also points
out that "Onrust" is the name of an island, the last bit of dry land sailors
see when leaving Holland. Jerry E. Patterson, *The City of New York: A History
Illustrated from the Collections of the Museum of the City of New York* (New York, 1978),
13–14.

53–54   Fort Nassau: For information about Fort Nassau see Jameson, *Narratives
of New Netherland*, 47.

54–55   remains of Adriaen Block's *Tijger*: For an excellent account of this event,
see Anne-Marie Cantwell and Diana diZerega Wall, *Unearthing Gotham: The
Archaeology of New York City* (New Haven, 2001), 150–53. Some archaeologists
have questioned if the artifacts found were indeed from the *Tijger*, but the
weight of the evidence suggests that they came from Block's ship.

Chapter 3. The Colonizers Arrive

56–57   Dutch had the good fortune: Many authors make this similar point. See
Paul Wilstach, *Hudson River Landings* (New York, 1933), chapter 3; Henri
Van der Zee and Barbara Van der Zee, *A Sweet and Alien Land: The Story of the
Dutch in New York* (New York, 1978), chapter 3.

58	The first true settlers: Van der Zee and Van der Zee, *A Sweet and Alien Land*, 11–18.
58–59	"dug outs": Edmund Bailey O'Callaghan, ed., *Documents Relating to the Colonial History of the State of New York* (Albany, 1856), 1:368.
60	Minuit's acquisition of Manhattan: Minuit was following orders from Holland: "In case said Island is inhabited by some Indians . . . these should not be driven away by force or threats, but should be persuaded by kind words or otherwise by giving them something to let us live amongst them"; quoted in Van der Zee and Van der Zee, *A Sweet and Alien Land*, 2. These authors have drawn from F. C. Wieder, *De Stichting van New York in 1625* (The Hague, 1925), 35.
60	He bought Eghquaous Island: Edmund Bailey O'Callaghan, *History of New Netherland; or New York Under the Dutch* (New York, 1846), 1:104.
60	"samples of summer grain": O'Callaghan, ed., *Documents Relating to the Colonial History of the State of New York*, 1:37–38. Wassenaer reports a similar number of skins; J. Franklin Jameson, *Narratives of New Netherland* (New York, 1909), 83.
61	"beginning to build new houses": The letter of Jonas Michaëlius is found in Jameson, *Narratives of New Netherland*, 122–33. Additional information about trade and living conditions comes from Wilstach, *Hudson River Landings*, 59–61; Van der Zee and Van der Zee, *A Sweet and Alien Land*, chapter 2.
61	the spine of New Netherland: Other authors, like Wilstach, *Hudson River Landings*, 23 and chapter 3, make this point in similar ways.
61	Michaëlius complained: Van der Zee and Van der Zee, *A Sweet and Alien Land*, 16–18.
62	Minuit embarked for Holland: Van der Zee and Van der Zee, *A Sweet and Alien Land*, 18.
63	"promote the peopling": Information here comes largely from A. J. F. Van Laer, trans. and ed., *Van Rensselaer Bowier Manuscripts* (Albany, 1908), 49. The 1629 charter was a revision of a 1628 charter; Oliver A. Rink, *Holland on the Hudson* (Ithaca, New York, 1986), 105.
63–64	Kiliaen van Rensselaer: Van Laer, ed., *Van Rensselaer Bowier Manuscripts*, 251. I have drawn from these manuscripts and the introduction and appendixes extensively in my discussion of the van Rensselaer family and Rensselaerwyck. See also Nancy Anne McClure Zeller, ed., *A Beautiful and Fruitful Place: Selected Rensselaerswijck Seminar Papers* (Albany, 1991).
64–65	"try to buy the lands": Van Laer, ed., *Van Rensselaer Bowier Manuscripts*; O'Callaghan, ed., *Documents Relating to the Colonial History of the State of New York*, 14:1–2.
65	Van Rensselaer's plan: The patroon might well have been thinking of the future, too, looking forward to a time when he would be allowed to trade for furs. If that should happen, and it did, then Rensselaerwyck would be very close to the source.

66   "discover any mines, minerals": Van Rensselaer was always worried lest someone should be stealing from him. "You might write me as to how far everyone acts to my advantage, I shall keep your name secret," he wrote to his relative Arent van Curler on July 18, 1641. Van Curler probably thought twice about disclosing such information, as the colony was so small. Van Laer, ed., *Van Rensselaer Bowier Manuscripts*, 557.

66   "a dead horse overboard": Journal of Antony de Hooges, who shipped on the *Conick David*, July 30 to November 29, 1641; Van Laer, ed., *Van Rensselaer Bowier Manuscripts*, 580–603.

66   "a few calves": "Memorial presented by Kiliaen van Rensselaer to the Assembly of the Nineteen of the West India Company, November 25, 1633; Van Laer, ed., *Van Rensselaer Bowier Manuscripts*, 235–50.

66   "If I cannot get animals": Van Rensselaer to van Twiller, July 27, 1632; Van Laer, ed., *Van Rensselaer Bowier Manuscripts*, 233.

67   the Nineteen named Wouter van Twiller: In a letter to Krol on July 20, 1632, van Rensselaer maintained that he did not speak to anyone in the company about van Twiller's appointment. Indeed, the patroon seems to have had some misgivings: "Whether they act prudently and wisely in this, I leave for others . . . to judge. The result will show it; and whether they are not recalling more efficient and faithful people than some of the new ones they send out; the Lord only knows." Van Laer, ed., *Van Rensselaer Bowier Manuscripts*, 218. Though there is no evidence, it is likely that van Rensselaer had actually recommended van Twiller to the Nineteen; that they appointed his nephew director-general very likely astounded him.

67   stock comic character: Historians have relied for the most part on the journal of David Pietersen De Vries, a merchant and captain who piloted his own boat on trading ventures about the globe. De Vries, however, was not always a reliable witness, as he had wanted the position of director-general in place of van Twiller. Still, when it came to alcohol, van Twiller, as was the case with so many Dutch in the New World, was intemperate. The actual title of the journal of De Vries is: "Short Historical and Journal-Notes of various Voyages performed in the Four Quarters of the Globe, viz., Europe, Africa, Asia and America, by David Pietersen de Vries, Artillery-Master to the Noble and Mighty Lords the Council of West Friesland and Northern Quarter [of the Province of Holland], wherein is set forth what Battles he delivered on the Water, Each Country, its Animals, its Birds, its Kinds of Fishes, and its Wild Men counterfeited to the Life, and its Woods and Rivers with their Products." Others, starting perhaps with Washington Irving, have used words like "ridiculous," "bombastic," and "foolish" to describe van Twiller; Van der Zee and Van der Zee, *A Sweet and Alien Land*, 53.

68   "one can not accomplish": Kiliaen van Rensselaer to Wouter van Twiller, April 23, 1634; Van Laer, ed., *Van Rensselaer Bowier Manuscripts*, 268.

68	"purchase for me": Van Laer, ed., *Van Rensselaer Bowier Manuscripts*, 230.
68	"their products of the soil": Van Laer, ed., *Van Rensselaer Bowier Manuscripts*, 266; S. G. Niessenson, *The Patroon's Domain* (New York, 1937), 81, 91.
68	reports of the director-general's bizarre behavior: It is likely that De Vries was responsible for some of these stories. He had hoped to replace Minuit as director-general. Contemptuous of van Twiller, he lost no opportunity to document his follies and failures.
68–69	"assembled all his forces": Jameson, *Narratives of New Netherland*, 188.
69	They found the captain: The depositions of several members of the crew of the *William*, including one by "Jacob Jacobsin Elikins," are found in O'Callaghan, ed., *Documents Relating to the Colonial History of the State of New York*, 1:71–81. Early in 1634, De Vries returned to Amsterdam from a trip to New Netherland with news of Wouter van Twiller's follies. While stopping at New Amsterdam before returning to the Netherlands, he had met van Twiller and witnessed his strange behavior in the face of the English. As soon as his ship reached the port of Amsterdam in late July, he spread through the streets and shipping offices the story of the man "whom they had made out of a clerk into a governor." Jameson, *Narratives of New Netherland*, 187.
69–70	"Such a shameful pot": Van Laer, ed., *Van Rensselaer Bowier Manuscripts*, 266–88.
70	van Twiller was accumulating land: O'Callaghan, ed., *Documents Relating to the Colonial History of the State of New York*, 14:3–5. Van Twiller also purchased "New" or "Nut" Island, today called Governors Island, from the Indians Cacapeteyno and Pewihas "in exchange for certain goods."
70	bucket brigade to drown the flames: Rink, *Holland on the Hudson*, 131. Apparently van Twiller was no stranger to such conflagrations, either. Shortly after his arrival in the New World, the director-general had rowed across the Hudson to sample a store of "good Bordeaux wines" in Pavonia. The drinking bout lasted through the afternoon and into the evening, and included a drunken quarrel and reconciliation. When it came time to leave, his host, wishing to give van Twiller a parting salute, "fired a pederero . . . when a spark flew upon the house, which was thatched with rushes, and in half an hour it was entirely consumed." Jameson, *Narratives of New Netherland*, 197–98.
70–71	Wouter van Twiller's quarrel: Van Rensselaer to van Twiller, September 21, 1637, in Van Laer, ed., *Van Rensselaer Bowier Manuscripts*, 352.
71	Fewer than two hundred people: Information compiled from Van Laer, ed., *Van Rensselaer Bowier Manuscripts*, 805–46. See also Nicolaas De Roever's brief biography of Kiliaen van Rensselaer in the same volume, 40–85.
71–72	"I am very anxious" . . . "and He will bless you": Van Laer, ed., *Van Rensselaer Bowier Manuscripts*, 513, 486, 509, 495, 454, 511.
73	"sturgeon, dunns, bass": Adriaen van der Donck, *A Description of New Nether-*

lands, ed. Thomas F. O'Donnell (Syracuse, New York, 1968), 10–11. Of the whales that swim into the river and became stranded at the Cohoes falls, van der Donck reported, "Although the citizens . . . broiled out a great quantity of train oil . . . the whole river . . . was oily for three weeks."

73 "such disorder and impertinence": Van Laer, ed., *Van Rensselaer Bowier Manuscripts,* 572.

74 "investigate who the man is": Van Laer, ed., *Van Rensselaer Bowier Manuscripts,* 636.

74 Kiliaen van Rensselaer's last acts: Van der Zee and Van der Zee, *A Sweet and Alien Land,* 205.

75 Slavery in the Hudson Valley: Edwin G. Burrows and Mike Wallace, *Gotham: A History of New York City to 1898* (New York, 1999), 31–33.

75–76 "Strange! that the science of government": I have quoted from Washington Irving's *Diedrich Knickerbocker's History of New York* (New York, 1940), 166.

76 Kieft governed by a council of two: O'Callaghan, ed., *Documents Relating to the Colonial History of the State of New York,* 1:183–84; Van der Zee and Van der Zee, *A Sweet and Alien Land,* 77–78.

76 "five and twenty morgens": O'Callaghan, ed., *Documents Relating to the Colonial History of the State of New York,* 14:14–15.

76–77 Kieft's brutal war: Allen W. Trelease, *Indian Affairs in Colonial New York: The Seventeenth Century* (Ithaca, New York, 1960), 61; O'Callaghan, ed., *Documents Relating to the Colonial History of the State of New York,* 1:119–20.

77 "unnatural, barbarous" acts: A report submitted to the States General in 1650, cited in Rink, *Holland on the Hudson,* 217.

77 "About midnight, I heard": Jameson, *Narratives of New Netherland,* 227–28. Another contemporary account, exaggerated to be sure (but there were eighty murders), stated: "Young children, some of them snatched from their mothers, were cut in pieces before the eyes of their parents, and the pieces were thrown into the fire or into the water; other babes were bound on planks and then cut through." The account by David De Vries copies from the *Breeden Raedt* (Grand Council), an anonymous anti-Kieft pamphlet published in Antwerp, 1649, found in O'Callaghan, ed., *Documents Relating to the Colonial History of the State of New York,* 4:103–4. Although the language of the document is colorful and no doubt overstates the case, at least eighty natives perished that night.

77 "Mine eyes did see": Trelease, *Indian Affairs in Colonial New York,* 74, quoting from the Plymouth Colony Records, 10:440.

77–78 "by cunning and numerous": Jameson, *Narratives of New Netherland,* 333.

78 "Is it right and proper": O'Callaghan, ed., *Documents Relating to the Colonial History of the State of New York,* 1:414–15.

78–79 "As regards the 12": O'Callaghan, ed., *Documents Relating to the Colonial History of the State of New York*, 1:202–3. The leader of the Twelve was none other than David Pietersen De Vries, who disliked Willem Kieft as much as he had his predecessor Wouter van Twiller. "I told Commander Kieft that no profit was to be derived from a war with the savages," De Vries remembered saying to the director-general, "that he was the means of my people being murdered, at the colony which I had commenced on Staten Island." Trelease, *Indian Affairs in Colonial New York*, 66–70; Jameson, *Narratives of New Netherland*, 214.

79   "We, wretched people": O'Callaghan, ed., *Documents Relating to the Colonial History of the State of New York*, 1:209–13; Van der Zee and Van der Zee, *A Sweet and Alien Land*, 133–34.

79   half a million guilders: Burrows and Wallace, *Gotham*, 40; for the sale of company property, see O'Callaghan, ed., *Documents Relating to the Colonial History of the State of New York*, 1:234.

79–80   another crisis of leadership: O'Callaghan, ed., *Documents Relating to the Colonial History of the State of New York*, 1:178.

80   "Friends, I have done wrong": Van der Zee and Van der Zee, *A Sweet and Alien Land*, 166–67.

80   Peter Stuyvesant: For information about Stuyvesant I have drawn from Burrows and Wallace, *Gotham*, chapter 4; Van der Zee and Van der Zee, *A Sweet and Alien Land*, chapter 15; and Henry H. Kessler and Eugene Rachlis, *Peter Stuyvesant and His New York* (New York, 1959).

80   Fort Amsterdam a "molehill": Kessler and Rachlis, *Peter Stuyvesant and His New York*, 7.

82   "Mijn Heer General": Rink, *Holland on the Hudson*, 226.

82   "rubbish, filth, ashes": I. N. Phelps Stokes, *The Iconography of Manhattan Island* (New York, 1916), 1:61–62.

82   standard weights and measures: Stokes, *The Iconography of Manhattan Island*, 1:69.

82   first speed limit: Stokes, *The Iconography of Manhattan Island*, 1:36; Milton M. Klein, ed., *The Empire State: A History of New York* (Ithaca, New York, 2001), 47.

83   military expedition against Fort Christina: The complicated story of the Swedish interest in the New World, the curious relationship Minuit had with diplomats in Stockholm, and Peter Stuyvesant's assault on Fort Christina appears in Van der Zee and Van der Zee, *A Sweet and Alien Land*, 79–82 and 267–70.

84–85   Brant van Slichtenhorst: For an account of the van Slichtenhorst disputes see Van der Zee and Van der Zee, *A Sweet and Alien Land*, 205–11.

86   ordered Lutherans imprisoned: O'Callaghan, ed., *Documents Relating to the Colonial History of the State of New York*, 14:369–70.

86   "the latrina of New England": Stokes, *The Iconography of Manhattan Island*, 4:180–81; John Romeyn Brodhead, *History of the State of New York* (New

York, 1853), 1:636; Jameson, *Narratives of New Netherland*, 400; Edward T. Corwin, comp. and ed., *Ecclesiastical Records of New York* (Albany, 1915), 1:399–400.

86   Lutherans treated "quietly and leniently": O'Callaghan, ed., *Documents Relating to the Colonial History of the State of New York*, 14:418, 526.

86–87   Sephardic Jews from Brazil: According to Edwin Burrows and Mike Wallace, "Mostly Sephardim, the newcomers—four couples, two widows, and thirteen children—had been trying to get to Holland since Recife fell to the Portuguese the previous January"; Burrows and Wallace, *Gotham*, 60; Jonathan D. Sarna, *American Judaism* (New Haven, 2004), 1–3.

87   "best as regards trade": O'Callaghan, ed., *Documents Relating to the Colonial History of the State of New York*, 1:294.

87   "evil consequences": O'Callaghan, ed., *Documents Relating to the Colonial History of the State of New York*, 1:298–302.

88   population of New Netherland: Burrows and Wallace, *Gotham*, 50.

89   "The country has arrived": O'Callaghan, ed., *Documents Relating to the Colonial History of the State of New York*, 1:263.

89   Peach War: Van der Zee and Van der Zee, *A Sweet and Alien Land*, 271–79.

90   "It would be best": O'Callaghan, ed., *Documents Relating to the Colonial History of the State of New York*, 13:84–86.

92   "If it has to be": A. J. F. Van Laer, trans. and ed., *Correspondence of Jeremias van Rensselaer* (Albany, 1932), 465.

Chapter 4. The Valley Transformed

94   court cases translated into Dutch: Milton M. Klein, ed., *The Empire State: A History of New York* (Ithaca, New York, 2001), 119.

95   Family legend suggests: Throughout my discussion of Robert Livingston and his family, I have relied heavily on Clare Brandt's superb *An American Aristocracy: The Livingstons* (New York, 1986), and Lawrence H. Leder's *Robert Livingston, 1654–1728, and the Politics of New York* (Chapel Hill, North Carolina, 1961). My debt to both authors is significant, and to Brandt especially, as she is careful to follow the family through to the late twentieth century. Readers will find Reuben Hyde Walworth's *Livingston Genealogy* (Rhinebeck, New York, 1982) useful when trying to follow the various members of the clan through its several generations. I have also benefited from conversations with Jeanne Hunter about the family and Clermont.

95   "No, no, send him away": This oft-repeated story may be found in Brandt, *An American Aristocracy*, 21, and Leder, *Robert Livingston*, 21.

97   "not much to write": A. J. F. Van Laer, trans. and ed., *Correspondence of Jeremias van Rensselaer* (Albany, 1932), 301.

98   "I cannot bear": A. J. F. Van Laer, trans. and ed., *Correspondence of Maria van Rensselaer* (Albany, 1932), 57.

99	"three hundred guilders in Zewant": Brandt, *An American Aristocracy*, 24.
99–101	patents issued to Livingston: Brandt, *An American Aristocracy*, 24–26.
102	"Ye vulgar sort": Quoted from Clare Brandt, "Robert R. Livingston Jr.: The Reluctant Revolutionary," a symposium paper delivered at "The Livingston Legacy: Three Centuries of American History," June 6–7, 1986. See also Brandt, *An American Aristocracy*, 31–36.
103	"This man by false insinuations": Edmund Bailey O'Callaghan, ed., *Documents Relating to the Colonial History of the State of New York* (Albany, 1856), 4:251.
103	"should not pass from our memory": Quoted from Robert Livingston, "The Schenectady Massacre," New-York Historical Society, Gilder Lehrman Document Number GLC 3107.
104	Bellomont ordered the arrest: O'Callaghan, ed., *Documents Relating to the Colonial History of the State of New York*, 4:762.
104	"intolerable corrupt selling": O'Callaghan, ed., *Documents Relating to the Colonial History of the State of New York*, 4:791. See also Irving Mark, *Agrarian Conflicts in Colonial New York* (New York, 1940), 23.
104	would he next move: There was considerable evidence that Bellomont would go after Livingston Manor and Rensselaerwyck. His bill vacating the grants that involved bribes states: "There do still remain in force several other exorbitant grants with the particulars whereof we shal forbear to trouble Your Majesty, til such time as it shal be judged proper by Your Majesty to have the like method taken for Vacating and annulling the said remaining grants by an Act to be passed in that Province, which however, from the reasons given by the Earl of Bellomont, We do apprehend may prove a work of great difficulty." O'Callaghan, ed., *Documents Relating to the Colonial History of the State of New York*, 5:22.
104	"Ambition and Avarice": Brandt, *An American Aristocracy*, 48.
105–6	Alida remained Livingston's anchorage: Again, I am indebted to Brandt, *An American Aristocracy*, 26–27, for much of the information for this paragraph.
107	victualing the settlers: O'Callaghan, ed., *Documents Relating to the Colonial History of the State of New York*, 5:171.
107	"tearing him apart": Cited in Linda Briggs Biemer, *Women and Property in Colonial New York: The Transition from Dutch to English Law, 1643–1727* (Ann Arbor, Michigan, 1983), 69. A revision of a 1979 doctoral dissertation, this work has a substantial chapter on Alida Schuyler Livingston.
108	Livingston finally achieved all: Brandt, *An American Aristocracy*, 66.
109	Philipse arrived in the Hudson Valley: The first time Philipse's name appears in official documents is in 1653 as a carpenter employed by the Dutch West India Company. In 1660, he became the director's carpenter. For information about Philipse and Margaret, I have drawn from Carol Berkin, *First Generations: Women in Colonial America* (New York, 1996), and

Biemer, *Women and Property in Colonial New York.* I have also profited from a term paper about Margaret Philipse by Kristin Nelson.

109   "Small Burgher Right": *American National Biography*, 17:439, and Berkin, *First Generations*, 80.

109–10   emotional and a commercial success: Information about Philipse and his holdings may be found in *American National Biography*, 14:439–40; O'Callaghan, ed., *Documents Relating to the Colonial History of the State of New York*, 3; Jacob Judd, "Frederick Philipse and the Madagascar Trade," *New-York Historical Society Quarterly* 55, no. 4 (October 1971), 354–74; Kathleen Eagen Johnson's notes for an exhibit entitled "Cross Roads and Cross Rivers: Diversity in Colonial New York," Philipsburg Manor in Sleepy Hollow, 1999–2000. Edwin G. Burrows and Mike Wallace provide a useful context for Philipse in *Gotham: A History of New York City to 1898* (New York, 1999), 77–82.

110   "Manor of Philipsborough": Edward Hagaman Hall, "The Manor of Philipsborough," address written for the New York Branch of the Order of Colonial Lords of Manors in America, 1920.

112   "For negroes in these times": Philipse's letter to his pirate broker in Madagascar is quoted in Judd, "Frederick Philipse and the Madagascar Trade," 358.

112   "It is by negroes": Judd, "Frederick Philipse and the Madagascar Trade," 358.

113   New York City ranked: Reliable population figures for slaves are somewhat difficult to come by, especially before the census of 1790, which counted 2,369 slaves in New York City and 1,101 free blacks. According to Milton M. Klein, ed., *The Empire State: A History of New York* (Ithaca, New York, 2001), 156, the state's slave population in 1771 stood at 9,247. Most lived in New York City and Albany.

114–15   Heaten's painting for Marten Van Bergen: My discussion of the Van Bergen overmantel owes much to my conversations with Marc Woodworth of Skidmore College. Readers should also see Alice P. Kenney, *Stubborn for Liberty: The Dutch in New York* (Syracuse, New York, 1975), 99–102. I have used Kenney to guide me through the history of the house and the family genealogy.

115–16   "even the dark aspect": Quoted from Anne Grant, *Memoirs of an American Lady, with Sketches of Manners and Scenes in America as They Existed Previous to the Revolution, by Anne Grant, with Unpublished Letters and a Memoir of Mrs. Grant by James Grant Wilson* (New York, 1901), 80.

117   New York slave "plot": Joel Tyler Headley, *The Great Riots of New York, 1712–1873: Including a Full and Complete Account of the Four Days' Draft Riot of 1863* (Miami, Florida, 1969), 43–44.

117–18   execution of Cuffee: O'Callaghan, ed., *Documents Relating to the Colonial History of the State of New York*, 6:197–98.

119	"They are a broken reed": Allen W. Trelease, *Indian Affairs in Colonial New York: The Seventeenth Century* (Ithaca, New York, 1960), 306.
120	Iroquois sachems to London: Included among the sachems was a Mohawk of legendary stature known to his fellow tribesmen as Tee Yee Neen Ho Ga Row, or Tiyanoga, and to the English as King Hendrick. Nelson Greene, *The Valley of the Hudson* (Chicago, 1931), 1:431–32.
121	"96 Knives, 12 gunns": Quoted from O'Callaghan, ed., *Documents Relating to the Colonial History of the State of New York*, 5:229.
122	"to renew, strengthen and brighten": "Conference Between Governor Clinton and the Indians," June 18, 1744, in O'Callaghan, ed., *Documents Relating to the Colonial History of the State of New York*, 6:262–66.
123	more precarious than ever: By 1753, Robert Dinwiddie, the governor of Virginia, grew alarmed. His colony claimed a western border far beyond the Alleghenies into the unexplored and unknown distance. Disregarding the encroaching winter, he sent a twenty-one-year-old major, George Washington from Williamsburg, in October on a mission to the French Fort Le Boeuf near Lake Erie. The major carried a message from the governor demanding that the French remove their settlement and withdraw to Canada. Slogging through "excessive Rains and a vast Quantity of Snow," and surviving an assassination attempt, Washington was politely and firmly dismissed.
123	Franklin's Albany Plan: Walter Isaacson, *Benjamin Franklin: An American Life* (New York, 2003), 159–60.
124	The English had neglected the Indians: Benson J. Lossing, *Pictorial Field Book of the Revolution* (New York, 1850), vol. 1, chapter 5.

Chapter 5. The Only Passage

126	"The importance of the North River": George Washington, *The Papers of George Washington, Revolutionary War Series*, ed. Philander D. Chase (Charlottesville, Virginia, 2001), 12:498–99.
128	Battle of Saratoga: For this discussion of the battle I have relied especially on Robert M. Ketchum, *Saratoga: Turning Point in America's Revolutionary War* (New York, 1997), and Max M. Mintz, *The Generals at Saratoga* (New Haven, 1990).
129	twenty-four days to travel: Don R. Gerlach, *Proud Patriot: Philip Schuyler and the War of Independence, 1775–1783* (Syracuse, New York, 1987), 260.
129	"unfortunate affair at Bennington": Marvin L. Brown, Jr., trans., *Baroness von Riedesel and the American Revolution: Journal and Correspondence of a Tour of Duty, 1776–1783* (Chapel Hill, North Carolina, 1965), 44.
129	"Britons never retreat": Brown, trans., *Baroness von Riedesel and the American Revolution,* 47.
130	"fifteen, sixteen, and twenty": Quoted from Ray Raphael, *A People's History*

of the American Revolution: How Common People Shaped the Fight for Independence (New York, 2001), 76.

130–31   "The army was in a pitiful situation": Helga Doblin, trans., and Mary C. Lynn, introduction, "The Battle of Saratoga from an Enemy Perspective," *Tamkang Journal of American Studies* 3, no. 3 (Spring 2001), 20–21. The German officer is unknown. This fragment of his journal was found in the Niedersächsisches Archiv in Wolfenbüttel, Germany. Quotations come from entries for September 21 and October 3, 1777.

131   "Oh fatal ambition!": Brown, trans., *Baroness von Riedesel and the American Revolution*, 51–52.

131   "There was no place of safety": Ketchum, *Saratoga*, 406–7; see also Helga Doblin, trans., Mary C. Lynn, ed., *The Specht Journal: A Military Journal of the Burgoyne Campaign* (Westport, Connecticut, 1995), 96–97.

131   "We had enemy on all sides": Doblin and Lynn, "The Battle of Saratoga from an Enemy Perspective," 24–25. The entry is for October 11, 1777, and obviously condenses a number of days of the battle.

131–32   "I am not glad to see you": Ketchum, *Saratoga*, 429. As Ketchum notes, "Several versions of the conversation exist, and whether these were the exact words spoken cannot be said for sure, but certainly this was the substance."

132   "Mother, is this the palace": Brown, trans., *Baroness von Riedesel and the American Revolution*, 65. The story originally appeared in Henry C. Van Schaack, *The Life of Peter Van Schaack* (New York, 1842), 93–94.

132   "a gill of rum": *The Papers of George Washington, Revolutionary War Series*, 11:237.

132–33   "Sir, is Philadelphia taken?": Walter Isaacson, *Benjamin Franklin: An American Life* (New York, 2003), 342–49; Benjamin Franklin, *The Papers of Benjamin Franklin*, ed. Leonard W. Labaree and Whitfield J. Bell, Jr. (New Haven, 1959), 25:234–37.

133   "meditat[ing] a serious blow": Israel Putnam worried, too, that Sir Henry Clinton meant to join Burgoyne: "My real & Sincere Opinion, is that they now Mean to join General Burgoyne with the utmost dispatch"; *The Papers of George Washington, Revolutionary War Series*, 11:449.

134   Vaughn reported: While he was at Kingston, John Vaughan learned of Burgoyne's impending surrender. "From the Accounts I had received of his Situation," he wrote, "I found it impracticable to give him any further Assistance." William Bell Clark, ed., *Naval Documents of the American Revolution* (Washington, 1996), vol. 10, American Theatre: October 1, 1777–December 1, 1777, [A]PRO, C.O. 5/94, 345–47, 350; [B]PRO, Admiralty 1/488, 58; [C]PRO, C.O. 5/95, 10–11.

134   "The complete captivity": Washington to Major General William Heath, October 22, 1777, in Washington, *The Papers of George Washington, Revolutionary War Series*, 11:574.

136	Livingston family's first names: Many others have made similar observations. See Clare Brandt, *An American Aristocracy: The Livingstons* (New York, 1986), 6, and throughout.
136	Almost all Livingston family members: Philip Livingston, Peter Van Brugh Livingston's son, quietly decided for the Loyalists.
137	"He stopt at Kingston": George Dangerfield, *Chancellor Robert R. Livingston of New York, 1746–1813* (New York, 1960), 105.
137–38	"When the King of Great Britain": Brandt, *An American Aristocracy*, 123.
138	"the key to America": Quoted in Richard L. Blanco, ed., *The American Revolution, 1775–1783: An Encyclopedia* (New York, 1993), 1773.
138–39	"Seize the present": Washington to Israel Putnam, December 2, 1777, in *The Papers of George Washington, Revolutionary War Series*, 11:498–99.
140	chain at West Point: The dimension of the chain is cited in United States Military Academy, History Department, West Point Fortifications Staff Ride Note Cards (2nd edition, 1998), Card 28.
140–45	Benedict Arnold: For this section I have drawn from James T. Flexner, *The Traitor and the Spy: Benedict Arnold and John André* (Boston, 1975).
146	"very limpingly": Washington in a letter to George Augustine Washington, November 14, 1782, in *The Writings of George Washington: Being His Correspondence, Addresses, Messages, and Other Papers, Official and Private, Selected and Published from the Original Manuscripts*, ed. Jared Sparks (Boston, 1839), 25:343.
146	"to procure justice": James T. Flexner, *Washington, the Indispensable Man* (Boston, 1974), 173.
146	Newburgh addresses: For this discussion of the Newburgh addresses I have relied on James T. Flexner, *George Washington in the American Revolution* (Boston, 1968), 500–518, and Joseph J. Ellis, *His Excellency, George Washington* (New York, 2004), 141–44.
147–49	Abandoned after seven years: A good picture of New York City in the aftermath of the Revolution is found in Edwin G. Burrows and Mike Wallace, *Gotham: A History of New York to 1898* (New York 1999), 259–61, 265–73.

Chapter 6. The Democratic River

150–52	Lafayette's visit: Information about Lafayette and his tour of the United States comes from Olivier Bernier, *Lafayette, Hero of Two Worlds* (New York, 1983), 292–98; Louis R. Gottschalk, *Lafayette Comes to America* (Chicago, 1965); and Marian Klamkin, *The Return of Lafayette* (New York, 1975).
153	population of New York City: Specifically, 23,614 in 1786; 123,706 in 1820. Philadelphia's population in 1820 was 62,802, and Boston's was 43,298.
154	New York's port: Specifically, of the port's domestic exports, cotton accounted for $3,925,000 of the total of $9,228,000; flour exports

were $794,000, and furs, $291,000; Robert Greenhalgh Albion, *The Rise of New York Port, 1815–1860* (New York, 1939), 100–101.

154–55   Across the Hudson at Troy: Robert Lowry, *Complete History of the Marquis de Lafayette, Major General in the Army of the United States of America, in the War of the Revolution; Embracing an Account of his Late Tour Through the United States to the Time of his Departure, September, 1825* (New York, 1846).

155   Robert Fulton and Robert R. Livingston: For the story of Fulton and Livingston I have relied especially on Clare Brandt, *An American Aristocracy: The Livingstons* (New York, 1986), George Dangerfield, *Chancellor Robert R. Livingston of New York, 1746–1813* (New York, 1960), Cynthia Owen Philip, *Robert Fulton* (New York, 1985), and James T. Flexner, *Steamboats Come True* (Boston, 1978).

157   "a cheap substitute for rags": Brandt, *An American Aristocracy*, 144–45.

160   sloops carried packages and mail: William E. Verplanck and Moses W. Collyer, *The Sloops of the Hudson* (Fleischmanns, New York, 1984), 7.

161   "beautiful scenery of the river": Cooper wrote these words in chapter 30 of *Afloat and Ashore: A Sea Tale* (New York, 1844). They are quoted in Verplanck and Collyer, *The Sloops of the Hudson*, 10.

162–63   Livingston-Fulton monopoly: Livingston and Fulton did not stop with the Hudson. They extended their monopoly to the Mississippi, where their Mississippi Steamboat Company obtained the exclusive right to operate a boat between New Orleans and Natchez.

164   "a brother agriculturalist": Dangerfield, *Chancellor Robert R. Livingston*, 437; Brandt, *An American Aristocracy*, 162.

164   "Apoplectic and paralytic seizures": Brandt, *An American Aristocracy*, 162; Dangerfield, *Chancellor Robert R. Livingston*, 437–38.

164   His pulse grew "feeble": Philip, *Robert Fulton*, 346; Flexner, *Steamboats Come True*, 361–63.

165   Cornelius Vanderbilt: Vanderbilt is a titanic figure who deserves a modern biography. Information for my brief portrait comes from Wayne Andrews, *The Vanderbilt Legend: The Story of the Vanderbilt Family, 1794–1940* (New York, 1941), Wheaton J. Lane, *Commodore Vanderbilt: An Epic of the Steam Age* (New York, 1942), and Meade Minnigerode, *Certain Rich Men: Stephen Girard, John Jacob Astor, Jay Cooke, Daniel Drew, Cornelius Vanderbilt, Jay Gould, Jim Fisk* (New York, 1927).

167   "I don't care half so much": Lane, *Commodore Vanderbilt*, 35.

168   Webster's arguments: There is an excellent and far more detailed synopsis of Webster's arguments in Lane, *Commodore Vanderbilt*, 100–107.

169–70   Erie Canal: Information on the Erie Canal comes from a number of sources, including Carol Sheriff, *The Artificial River: The Erie Canal and the Paradox of Progress, 1817–1862* (New York, 1996), Dorothie De Bear Bobbé, *De Witt Clinton* (Port Washington, New York, 1962), Evan Cornog, *The Birth of*

Empire: DeWitt Clinton and the American Experience, 1769–1828, and my collection of pamphlets and clippings.

170   "vast inland navigation": Washington's heart, however, lay in improvements to Virginia and the Potomac River.

172   "bringing the achievements": George Wilson Pierson, *Tocqueville in America* (Gloucester, Massachusetts, 1969), 376–77.

172   "Surely the water": Hawthorne wrote "The Canal Boat" for the *New-England Magazine*, no. 9, December 1835, 398–409.

172–73   The canal changed the economy: Milton M. Klein, ed., *The Empire State: A History of New York* (Ithaca, New York, 2001), 310–11.

173   John Maude's log: Roland Van Zandt, *Chronicles of the Hudson* (Hensonville, New York, 1992), 131–42.

174   looked west for cheaper flour: Albion, *The Rise of New York Port*, 89.

175–76   "Kiss his Ass": Edmund Bailey O'Callaghan, ed., *Documents Relating to the Colonial History of the State of New York* (Albany, 1856), 3:153; Brandt, *An American Aristocracy*, 89.

176   Many chose default: "Rent default was inherent in the nature of the leasehold system," one historian has observed, "and a tenant's conscientious fulfillment of his obligation was more an exception than the norm"; Sung Bok Kim, *Landlord and Tenant in Colonial New York: Manorial Society, 1664–1775* (Chapel Hill, North Carolina, 1978), 214. Kim's rigorous analysis of various leaseholder documents up to 1775 is excellent.

177   anti-renters as "Indians": David Maldwyn Ellis, *Landlords and Farmers in the Hudson-Mohawk Region, 1790–1850* (Ithaca, New York, 1946), 233; Charles W. McCurdy, *The Anti-Rent Era in New York Law and Politics, 1839–1865* (Chapel Hill, North Carolina, 2001), 9–13.

177   "Strike till the last armed foe expires": Brandt, *An American Aristocracy*, 184.

177–78   "Unequal ratio of taxation": J. Priest, *The Dutch and English Grants of the Rensselaer and Livingston Manors Together with a History of the Settlement of Albany* (Albany, 1844), 33–34.

178   Boughton arrested and convicted: Much of this information comes from Ellis, *Landlords and Farmers in the Hudson-Mohawk Region*, 260–62, and Brandt, *An American Aristocracy*, 186–87.

178   "Indian" raids: Henry Christman, *Tin Horns and Calico: A Decisive Episode in the Emergence of Democracy* (New York, 1945), 50.

181   A new era in travel: The Hudson River Railroad faltered until Cornelius Vanderbilt acquired the line in 1864. In 1869 he combined it with the New York Central to form the New York Central and Hudson River Railroad. Kurt C. Schlichting, *Grand Central Terminal: Railroads, Engineering, and Architecture in New York City* (Baltimore, 2001), 14–17, 25–26.

181–82   "Lo, soul, seest thou not God's purpose": These lines come from Whitman's "Passage to India!"

182–83	Washington Irving grumbled: Quotations about the disruption of the railroad are from Pierre M. Irving, *The Life and Letters of Washington Irving* (New York, 1883), 3:90; quotations about Sunnyside are from Ralph M. Aderman, Herbert L. Kleinfield, and Jennifer S. Banks, eds., *Letters of Washington Irving* (Boston, 1982), 4:1846.
184	"the length and volume": Edward Waldo Emerson and Waldo Emerson Forbes, eds., *Journals of Ralph Waldo Emerson, 1820–1872* (Cambridge, 1909), vol. 10, April 10, 1867.
185	"I experienced a sensation": Van Zandt, *Chronicles of the Hudson*, 213.

Chapter 7. Definers of the Landscape

188	"Never shall I forget": This manuscript of an unfinished article for *The Home Book of the Picturesque* appears in Stanley T. Williams, *The Life of Washington Irving* (New York, 1935), 1:28. See also Washington Irving, *Miscellaneous Writings, 1803–1859*, ed. Wayne R. Kime (Boston, 1981), 344–45.
189	Walter the Doubter: Washington Irving, *Diedrich Knickerbocker's History of New York* (New York, 1940), 170.
189	"adamantine chains": Irving, *Diedrich Knickerbocker's History of New York*, 622–27.
189	families "never forgave" him: Williams, *The Life of Washington Irving*, 1:119.
189	"I was . . . caressed": Williams, *The Life of Washington Irving*, 2:275.
190	"Sun not up yet": Williams, *The Life of Washington Irving*, 1:124.
192	Charles Dickens rose: Andrew B. Myers, ed., *A Century of Commentary on the Works of Washington Irving, 1860–1974* (Tarrytown, New York, c. 1976), 11.
192–93	Sunnyside: Much of the information about Sunnyside is found in Kathleen Eagen Johnson, *Washington Irving's Sunnyside* (Tarrytown, New York, 1995). See also Benson J. Lossing, *The Hudson: From the Wilderness to the Sea* (Hensonville, New York, 2000), 341–49.
193–94	"I have made more openings": Quoted from Irving's letter to Sarah Paris Storrow, in Johnson, *Washington Irving's Sunnyside*, 32.
195	Matilda Hoffman's Bible: Lossing, *The Hudson*, 343–44.
195	Even in this small way: Louis L. Noble has expressed this thought about Cole similarly: "Hitherto he had been trying mainly to make up nature from his own mind instead of making up his mind from nature. This now [in 1823] flashed upon him as a radical mistake." Louis Legrand Noble, *The Life and Works of Thomas Cole*, Elliot S. Vesell, ed. (Cambridge, 1964), 41. That said, other artists like William Guy Wall did journey up the Hudson before Cole. In addition to Noble's work, this discussion of Cole also draws from James T. Flexner, *That Wilder Image: The Painting of America's Native School from Thomas Cole to Winslow Homer* (New York, 1970), Earl A. Powell, *Thomas Cole* (New York, 1990), and Matthew Baigell, *Thomas Cole* (New York, 1981).

195   Kaaterskill Creek: The name is variously spelled, including "Caterskill," in Noble, *The Life and Works of Thomas Cole,* 35.

195   "I saw / The idle River": Marshall B. Tymn, ed., *Thomas Cole's Poetry* (York, Pennsylvania, 1972), 41.

197   "You have already done": Noble, *The Life and Works of Thomas Cole,* 35. See also Carrie Rebora Barratt, "Mapping the Venues: New York City Art Exhibitions," in *Art and the Empire City: New York, 1825–1861,* ed. Catherine Hoover Voorsanger and John K. Howat (New Haven, 2000), 47–81. Barratt's excellent essay presents the story in vivid detail, including, among other things, that Trumbull never actually paid Coleman the twenty-five dollars for his painting, because the shop owner was in debt to the artist.

197   Philip Hone bought: Such sales were common, because the American Academy of Fine Arts was a sales gallery, and "taking the paintings from Colemans to the Academy did not remove them from the market but transferred them to a more advantageous venue"; Barratt, "Mapping the Venues," 49.

197   endorsement started Cole's career: Noble, *The Life and Works of Thomas Cole,* 35.

197   "The painter of American scenery": Thomas Cole, "Essay on American Scenery," *American Monthly Magazine* 1 (January 1836), 1–12; reprinted in John W. McCoubrey, *American Art, 1700–1960: Sources and Documents* (Englewood Cliffs, New Jersey, 1965), 98–110.

197   "The woods are dark": The opening lines of "Twilight," Tymn, ed., *Thomas Cole's Poetry,* 38.

197   "Midnight hath loosed": Tymn, ed., *Thomas Cole's Poetry,* 175.

198   "in its majesty": Noble, *The Life and Works of Thomas Cole,* 43–45.

198   "The scenery is not grand": Cole, "Essay on American Scenery."

198   "The great struggle for freedom": Cole, "Essay on American Scenery."

198   *A View of Fort Putnam:* Lost for many years, this painting has recently reappeared in the Philadelphia Museum of Art, the promised gift of Charlene Sussel.

201   "broken into fleecy forms": John K. Howat, "A Picturesque Site in the Catskills: The Kaaterskill Falls as Painted by William Guy Wall," *Honolulu Academy of Arts Journal* 1 (1974).

202   "The mist below the mountain": Noble, *The Life and Works of Thomas Cole,* 39.

202   "natural magnificence . . . is unsurpassed": Cole, "Essay on American Scenery."

202   "When the morning lights the sky": Tymn, ed., *Thomas Cole's Poetry,* 178.

202   "Thine eyes shall see": The title of this poem is "Sonnet—To an American Painter Departing for Europe"; Parke Godwin, ed., *The Life and Works of William Cullen Bryant, Poetical Works* (New York, 1883).

202–3	"I wish to take": Cole's letter to Robert Gilmor, April 26, 1829, reprinted in Noble, *The Life and Works of Thomas Cole*, 72.
203	"the picturesque": William Cullen Bryant, "Funeral Oration on the Death of Thomas Cole Before the National Academy of Design," in McCoubrey, *American Art, 1700–1960*, 96–97.
203	"I want to be quiet": Noble, *The Life and Works of Thomas Cole*, 306.
205	"dark summits of the distant mountains": Noble, *The Life and Works of Thomas Cole*, 43–45.
205	"landscape of mood": William Cullen Bryant II, "Poetry and Painting: A Love Affair of Long Ago," *American Quarterly* 22, no. 4 (Winter 1970), 864–65.
205–6	"All, save this little nook of land": The poem's title is "A Scene on the Banks of the Hudson"; Godwin, ed., *The Life and Works of William Cullen Bryant*.
206	Asher Durand: John Durand, *The Life and Times of A. B. Durand* (New York, 1894), 223–25.
206	"I am pleased": Noble, *The Life and Works of Thomas Cole*, 163.
206	a "chord that vibrates": Asher B. Durand, "Letters on Landscape Painting," letter 4, *Crayon* no. 7 (February 14, 1855), 98. Consider also these words of Durand: "To the rich merchant and capitalist . . . released from the world-struggle, so far as to allow a little time to rest and reflect in, landscape art especially appeals. . . . In spite of the discordant clamor and conflict of the crowded city, the true landscape becomes a thing of more than outward beauty. . . . It becomes companionable, holding silent converse with the feelings . . . touching a chord that vibrates to the inmost recesses of the heart." "Letters on Landscape Painting," reprinted in McCoubrey, *American Art, 1700–1960*, 113–15.
208	"He may be regarded": Quoted in Eleanor Jones Harvey, *The Painted Sketch: American Impressions from Nature, 1830–1880* (Dallas, Texas, 1998), 20.
210	discerning collectors quietly moved: "Sale of the Baker Collection; Competition Not Very Spirited—The 'Cole' Paintings," *New York Times*, February 19, 1880, 2; "Selling the Durr Pictures," *New York Times*, January 28, 1881, 5. I am also indebted to Kenneth J. Avery, "A Historiography of the Hudson River School," and Doreen Bolger Burke and Catherine Hoover Voorsanger, "The Hudson River School in Eclipse," in *American Paradise: The World of the Hudson River School*, ed. John K. Howat (New York, 1998).
210–11	Andrew Jackson Downing: This discussion of Downing draws from his *Architecture of Country Houses* (New York, 1850) and *Victorian Cottage Residences* (New York, 1873), as well as George William Curtis, ed., *Rural Essays* (New York, 1974). In addition I have also consulted David Schuyler, *Apostle of Taste: Andrew Jackson Downing, 1815–1852* (Baltimore, 1996), Judith K. Major, *To Live in the New World: A. J. Downing and American Landscape Gardening* (Cambridge,

1997), and George B. Tatum and Elisabeth Blair MacDougall, eds., *Prophet with Honor: The Career of Andrew Jackson Downing, 1815–1852* (Washington, 1989). Carl Carmer also has an excellent chapter on Downing in *The Hudson* (New York, 1939).

211–12 "spirit and grace": Andrew Jackson Downing, *Victorian Cottage Residences* (New York, 1873), 50.

213 "wild sympathy of nature": Curtis wrote a brilliant memoir of Downing for his edition of *Rural Essays*; this quotation is taken from p. lvii.

214 "I was kindly allowed": "Rival Mountain Houses; The New Hotel on the Summit of the Catskills," *New York Times*, August 1, 1881, 5. There were numerous advertisements for Catskill resorts in New York papers during this period, for example in the *New York Times*, July 7, 1880, 7, and June 28, 1881, 7.

214 South Mountain: South Mountain was also referred to as Pine Orchard Mountain, and the Catskill Mountain House was sometimes called the Pine Orchard House in its early years. For information about pitch pine, see Alf Evers, *The Catskills: From Wilderness to Woodstock* (Garden City, New York, 1972), 349–50.

214 "large and commodious hotel": Roland Van Zandt, *The Catskill Mountain House* (Hensonville, New York, 1993), 37.

214 "bright as a diamond": "Rival Mountain Houses," *New York Times*, 5.

215 "situated 2500 feet above": Quoted in Roland Van Zandt, *Chronicles of the Hudson* (Hensonville, New York, 1992), 328, note 7; see also Van Zandt, *The Catskill Mountain House*, 29.

215 "an illuminated fairy palace": Van Zandt, *Chronicles of the Hudson*, 217.

216 "It shows beautifully": "Catskill Mountain Life; Looking Down on the Busy World Below," *New York Times*, July 4, 1885, 2.

216 "little, if at all, inferior": Karl Baedeker, ed., *The United States, With an Excursion into Mexico; Handbook for Travellers* (New York, 1899), 179.

217 seventy-five trees per acre: Seventy-five trees to produce fifteen cords is a bit conservative. Zadock Pratt computed 4 trees to a cord, 18 cords to the acre, or 120,000 hemlocks in 10 square miles. Barbara McMartin, *Hides, Hemlocks, and Adirondack History: How the Tanning Industry Influenced the Growth of the Region* (Utica, New York, 1992), 320.

217 The remaining trunks: The tanners actually left 95 percent of the hemlocks to rot; Field Horne, *Greene County and the Catskills: A History* (Hensonville, New York, 1994), 57. I have drawn most of my information about tanning from McMartin's and Horne's books.

218 "low pursuits of avarice": Cole, "Essay on American Scenery," introduction.

218–19 Zadock Pratt: Much of the information about Pratt comes from Evers, *The Catskills*, 340–49, and Horne, *Greene County and the Catskills*, 57–60.

219	"more than 6000 cords": McMartin, *Hides, Hemlocks, and Adirondack History,* 316–20.
220	a tannery "is not at all calculated": T. Addison Richards, "The Catskills," *Harper's Monthly,* July 1854, 153. On a sketching trip through the Catskills, Richards was appalled by the destruction he saw.
220–21	Elam Lynds: Information about Elam Lynds's features comes specifically from Scott Christianson's *With Liberty for Some* (Boston, 1998), 111. For this discussion of Sing Sing, I have drawn on Christianson's excellent chapter "Little Man in the Big House," 110ff., as well as Lewis E. Lawes, *Twenty Thousand Years in Sing Sing* (New York, 1932), 71ff.
221	a "Catocracy": For more on the "cat," as it was called, see Lawes, *Twenty Thousand Years in Sing Sing,* 74–76.
223	"Pronounce the Nightingale": Nash's poem is titled "Flow gently, sweet etymology, ornithology, and penology."
224	"How to live without waterfalls": T. Morris Longstreth, *The Catskills* (New York, 1918), 87; Horne, *Greene County and the Catskills,* 82.
224	"I don't know as I can": "A Long Mountain Drive: Queer Places and People in the Catskills," *New York Times,* August 20, 1882, 5.

Chapter 8. River of Fortunes

225–26	Lincoln's train journey: Most of the material about this trip in 1861 comes from accounts in the *New York Times:* "Affairs of the Nation," and "From the State Capital," February 19, 1861, and "Arrival and Reception in New-York; Starting of the Procession"; also Carl Sandburg, *Abraham Lincoln: The War Years* (New York, 1939), 4:53–61, and Abraham Lincoln, *Collected Works,* Roy P. Basler, ed. (New Brunswick, New Jersey, 1953), 4:224–31.
227	"one of the finest actors": Cited in William Kennedy, *O Albany! Improbable City of Political Wizards, Fearless Ethnics, Spectacular Aristocrats, Splendid Nobodies, and Underrated Scoundrels* (New York, 1983), 69.
227	A riot in Troy: "The Slave Rescue at Troy; Details and Particulars of an Exciting Scene," *New York Times,* May 1, 1860, 8.
227–28	John A. Bolding: Information on John Bolding may be found in the vertical file, Adriance Memorial Library, Poughkeepsie, New York.
230	"contrived over twenty ways": Quoted from Edgar Mayhew Bacon, *The Hudson River from Ocean to Source, Historical—Legendary—Picturesque* (New York, 1903), 426.
231	"Paradise could scarcely": Quoted from Harvey K. Flad, "Matthew Vassar's Springside: ' . . . the hand of Art, when guided by Taste,'" in *Prophet with Honor: The Career of Andrew Jackson Downing, 1815–1852,* ed. George B. Tatum and Elisabeth Blair MacDougall (Washington, 1989), 219.
232	"annals of philanthropy": Valice F. Ruge, ed., *Life Along the Hudson: Wood*

Engravings of Hudson River Subjects from Harper's Weekly, 1859–1903 (Woodstock, New York, 1994), 8.

234   "I'm hungry": Ralph Gary, *Following in Lincoln's Footsteps: A Complete Annotated Reference to Hundreds of Historical Sites Visited by Abraham Lincoln* (New York, 2001), 273.

235   "Fear not, Abraham": Sandburg, *Abraham Lincoln: The War Years*, 55–64. See also the report in the *New York Times*, February 20, 1861, 1. George Templeton Strong recorded, "Broadway crowded, though not quite so densely as on the Prince of Wales's *avatar* last October"; Strong, *Diary*, ed. Allan Nevins and Milton Halsey Thomas (New York, 1952), 3:101.

235   "not a voice—not a sound": Walt Whitman, *Prose Works, 1892*, ed. Ralph Stovall (New York, 1964), 500–501.

236   Changing fashion demanded more: For information about the relation between cotton and fashion, see Robert Greenhalgh Albion, *The Rise of New York Port, 1815–1860* (New York, 1939), especially 55–57 and 95–121. See also Philip S. Foner, *Business and Slavery: The New York Merchants and the Irrepressible Conflict* (New York, 1968), 139ff.

236–37   "Your insular city": Herman Melville, *Moby Dick*, chapter 1.

237   population of New York City: Kenneth T. Jackson, ed., *The Encyclopedia of New York City* (New Haven, 1995), 920–23. The boroughs that New York City now comprises (Manhattan, Brooklyn, Queens, Staten Island, and the Bronx) were not consolidated into one city until 1898.

237   William Backhouse Astor: Harvey O'Connor, *The Astors* (New York, 1941), 104.

237   Wood even proposed: Foner, *Business and Slavery*, 285ff. Foner shows that in reaction to the Morrill tariffs, Wood proposed creating a "Republic of New York," and cites a letter from John Forsyth, a Confederate commissioner, to Jefferson Davis: "While in New York last week, I learned some particulars of a contemplated revolutionary movement in that city" (291). Foner concludes that there is no way of knowing how serious the movement was.

240   nine of the ten wealthiest: Information about the wealth of individuals comes from biographies of those mentioned and various reliable genealogical sites on the Internet.

241   Census enumerators: Census figures about immigrants may be found in Jackson, ed., *Encyclopedia of New York City*, 581–87.

241   "working men and their families": "Music in Central Park," *New York Times*, May 30, 1880, 5; "No Rigid Enforcement; The Spasm of Virtue Apparently Passing Off," *New York Times*, December 18, 1882, 5.

242–43   landslide of 1906: "Mayor Foss said tonight that this clay is worth nearly $200,000, and that it will form a new source of supply for their brickyards for years to come"; "22 Die in Landslide; More Houses in Peril; Haverstraw Residences and Occupants Engulfed in Great Pit.

Brickmakers Will Profit; Disaster Laid to Their Encroachments and $200,000 Worth of Clay Dumped on Their Property," *New York Times*, January 10, 1906, 2.

243   "Crystal, like that of Muscovy": Adriaen van der Donck, *A Description of the New Netherlands*, ed. Thomas F. O'Donnell (Syracuse, New York, 1968), 37.

243   "It is fast becoming a necessary": *New York Times*, February 14, 1857, 10.

244   The Hudson provided more ice: Information about the ice industry comes from Richard O. Cummings, *The American Ice Harvest: A Historical Study in Technology, 1800–1918* (Berkeley, California, 1949), and numerous newspaper articles of the period. Throughout the valley, people eagerly followed the harvesting of each year's ice crop, as evidenced by a sampling of articles from the *New York Times*: "The Ice Trade; The Crop Excessive, the Price Outrageous, the Dealers a Monopoly," May 3, 1865, 8; "The Ice Crop of the North River," January 27, 1868, 5; "The Hudson River Ice Crop," February 11, 1869, 5; "Quantity of Ice Stored on the Hudson," February 14, 1869, 3; "Harvesting the Ice Crop, An Encouraging Change in Affairs—Brisk Work Along the Hudson—Men Employed Nights and Sundays," March 13, 1870, 8; "The Ice Crop, A Splendid Report from Up the River; Extended Fields of Clear, Clean, Thick Ice; Large Gangs Busily Engaged in Harvesting It; Preparations for Night Work by Calcium Lights," January 11, 1871, 1; "The Ice Crop; A Review of the Situation. What the Officers of the Local Companies Say About It; Ice From Maine and Massachusetts for This Market," February 1, 1874, 3; "Strike on the Ice-Fields, A Fine Crop and No Men to Harvest It; Suspension of Work at Icehouses; Demands for Higher Wages," January 15, 1875, 8; "The Ice Crop, Reports from Different Parts of the Hudson River, Prospects of the Harvest," January 31, 1878, 5; "Reaping the Ice Harvest; An Unusually Large Yield from the Hudson River. The Gathering to Be Finished Probably This Week—Expectation that 3,000,000 Tons Will Be Obtained, or Enough for Two Seasons," January 28, 1879, 2. The last article reports on the number of icehouses along the river. Wendy Harris and Arnold Pickman, "Landscape, Landuse, and the Iconography of Space in the Hudson River Valley: The Nineteenth and Early Twentieth Century," paper presented at the New York Academy of Sciences, December 9, 1996, assesses the number of icehouses on the river and the way they changed the landscape.

244   "No man sows, yet many men reap": Ernest Ingersoll, *Illustrated Guide to the Hudson River and Catskill Mountains* (New York, 1910), 129. Ingersoll quoted from John Burroughs, *Signs and Seasons* (New York, 1886), 183–200.

245   "to regulate prices and the amount harvested": "Competition in the Ice Business; A New Company Buying Houses and Fields Along the Hudson," *New York Times*, January 2, 1896, 9; "Ice Trust Formed Under Maine Laws," *New York Times*, June 8, 1895, 3; "Means Death to Poor; Ice Combination's Advanced Prices Beyond Their Reach," *New York Times*,

April 19, 1896, 2; "Must Suffer for Ice; The Price Forced Beyond the Reach of the Poor," *New York Times*, April 21, 1896, 9.

249   "like the Trianon": Clare Brandt, *An American Aristocracy: The Livingstons* (New York, 1986), 213.

250   "Fifteen hundred people": James Stuart, *Three Years in North America* (New York, 1833), 38.

250   Saratoga hotels expanded: Karl Baedeker, ed., *The United States, With an Excursion into Mexico; Handbook for Travellers* (New York, 1899), 199.

251   "everybody wore what they pleased": Edith Wharton, *The Buccaneers: A Novel by Edith Wharton; Completed by Marion Mainwaring* (New York, 1994), 4.

251   "democratic, vulgar Saratoga": Field Horne, *The Saratoga Reader* (Saratoga Springs, 2004), 207–15. James originally published his remarks about the resort in the *Nation*, August 11, 1870.

251   1.3 million foreign born: I have extrapolated these figures from the 1880 and 1900 census.

252   "dauntless power" of the city: Henry James, *The American Scene*, introduction and notes by Leon Edel (Bloomington, Indiana, 1968), 76ff.

253   "in an old house at Albany": Henry James, *The Portrait of a Lady*, ed. Leon Edel (Cambridge, 1963), 47.

253   "a peculiar romance": James, *The American Scene*, 148. Of course James had forgotten that the rivermen who piloted their sloops along the Hudson had made the very same case against the intrusion of the steamboats.

253   a "wet and windy day": James, *The American Scene*, 149–51.

Chapter 9. Twentieth-Century Waters

254–56   Hudson-Fulton Celebration: Most of the information on the celebration comes from daily reports in the *New York Times* as well as Edward Hagaman Hall, *The Hudson-Fulton celebration, 1909, the fourth annual report of the Hudson-Fulton celebration commission to the Legislature of the state of New York.* Published in 1910, these two immense volumes are filled with photographs and accounts of every celebration on the river.

258   Tunnels from Manhattan to New Jersey: The tunnel construction and opening were of great interest to all who lived along the lower Hudson. See "Twenty Men Buried Alive; Caving in of the Hudson River Tunnel. The Story of the Disaster. Story of a Survivor. What Another Workman Says. The Lost and the Saved. What the Superintendent Says. Character of the Enterprise. Where the 'Blow-Out' Occurred. Consultation of Engineers. Who Is at Fault?" *New York Times*, July 22, 1880, 1; "Trolley Tunnel Open to Jersey; President Turns On Power for First Official Train Between This City and Hoboken," *New York Times*, February 26, 1908, 1.

258   the Bear Mountain Bridge: Information about the Bear Mountain and

other bridges spanning the Hudson comes from numerous books and pamphlets as well as notes taken over twenty years. Three useful books on the subject are Sharon Reier, *The Bridges of New York* (New York, 1977), David Steinman, *Bridges and Their Builders* (New York, 1977), and Darl Rastorfer, *Six Bridges: The Legacy of Othmar H. Ammann* (New Haven, 2000). Othmar Amman designed the George Washington Bridge and the Verrazano Narrows Bridge.

259   Roosevelt looked with pride: Geoffrey C. Ward, *Before the Trumpet: Young Franklin Roosevelt, 1882–1905* (New York, 1985), 16–18, 230–31.

259   "the march of modern civilization": Helen Wilkinson Reynolds, *Dutch Houses in the Hudson Valley Before 1776* (New York, 1965).

260   "historical afternoons": Thomas W. Casey, "FDR Always Proud of Valley Roots; Boyhood, River, Friends Stay in His Thoughts," *Poughkeepsie Journal,* Spring 2005.

260   he named it Val-Kill: Ward, *Before the Trumpet,* 736–37.

260   "We are seeking . . . to adapt": Information about the post office dedication may be found in the Franklin Delano Roosevelt Library, Hyde Park, New York. See also Geoffrey C. Ward, ed., *Closest Companion: The Unknown Story of the Intimate Friendship Between Franklin Roosevelt and Margaret Suckley* (Boston, 1995).

261   "a point on the *east* side": Geoffrey C. Ward, *A First-Class Temperament: The Emergence of Franklin Roosevelt* (New York, 1989), 268–69.

261   King George VI and Queen Elizabeth: "The Hot Dog: A Success Story," *New York Times,* July 9, 1939, 84; "King Tries Hot Dog and Asks for More," *New York Times,* June 12, 1939, 1. Roosevelt took a quiet delight in addressing royalty by their first names; Ward, *A First-Class Temperament,* 760.

261   "All that is in me goes back": Joseph P. Lash, *Eleanor and Franklin: The Story of Their Relationship* (New York, 1971), 116.

261–62 a special seventeen-car funeral train: Ward, *Before the Trumpet,* 3–4, 7–11.

262   By midcentury the pollution was horrendous: Information about pollution comes from numerous clippings and publications by such organizations as Scenic Hudson, as well as Robert Boyle, *The Hudson River: A Natural and Unnatural History* (New York, 1969). Boyle is an invaluable source of information about the state of the Hudson at midcentury.

262–63 Consolidated Edison's proposed power plant: For this account of the Storm King controversy I have drawn from Boyle, *The Hudson River,* 153–74, and Allan R. Talbot, *Power Along the Hudson: The Storm King Case and the Birth of Environmentalism* (New York, 1972), especially 72–89 for Con Ed's plan. Talbot's book is the best single source on the subject.

263–64 Mowton Le Compte Waring: Talbot, *Power Along the Hudson,* 72–74, 76–80, 82–89, 190–91.

265–66 Those who were opposed to the project: Boyle, *The Hudson River,* 156.

267   comparing the boats at Storm King with those at Dunkirk: "Armada of Foes Invades Site of Con Ed Project on Hudson; Beachhead Established

and Sign Planted Before Fleet Retires Downstream," *New York Times*, September 7, 1964, 21. See also Talbot, *Power Along the Hudson*, 109–12.

268   Scenic Hudson won: Boyle, *The Hudson River*, 169; Talbot, *Power Along the Hudson*, 134–35.

269   "We lost the Fight": "Con Ed to Drop Storm King Plant as Part of Pact to Protect Hudson; 20 Months of Negotiations Con Ed Agrees to Halt Storm King Plant on Hudson; PSC Approval Needed; Indian Point Violation Alleged," *New York Times*, December 20, 1980, 1.

269   Waring moved from the Hudson: Talbot, *Power Along the Hudson*, 152.

270   The *Clearwater* and Pete Seeger: Pete Seeger's inspiration to create the *Clearwater* is well documented, of course, but perhaps nowhere better than in John Cronin's memoir that forms chapter 2 of John Cronin and Robert F. Kennedy, Jr., *The Riverkeepers* (New York, 1997).

271   increased levels of PCBs: Information on PCBs comes from many sources, including Cronin and Kennedy, *The Riverkeepers*, 58–61, as well as a large personal collection of newspapers.

273   Hudson Riverkeeper: Cronin and Kennedy, *The Riverkeepers*.

273   The Livingston genetic web: Clare Brandt, *An American Aristocracy: The Livingstons* (New York, 1986), chapter 33.

273   Clermont showed the strain: Brandt, *An American Aristocracy*, 187–89.

274   marriage of Honoria Alice Livingston: "Honoria Livingston Engaged to Marry; Will Become the Bride of Reginald L. M. McVitty, Formerly of Ireland. Fiancee's Family Noted; Miss Livingston a Great-Granddaughter of Signer of Declaration—Kin of Mr. McVitty Prominent," *New York Times*, April 6, 1931, 28; "Honoria Livingston Has Church Bridal; Descendant of a Declaration Signer Wed to Reginald L. M. McVitty. On Historic Anniversary; Clermont, Home of Bride's Mother, Built 200 Years Ago by First Lord of Livingston Manor," *New York Times*, September 13, 1931, N7.

274–75   a peculiar arrogance: Brandt, *An American Aristocracy*, chapter 34.

275   "the privilege of a Hudson River estate": Brandt, *An American Aristocracy*, 238.

275   Honoria and her partner: Brandt, *An American Aristocracy*, 250–51.

277   On Mount Merino: David C. Huntington, *The Landscapes of Frederic Edwin Church: Vision of an American Era* (New York, 1966), presents an excellent account of Church and his creation of Olana, especially in chapter 8.

277   a treasure house in Persia: The name Olana may also be a Latin corruption of the Arabic word *Al'ana*, meaning "our place on high"; Huntington, *The Landscapes of Frederic Edwin Church*, 114.

277   "About an hour this side": Huntington writes, "Olana stands above the very spot where Henry Hudson gave up his quest for a real passage. In symbolic terms Church fulfilled the navigator's urge." Of course Hun-

tington isn't entirely accurate, but I am indebted to him for the observation, as I am for his mention of Whitman and "Passage to India." Huntington, *The Landscapes of Frederic Edwin Church*, 115.

279   Church's sketching trips in the field: A number of these plein-air sketches show the perspective from Olana looking south down the Hudson to a bend in the river at Germantown and the start of Clover Reach, and west toward the mountains, the town of Catskill, and the home of his late mentor Thomas Cole. From his vantage point Church set out to capture the moment, the effect of a setting sun on the cloud formations and mountains, and the contours of the snow-capped landscape in *Sunset Across the Hudson Valley, Winter*, or the peculiar play of clouds and gray light on the pale Hudson in *The Bend in the River from Olana*. At Olana, Frederic Church was never far from the main source of his inspiration. Huntington makes this point in *The Landscapes of Frederic Edwin Church*, chapter 8, as does Eleanor Jones Harvey in *The Painted Sketch: American Impressions from Nature, 1830–1880* (Dallas, Texas, 1998), 106–9.

279   "Xanadu on the Hudson": Editorial, *New York Times*, June 10, 1966, 44.

279–80   preservation of Olana: A perusal of *New York Times* articles about Olana's brush with destruction provides an excellent lesson in grassroots preservation efforts in the Hudson Valley. David Huntington was the hero, but he had help from sympathetic politicians in Albany and the valley, including Alexander Aldrich, Winthrop Aldrich, and Governor Nelson Rockefeller. See especially these articles in the *New York Times*: "Fund Drive Is Begun to Save Estate on Hudson," November 12, 1964, 31; "Drive on to Save Artist's Mansion," January 20, 1965, 29; "$100,000 Is Raised to Prevent Destruction of Olana Mansion," January 31, 1966, 18; "Benefits Planned to Make Shrine of Upstate Home," May 17, 1966, 54; "State Will Operate an Artist's Mansion as a Museum," June 28, 1966, 26.

Acknowledgments

It is a happy task to discharge some of the many debts I have accumulated while writing this book. From the beginning I have received sage advice from Chris Calhoun, at Sterling Lord Literistic, who has continued to encourage me throughout the writing.

The history of a river is a very large topic indeed. Without the help of my editor at Yale, Lara Heimert, I would have been lost. More than anyone she has helped me shape the substance of this book. I am grateful to her for careful readings, judicious criticism, and extraordinary forbearance. I am grateful as well to Yale's manuscript editor Philip King, whose close reading of every chapter has added immeasurably to this book's clarity and grace. I also appreciate the help Molly Egland of Yale has given with the production of this book.

A number of friends have read the various drafts of the book's manuscript or have answered my numerous questions. Among them are Peggy Boyers, Thomas J. Condon, Anne Diggory, Robert Foulke, Judith Halstead, Field Horne, Kenneth Johnson, Bernard Kastory, Karen Kellogg, Colin Lewis, John Lukacs, Deane Pfeil, Bill Schmidt, Marc Woodworth, and Jan Young. I want to thank especially Alan and Renate Wheelock for their incisive comments. They have provided me with ideas, quotations, images, and books. I value their friendship.

Countless librarians and archivists at numerous libraries have served me in my work. I want to thank especially those at Columbia University, the New-York Historical Society, the Adriance Memorial Library, Poughkeepsie, Rensselaer Polytechnic Institute, Williams College, Vedder Memorial Research Library at the Greene County Historical Society, the Columbia

County Historical Society research library, the Saratoga County Supreme Court Law Library, Scenic Hudson, Union College, Skidmore College, the New York State Library at Albany, the Bannerman Castle Trust, the Franklin Delano Roosevelt Library, and the New York Public Library. Special thanks to Marilyn Sheffer, at the Lucy Scribner Library, who has located scores of interlibrary loan materials for me.

I also appreciate the help I have received from many others including Larry Hott from Florentine Films; Michael Moore, a dear friend; Robert Boyers, Heather Caney, Ralph Ciancio, Hunt Conard, John Danison, Steve Dinyer, Meagan Magrath, Stephen Otrembiak, Michael Popowsky, and Charlotte Walker.

My greatest debt, as always, is to my wife, Jill, steadfast companion, kind critic, wise editor, patient listener. Without her, this book would not be.

Index

Juet, Robert, 51
    abandons Henry Hudson, 49
    death, 49
    journal about the Hudson, 42–46,
        47–48, 173, 186
    murder of Native American, 44

Kaaterskill Creek, 113, 195
Kaaterskill Falls, 113, 195, 224
Kalm, Peter, 7, 22
    Kalmia latifolia, 7
    on porpoises, 19
    quoted, 13
    on trees, 20
    on wheat, 21
Kemble, Fanny, 185, 265
Kemble, Gouverneur, 233–34
Kempshall Mountain, 31
Kennebec River (Maine), 245
Kennedy, Mrs. John F., 281
Kensett, John Frederick, 208
Kidd, William, 103–5, 112
Kieft, Willem
    Committee of Eight (later nine),
        79–80, 87
    Committee of Twelve, 78–79
    death, 80
    director-general of New Nether-
        land, 75–80, 81, 82, 87
    Irving lampoons, 189
    war against Native Americans,
        76–78, 79, 111
Kindred Spirits (Durand), 203–5
King George's War, 122–23
King's College, 22, 136. *See also* Co-
    lumbia College (University)
Kingston, 89, 91, 94, 114, 179, 180,
    212, 227, 240, 243, 249, 258,
    274, 280
    Lafayette's visit to, 152
    razed in American Revolution, 134,
        149, 230
King William's War, 119
Knickerbocker Ice Company, 243–45
Kosciusko, Thaddeus

and Burgoyne's route to Saratoga,
    129
    fortifications at Saratoga, 130
    fortifications at West Point, 139–40
Kosciusko (steamboat), 182
Kossuth, Louis, 235
Krol, Bastian Jansz, 66, 68

Laet, Johannes de
    *New World, or Description of Dutch West-
        India*, 46, 47
Lafayette, Marquis de (Marie-Joseph-
        Paul-Yves-Roch-Gilbert du
        Motier de Lafayette), 265
    and Arnold treason, 142, 144, 152
    and Erie Canal, 169, 170
    tour of United States (in 1824–25),
        150–55, 169, 172, 215, 235
    victory at Yorktown, 152
Lake Avalanche, 33
Lake Champlain, 31, 119, 121, 124,
    128, 215
Lake Colden, 33
Lake Erie, 18
Lake George, 124
Lake Harris, 34
Lake Placid, 11
Lake Sally, 12
Lake Tear of the Clouds
    discovery, 32, 33
    source of the Hudson River, 11–12,
        17
Lake with Dead Trees (Cole), 11, 196, 197,
    198
Lander, Frederick W., 30
Lange Rack, 14
Laurel House Hotel, 216, 224
Lee, Robert E., 232
Leeds, 113
Legislator (steamboat), 229
Le Havre, 236
Leisler, Jacob, 101–2, 105, 119, 120
Lincoln, Abraham, 239
    Emancipation Proclamation, 238
    and Parrott Gun, 234

New York City, 8, 9, 11, 25, 27, 30,
102, 179, 195, 196, 213, 218,
227, 229, 230, 240, 242, 253,
259, 281
and American Revolution, 127,
128, 129, 135, 145, 147–49, 181
buildings and institutions: Astor House, 235; Bloomingdale
Insane Asylum, 154; Cathedral
of St. John the Divine, 243;
City Bank, 240; City Hall,
237; Cooper Union, 235; Deaf
and Dumb Asylum, 154; Grace
Church, 223, 231; Grant's
Tomb, 8, 252, 255; New York
Asylum for Lying-In-Women,
154; New York Tribune building, 251; orphan asylum, 239;
Riverside Church, 8; Rockefeller Center, 25; St. Patrick's
Cathedral, 231; United States
Treasury building, 223; Western
Union building, 251; World
Trade Center, 47, 53, 55
and Civil War, 239
Collect Pond, 217
draft riot, 238–39
and 1860 election, 237
financial center, 153
Henry James on, 251–52
and Hudson-Fulton Celebration,
254–55
immigration, 241–42
Lincoln's visit (in 1861), 235,
237–38
meat production in, 239
named, 91, 94
named New Orange, 92
population, 153, 214, 237, 241,
258
port of, 154, 236–37
and railroad, 180–83
slavery in, 113, 235–38
and steamboats, 158–61, 163,
179–80, 184–85

streets and avenues: Broadway,
1, 82, 89, 196–97, 235, 238,
252; Dey Street, 54; Eighty-
ninth Street, 252; Fifth Avenue,
239, 241; Forty-ninth Street,
252; Forty-second Street, 239;
Greenwich Street, 54, 151;
Madison Avenue, 252; Ninth
Avenue, 235, 241; 155th Street,
241; 110th Street, 241; 122nd
Street, 252; Riverside Drive,
252, 282; Sixty-fifth Street,
241; Sixty-fourth Street, 19;
Thirtieth Street, 235, 241;
Thirty-fourth Street, 258;
Twenty-third Street, 252; Wall
Street, 83, 239; Water Street, 47
"The Swamp," 217
and Tammany Hall, 237, 245
Wood's proposed separation from
the Union, 237
New York Elevated Railroad Company,
241
New Yorker, 223
New York Evening Post, 205
New York Journal, 248
New York Society for the Promotion
of Agriculture, Manufactures,
and the Useful Arts, 156
New York State National Bank
(Albany), 154
New York State Thruway, 274
New York Stock Exchange, 153
New York Tannery, 218
New York Times, 30, 36, 216, 243, 248
New York Tribune building, 251
New York University, 223
Niagara Falls, 263
Nicolls, Richard
captures New Netherland, 91, 110
governor of New York, 94
Nieu Dorp, 90
The Nineteen. *See* Dutch West India
Company: Assembly of XIX
Niskayuna (Schenectady County), 227